S0-BOI-729

PRINTED IN GREAT BRITAIN

A HISTORY OF RUSSIA

All rights reserved.

A
HISTORY *of* RUSSIA

BY

V. O. KLUCHEVSKY

LATE PROFESSOR OF RUSSIAN HISTORY IN THE UNIVERSITY OF MOSCOW

TRANSLATED BY

C. J. HOGARTH

VOLUME THREE

LONDON: J. M. DENT & SONS, LTD.
NEW YORK: E. P. DUTTON & CO.   1913

Printed by BALLANTYNE, HANSON & Co.
at the Ballantyne Press, Edinburgh

CONTENTS

CHAPTER I

CHAPTER II

CHAPTER III

CHAPTER IV

v

CONTENTS

CHAPTER X

CHAPTER XI

CHAPTER XII

CHAPTER XIII

CHAPTER XIV

CONTENTS

CHAPTER XV

CHAPTER XVI

CHAPTER XVII

CHAPTER XVIII

HISTORY OF RUSSIA

CHAPTER I

Survey of the fourth period of Russian history—The chief factors of the period—Manifest
contradictions in the correlation of those factors—Influence of foreign policy upon the
domestic life of the State—Course of affairs during the fourth period in connection with
that influence—The State and the political sense of the community—The beginning of
the Period of Troubles—The end of the dynasty—Tsar Theodor and Boris Godunov—
Circumstances which contributed to the Period of Troubles—The Pretendership.

In the last volume we stopped at the fourth period of Russian history—
the last period, and the only one accessible to study throughout the whole
of its length. By the fourth period I mean the epoch extending from
the beginning of the seventeenth century to the beginning of the reign of
the Emperor Alexander II. (to be precise, from the year 1613 to the year
1855).[1] As its actual starting point we may take the year of the accession
of the first Tsar of the new dynasty, while the Period of Troubles figures
merely as a transitional interval between two adjoining epochs with the
former of which it was connected by its causes, and with the latter by its
effects.

The fourth period has for us a special interest, in that it is not merely
an historical space of time, but a whole chain of epochs through which
there runs a series of important factors constituting the secret basis of
our life of to-day—a basis which, though variable, never changes. I
repeat that the fourth period is more than one of the epochs of our
history: *it is the whole of our modern history.* In the ideas and relations
formed during those two centuries and a half we can detect the first
germs of ideas which coincide with our own; we can observe, in due order,
the institutions which constituted the first social impressions of the men
of my own generation. As one studies the phenomena of the period one

[1] Since the author's death this history has been written up to date, with the aid of notes
which he left behind him.

feels that, the further one goes, the more does one enter into the province of autobiography and approach the study of oneself, of one's own intellectual outlook, in so far as it is bound up with the past of our country. All this tends to keep the attention engaged, and to guard the thoughts from straying.   Bound ever to be sincere seekers after the truth, we cannot deceive ourselves when it is *our own* historical growth that we attempt to measure, *our own* social maturity that we seek to define.

In passing to a review of the phenomena of the period now awaiting us, let us first of all throw another glance at the centuries of our history already studied, and picture to ourselves, in a short sketch, their course. We have seen that the forms of political life which arose in Russia up to the close of the sixteenth century were closely bound up with the geographical distribution of the population.   The Muscovite Empire was created by the Russian people, as concentrated at the exact centre of the Eastern European plain, at the exact focus-point of its water system (*i.e.* the region of the Upper Volga), where it came to form the Great Russian stock.   In this Empire, under the sway of the house of Ivan Kalita, the Great Russian stock became united into a political nationality. The Tsar of Moscow ruled a united Great Rus, with the help of the Muscovite boyars; who consisted of the old Muscovite noble stocks, as represented by erstwhile appanage princes and their retainers.   Meanwhile the order of State kept passing more and more to a basis of *tiaglo* or cess —*i.e.* of compulsory apportionment of State dues among the several classes of the community.   Yet, though this apportionment left peasant labour— still the chief productive force in the country—legally free, a large portion of the peasant population had, in reality, become dependent, through debt, upon the landowners, who were likewise threatening it with legal serfdom.

With the second decade of the seventeenth century, however, there enters into our history a series of new factors which markedly differentiate the succeeding epoch from the preceding one.   In the first place, a new dynasty takes its seat on the Muscovite throne.   Furthermore, it is a dynasty which acts over an ever-widening area.   The Imperial territory, hitherto limited to the confines of the original settlement of the Great Russian stock, now passes far beyond those confines, until it has absorbed the whole of the Russian plain, and has come to extend both to that plain's geographical boundaries and (in most directions) to the limits of Russian popular migration.   Thus to the Russian Empire there gradually become added Little Russia, White Russia, and New Russia (the latter a region formed by colonisation of the Southern Steppes). Stretching from the shores of the White Sea and the Baltic to those of the Black Sea and the Caspian, the territory of the State overflows southward beyond the Caucasus, and eastward beyond the Urals and the Caspian. In the internal organisation also of the State there takes place an important change, since hand in hand with the new dynasty we see arise and flourish a new ruling class. Gradually decaying, through genealogical paucity and economic poverty, the old order of boyars disappears, and with it go those political relations which custom had hitherto enabled to maintain the supreme power in its place. Into the position of that order at the head of the community there steps a new order—the order of *dvorianstvo* or nobility ; which *stratum* is composed of the old metropolitan and provincial servitors of the State, and finally absorbs into its variegated, heterogeneous body the last remaining fragments of the old boyar aristocracy. Meanwhile the original basis of the political edifice, the class apportionment of imposts, becomes strengthened, and converts the social classes into a number of inter-differentiated corporations. Gradually (though more especially during the reign of Peter the Great) that basis becomes widened, and complicates the existing aggregate of special dues with new imposts which fall upon classes individually. Finally this ceaseless tension of the popular forces ends in the freedom of peasant labour becoming finally extinguished. The seigniorial *krestianin* lapses into serfdom, and that serfdom becomes a new State obligation that is incident only upon the class in question. Yet, though restricted in political rights, the labour of the masses becomes broadened in its economic scope. To the old purely agricultural exploitation of Rus there becomes added an industrial working of the country, since, side by side with husbandry (which still remains the chief productive force in the State), there appears, with ever-growing importance in the popular *ménage*, the task of obtaining, elaborating, and perfecting certain natural resources of the country which hitherto have been left untouched.

Such are the principal new features revealed in the period which we are about to study. They comprise (1) a new dynasty, (2) new boundaries to the territory of the State, (3) a new organisation of the community, with a new ruling class at its head, and (4) a new adjustment of popular industry. Of these factors, however, the correlation may give rise to a certain misapprehension. At the first glance we can distinguish in them two parallel tendencies, namely, (1) the tendency that up to the middle of the nineteenth century the external territorial expansion of the Empire marched in inverse proportion to the growth of the internal freedom of the people, and (2) the tendency that the political position of the labouring classes became established in inverse proportion to the economic productiveness of their labour (*i.e.* their labour became less free in proportion as it became more productive). The relation of popular industry to the social organisation of the people which we see revealed in the latter process contradicts our customary notion of the existence of a connection between the productiveness of popular labour and that labour's freedom. It is our custom to think that servile labour can never equal free labour in energy, and that labour efficiency can never in any way prove detrimental to the juridical position of the labouring classes. This economic contradiction is emphasized by a political contradiction. In comparing the psychology of nations with the life of individuals, we are accustomed to think that, in proportion to the growth of activity in the masses and in individuals, as also in proportion to the extension of that activity in the masses and in individuals, consciousness of political strength grows more acute, and acts as the source of the sense of political freedom. Yet the influence which our history shows to have been exercised by the territorial expansion of the Empire upon the relation of the State power to the community does not justify this notion. On the contrary, in proportion as Russian territory expanded with the growth of the external strength of the nation, the nation's internal freedom became restricted. The strain thrown upon the national activity tended to absorb the nation's strength, and while the scope of national power developed with success in war, the lifting force of the national spirit became diminished. Indeed, the external progress of modern Russia reminds one of the flight of a bird which, driven before the wind, cannot make full use of its wings. With the contradictions mentioned there was bound up a third. I have just spoken of the absorption of the old Muscovite boyars by the *dvorianstvo* or gentry. That process was hastened by a law of 1682, which abolished the *miestnichestvo*, and formally placed the two State service classes on an equal footing. Hitherto the boyars—the aristocracy of birth—had been the ruling class ; but with the abolition of the *miestnichestvo* a first step was taken towards effecting democratisation of the Government. Moreover, the movement did not stop here, since further steps followed upon the first. During the time of Peter the Great the old Muscovite *po otechestvu* [1] nobility became reinforced from all sections of the community (including the

[1] By descent.

alien section) and all *tchini* or ranks—not only the "white" or untaxed ranks, but also the "black" or taxed, including slaves who had been promoted for meritorious service. To these *raznotchintsi* or members of various *tchini* the table of ranks of 1722 opened the door (through State service), to "the better and olden *dvorianstvo*." Although it might have been supposed that this social shuffling and reshuffling of the ruling class would have led to a more democratic administration of the community, the ruling class, though gradually weakening from the genealogical point of view, was growing immensely stronger from the political standpoint, owing to the fact that the newly ennobled *raznotchintsi* acquired personal and public rights which the old "born" boyars had never enjoyed. *Pomiestia* became the absolute property of their holders, the *dvoriané*, and *krestiané* absolute serfs to the latter. Under Peter III. the *dvoriané*, as a corporation, were forced to render compulsory State service, but under Catherine II. they acquired a new corporate organisation, corporate self-government, a considerable participation in the administration of local affairs and local justice, and the right to "offer pleas and representations" to the supreme power itself. Finally, under Nicholas I. there became added to the last-mentioned privilege a right whereby assemblies of *dvoriané* could "offer representations" to the supreme power concerning the needs of the other classes in their local communities. These corporate acquisitions were accompanied by an increase in the political strength of the *dvorianin* corporation. The Muscovite Government began to administer the community through the *dvorianstvo* in the seventeenth century, while the eighteenth century saw the same *dvorianstvo* attempt to administer the community through the Government. But the political principle under cover of which it attempted so to administer at length permeated the whole, until by the nineteenth century the *dvorianstvo* had become added to the *tchinovnichestvo*,[1] as its most flourishing offshoot. Thus the middle of the nineteenth century saw Russia under the administration, not of an aristocracy, nor of a democracy, but of a bureaucracy— *i.e.* of an army of officials of heterogeneous origin, who acted externally to the community, had no particular social characteristic to distinguish them, and were bound together only by their common status as *tchinovniki*. The democratisation of the administration, therefore, was accompanied by an increase of social cleavage and inequality; which social disintegration was further added to by the moral estrangement of the ruling class from the masses whom that class administered. It is said that culture draws

[1] The order of officials of the civil service.

all men together, and levels a community; yet with us it has been otherwise. Although ever-growing intercourse with Western Europe has brought us abundance of ideas, morals, learning, and culture, the influx has swept over the heads of the community, leaving a sediment of partial reforms which have ever been more or less fruitless and niggardly. Enlightenment has become a class monopoly which, so long as they remain in darkness, the unenlightened masses may not touch without danger to the State. At the close of the seventeenth century the men who conceived the idea of instituting the Moscow Academy of Sciences (the earliest of our higher educational establishments), found it possible to admit thereto "every grade and rank and age of men"; but, a hundred and fifty years later, in the time of Nicholas I., Kotchube's secret committee—a purely reforming commission—decided, when the court official who was then acting as Professor of Painting at the Academy committed suicide because of the harm which he conceived to be done to the institution by the admission of serfs, that the latter ought not to be received "into such schools, where they only learn a fashion of life, a mode of thought, and a form of ideas which are unsuited to their condition."

Though full of such contradictions embracing the principal phenomena of the period, the three processes which I have expounded were not anomalies, were not mere negations of historical rules. Rather they were historical *antinomies*, or exceptions from the rules of historical life—*i.e.* products of such a peculiar local adjustment of conditions as, once compounded, obeyed, in its further working, the general laws of human life, even as an organism which suffers from a disordered nervous system still performs its functions according to the general norms of organic life, yet produces abnormal phenomena in harmony with its disorder.

For an explanation of these antinomies in our modern history we must turn to the relation which became established between the needs of the State and the means which lay at the disposal of the nation for their fulfilment. When a European State finds itself confronted with new and difficult problems, it proceeds to seek new resources among its people, and usually succeeds in finding them, since a European nation which lives the normal, conservative life of free labour and thought can easily make the results of that labour and thought serve as a means for aiding the State power. Those results consist, in the matter of labour, of increased taxatory capacity, and, in the matter of thought, of trained, capable, and conscientious State workers. The important point is that, in such a nation, cultural work should be carried on through the covert and intangible, yet friendly, efforts of individual persons and private associations, independently of the State and (usually) in anticipation of its needs. But with us the reverse has been the case. When Michael acceded to the shattered Tsarship, and, through the agency of the *Zemski Sobor*,[1] turned to the land for help, he found in his chosen territorial representatives humble and devoted subjects, but not capable assistants or substantial tax payers. Accordingly he was led to think both of the necessity and of the best means of providing both the one and the other—*i.e.* of obtaining both public workers and money where abundance of each existed: and in that connection the Mercantile Association of Moscow stepped forward with a proposal to import foreigners capable of affording a "feeding" (*i.e.* a livelihood) to the poorer Russian folk by teaching the latter their (the foreigners') crafts and industries. Since then this peculiar phenomena has more than once been repeated. Nevertheless the State continued to find itself entangled in growing difficulties, until the Government (which in few cases had foreseen or provided for those difficulties) began once more to search the community for men and ideas capable of extricating it from its position. Finding neither the one nor the other, it hardened its heart, and turned to the West, where it saw in operation an old and complex apparatus of culture capable of furnishing the desiderated men and ideas. Hurriedly summoning thence suitable craftsmen and *savants*, it erected factories, and founded schools which it compelled its students to enter. The exigency of the State admitted of no delay; it could not wait until its compulsory scholars had learned their letters. Consequently it had, so to speak, to rest satisfied with cheese—with forced sacrifices which sapped the popular substance and restricted the public freedom. The demands of the State, while putting the greatest possible tension upon the popular forces, did nothing to increase them, but only exhausted their strength. Enlightenment diffused at the behest of State necessity, and not at that of some internal demand, only brought forth scanty, frostbitten fruit. Feverish impulses towards education only aroused in the rising generation weariness and aversion to learning as a conscriptory obligation. Thus popular education acquired the character of a Government behest—a fiscal provision of pupils, to be educated according to a stereotyped programme. Expensive cadet corps for noblemen's sons were instituted; engineering schools, select ladies' academies, schools of art, and gymnasia sprang up with tropical

---

[1] See vol. ii. chap. xvi.

growth in the warmth of a lordly atmosphere: yet for two centuries not a single purely popular educational establishment or a single agricultural college was opened. New Europeanised Russia was, for four or five generations, a Russia merely of Guards' barracks, Government offices, and country houses; the latter leading to the first and the second through an easy course of scions through native schools or exotic *pensions*, whence she received, in exchange, retired brigadiers in uniform. By this process of extracting the necessary State workers from the population the State implanted in the community a profoundly utilitarian view of learning, as a mere road to ranks and perquisites. Also, it formed of the upper classes—most of all, of the *dvorianstvo*—a new service caste which was divorced from the people not only by its possessions and its prejudices of rank and class, but also, and to an even greater degree, by its class abuses. Thus, by placing an immense strain and drain upon the popular resources, the expansion of the State's territory increased the State's power without also stimulating the popular consciousness; while at the same time it drew into the composition of the administration new and more democratic elements. The result was that it accentuated the inequality and inter-differentiation of the social composition, and complicated the industrial labour of the nation with new products, since the expansion of the State enriched, not the nation as a whole, but the treasury and individual *entrepreneurs*—thus lowering the labouring classes *politically*. All these irregularities came of a common source—namely, of the unnatural relation of the external policy of the State to the internal growth of the nation. That is to say, in proportion as the popular forces increased, they came to take a smaller part in the tasks which confronted the State through the rapid external expansion of its territory; while at the same time the intellectual activity of the nation failed to keep pace with the material activity of the State. Thus the State grew swollen, and the people fat.

In the history of but few countries has the influence of the international position of the State upon the State's internal organisation been more potent than was the case in Russia at the period which we are now approaching. Nor at any period of our history has that influence been more clearly displayed than in the period named. Let us once more recall the chief problems involved by the external policy of the Muscovite Empire during the fifteenth and sixteenth centuries, and also their origin, and their connection with the past fortunes of our country. During the first period of our history, under the pressure of foreign foes, the multi-racial and scattered elements of the population became compounded into a sort of whole, and therefrom there arose the Great Russian nationality. During the second period of our history the ever-increasing shower of blows from Tartar and Lithuanian quarters caused that nationality to divide into two branches, the Great Russian and the Little Russian: from which time onwards each of them had its own peculiar fortunes. The Great Russian branch contrived to preserve its virility in the wilds of the Upper Volga, and to develop that virility in a patient struggle with grim nature and external foes. Thanks to that circumstance, the Great Russian branch succeeded in welding itself into a fairly stable military State. During the third period the State referred to—now become united Great Rus— entered upon the solidification, popular and political, of the whole of the Russian land; and the assumption of this task, as well as the approach to its accomplishment, constitutes the principal work performed by the old dynasty of Muscovite Tsars. We have seen the national efforts which were devoted to this work, and the success which, by the close of the sixteenth century, had been attained in this direction; but, unfortunately, in pressing forward to the desired goal, the community of the Muscovite Empire adopted the disastrous political organisation of the period to which we have just devoted our attention. In the seventeenth century the territorial losses of the Period of Troubles caused the external struggle to become still more onerous, and the social organisation to change in the same direction. Under the burden of the wars with Sweden and Poland the old petty economic grades, the *tchini* (which still preserved the outward tokens of freedom of labour and mobility), became welded, in the interests of the treasury and State service, into large corporations, while a considerable majority of the peasant population became bound to serfdom. Under Peter the Great the fundamental spring of the State order attained an even higher degree of tension, and the corporate apportionment of special dues became even heavier than it had been in the seventeenth century; since to the old corporate imposts the State added certain new ones, while the old obligations of conscription and tax-payment were apportioned among classes which had hitherto stood exempt from State burdens—namely, among the "free men" and the slaves. Thus there arose in Russian legislation a dim idea of "general dues" which, if not pan-corporate, were at all events multi-corporate, and which, in their further development, presaged a notable change in the social structure. At the same time there took place a break in the external policy of the State. Hitherto Russian wars in the West had been essentially defensive

—had had for their aim the recovery of territory either more or less recently bartered away or looked upon as the pristine property of Rus; but from Poltava [1] onwards these wars acquired an *offensive* character, and were directed either to strengthening possessions of Rus which Peter had won in Eastern Europe or to maintaining the European equilibrium (so our diplomatists elegantly express it). Once started upon this pretentious road, the State began to cost the nation far dearer than it had done before: with the result that, but for the potent fillip which Peter the Great gave to the productive forces of the country, the nation would have failed to foot the bill for the rôle which it was called upon to play in Europe. After Peter's time a new and important condition became introduced into the internal life of the State. That is to say, under certain of the unworthy successors, male and female, of the Great Reformer, the throne tottered for a while, until it found itself forced to seek support among the community—most of all among the *dvorianstvo;* while to pay for the upkeep of the throne the legislature had to discard the idea of pan-corporate dues which had glimmered in Peter's day, and to adopt, rather, the idea of *special corporate rights.* That is to say, the *dvorianstvo* became emancipated from the heavy burden of compulsory State service, while at the same time it not only retained its old rights, but acquired new ones of an extensive character. Crumbs from the same table fell to the lot of the superior mercantile grade, and in this fashion the leading sections of the community were loaded with every exemption and advantage with which the supreme power could dower them, while the sections at the foot received but burdens and disabilities. If the nation had continued patiently to bear this system Russia would soon have dropped out of the circle of European countries; but, as a matter of fact, the middle of the eighteenth century witnessed the beginning of a very peculiar and insistent ferment among the masses. Although the seventeenth century had been fertile in rebellions, those risings had been directed against the Government—against the boyars, *voievodi,* and officials of the public service. Now, however, they took on a *social* tinge, as having for their object rather the masters, the serf owners. For instance, it was under the standard of legality that Pugachev [2] initiated his movement, as representing the idea of lawful power against its usurpation by Catherine II. and her *dvoriané;* until, finally, when they felt the ground shaking

---

[1] Here, in 1709, the Russian General Menshikov defeated the Swedish forces under Charles XII.

[2] Leader of a great Cossack rebellion during the years 1773-1775.

under their feet, Government circles revived the idea of levelling the community and mitigating serf law. Starting and trembling, chewing the cud of a given scheme over and over again, deferring the question from one reign to another, making faint-hearted attempts at improvement which did nothing to justify the grandiose title of the supreme power,—the affair reached the point, by the middle of the nineteenth century, of its decision becoming an urgent necessity, especially after Sevastopol had struck home the truth to even the most stagnant of minds.

Thus the course of events during the fourth period might be set forth as follows. In proportion as the tension of the struggle for the defence of the country became greater, the special State obligations which were incident upon the several classes of the community became more complex; while, in proportion as the defensive struggle became converted into an offensive movement, the superior social classes of the community became relieved of their special obligations, and were, instead, dowered with special corporate rights, while their late obligations became heaped upon the inferior classes. In proportion, however, as the feeling of popular dissatisfaction with this system of inequality grew stronger, the Government began to reconsider the question of effecting a more equitable adjustment of the community. This outline of the matter we must try to lay to heart, since it contains the real meaning of the epoch, the key to an explanation of the more important phenomena of the period. It is an outline which will serve as a *formula* to the interpretation of which we must devote the whole of our study of the fourth period.

Such was the sequence of phenomena during this fourth period, as well as their inter-relation. With the sequence referred to was bound up a growth of the political sense in the Russian community, and a certain progress in the ideas which are manifested in those phenomena. Towards the close of the sixteenth century the Muscovite Empire became fully organised, fitted with the customary forms and instruments of State life, and provided with a supreme power, a legislature, a central and a provincial administration, a huge and an ever-increasing body of public officials, a growing system of social differentiation, an army, and even a certain dim idea of public representation. Of State debts alone is there no trace to be discerned. Yet institutions, by themselves, are merely forms, since for their successful working both scope, ideas to help their workers to make clear their meaning and purpose, and norms and moral standards to direct the activity of those workers are needed. Such requisites are never to be found ready-made, but must be elaborated by a process of tense thought and of slow, arduous, often painful, experiment. Although the institutions of the Muscovite Empire had been prepared by the time that the old dynasty was extinguished, it may be questioned whether the *intellects* of the Empire were then ready to transact business in them in consonance with State problems and aims of public weal. Suppose we make what might be called "a summary estimate" of the political consciousness of the Muscovite statesmen of those days, and suppose that for that purpose we attribute to their powers of political conception the simplest possible idea of a State, so that we may see how far they understood the fundamental, the indispensable elements of a State order in consonance with the nature and tasks of the same. The fundamental elements of a State order are a supreme power, a nation, a system of law, and public welfare. Although we have seen [1] that the supreme power in the Muscovite Empire adopted titles and expressions of the most exalted order, these were not political assumptions, but mere grandiose embellishments, or diplomatic enhancements, after the style of "Tsar of All Rus." In the workaday round, in the daily interchange of ideas and relations there still prevailed the old appanage norm which hitherto had served as the real, the historically compounded basis of that power—namely, the norm contained in the view that the realm of the Muscovite Tsar was his absolute, hereditary property. Consequently, according as new political ideas became born of the course of events, they tended, through the then bent of Muscovite political thought, to conform to that time-hallowed norm. That is to say, although Moscow's unification of Great Rus aroused in men's minds the idea of a national Russian State, that idea—a direct negation of the idea of the State as the *otchina* of its ruler—found expression in the old *otchina* system which had hitherto led the "Tsar of All Rus" to look upon himself, not as the supreme ruler of the Russian nation, but as the hereditary seignior, the territorial squire, of the Russian Imperial manor. "From olden time and from our forefathers all the Russian land hath been our *otchina*," asserted Ivan III. Political thought discounted territorial acquisitions and dynastic claims by converting appanage prejudices into political misunderstandings. Under the action of the anomaly referred to—an anomaly which united in the one essence of the supreme power the two incommensurable qualities of Tsar and *otchinnik* (hereditary proprietor)—the rest of the above elements of a State order also underwent deflection in the political thought of the day. For instance, the idea of the nation had not yet become identified with the idea of the State. That

[1] In vol. ii. chap. ii.

is to say, the State connoted not so much a national union, administered by the supreme power, as a manorial property which included among its manorial assets all classes of the population by which the territory of the Tsar's *otchina* was inhabited. For that reason the popular welfare, as an aim of the State, was subordinated to the dynastic interest of the lord of the manor, and even a new law bore the character of an estate order issued from the manor-house of the Kremlin for the guidance of an underling staff—more particularly in the matter of insuring that all the tenants should perform their several obligations to the landlord. In Muscovite legislation anterior to the seventeenth century not a single regulation which is recognisable as a fundamental law for defining either the organisation and rights of the supreme power or the fundamental rights and obligations of the citizens is to be met with. In this manner the basic elements of the State order remained unsupported by any conceptions in consonance with their nature. The forms of State organisation, though compounded historically, and through the elemental instinct for law of the Russian people, were not yet filled out—they still seemed, as it were, to be superior to the existing political sense of the statesmen who acted through their means. In this lies the chief interest of the period which we are about to study—the interest which lies in tracing the process whereby the ideas which constituted the soul of the political order finally became perfected in the public consciousness, and developed into the forms of which I have spoken; while at the same time, under their stimulus and support, the skeleton of the State gradually became converted into a living State organism. In this process we see the antinomies already referred to not only lose their manifest disparity, but attain their historical explanation.

Such is the series of factors which we are about to study, as well as the series of problems which we are about to resolve. Those factors let us observe from the moment when the new dynasty first took its seat upon the Muscovite throne.

But before that accession came about, the Muscovite Empire experienced an upheaval which shook it to its foundations, and gave the first, and a very serious, check to the onward march of the ideas of which the majority of State orders built upon the extinction of dynasties stand most in need. This upheaval took place during the early years of the seventeenth century, and is usually known in our history as the Period of Troubles; though certain Russian writers who were contemporary with that grievous time have also called it (more especially with reference to its later years) " the Great Destruction of the Muscovite State." The first signs of the Period showed themselves immediately after the death of the last Tsar of the old dynasty (Theodor Ivanovitch),[1] and the Period came to an end when the territorial magnates, assembled in council in Moscow early in the year 1613, elected to the throne the founder of the new dynasty, the Tsar Michael. Consequently the *Smuta* or *Smutnöe Vremia*[2] of our history may be taken to have covered the fourteen years between 1598 and 1613; and the same number of years is assigned to it also by a contemporary writer—one Abraham Palitsin, Abbot of the Troitski Monastery, and author of an account of a siege of that establishment by the Poles. Let us halt at the origin and meaning of the upheaval before passing to the study of the fourth period, and ask ourselves whence came this Terror—whence came what certain foreigners of the day have called the " Tragœdia Moscovitica." The following is its outline.

In 1581—*i.e.* a little more than two years before his death—one of those evil moments which were so frequent with him led Ivan IV. to have his daughter-in-law punished for appearing to him, on his entering her room, too lightly clad for a woman who was in a condition of pregnancy ("Nimis simplici veste induta" is how the Jesuit missionary, Anthony Possevino, who visited Moscow three months after the event, and therefore found the traces of it still warm, describes her toilet); and upon the aggrieved lady's husband—the Tsarevitch Ivan, heir to the throne—resenting his father's action, the enraged parent dealt him a fatal blow with the iron-headed cane which he was carrying at the time. Instantly overcome with remorse for what he had done, the Tsar spent several days and nights in wild lamentation; declaring that he would retire from the throne and assume the cowl. True, he never carried this actually into effect, but the upshot of the murder was that his second son, the Tsarevitch Theodor, became his heir.

Theodor, the last Tsar of the old Muscovite dynasty, constitutes an instructive phenomenon in our history. Although Kalita's stock, who built the Empire of Moscow, were consistently remarkable for their ability to feather their nests and their excessive family solicitude for mundane matters, the dynasty made amends in its last moments by expiring with Tsar Theodor, who, to quote certain of his contemporaries, " did all his life shun the baubles and vanities of this world, and think of things heavenly." Sapiega, then Polish Ambassador to Rus, has described him thus : " The Tsar is short of stature, and meagre withal, and hath a

---

[1] Son of Ivan IV.   [2] Disturbance or Disturbed Epoch.

gentle voice as of one who doth suffer, and likewise a simple countenance. Of mind hath he but little—or (so I have heard from other men, as well as have remarked of myself) he hath none at all, inasmuch as, when seated upon the throne and receiving an ambassador, he refraineth not from smiling, nor from gazing first upon his sceptre, and then upon his orb." Another contemporary, the Swedish envoy Petreius, says, in his description of the Muscovite Empire between 1608 and 1611, that Theodor was by nature practically an imbecile, that he took pleasure only in spiritual matters, and that it was his frequent custom to run from church to church, for the purpose of ringing the bells and having Mass celebrated. For this Theodor's father used to reproach him bitterly, saying that he was more like a sexton than the son of a Tsar. Yet in these descriptions of the monarch there is undoubtedly some exaggeration, a spice of caricature. Probably contemporary Russian thought attempted, in its equal reverence to God and to the throne, to fashion of Theodor that particular model of religious protagonism which was most grateful to its heart. We have seen[1] the significance which was attributed to *urodstvo* or devout idiocy, and the respect in which it was held by the faithful. The idiot or " blessed one " not only renounced the good things of life (both temporal possessions and such spiritual amenities and allurements as honours, fame, respect, and the love of kinsfolk), but also directly challenged those possessions and amenities. Poor and homeless, roaming the streets barefooted and in rags, acting neither like man nor beast, speaking a sort of incoherent jargon, and despising the generally accepted conventions of life, he strove to be a butt for the thoughtless, and mocked at the blessings which men love and value, and at the men who love and value them. In this humility, carried to the point of self-abasement, ancient Rus saw a practical fulfilment of the divine ordinance that unto those who do humble themselves shall the Kingdom of Heaven belong. To the lay conscience of the age such spiritual poverty as was represented in the person of the *urodivi* or devout idiot seemed a living searchlight thrown upon the passions and vices of humanity. Consequently the *urodivi* enjoyed extensive rights and full freedom of speech among the community ; and even the powers that were—the Tsars and their nobles—would listen to the audacious, mocking, even insolent speeches of such a sanctified street mendicant without daring to raise a finger against him. It was this well-known, familiar mien of the *urodivi* that his contemporaries attributed to Theodor. In

[1] In vol. ii. p. 156.

their eyes he was an enthroned imbecile—one of those persons, humble in spirit, to whom shall be given, not an earthly, but a celestial kingdom— one of those beings whom the Church has always loved to add to the number of her saints, as a standing reproach to the gross thoughts and sinful frailties of the Russian layman. "Oh but to be holy and bereft of sense from one's mother's womb, and to take no thought save for the salvation of one's soul!" exclaims Prince Katirev Rostovski, one of Theodor's courtiers, concerning his master. Another contemporary says that, in Theodor, monasticism was inseparably bound up with sovereignty; so that the one served as an embellishment to the other, and Theodor became known as the "Sanctified Tsar," divinely foreordained to holiness and a heavenly crown. In short, I may quote Karamzin in saying that Theodor's rightful place was a cell or a catacomb rather than a palace. Even in our own day he has served as a subject for poetic fancy. For instance, Tolstoi devotes to him the second tragedy of his dramatic trilogy—a work wherein Theodor's image approximates so closely to its ancient Russian model that the poet would seem to have drawn his portrait of the "Blessed Tsar" direct from some old manuscript presentment of the same. Yet, though, in Tolstoi's picture, we can discern that disposition towards kindly jesting with which the ancient Russian *urodivi* always tempered his grim protest, there still projects through the external piety which moved Theodor's contemporaries to such admiration the *moral* sense, in the shape of a wise simplicity which, by some unconscious, mysteriously enlightened instinct, was able to understand matters which the greatest intellects of the day could not envisage. In Tolstoi's pages we read that Theodor was grieved to hear of party dissensions and the enmity which existed between the partisans of Boris Godunov and the adherents of Prince Shuiski; that he yearned to see the day when all men should be partisans only of *Rus*, and when strife of every kind should be reconciled; and that to Godunov's doubts as to whether such a general pacification was ever likely to come about in the State he retorted warmly:

> "Nay, nay!
> Thou dost not mean this, Boris.
> Guard thou the State as thou dost well know how.
> Use all thy skill,—though more of skill, methinks,
> The heart doth need to guard its erring thought."

And again:

> "For am I Tsar, forsooth? In everything
> To fool my senses is no hardy feat.

> Yet hold! In one regard am I no fool:
> When choice, for me, doth lie 'tween black and white,
> Choose I with wit."

Of these edificatory, or poetic, pictures of an historic figure, whether drawn by contemporary or later writers, we must not overlook the historical inwardness. As Tsarevitch, Theodor was reared in the suburb of Alexandrov, amid all the indecencies and horrors of the *Oprichnina*, and early each morning his father, the "Abbot" of the mock suburban monastery, would dispatch him up the belfry to ring for Matins. Weakly from birth (owing to the latterly failing health of his mother, Anastasia Romanovna), he grew up a motherless orphan, surrounded by the repellent scenes of the *Oprichinina*—grew up an undersized, whitefaced stripling who was disposed to dropsy and possessed of an unsteady, quasi-senile gait, due to a congenital affection of the lower limbs. Such, at all events, is the description of the Tsar at thirty-two given by the English Ambassador Fletcher. In Theodor's person the dynasty expired, so to speak, obviously. Though on his face there was a constant smile, it was a lifeless one. It was the same smile with which, in his youth, he had had to defend himself from the capricious anger of his father; until, in time, and more especially after the terrible death of his elder brother, that smile became converted, through the force of habit, into an involuntary, automatic grimace. Often goaded to madness by his father, he gradually lost all will-power, yet never quite dropped the look of crushed abasement which he had learnt so persistently to wear. Finally, when seated upon the throne, he found that he needed some one to act as the keeper of his conscience: and into the vacant place of the late demented parent there stepped, though cautiously, Boris Godunov.

When at the point of death, Ivan IV. had recognised that his "humbly-gifted" successor was incompetent to rule the State, and so had appointed, for his guidance, an administrative commission—a sort of regency composed of certain of his most trusted lords. At first the leadership among these officials was held by the new Tsar's maternal uncle, Nikita Romanovitch Yuriev; but, before long, the illness and death of the latter cleared the way to power for a second guardian, the Tsar's brother-in-law, Boris Godunov. Taking advantage of the Tsar's character, as well as of the support of his (Boris') sister, the Tsaritsa, Boris gradually ousted his fellow regents, and began to administer the State in the name of his kinsman-at-law. We should scarcely call him a prime minister; rather, he was a kind of dictator or co-regent. The Tsar, to use Kotoshikhin's expression, appointed him general administrator of the State, and himself engaged "only in prayer and humbleness." So far did Boris exercise an influence over the Tsar and affairs generally, and so far (to quote the Prince Katirev Rostovski whom I have mentioned) did he usurp power and come to "be hearkened to like unto the Tsar," that, hedged about almost with imperial pomp, he received foreign ambassadors in his residence with all the glitter and magnificence of a real potentate. "He was honoured," so we read, "with no less homage than was rendered unto the Tsar himself." Yet he ruled wisely, and with caution; the result being that the fourteen years of Theodor's reign were a time of rest for the State after the alarms and excursions of the *Oprichnina.* "The Lord did soften His heart unto His people," writes the same contemporary, "and did grant unto them a time of grace. Yea, He did suffer the Tsar so to rule in peace and quietness that all orthodox Christendom did begin to live at rest, and to dwell together without fear or strife." Nor was the general tendency in any way interrupted by a successful war with Sweden. Yet suddenly disturbing reports began to circulate in Moscow. Ivan had left behind him a younger son, Dmitri, who, in accordance with the age-long custom of the Muscovite Tsars, had been dowered with a small appanage, in the shape of Uglitch and its canton. To prevent intrigues and *révolutions de palais,* the Tsarevitch and his maternal relatives were, at the beginning of Theodor's reign, entirely segregated from Moscow, although it was commonly said in the capital that the seven-year-old Dmitri—who was the son of Ivan's fifth crowned wife[1] (we need not take into account the two uncrowned) and, consequently, beyond doubt, the lawful Tsarevitch from a canonical point of view—would not only develop into a tyrant suitable to the age of the *Oprichnina,* but also be threatened with grave danger from certain persons who meditated placing themselves upon the throne in the not unlikely event of Theodor dying without issue; and, as though to justify these rumours, the year 1591 saw the news run through Moscow that the Appanage Prince, Dmitri, had been murdered in broad daylight, and that his murderers themselves had been put to death by the enraged populace, and none remained to testify to the Tsarevitch's killing. A commission of inquiry, with, at its head, Prince Shuiski (a secret enemy and rival of Godunov's), was forthwith dispatched to Uglitch, but pursued the matter without ordinary zeal or care, since, though it asked the most minute questions about trifles, it overlooked more important circumstances, took

---

[1] Maria Nagoi, seventh and last spouse of Ivan IV.

no trouble to unravel the various contradictions in the evidence, and, in general, bungled its task. In particular it tried to persuade itself and others that the Tsarevitch had not had his throat cut, but that he had been seized with a fit, which had caused him to fall upon the point of a knife with which he and some other children had happened to be playing some childish game. For that reason the citizens of Uglitch were subjected to severe chastisement for the voluntary revenge which they had wreaked upon the supposed murderers. On receipt of the commission's report, the patriarch Yov,[1] who was a friend of Godunov's, and who, two years ago, had acquired his ecclesiastical rank with Godunov's help, explained to the Synod that the death of the Tsarevitch must be assigned to the judgment of God; and there the affair ended for a while. In January 1598 Tsar Theodor died, and of his dynasty none remained to fill the vacant throne. True, allegiance was sworn to the late monarch's widow, but soon afterwards she took the veil, and the dynasty closed raggedly, through a death not its own. Finally the Tsarship was re-established by the *Zemski Sobor* (headed by the patriarch Yov), which elected the minister, Boris Godunov, to the throne.

On the throne Boris proved as wise and cautious an administrator as he had shown himself to be when standing beside it, under Tsar Theodor. By origin he belonged to a high, though not a leading, rank of boyars, since the Godunovs were a junior branch of an old and important Muscovite boyar house which derived from a Tartar mirzha named Tchet, who had left the Horde for Moscow in Kalita's time.[2] The senior branch of that house, the Saburovs, occupied a prominent place in Muscovite boyardom, while the Godunovs had attained their promotion only recently (*i.e.* during the reign of Ivan IV.), and principally with the help of the *Oprichnina*. This was because Boris had not only attended Ivan at one of the numerous unions consummated by that monarch during the period of the *Oprichnina*, but himself had become son-in-law to Maliuta Skuratov, the chief of the corps; while the marriage of his (Boris') sister to Theodor still further strengthened his position at Court. Up to the institution of the *Oprichnina* we meet with no Godunovs in the *Boyarskaia Duma*; it is only in 1573 that they first begin to make their appearance there. After the death of Ivan IV., however, they are constantly to be found receiving summonses to the Council, and always in the important rank of boyars or *okolnichi*. Boris did nothing to distinguish himself in the records of his fellow *oprichniki*, and thereby lost

[1] Job.   [2] See vol. ii. p. 109.

nothing in the eyes of the community, who looked upon the members of the *Oprichnina* as so many *kromiestchiki* or outcasts (thus making a pun upon the synonyms of *oprich* and *kromïe* [1]). Boris began his reign with success, and even with *éclat ;* his first acts on the throne evoked the popular approval. Contemporary chroniclers have written of him, in florid style, that by his foreign and domestic policy he "did set forth much prudent and right counsel unto the nations," that he possessed a mind "exceeding wise and able to judge in all things," and that he was a man who, though courteous of speech, was a masterful lord, and one ever mindful of his power. In these eulogies of his exterior man, as well as of his inward qualities as Tsar, they further write that "no man of the boyar *sinklit* was like unto him for the splendour of his countenance, nor yet for the judgment of his mind,"—though they also note with some surprise that he was the first non-princely Tsar of Rus, and one who "from his youth up had had no skill in book learning, nor been used even to simple letters." Nevertheless, though recognising that he excelled his fellows in exterior and in intellect, as also that he accomplished much in the State that was praiseworthy—that he was of liberal views, gracious, and good to the poor (though unskilled in the art of war)—these writers discover in him certain faults. For instance, they find that, though rich in the graces, so that he might easily have come to resemble the olden Tsars, he allowed those virtues to be overshadowed by malice and envy. Moreover, they accuse him of inordinate power, and of an over-readiness to pay heed to slanderers and to fall foul of the slandered. Also, considering himself incompetent to transact military matters, yet distrusting his *voievodi*, he pursued an indeterminate, ambiguous foreign policy, and did not avail himself (so these writers say) of the inveterate hostility between Poland and Sweden to form an alliance with the Swedish King, and so wrest Livonia from the former. Rather, he devoted his attention mostly to organising the *internal* order of the State—to "amending all things needful unto his realm," to quote Palitsin. Indeed, during the first two years of his reign (says the same chronicler) Rus was rich in every kind of blessing. The Tsar paid great attention to the poor and needy, and lavished his bounty upon them, yet adopted the sternest measures towards the evilly disposed. Consequently he earned immense popularity—"was beloved of all men." Furthermore, in his ordering of

---

[1] Both these prepositions mean "except" or "outside." Consequently, in the sense of the pun, an *oprichnik* or a *kromiestchik* connoted an exception to the rest of the community—an "outsider," or a person who stood beyond the pale.

the State's internal system he displayed an unusual power of initiative. When expounding the history of the peasantry of the sixteenth century I had occasion to show that the idea of Boris being the founder of serf-dom must be relegated to the limbo of our historical legends.[1] So far from that being the case, he was the author of a measure which, if it had ever materialised, would have gone far to consolidate the freedom and prosperity of the *krestianin ;* for he seems to have prepared a *ukaz* which was intended to make exact definition of the taxes and obligations which the *krestianin* was to render to the landowner. It was the same law that the Russian Government decided upon only when it finally liberated the serf.[2]

Thus did Boris begin his reign. Yet, despite his many years' adminis-trative experience, the generous favours which he bestowed upon all classes at his accession, and the governing ability which so surprised his contemporaries, his popularity was not a lasting one. As a matter of fact, he belonged to the number of individuals who at once attract and repel. By his obvious qualities of intellect and ability he attracted, yet by his unseen, though dimly apprehended, faults of heart and conscience he repelled. He could evoke astonishment and admiration, yet could not inspire confidence, since he was never free from suspicion of double-facedness and cunning, as being capable of any deceit. Undoubtedly the terrible school of Ivan IV. through which he had passed had left its indelible mark upon him. Even while Theodor was still occupying the throne many persons formed the idea that Boris was a man prudent and clever, yet a man capable of anything—a man who would not stick at any moral difficulty. Indeed, certain observant and impartial re-corders, such as the clerk Ivan Timothëev (author of some curious notes on the Period of Troubles), pass straight from stern censure of Boris to solemn eulogy, yet cannot decide whether the good in him came of nature or was the work of a strong will able to wear a pleasing mask with *aplomb.* To them the *Rabotsar,*[3] as they called him, seemed an incom-prehensible mixture of good and evil—a gamester whose conscience was for ever trembling in the balance. Yet this view did not prevent popular rumour from attaching to his name every kind of odium and suspicion. For instance, it was said of him that it was he who induced the Khan of the Crimea to make another raid upon Moscow ; that he put the good Tsar Theodor and his infant daughter (Boris' own niece, Theodosia) to death by starvation ; that he poisoned his sister, the Tsaritsa Alexandra ;

---

[1] See vol. ii. p. 219 *et seq.* [2] In 1861. [3] Tsar of *rabi* (slaves).

that he blinded the ex-"Tsar" of Ivan's *Zemstchina*,[1] Simeon Bekbulato-
vitch (who had long been losing his sight from senile decay); and that
of set purpose he caused the fire in Moscow which followed upon the
murder of the Tsarevitch Dmitri, in order to divert the attention of the
Tsar and the metropolitan community from the crime committed at
Uglitch.   In fact, he became the favourite mark for every sort of political
calumny.   "Who, if not he, murdered the Tsarevitch Dmitri?" said
common report, and openly enough, since unseen tongues bore the fatal
insinuation far and wide over the world.   It was declared that, though
he had not actually borne a hand in that deed of darkness, he had none
the less sent assassins to kill the boy, in order to clear his own road
to the throne.   This alleged share of Boris in the affair is openly dis-
cussed by contemporary chroniclers—though, of course, only on the
strength of hearsay and conjecture.   Of direct evidence there was not
a particle, nor could there be any, seeing that the chief actors in such a
matter always know how to avoid the consequences.   Yet these chronicled
rumours do not reveal all the contradictions and confusion which marked
the report of the commission of inquiry, for the chroniclers understood
Boris' difficult position, as well as that of his adherents, under Tsar
Theodor.   It was necessary for Boris to kill in order not himself to
be killed.   Without doubt the Nagoi family would have shown no mercy
to the Godunovs if the Tsarevitch of Uglitch had acceded to the crown.
Boris himself knew that persons who would ascend the steps of a throne
know neither mercy nor magnanimity.   Yet in one respect contemporary
writers raise a doubt, since Boris bears himself in their pages with
such unguarded frankness.   To him they attribute not only a direct and
active share, but also the *initiative*, in the Uglitch crime, although such
details as unsuccessful attempts to poison the Tsarevitch, periodical
consultations with relatives and intimates as to alternative methods of
removing Dmitri, an unlucky first selection of agents, Boris' chagrin
over this *contretemps*, his comforting by Kleshnin (who promised to carry
out his wishes), and so on, are details with which men so inured to
intrigue as Boris and his friends might have been thought able to dispense.   With such a master in his own line as Kleshnin (a man entirely
devoted to Boris, and, apparently, the prime engineer of the Uglitch
affair) there can have been no need for open speech at all.   A mere hint,
a mere gesture of inspiration, would suffice to ensure comprehension.
Yet it is difficult to suppose that the deed was perpetrated altogether

[1] See vol. ii. pp. 80, 81.

without Boris' knowledge—to suppose that it was not led up to by some underling who had guessed Boris' secret thoughts, wished to do him a good turn, and hoped to secure the fortunes of his (the underling's) party by support of Boris. However, seven years now passed, and were seven years of tranquil rule under Boris. Indeed, time had almost begun to cleanse the stain of Uglitch from his person when the death of Theodor proved the signal for a revival of popular rumour and suspicion. Report now had it that the election of Boris to the Tsarship had been corrupt —that, after poisoning Theodor, Boris had attained the throne by police stratagems which rumour magnified into an organised plot. It was commonly said that every quarter of Moscow, as well as every provincial town, had been worked by agents (including monks from the different monasteries) who had urged the people to petition for Boris as Tsar. Even the widowed Tsaritsa, it was said, had assisted her brother by offering money and favours to the officers of the *Strieltsi*,[1] on condition that they would act on Boris' behalf. The story had it that, under threat of a heavy fine for opposition, the Muscovite police drove the people to the Novodievitchi Monastery, and forced them to make humble petition to the Imperial inmate that she would nominate her brother to the Tsarship. Innumerable constables saw to it that the act of petitioning was carried through with copious tears and lamentation,—so much so that a large number of persons who did not happen at the moment to have any tears ready were forced to daub their eyes with their spittle, in order to avert the batons of the police. When the Tsaritsa appeared at the window of her cell, to assure herself of the national supplication and woe, a signal was made, and at once the populace fell upon their faces to the ground. Persons who could not or would not so prostrate themselves were pricked in the neck from behind with javelins until they had complied, and thereafter the whole assemblage rose to their feet, and started howling like wolves, with stomachs distended and faces purple with the effort, so that the ear could scarcely bear the din. All this was repeated several times until the Tsaritsa, softened by the spectacle of the national devotion, consented to nominate her brother to the Tsarship.

The bitterness underlying these accounts—much, of course, exaggerated—speaks eloquently of the resentment against themselves which Godunov and his partisans did all they could to sow among the community; but it was in 1604 that the worst rumour got about. For the last three years it had been whispered in Moscow that an unknown man

---

[1] Musketeers or Imperial Bodyguard.

had appeared who called himself the Tsarevitch Dmitri. Now the news was openly bruited that the agents whom Boris had dispatched to Uglitch had missed their mark, and had cut the throat of the wrong child—that the real Tsarevitch was still alive, and was about to return from Lithuania to Russia, to regain the throne of his fathers. All minds in Russia were profoundly agitated by the news, and the Period of Troubles began. Boris died in the spring of 1605, his spirit broken by the success which the Pretender had attained : yet, though the latter duly acceded at Moscow, he was shortly afterwards assassinated.

Such were the prelude to and the beginning of the *Smuta* or Period of Troubles. It was evoked, as we have seen, by two circumstances— namely, (1) by the violent and mysterious ending of the old dynasty, and (2) by the artificial resurrection of that dynasty in the person of the First Pretender. The violent and mysterious ending of the dynasty was what started the *Smuta*, since the extinction of a dynasty is necessarily a break in the history of a monarchical State. Yet nowhere has such an extinction been accompanied by more disruptive consequences than was the case in Russia. Usually, when a dynasty expires, another one is chosen, and the State re-establishes itself. Pretenders seldom appear, or, if they do so, no attention whatever is paid them, and they vanish of themselves. With us, however, the light hand of the first false Dmitri allowed the business of pretendership to become a chronic malady in the State ; so that almost until the close of the eighteenth century few reigns passed without a claimant arising. In Peter's time the *lack* of a pretender caused popular rumour even to convert the true Tsar into a usurper. That being so, neither the extinction of the old dynasty nor the appearance of the First Pretender can well have been the actual causes of the *Smuta*. What communicated to those events their disruptive force were conditions of another kind altogether ; and those real mainsprings of the *Smuta* must be sought for in the external circumstances which evoked the Period.

CHAPTER II

As we survey the events of the Period of Troubles we discern its secret causes both in the consecutive development of those events and in their internal connection. The distinguishing feature of the Period is the circumstance that consecutively there figured in it all classes of the Russian community, in the precise order in which they stood in the composition of the community, and precisely as they stood disposed (relatively to their comparative importance in the State) in the scale of social ranks. At the head of that scale stood the boyars, and it was they who initiated the disturbance.

Boris acceded to the throne through the legal method of election by the *Zemski Sobor*. By his personal qualities, as well as by his political services, he was entitled to become the founder of a new dynasty; yet no sooner had a Tsar been elected of their own company than the boyars —who had suffered many things under Ivan IV.—found themselves unable to rest satisfied with the simple customs on which their political status under the old dynasty had been based, and looked to Boris to grant them more secure warranty of that status, and to allow his power to undergo limitation by a formal undertaking that he would "kiss the cross unto the State according unto a charter forewritten" (to quote a passage which has come down to us among the writings of the eighteenth-century historian, Tatistchev). Boris acted in his usual ambiguous manner. Though well aware what the boyars really wanted of him, he made up his mind neither to yield nor to return them a direct refusal. All his calculated comedy of directly declining the proffered power was a mere trick to evade the conditions on which that power was proffered. On the one hand, the boyars remained silent, in the hope that Godunov would of himself come to terms with them on the question of conditions—on the question of the "kissing of the cross"; while, for his part, Boris silently refused the throne, in the hope that the *Zemski Sobor* would elect him without attaching thereto *any* conditions. In this lay Godunov's greatest mistake—a mistake for which, in the end, he and his house paid dearly. This was because from the start his action gave his authority a false basis. Whereas he ought to have held strictly to his mere status as the candidate of the *Sobor*, he attempted to tack himself on to the old dynasty by means of a number of invented testamentary dispositions. The Council's resolution stated, without beating about the bush, that, at the moment when Ivan IV. entrusted the young Theodor to Boris' care, the former addressed to the latter the words, "On his death I do assign unto thee this realm." This was as though Ivan could have foreseen the murder of the young Dmitri and Theodor's childless death! Moreover, the resolution represented Theodor as also having "entrusted his realm," at his decease, to Boris. As a matter of fact, these inventions were due to the friendly zeal of the Patriarch Yov, who composed the resolution just quoted. Boris was not the hereditary *otchinnik* of the Muscovite Empire, but only the chosen candidate of the people. Consequently he began a new line of Tsars which was possessed of a new State significance. Had he wished to avoid becoming an object of scorn or hate, he should have adopted a different line altogether, and not have parodied the extinct dynasty, with its appanage prejudices and traditions. The "great" or leading boyars, headed by the Princes Shuiski, were opposed to Boris' election, on the ground that they feared (so says an ancient manuscript) "that for them (the boyars) and for all men there would come of him oppression." This apprehension Boris ought to have dissipated; indeed, for a time, apparently, the leading boyars expected that he would do so. Consequently we find an adherent of Prince Vassilii Shuiski writing, at the instigation of the latter, that those of the "great" boyars who came of the stock of Rurik, and thus were kinsfolk and accredited descendants of the old Muscovite Tsars according to the *Rodoslovetz*,[1] had no wish to elect a Tsar from among their own circle, but were willing to leave the matter in the hands of the people; since, even without such adventitious aid, they had always been great and glorious, not only in the land of the old-time Tsars, but also in distant countries. Yet that condition of greatness and glory ought to have sought its warranty in a dispensation which took

---

[1] Register of boyar genealogies.

no account of either: and that warranty was to be found only in a limitation of the power of an elected Tsar whom the boyars themselves desiderated. It was a matter in which Boris ought to have taken the initiative, by converting the *Zemski Sobor* from a gathering of service officials into a permanent, popular, and representative parliament of the kind which we have seen glimmering as an idea, in Muscovite minds as early as the reign of Ivan IV. To give him his due, Boris demanded the convocation of such a parliament, for the purpose of ensuring that a Tsar should be elected of all the people; and, had this been done, it might have reconciled the disaffected boyars, and even averted the misfortunes which overtook Boris' family and the country. In other words, it might have caused him to become the founder of a new dynasty. However, the "cunning dissembler" lacked sufficient political acumen to avoid overreaching himself. As soon as the boyars perceived that their hopes were vain, and that the new Tsar intended to rule in the same autocratic manner as Ivan the Terrible had done, they secretly decided to act accordingly. More than one Russian writer of the day explains Boris' misfortunes by the dissatisfaction felt by all the leading men in the country. At the same time, realising this profound resentment of the boyars, Boris took steps to guard himself against their machinations. In the first place, he wove an intricate net of police supervision, wherein the chief part was played by the boyars' own slaves, who had instructions to inform against their masters. Also, a number of released felons were commissioned to haunt the streets of Moscow, in order that they might hear what was being said of the Tsar, and arrest anyone who uttered an unguarded word. Thus denunciation and calumny came to be terrible sources of social division. Men of all classes, including even the clergy, gave information against one another; members of one and the same family feared to hold communication with their fellows; and even to pronounce the Tsar's name became a misdemeanour for which a detective could seize the delinquent and hale him to prison. With this system of denunciation there went court disgrace, torture, capital punishment, and the destruction of homes. "Never before in any State whatsoever have there been such calamities," said men of the day. In particular, great animus marked Boris' operations against the eminent boyar clique which was headed by the Romanovs—a clique wherein he discerned, as he had done in the case of Theodor's cousins, his ill-wishers and rivals. The five Nikitisches, with their kinsmen, friends, and the wives, children, sisters, and nephews of those kinsmen and friends, he banished to different quarters of the Empire; while the head of the family himself—the future Patriarch Philaret—he immured, together with his wife, in a monastery. In short, he was foolish enough to attempt to know the secrets of every hearth, to read the thoughts of every heart, and to lord it over every conscience. He ordained a special prayer which was to be recited at table whenever the health of the Tsar and his family was drunk : and as one reads this hypocritical, fulsome petition, one realises with a pang to what depths a man—even though he be a Tsar—may sink. By such measures Boris created for himself an unenviable position. Although he succeeded in interning the boyar order, with its agelong traditions, in town mansion, country house, and sequestered gaol, it was not long before there stepped into its place, from hole and crevice, the obscure family of the Godunovs, who surrounded the throne, and thronged the palace, of their kinsman with a jealous retinue. Thus the old dynasty became replaced by a family at whose head stood the chosen nominee of the *Zemski Sobor*—a *parvenu* converted into a poltroon with all the petty instincts of a constable. Lying *perdu* in his palace, he seldom appeared before the public eye, and even declined to accord personal interviews to petitioners, although such receptions had been the unvarying custom of the oldtime Tsars. In short, suspicious of every man, and tortured with fears and fancies, he could not have dreaded his fellows more if he had been a thief standing in momentary dread of arrest (to quote the apt phrase of a foreigner then resident in Moscow).

In all probability it was in the *côterie* of boyars most persecuted by Boris—*i.e.* the *côterie* headed by the Romanovs—that the idea of a pretender was first hatched. True, the blame for its incubation was laid upon the Poles, but, though it was baked upon a Polish stove, it was mixed in Moscow. It was not for nothing that, as soon as Boris heard of the false Dmitri, he told the boyars that it was *their* work—that it was *they* who had put forward the Pretender. Of the unknown individual who succeeded Boris on the throne many interesting anecdotes exist. In the first place, his identity has never been aught but conjectural, despite the best efforts of *savants* to unravel it. For a long while there prevailed an idea which emanated from Boris himself—namely, that the Pretender was a certain Yuri Otrepiev, monastically known as Gregory Otrepiev, whose father had been a small burgher of Galitch. Of this Gregory's adventures I need not speak, since they are well known. I need only recall that, at first a slave in the service of certain of the Romanov family and a Prince Tcherkasski, he subsequently entered the priesthood; that, later, his knowledge of literature—in particular, his composition of a work in praise of certain miracle-workers of Moscow—led to his being appointed amanuensis on the staff of the Patriarch; and that in this position he, for some reason or another, went on to declare that he would one day be Tsar of Moscow. For this he would have been interned in a sequestered monastery had he not had powerful friends to protect him who enabled him to escape to Lithuania just at the time when the ban against the Romanov faction was removed. On the other hand, the man who, in Poland, called himself the Tsarevitch Dmitri averred that his chief supporter was a leading *diak* named Shtchelkalov, who also had fallen under Godunov's ban. Whether or not the First Pretender was Gregory Otrepiev, or whether (as seems to me the more probable) he was altogether someone else, it is difficult to say. The important point for us is, not his identity, but the masked *rôle* which he played. On the throne of the Muscovite Tsars he constituted an unprecedented phenomenon. A young man of under medium height, with an uncouth red face and a pensive, downcast air, he expressed in his outward person nothing of his inward nature. Yet he was richly gifted. Possessed both of a vigorous mind which could easily resolve the most difficult questions in the *Boyarskaia Duma* and of a lively—even an ardent—temperament which could snatch success at moments of peril (though it was none the less prone to fits of abstraction), he was a master of the art of speaking, and frequently evinced signs of great erudition. He entirely abolished the old affected order of life of the Muscovite monarchs, with its strained, overbearing relation to the people; he broke through many other customs sanctified by old Muscovite tradition; he never went to sleep after dinner or indulged in baths; and he bore himself towards all men in a simple, approachable manner rather than as Tsar. From the outset he proved himself an active administrator, free from severity, ready to make personal enquiry into everything, constant in his attendance in the *Duma*, and capable of personally training his military forces. Such a form of policy won for him widespread and enthusiastic popularity among the masses. Yet in Moscow not a few persons were to be found who looked upon him with suspicion, or openly accused him of being a usurper. Nay, his best and most devoted adherent, one Basmanov, made secret confession to some foreigners that the Tsar was not the son of Ivan the Terrible, as reputed, but a man who was recognised as Tsar only because allegiance had been sworn to him, and no better Tsar was to be found. Yet the false Dmitri looked upon himself in a very different light. Throughout he acted as though he were the legal, the natural Tsar, and were fully persuaded of his Imperial position. No one who knew him ever discerned on his face the least shadow of doubt on that head, nor had he any misgiving but that the rest of the world looked upon him in the same way. Though the trial of the Princes Shuiski for spreading rumours of his being a usurper was his personal concern alone, he yielded to the general judgment of the country, and convened, for their impeachment, the first *Zemski Sobor* to approximate to the popular representative type—*i.e.* to the type which included delegates chosen from all ranks and all classes of the community. Nevertheless the death sentence which that *Sobor* pronounced upon the Princes he commuted to banishment, and followed that up by restoring the exiles to rank and fatherland. No Tsar who viewed himself in the light of a charlatan-ravisher of the throne could well have acted in such a confident, unguarded manner. Such a man as Boris Godunov would, in similar circumstances, have proceeded, first of all to apportion his victims a cell in a torture establishment, and then to immure them in different prisons. How the false Dmitri came to adopt this view of himself is a problem equally historical and psychological. In any case he did not accept the vacant throne merely in order to justify the expectations of the boyars. Determined not to be a passive instrument in their hands, he carried his independence to excess in the development of his political schemes—schemes which, in the field of foreign policy, were overdaring and comprehensive, since they included a plan to raise all the Catholic powers, headed by Orthodox Rus, against the Turks and the Tartars. At intervals, also, he would intimate to his councillors in the *Duma* that they were poor, blind, ignorant persons—that they ought to travel abroad and improve themselves; but this he did goodhumouredly, and without giving offence. More irritating to the highly born boyars was the familiarity which existed between the throne and the Tsar's presumptuous, ill-educated relatives, as well as the weakness of the latter for foreigners—especially for foreigners who were Catholics. In the *Boyarskaia Duma* as many as five of the Nagoi family held seats as boyars, while three more of that clan were included among the *okolnichi*,[1] as *diaki* or heads of State departments. Even greater offence was caused, not only to the boyars, but also to Muscovite citizens at large, by the throng of unattached, peripatetic Poles with whom the new Tsar flooded Moscow. In the memoirs of the Polish *hettman* Zholkevski (who took an active part in Muscovite doings during the Period of Troubles) there is recorded

[1] See vol. ii. p. 258.

an incident in Cracow which forcibly illustrates the position of affairs in the Russian capital. At the beginning of the year 1606 the false Dmitri dispatched to Cracow a commissioner named Bezobrazov, for the purpose of acquainting the Polish King with the accession of the new Tsar to the Muscovite throne. Justified as ambassador by his rank, Bezobrazov gave the Polish Chancellor a secret intimation that he wished to speak to him alone; and when an equerry was sent to listen to his tale he delivered himself of the message which had been entrusted to him by the Princes Shuiski and Golitzin—namely, that they (the boyars) greatly blamed the King of Poland for having given them for their Tsar a man who was not only a low, thoughtless, cruel, dissolute rascal, but also a man who was both unfit to occupy the Muscovite throne and unable to treat his boyars with common decency. They (the boyars)—so said the message—could not think how to get rid of him, nor whether it would not be better for them to recognise as their Tsar the King's son Vladislav. From this it is clear that at that time the aristocracy in Moscow were contemplating some move against Dmitri, and that they were only deterred therefrom by a fear lest the Polish King might take the part of his nominee. Thus the false Dmitri's customs and departures from custom (in particular, his frivolous treatment of all ceremonial, certain individual acts and dispositions of his, and his foreign policy) brought down upon his head a storm of curses and reproaches on the part of more than one class in the Muscovite community; though, outside the walls of the capital, and among the masses at large, no perceptible weakening of his popularity was to be detected. The chief cause of his downfall was quite different. To it Prince Vassilii Shuiski, principal director of the boyar conspiracy against the Pretender, gave concise testimony when, at a meeting of his fellow-conspirators on the eve of the affair, he declared that he had recognised the false Dmitri as Tsar only in order to be delivered from Godunov. The "great" boyars were forced to create a pretender for the purpose of dislodging Boris, and thereafter to dislodge that pretender for the purpose of clearing the road to the throne for a member of their own circle. In this policy they made equal division of the work. The former portion was entrusted to the Romanov faction, and the latter to the titled faction which was headed by Prince Vassilii Shuiski. Both the two factions saw in the Pretender a puppet which was to be held on the throne for a while, and then cast aside as done with. Yet the conspirators could not hope to cause a rising without the aid of chicanery. Those who murmured most bitterly against the Pretender were the Poles; yet, in lieu of deciding to raise the people simultaneously against both the Pretender and the Poles, the boyars separated the two objectives, and on the 17th of May, 1606, led the populace to the Kremlin with the cry, "The Poles are killing the boyars and our Tsar!"—their real object being to surround the false Dmitri, under pretence of defending him, and then put him to death.

The Usurper Tsar was succeeded on the throne by the Conspirator Tsar, Vassilii Shuiski. Shuiski was then a middle-aged boyar of fifty-four —a man who, though small of stature, plain of exterior, and short of sight, was nevertheless no fool. Yet he was cunning rather than clever; an inveterate liar and intriguer who would go through fire and water to attain his ends; a conspirator who had looked upon the block, and escaped it only by favour of the Pretender against whom he had been working in secret; an assiduous devotee of the society of the learned; and a convinced dreader of the power of wizards. He opened his reign with a series of proclamations which were published broadcast through-out the Empire, and included, in each case, at least one falsehood. Thus in the rescript whereby he announced his taking the oath of accession he wrote of himself: "It seemed good unto him to kiss the cross, in token that he will deliver no man over unto death save that he (the Tsar) do first judge him with true judgement, in company of all the boyars." As a matter of fact (as we shall presently see) Shuiski said nothing of the kind when subscribing the oath. In another proclamation, written in the name of the boyars and the various ranks of officialdom, we read that, on the overthrow of Gregory Otrepiev, the Holy Synod, boyars, and others " did choose a Tsar for all the State of Moscow," and selected for that purpose the Prince Vassilii Ivanovitch, "Autocrat of All Rus." The document is clear as to election by a council: yet, as a matter of fact, no such election was held. True, on the downfall of the Pretender, the boyars decided to make a general appeal to the country, and to summon to Moscow delegates from every town, "to the end that by concord there be chosen a Tsar who shall be beloved of all men"; but Shuiski was afraid of the townsmen, the provincial electors, and made a counter proposal that the pan-territorial convention should be dispensed with. A few of the great titled boyars tacitly recognised him as Tsar, and his name was publicly acclaimed in the Red Square by the large and devoted band of Muscovite citizens whom he had raised against the Pretender and the Poles; yet in that same Moscow—so an old chronicle tells us—there were persons who had not even an inkling of what was happening. In a third proclamation issued in his name the new Tsar did not scruple to adduce false or forged Polish evidence concerning an alleged design on the part of the Pretender to effect a wholesale massacre of the boyars, and to convert all Orthodox Christians to the Lutheran or the Latin faith. None the less, the accession of Tsar Shuiski constitutes a landmark in our political history, since, in acceding to the throne, he not only put limits to his authority, but formally expounded the conditions of such limitation in the proclamation concerning the taking of the oath of succession which he published broadcast throughout the country.

The proclamation referred to is so vague and compressed in its wording as almost to convey the impression of having been a rough draft, hastily composed. At its close the Tsar gives all Orthodox Christians a general undertaking that he will "judge them with true and lawful judgement"—*i.e.* in accordance with law, not at his individual discretion; yet in the body of the document we find this condition rather disjointed. Cases of more serious crime, such as were punishable with death and confiscation of property, the Tsar binds himself to deal with "in company with his boyars"—*i.e.* with the *Duma;* while he also renounces his Imperial right to sequestrate the property of those relatives of the delinquent who might not have taken any part in the crime. Then the Tsar continues: "Unto false witnesses will I lend not mine ear, but will ever pursue steadfastly with all pursuance, and will set them (the witnesses) before mine eyes"; while the said false witnesses, on conviction, he undertakes to punish according to the amount of guilt brought home to the perjured. This would seem to refer to less criminal offences—to offences which were to be dealt with by the Tsar alone, without the aid of the *Duma.* Also, it gives a more exact definition of the term "true judgement." Thus the proclamation distinguishes two forms of the supreme court—namely, trial by the Tsar in conjunction with the *Duma,* and trial by the Tsar alone. The document ends with a rather peculiar condition —namely, that the Tsar will not "upon any man lay his ban without cause." The *opala* or Imperial ban referred to was imposed upon State servitors who had incurred the Sovereign's censure, and was accompanied by service deprivations which corresponded to the dereliction of the individual banned or to the depth of the Imperial displeasure; such deprivations consisting either of banishment from court ("from before the serene eyes of the Tsar"), abasement in rank or in post, sequestration of property, or eviction from *pomiestïe* or town mansion. In this connection the Tsar acted, not on judicial, but on disciplinary, authority—for the preservation of the interests of, and the maintenance of good order in, the service. Consequently, as an expression of the master will of the Sovereign, the ban needed no justification, and, in the then state of Muscovite society, it sometimes assumed barbarous and capricious forms which converted a disciplinary measure into capital punishment. Under Ivan the Terrible the merest doubt concerning the professional devotion of an official was sufficient to bring the delinquent to the scaffold. For that reason Tsar Shuiski was giving a bold undertaking (though, of course, one which he never fulfilled) when he said that he would impose his ban only on due conviction of guilt, seeing that for the preliminary detection of guilt there still remained the necessity of establishing special disciplinary procedure.

From this it will be seen that the proclamation was a very one-sided affair, since the whole of the obligations which Shuiski assumed therein were directed exclusively to limiting the security of the person and property of the subject against the freewill of the Sovereign ; while at the same time they in no way bore directly upon the general bases of the State order, or changed, or gave more exact definition of, the status, powers, and mutual relations of the Tsar and the superior administrative institutions. Although the proclamation subjected the Imperial authority to the consultative voice of the boyars, with whom the Sovereign had always hitherto acted, that limitation had little binding force upon the Tsar in judicial matters, or in his relation to individuals. At the same time, the origin of the accession proclamation is of even more complex nature than the contents of the document, since the document had a secret history of its own. A chronicler tells us that, immediately upon being proclaimed Tsar, Shuiski repaired to the Usspenski Cathedral, where he made a declaration which had never once, during the centuries, been honoured in the State of Moscow. "Hereby," he said, " I do kiss the cross *unto all the land*, in token that ill shall unto no man be done *without the Council*"; and, upon the boyars representing to him that he ought not to give such an undertaking, seeing that it had never before obtained in the history of the Muscovite Empire, he declined to listen to them. Shuiski's step seemed to the boyars a revolutionary departure in that the Sovereign summoned to participate in his judicial practice as Tsar, not the *Boyarskaia Duma*, the agelong coadjutor of the Sovereigns in all matters of legal and general administration, but the *Zemski Sobor* or Territorial Council—an institution recently established, and one which was convoked only at rare intervals for the consideration of extraordinary questions of State life. In this departure they saw an unprecedented innovation, an attempt to supplant the *Duma* with the *Sobor*, a design to shift the centre of gravity of State life from the boyar ring to popular representation. Eventually the Tsar decided to govern with the help of the *Sobor*, although he had been afraid to make use of that body to gain the throne. Yet he knew quite well what he was about. By binding himself, ere he headed the revolt against the Pretender, to govern " by common counsel " with his fellow-boyars he contrived to figure as a Tsar who was imposed upon the country by a clique of the leading nobles, and therefore as a boyar, a partisan, Sovereign who was forced to act always at the dictation of others. Yet in reality his quest was provincial support for his irregular authority, and in the *Zemski Sobor* he hoped to find a counterpoise to the *Boyarskaia Duma*. In swearing before the country at large that he would award no penalty whatever save with the co-operation of the *Sobor*, he reckoned to rid himself of boyar tutelage, to become a pan-territorial ruler, and to limit his authority with a stipu-lation hitherto unprecedented — in other words, to free it from *all* practical limitation. Consequently, in the form in which it was published to the nation, the proclamation of which we are speaking was the fruit of a deal between Tsar and boyars. By tacit agreement of long standing the Sovereign had always been accustomed to share his authority with his boyars in matters of legislation, administration, and legal practice. Now, however, that it was a case of pitting their *Duma* against the *Zemski Sobor*, the boyars did not insist upon the publication of all the concessions which they had demanded of the Tsar, for the reason that it would have been indiscreet to reveal to the community at large how cleanly their cock had been plucked. - No ; the accession proclamation merely emphasised the status of the *Boyarskaia Duma* as a plenipotentiary assistant to the Tsar in cases remitted to the supreme court. At the time this was all that the boyars required. Although, as the ruling class, they had, throughout the sixteenth century, shared authority with the Sovereign, individual members of that class had suffered many things from the Imperial freewill of Tsars Ivan IV. and Boris Godunov. Consequently the boyars seized the present opportunity to abolish that freewill, and to safeguard private persons (*i.e.* themselves) from any possible repetition of the misfortunes which they had suffered in the past, by binding the Tsar to consult the *Boyarskaia Duma* in all political cases. At the same time they secretly hoped that, in virtue of ancient custom, the administrative power would remain in their hands, as of old.

The lack of detail in Shuiski's accession proclamation causes it to constitute a new and unprecedented State document in Muscovite Imperial law, since it represents a first attempt to build a State order on the basis of a formally limited supreme power. Into the composition of that power it introduced an element—more precisely, an instrument—which effected a radical change in the character and structure of the power in question. The point lies, not in Shuiski's putting limits to his authority, but in the fact that by his oath of accession he put limits to that authority which caused him to figure both as an elected and as a sworn Sovereign. In its very essence the oath negatived that personal authority of a Tsar of the old dynasty which had grown up out of the appanage relations of the manorial Sovereign of past ages. At the same time, Shuiski renounced three of the prerogatives wherein that personal authority of a Tsar had found its clearest expression. Those prerogatives were (1) "ban without cause"—*i.e.* the Sovereign's displeasure without due occasion and at his individual discretion alone, (2) confiscation of the property of such of the relatives of an incriminated person as had not participated in the given crime (abjuration of this right rendered nugatory also the old institution whereby a family was made politically responsible for all its members), and (3) the right of extraordinary trial of criminal cases on mere denunciation, accompanied by torture and *ogovor* (forced incrimination of accomplices),[1] but without confrontation, evidence of eye-witnesses, and certain other resources of the normal process. These prerogatives had constituted the essential *nucleus* of the authority of the Muscovite Sovereign as expressed in the *formulæ* of Ivan III. and Ivan IV. when the former said, "To whom I will, to him will I give the Princeship," and the latter declared, "We are free to reward our slaves, even as we are free to punish them." By forswearing these prerogatives Tsar Shuiski became converted from a master of bondsmen into a constitutional monarch of subjects—a Sovereign who ruled by law.

Yet the boyars did not act as an unanimous ruling class during the Period of Troubles, but split asunder into two sections. From the higher grade of the order there broke off the "middle boyars," to whom there afterwards became added the metropolitan *dvoriané* and the officials of *prikazi*[2] (*diaki* or State clerks): and from the time of the accession of Shuiski onwards this section played a large part in the upheaval. For one thing it elaborated yet another plan for the reorganisation of the State—a plan which, like Shuiski's, was founded upon a limitation of

---

[1] See vol. ii. p. 275.   [2] See vol. ii. chap. xiv.

the supreme power, but included in its scope a much wider circle of political relations than had been the case in Shuiski's manifesto. The deed wherein the plan was embodied was composed under the following circumstances. Few persons felt satisfied with Shuiski—the chief reasons for this being his irregular progress to the throne and his dependence upon a clique of boyars who, like children, had taken him for a plaything (to quote the phrase of a contemporary writer). When men are dissatisfied with the powers that be, the way begins to lie open for a pretender. Accordingly pretendership soon became the stereotyped form of Muscovite political thought, and into it every social grudge resolved itself. From the earliest moments of Shuiski's reign there arose rumours of the escape of the first false Dmitri—*i.e.* rumours of a second pretender, even though no second false Dmitri was yet preparing. In 1606 this phantom brought about a rising of the Northern Territory and the Trans-Okan towns, headed by Putivl, Tula, and Riazan. Defeated by the Tsar's forces near Moscow, the insurgents next took refuge in Tula, whence they sent to Prince Mnizhek [1] a request that from his factory of pretenders he should send them a man of some sort to masquerade as the Tsarevitch Dmitri. At length a second false Dmitri of the kind was found, and, on being reinforced by Polish-Lithuanian and Cossack bands, he, in the summer of 1608, took up his position at the suburban village of Tushino, where he held under his thievish thumb the very centre of the Muscovite Empire—namely, the region enclosed by the rivers Oka and Volga. The course of affairs in Moscow was the further complicated by international relations. Already I have mentioned the enmity which existed between Poland and Sweden, owing to the fact that Sigismund III., elected King of Poland, had been ousted from the hereditary Swedish throne by his uncle, Charles IX. Since the Polish Government secretly, if not openly, supported the second Pretender, Shuiski turned to Charles for help against the brigand of Tushino, and the negotiations conducted by the Tsar's nephew, Prince Skopin Shuiski, ended in the dispatch of an auxiliary Swedish force, under the leadership of General Delagarde. Upon this the Tsar had no choice but to make a permanent alliance with Sweden against Poland, as well as to agree to various other onerous concessions ; which direct challenge was met by Sigismund with an open rupture, and in the autumn of 1609 he laid siege to Smolensk. In the camp of the Pretender at Tushino there were serving a large number of

---

[1] Palatine of Sandomir in Poland, who had supported the cause of the First Pretender, and given him his daughter, Marina, in marriage.

Poles, under the command of one Prince Rozhinski, *hettman* of the Tushino district; but these Polish allies looked with scorn upon the would-be Tsar, who, dressed in a peasant's costume and mud-bespattered boots, was only too glad to remove himself to Kaluga, where he could escape the close watch that was set upon him at Tushino. Subsequently Prince Rozhinski made an agreement with the Polish King, and thereupon the latter ordered his men to join him at Smolensk. This example obliged the Russian contingent of the Tushino band to follow suit, while at the same time it chose a deputation for the purpose of treating with Sigismund for the nomination of his son, Vladislav, to the throne of Moscow. The mission in question was composed of a boyar named Michael Saltikov, a few metropolitan *dvoriané*, and half-a-dozen of the leading *diaki* of the Muscovite *prikazi*. Yet among these commissioners we meet with not a single name of standing, although most of the delegates were at least men of good family. Thrust by their own self-assurance, or by the general upheaval, into the turbulent Russo-Polish camp at Tushino, they none the less did not scruple to figure as representative of the Muscovite Empire and Russian land at large. This was sheer presumption on their part—a presumption which gave them no right to general recognition of their fictitious credentials ; yet the fact does not deprive their proceedings of all historical importance, since intercourse with the Poles and better acquaintance with their freedom-loving manners and ideas so widened the political outlook of these Russian adventurers that they suggested to the King, as a condition of the nomination of his son to the Tsarship, that not only should the old rights and privileges of the Muscovite nation be preserved, but that to those rights and privileges there should be added certain new ones which the said nation had never hitherto enjoyed. At the same time, this intercourse, though delighting the Muscovite delegates with a view of foreign freedom, awoke in them also a sense of the national and religious perils which freedom of that kind was likely to entail : so much so that Saltikov actually burst into tears when speaking to the King concerning the maintenance of Russian Orthodoxy. In the end this dual consideration found expression in certain precautions wherewith the commissioners from Tushino sought to safeguard their fatherland against the power—alien alike in faith and in race—which they were engaged in invoking from abroad.

In no State instrument of the Period of Troubles does Russian political thought attain so high a level as it does in the treaty made by

Michael Saltikov and his companions with King Sigismund. Concluded at Smolensk on February 4th, 1619, the document both sets forth the conditions on which the Tushino plenipotentiaries were prepared to recognise the King's son, Vladislav, as Tsar of Moscow and constitutes a political deed wherein there is expounded an elaborate scheme for the re-organisation of the Muscovite State. By way of preamble it formulates the rights and privileges of the Muscovite nation at large, as well as of individual classes therein. Next, it establishes a system of superior administration. Beginning by insisting upon the inviolability of the Russian Orthodox faith, it goes on to define the rights of the people in general and of individual classes in particular. In it rights for safeguarding the personal freedom of the subject from the freewill of the supreme power are worked out from many more points of view than is the case in the accession manifesto of Tsar Shuiski. Indeed, it may be said that in this treaty of February 4th the idea of personal rights—hitherto so little remarked by us—first appears in definite outline. All men are to be judged according to law, and no man is to be punished without trial. This condition the treaty insists upon with especial force, and with repeated demands that, without conviction of guilt, and without trial by a court "wherein are all the boyars," no man shall be subjected to a penalty. Evidently the custom of administering punishment without trial or process of law was a very grievous sore in the organism of the State, and one which called for radical treatment by the supreme power. Moreover, in this treaty, as in Shuiski's manifesto, responsibility for the misdemeanour of a political offender is not to fall also upon his innocent brethren, wife, or children, nor to lead to the confiscation of their property. Two other conditions relative to personal rights strike one as novelties — namely (1) that persons of the superior *tchini* or service ranks are not to be degraded without cause, or persons of the inferior *tchini* to be left without promotion for meritorious service; and (2) that every individual in the Muscovite nation is to be free to visit other Christian States for purposes of study, as also to have his property exempt from sequestration by the Tsar. Also, the document contains glimmerings of the ideas of religious tolerance and freedom of conscience. For instance, the treaty binds the King and his son to seduce no one from the Greek to the Roman, or any other, faith, since faith is a gift of God, and it is not befitting that a man should be subjected to duress or oppression on account of his religious tenets. The Russian subject is to be free to hold the Russian faith, and the Lech subject to hold the faith of the

Lechs. In defining *corporate* rights, however, the envoys from Tushino display less broad-mindedness and sense of equity. The treaty binds the King to preserve, and to augment for meritorious service, the rights and property both of the clergy, of "men of the *Duma* and the *prikazi*," of metropolitan and provincial-urban *dvoriané*, and of "sons of boyars"—as well as, partially, of the trading classes; but to the peasantry the King is to refuse right of migration, whether from Rus to Lithuania, or from Lithuania to Rus, or from one landowner to another. Slaves are to be left in their old dependence upon their masters, and the Sovereign is not to award any slave his freedom. Furthermore (as stated above), the treaty establishes a system of superior administration. The Sovereign is to share his authority with two institutions—namely, with the *Zemski Sobor* and with the *Boyarskaia Duma*. Yet, inasmuch as the latter had now become part of the former, the combined *Sobor* figures, in a Muscovite edition of the treaty to which I shall presently refer, as the *Duma Boyar i Vsei Zemli*, or "Council of the Boyars and All the Land." For the first time, also, this treaty draws a distinction between the political powers of the two bodies named. The status of the *Zemski Sobor* is defined by two functions. In the first place, the task of revising or supplementing judicial custom and the *Sudebnik* is to lie in the hands of "the boyars and all the land,"—the Sovereign merely being called upon to give his assent thereto; and inasmuch as judicial custom and the *Sudebnik* of Moscow were then the two guiding authorities in Muscovite jurisprudence, and were possessed of the force of fundamental laws, we see that the treaty conferred upon the *Zemski Sobor* certain revisory powers. To the *Sobor* also was to belong the legislative initiative. In case the Patriarch and the Holy Synod, together with the *Boyarskaia Duma* and representatives of the various *tchini*, should present a petition to the Tsar on matters which were not provided for in the treaty, the Sovereign was to decide the questions raised in company with the Synod, the boyars, and "all the land," as well as "according unto the custom of the Muscovite State." On the other hand, the *Boyarskaia Duma* was to possess legislative authority; with the *Duma* the Sovereign was to transact all current lawmaking, and to promulgate all ordinary laws. Questions of taxation and the remuneration of State servitors (questions which referred to *pomiestia* and *otchini*) were to be decided by the Tsar in company with the boyars and the *dumnie liudi*;[1] and in default of their consent the Tsar was not to introduce any new taxes, nor, in general, to make any

[1] See vol. ii. p. 258.

changes in the taxes which former Sovereigns had established. Lastly, to the *Duma* was to belong the supreme judicial authority. Without prosecutory evidence, and without trial by the Tsar "in company with all the boyars," the Sovereign was not to sentence any man to death, nor to deprive him of honour, nor to send him into exile, nor to degrade him in rank. At this point the treaty once more reiterates that all such matters, as also all matters of succession in the case of persons who should die without issue, are to be dealt with by the Sovereign only in agreement with, and by the advice of, his boyars and *dumnïe liudi;* and that without such agreement and such advice nothing whatever is to be done.

The document was the work of a party or a class—or, rather, the work of the middle classes, especially the metropolitan *dvoriané* and the metropolitan *diaki.* Yet the course of events gave it a wider importance. With the aid of the Swedish auxiliary force the Tsar's nephew, Prince Skopin Shuiski, wrested the northern towns from the insurgents of Tushino, and, in March, 1610, arrived in Moscow. The people were eagerly hoping to see this young and gifted leader succeed his old and childless uncle, but he died suddenly, and, shortly afterwards, the force which Tsar Shuiski had dispatched against Sigismund at Smolensk was defeated at Klushino by the Polish general Zholkovski. Upon this the *dvoriané,* headed by Zachariah Liapunov, dethroned Shuiski and put him to death. Moscow then swore allegiance to the *Boyarskaia Duma* as a temporary Government, since now a choice had to be made between two competitors for the throne—namely, between Vladislav, whose recognition was demanded by General Zholkovski (the latter had by this time arrived in Moscow) and the Pretender (who also had made his way to the capital, on the strength of what he conceived to be the popular feeling for himself). Fear of the latter caused the boyars to come to an agreement with Zholkovski, on terms which Sigismund also accepted at Smolensk; yet the treaty in which, on August 17th, 1610, Moscow took the oath to Vladislav was by no means an exact repetition of the treaty of the previous February. Although most of the articles in the former are set forth in fair approximation to the original, others of them are abbreviated or extended, while yet others are omitted, or interpolated as new additions. These omissions and additions are exceedingly characteristic. For instance, we find that the superior grade of boyars deleted the article concerning the promotion of commoners for meritorious service, and interpolated in its place a new condition whereby "Muscovite houses of

princely and noble degree shall not be oppressed or abased in *otechestvo*,[1]
nor in honour, by men from foreign parts." Also, the leading grade of
boyars deleted the article concerning the right of Muscovites to visit
other Christian countries for purposes of study. Evidently the Muscovite
aristocracy considered such a right to be charged with too much peril
for the established domestic order, since the ruling class of the day stood
on a low level of ideas as compared with their immediate executive
instruments, the middle classes of the service — a fate which usually
overtakes social circles which over-exalt their heads above the activity
of the masses. Thus the treaty of February 4th constituted a complete
fundamental law for establishing a constitutional monarchy; a law which
provided for a reconstruction both of the supreme power and of the fundamental rights of the subject; a law which was eminently conservative
in its nature, as steadfastly maintaining all that had held good under
previous Tsars, according to the old-established customs of the Muscovite
State. When men feel that the habits of life wherein they have hitherto
walked are slipping beneath their feet they grasp at a written law. Saltikov
and his companions had a far livelier sense of the changes that were in
progress than had the boyar aristocracy—they had suffered far more from
the lack of a political charter and the freewill of the supreme power;
while the revolutions and collisions with alien States which they had
experienced not only moved them strongly to seek future resources
against such calamities, but also communicated to their political ideas
a greater breadth and clarity. In short, these commissioners strove to
underpin ancient and tottering customs with a written law wherein those
customs were thought out anew.

In the wake of the upper and middle *dvoriané* of the capital, the
dvoriané "of the line"—the provincial *dvoriané*—were drawn into the
upheaval. Their participation in the unrest first becomes noticeable, like
that of their superiors, in the beginning of the reign of Tsar Shuiski.
The first to take the field were the *dvoriané* of the Trans-Okan and
Sieversskan towns—*i.e.* the towns of southern cantons which lay contiguous to the Steppes, where the perils and alarms of life had bred in
the gentry of the region a warlike and venturesome spirit. In this movement the *dvoriané* of the towns of Putivl, Venev, Kashira, Tula, and
Riazan led the way—the first leader to become prominent being Prince
Shakhovski of remote Putivl—a man of no birth, though titled; and soon
his work was taken up by the descendants of a line of oldtime Riazan

[1] See vol. ii. p. 46.

boyars, who had now sunk to be plain *dvoriané*—namely, the Liapunovs and the Sunbulovs. But the real directors of these bold, half-savage gentry of the Steppes was Procopi Liapunov, a magnate of the town of Riazan, and a resolute, overbearing, tempestuous man. He was the first malcontent to see how the wind blew. But his hand usually put itself to a piece of work before his head had fully considered it. Even while Prince Skopin Shuiski was still *en route* for Moscow, Liapunov sent to hail him as Tsar, despite the fact that the elder Shuiski was still alive : which action ruined the position of the nephew at his uncle's court. In the previous year Sunbulov, a friend of Liapunov's, raised a rebellion in Moscow; on which occasion the insurgents cried out that the Tsar was a gross and dishonourable man, a drunkard and a fornicator, and that they had risen to avenge their brethren, the *dvoriané* and "sons of boyars" whom they alleged to have been drowned or put to the sword by the Tsar and his favourites, the "great boyars." This was a rising of the inferior *dvoriané* against the aristocracy. At length, in July, 1610, Liapunov's brother, Zachariah, assisted by a band of his fellow *dvoriané* (all of them men of no considerable standing), succeeded in dethroning the Tsar. In this they were opposed by the clergy and the "great boyars"; wherefore the political aspirations of the inferior provincial gentry are a little hard to understand. At first they joined with the clergy in spiting the boyars by electing Boris Godunov to the throne, and had shown themselves delighted with that ruler, since he was *of* the boyars, yet not *for* them. Nevertheless we see them again rising— this time against Tsar Shuiski, although he too was a purely boyar Tsar. Their own candidates for the throne were, first of all, Prince Skopin Shuiski and, subsequently, Prince V. Golitzin. At the same time, a State document exists which throws a certain light upon the political attitude of this class. After deciding to swear allegiance to Vladislav, the Muscovite boyar Government sent an embassy to Sigismund, to beg of him his son for the Tsarship; whereafter, through fear of the Muscovite populace (whose sympathies lay wholly with the Second Pretender), the Government induced the Polish general Zholkovski to move with his contingent upon the capital. At the close of 1610 the death of the brigand of Tushino[1] united the hands of all, and a strong popular movement set in against the Poles. Towns were united and banded together to clear the Empire of foreigners, and among the first to rise was the city of Riazan, headed by its leading spirit, Procopi Liapunov. Yet before

---

[1] *i.e.* the Second Pretender.

the massed contingents could reach Moscow the Poles had drawn the sword upon the Muscovites, and fired the capital (March, 1611). Thereupon, investing what remained of the city—namely, the Kremlin and the Kitaigorod (the latter the quarter where the Poles had entrenched themselves)—the contingent elected a temporary Government of three persons—namely, two leaders of Cossacks (the Princes Trubetskoi and Zarutski) and the president of *dvoriané*, Procopi Liapunov. As a guide to these three governors there was framed a treaty, which was signed by them on June 30th, 1611. The bulk of the insurgent force consisted of provincial State servitors, whose armament and support depended upon what they could wring from the cesspayers, urban and rural; yet, though it was only in the camp of these *dvoriané* that the treaty was composed, the document is none the less styled "a treaty of all the land." Similarly, the three governors purported to be elected "by all the land." Thus we see men of a single class—the armsbearing *dvoriané* —figuring as representatives of the nation at large. Of political ideas few can be remarked in this treaty; wherefore class claims bulk in it the more. The three elected governors were bound "to order the land, and to give thought unto all matters of territory and of war"; yet the treaty permitted of their taking no important step without first of all calling a council of the whole camp. This council appears to have been the supreme dispositive authority, and to have arrogated to itself powers far in excess of those conferred upon the *Zemski Sobor* by the treaty of February 4th. In general the document of June 30th concerns itself mostly with safeguarding the interests of the State service class. It regulates their relations, service and agrarian, and refers to their *pomiestia* and *otchini;* yet of the peasantry and the small homesteaders we find no mention made, save to ordain that peasants who had absconded or had been abducted[1] during the Disturbed Period should forthwith be returned to their old masters. The contingent remained two months before Moscow, yet did nothing during that time to deliver the city from the Poles. All that it did was to masquerade as the all-powerful directory of the country. At length, on Liapunov chancing to fall out with his Cossack allies, the camp of the Russian *dvoriané* found itself powerless to defend its leader, and so fell an easy prey to Cossack swords.

Finally, in the train of the provincial State servitors, as well as immediately in sequence to them, there entered into the general upheaval the *liudi zhiletskie* or tenant folk—*i.e.* the simple people, both cesspaying

[1] See vol. ii. chap. xiii.

and non-cesspaying. Beginning by marching hand in hand with the *dvoriané* of the provinces, these classes subsequently separated from the latter, and acted in pure hostility to the boyars and to the gentry. The ringleader of the rising of the southern *dvoriané*—Prince Shakhovski ("a *zavodchik*[1] of full blood," to quote the expression of a writer of the day)—selected as his lieutenant an agent of anything but gentle degree. This was Bolotnikov—a man of very determined nature and an ex-slave, who, in addition, had been a prisoner in the hands of the Turks, had experienced a Turkish galley, and had returned to his native land as an agent of the Second Pretender at the time when the latter had not yet materialised, but was still being thought of. The movement initiated by the *dvoriané* this Bolotnikov introduced into the social depths whence he himself had sprung. Selecting his forces from among the poorer burghers, homeless Cossacks, and runaway peasants and slaves—in short, from among the *strata* which lay at the very foot of the social scale—he hounded them on against the *voievodi*, the masters, and all who were in authority; until, supported by the insurgent *dvoriané* of the southern districts, he and his rabble army were able to make a triumphal march upon Moscow without exchanging even a blow with the Tsar's troops. At this point a cleavage took place between the two temporarily and incongruously united classes : yet Bolotnikov still persisted in his enterprise. From his camp near Moscow he distributed proclamations wherein slaves were invited to slay their masters (in return the slaves were to be awarded the wives and property of the slain), and to rob and beat traders. In fact, he promised all thieves and rogues the status of boyars or *voievodi*, and, in addition, honours and riches without stint. On perceiving whom they had to deal with, as well as that Bolotnikov's force was only for the people, Procopi Liapunov and his fellow leaders of *dvoriané* deserted the popular general, transferred their services to Tsar Shuiski, and assisted the Imperial troops in dealing the rabble contingents a crushing blow. Bolotnikov himself was killed, but his efforts found a universal echo. Everywhere the peasantry, slaves, and alien settlers of the Volga region—in short, everyone who was either fugitive or without substance—rose for the Pretender. The interposition of these classes not only served to prolong the Period of Troubles, but also communicated to it another character. Hitherto it had been a *political* struggle—a quarrel concerning a form of government, concerning the reorganisation of the State ; but as soon as ever the social depths arose

---

[1] See vol. ii. chap. xiii.

the upheaval became converted into a *war of society*, an extermination of the upper classes by the lower.   Even the candidature of the Pole, Vladislav, attained a certain measure of success only because the lower classes took part in the struggle.   That is to say, the aristocracy hardened their hearts, and agreed among themselves to accept the King's son rather than let the throne slip into the hands of the mob's candidate, the brigand of Tushino.   At a conference held with Sigismund at Smolensk in 1610 the Polish magnates who were present stated that the populace had risen all over the Muscovite Empire, that the people were opposed to the boyars, and that practically all authority was in their hands.   Everywhere at that period we perceive sharp social disintegration; everywhere we see the more important of the towns becoming arenas of strife between the summit and the foot of the community; everywhere we hear "honourable" (*i.e.* wealthy) citizens saying (to quote a contemporary) that it were better to serve the King's son than to be murdered by one's own slaves, or to become permanent serfs to the latter.   On the other hand, we see all the men of lesser substance in the towns joining the slaves in flocking to the camp of the Tushino adventurer, in expectation of being delivered from their misfortunes.   Of these classes the political aspirations are difficult to conjecture.   Indeed, one could scarcely attribute to them anything resembling political thought at all.   In the upheaval they were seeking, not a new State order, but an escape from their grievous position ; they were yearning, not for corporate warranties, but for personal relief. The slaves rose in order to rid themselves of their slavery, and to become free Cossacks ; the peasants rose in order to do away with the taxes which fell upon their class, and also to become State servitors or *prikaznïe liudi*.[1] In short, Bolotnikov summoned to his standard all who desired to attain freedom, distinction, and wealth.   For such folk the Pretender was the real Tsar, although in the eyes of more respectable citizens he was only the embodiment of lawlessness and disorder.

Such was the course of the Period of Troubles.   Next let us examine its principal causes and immediate effects.

---

[1] Officials of government departments.

CHAPTER III

To explain the causes of the Period of Troubles is to point out the circumstances which brought it about and the conditions which so long maintained it in being. Of the circumstances which conduced to the Period we already know. They were the violent and mysterious ending of the old dynasty, and its artificial resurrection in the person of various pretenders. Yet the circumstances which conduced to the upheaval, as well as its profound inward causes, attained their force only because they sprouted on a favourable soil which had been worked by the assiduous, though improvident, efforts both of Ivan IV. and of Boris Godunov during the time that the latter was chief administrator of the State under Tsar Theodor. That soil was the depressed, mystified attitude of the community—an attitude which had been created by the enormities of the *Oprichnina* and the secret intrigues of Godunov.

The course of the Period reveals also its causes. The Period was evoked by a fortuitous incident—by the cutting off of the old dynasty. Whether due to force or to nature, the extinction of a family, of a stock, is a phenomenon almost daily to be observed among us. In private life it excites little notice, but the foreclosure of a whole dynasty is a very different matter. At the close of the sixteenth century an event of this kind in Russia led to a political and social struggle: to a struggle at first *political—i.e.* for a form of rule—and, subsequently, to a struggle *social* —*i.e.* to a feud between different classes of the community. In this upheaval a clashing of political ideas was accompanied by a contest of economic conditions;[1] while, as the forces which stood behind the ever-

[1] In the sense of grades or statuses.

47

changing Tsars and the ever-aspiring pretenders, we see the various social *strata* of the Muscovite Empire. Each class was for a Tsar or a would-be Tsar of its own. Such Tsars and candidates were the standards under which the different political aspirations (with, behind them, the different classes of the Russian community) marched. The disturbance began with the aristocratic intrigues of the "great boyars," who rose against the unlimited powers of the new Tsars, and was continued with the political aspirations of the *dvoriané*—the guards' corps—of the capital, who took up arms against the oligarchic schemes of the "great boyars" in the name of political freedom for the military caste. The rising of the metropolitan *dvoriané* was followed by one of the provincial *dvoriané*, who had a mind to rule the country. These, in turn, attracted to their standard the non-official classes of the provinces (who were against a State order of *any* kind), in the name of personal emancipation—*i.e.* of anarchy. Each of these stages in the upheaval was accompanied by the interposition of Cossack and Polish offscourings of the Muscovite and Lithuanian Empires, who seized upon the unsettled state of the Russian land as an excuse to come from their lairs on the Don, the Dnieper, and the Vistula, and to rob and pillage at their ease. At first, in view of the imminent disruption of the community, the boyars tried to unite all classes on behalf of a new State order; but, unfortunately, that order did not conform to the ideas of the other classes in the community. Next, an attempt was made to avert the catastrophe by artificially recreating the late defunct dynasty (hitherto the only factor which had served to curb dissension) in the hope of reconciling the divergent interests of the several classes in the person of a pretender. In fact, pretendership was resorted to as a means of escape from the warring of those interests. When the attempt proved unsuccessful, even on second trial, there seemed to remain no political tie, no political interest, which could avert the disruption of the community. Yet that disruption never came about: only the State order tottered. Though the political fastenings of the social system burst asunder, there remained the stronger clamps of nationality and religion to preserve the fabric. Slowly, but surely, educating the population which they ravaged, Cossack and Polish bands forced the mutually hostile classes of Russian society to combine, not on behalf of a State order, but on behalf of the national, religious, and civic security which was menaced by those Cossacks and Poles. Thus, though the upheaval derived its strength from universal social dissension, it reached its end through the fact that the entire community was forced to enter upon a struggle with the extraneous forces—alien and destructive to Russian nationality—which had ventured to intrude themselves into the domestic feud.

Thus we see that the course of the Period of Troubles very clearly reveals two of the conditions which maintained it. Those two conditions were pretendership and social discord. To them we must look for guidance to the principal causes of the unrest. Already I have had occasion to point out one misapprehension in the political consciousness of the Muscovites—namely, the misapprehension that, though, as the union of a nation, a State can belong to none but the nation itself, both the Muscovite Tsar and the Muscovite people looked upon the Muscovite Empire as the hereditary manor of the princely dynasty from whose property it had developed. In this manorial-dynastic view of the Empire I see one of the fundamental causes of the Troubled Period. The misapprehension to which I have referred was bound up with a certain poverty or immaturity of political ideas, since the latter were altogether divorced from the elemental working of the national life. In the public conception the Muscovite Empire was still understood only in the old appanage sense—*i.e.* in the sense of being the estate of the Muscovite Tsars, the family property of Kalita's stock, by whom that property had been directed, extended, and consolidated during a space of three centuries. In reality the Empire was a union of the Great Russian race. True, men's minds had grasped the idea of the Russian land as an integral entity, but those minds had not risen to the idea of the nation as a union of State. The real ties of that union were still the free-will and the interests of the lord of the Imperial Manor. To this it may be added that such a manorial view of the State was no dynastic claim of the Muscovite Tsars, but a part of the political thought of the day, as inherited from the appanage period. At that time a State was looked upon in Russia as the *otchina* or heritable property—the manor—of the Tsar of a given dynasty; and if the average Muscovite citizen of those days had been told that the authority of the Tsar was also the Tsar's obligation or duty, and that, in administering the nation, the Tsar also served the State and the public weal, such a statement would have seemed to the hearer a confusion of ideas, a sheer anarchy of thought. This enables us to understand the conception of the relation of the Tsar and the nation to the State which the then Muscovite population had worked out for itself. That conception was the view that the Muscovite Empire wherein the Muscovite population had its being was the Empire of the Muscovite Emperor, and not of the Muscovite, the Russian, nation. The two inseparable ideas in the matter were, not the State and the nation, but the State and a lord of that State who belonged to a given dynasty. It was easier for Moscow to imagine an Emperor without a people than an Empire without an Emperor. This view found characteristic expression in the political life of the Muscovite nation. When a people, hitherto associated with its Government through the idea of the welfare of the State, becomes dissatisfied with the ruling authority, on seeing that such authority does not properly safeguard the public welfare, it usually rises against it. Similarly, when servants or lodgers who are associated with a master or a landlord through temporary and conditional amenities perceive that they have ceased to receive those amenities they usually quit his establishment. Yet, when rising against authority, a people seldom also abandons its State, since it looks upon that State as one with itself ; whereas a servant or a lodger who is dissatisfied with his master or his landlord ceases to remain in the house of the latter, for the reason that he (the servant or the lodger) does not look upon that house as his own. The population of the Muscovite Empire acted rather as servants or lodgers who are dissatisfied with their landlord than as citizens who rebel against a Government. They murmured against the acts of the authority which ruled them : yet never once during the time that the old dynasty was still alive did they allow popular dissatisfaction to attain the point of rebelling against the authority itself. On the contrary, the Muscovite nation ended by devising a special form of political protest. Malcontents who could not stomach the existing order of things did not *rise* against it, but simply *left* it—" wandered afar," *i.e.* departed out of the State. The Muscovite of the age seemed to feel that he was only a temporary sojourner in the Empire—a mere chance, removable inmate of another's man's house. In the event of his finding the position irksome he considered it possible to leave the uncongenial landlord, yet never quite to reconcile himself to the idea of *rebelling* against that landlord, or of establishing another *régime* in the mansion. Thus the central knot of all relations in the Muscovite Empire was, not the thought of the popular weal, but the person of a member of a given dynasty ; and a State order was considered possible only under a Tsar of that particular dynasty. Consequently, when the dynasty came to an end and the State appeared to be no man's property, men felt at a loss, and, abandoning their old conceptions of who or where they were, took to roaming afield, and living in anarchistic fashion. They felt themselves to be anarchists against their will and through an obligation which, though calamitous, was also inevitable : and since no one was to blame for this state of affairs, they felt it incumbent upon them to run amok.

The next event was the election of a Tsar by a *Zemski Sobor* or Territorial Council. Yet the very novelty of such an election by such a body caused it to be looked upon as an insufficient justification for a new power in the State. Thus it gave rise to doubt and alarm. The Council's decree announcing its choice of Boris Godunov shows, in itself, that the Council had foreseen what men would say of the electors who were responsible— namely, that " we do stand apart from them (the electors), in that they have appointed a Tsar unto themselves." At the same time, we find the document dubbing anyone who so expressed himself " both foolish and accursed." Also, in a lengthy pamphlet of 1611 it is related that the author of the script was vouchsafed a miraculous vision wherein he was informed that God Himself would show who was to rule the Russian State, and that any ruler whom the State might appoint on its own account " would never be Tsar." In short, never during the course of the Period of Troubles did men grow accustomed to the idea of an elected Sovereign. They thought that such a ruler could not be Tsar at all—that the only true, legal Tsar must of necessity be a born, hereditary scion of the line of Ivan Kalita. Consequently they strove by every manner of means to connect their elected Sovereign with that line—both by juridical devices, by a stretching of genealogical points, and by rhetorical exaggeration. Thus, Boris Godunov, when elected, was greeted by clergy and people as " hereditary Tsar " ("they offered unto him greetings touching his *otchina*, the State "); while Vassilii Shuiski, though formally limiting his own power, was none the less described in official documents as *Samoderzetz* or " Autocrat " (after the manner of the title usually ascribed to the old *born* Tsars of Moscow). In view of this unyielding bent of governing circles, the phenomenon of an elected Tsar on the throne must have seemed to the masses of the people less the result of political necessity, however pressing, than something akin to an infringement of the laws of nature. To the masses an elected Tsar would seem as grave an irregularity as an elected father or an elected mother. Consequently simple minds were powerless—were intellectually unable—to fit the idea of a " true Tsar " either to Boris Godunov or to Vassilii Shuiski—still less to the Polish King's son, Vladislav. In such rulers they could see only usurpers, while, on the other hand, even a single sign of a " born Tsar " in the person of a newcomer, however unknown his origin, was sufficient to quiet their dynastic conscience, and to inspire them with respect. The

Period of Troubles ended only when the nation had succeeded in finding a Tsar whom it could connect by birth, however indirect, with the extinct line of Sovereigns.   Tsar Michael established himself on the throne less through the fact that he was the candidate of the country and of the people at large than through the fact that he turned out to be a nephew of the concluding Tsar of the old dynasty.   Such a doubt as to the efficacy of popular election as a regular source of supreme power was the condition which, more than all others, nourished the unrest of the period : which doubt proceeded from a rooted belief that, properly, such a source could only be hereditary, proprietary succession in a given dynasty. Consequently as the first derivative cause of the upheaval which arose from the basis just expounded we must name this inability to adopt the idea of an elected Sovereign.

Furthermore, I have shown that social discord was one of the out-standing features of the Troubled Period.   That discord had its root in the *taxatory character* of the Muscovite State order, and was the second fundamental cause of the disturbance.   In every regularly organised State order there is presupposed, as one of the bases of its regularity, an incumbent correspondence of personal and class rights to obligations : yet in this respect the Muscovite Empire of the sixteenth century was remarkable for a heterogeneous intermingling of socio-political relations of different periods and characteristics.   In the Muscovite Empire there existed neither persons' free and full rights nor free and autonomous classes. Yet the community was not an impersonal mass of population, as in the case of Oriental despotisms, where general equality rests upon a general lack of rights : on the contrary, the Muscovite nation was a dismembered community—a community that was divided into classes whose formation dated from the appanage period.   In appanage days classes had possessed only a civic standing—they had been economic grades, divided strictly by their avocations.   Now, however, they acquired a political character, and were apportioned special State obligations in harmony with their avocations.   Yet still they remained, not corporations, but service divi-sions or grades which were known in the official jargon of Moscow as *tchini*, while the State service that fell upon them was not identical in all cases, since one kind of service gave the classes which were subject to it greater or less powers of disposition or official management, and another kind of service conferred upon the classes which were subject to it a mere obligation of obedience, of execution.   Again, one class had imposed upon it an obligation of government ; other classes served either as the

instruments of the supreme administration or material for military conscription; while yet other classes were called upon to perform certain
taxatory functions. This unequal appraisement of different forms of
State service gave rise to inequality of State and social position among
the several *strata*. Needless to say, the lower *strata*, whereon the upper
rested, had to bear the heaviest burdens; and, needless to say, those
burdens were too heavy for them. Yet even the superior administrative
class, upon which State service conferred the power of commanding the
rest, never acquired direct legislative warranty of its political privileges.
It ruled, not by virtue of right received, but by a *de facto* authority, or
on the strength of agelong custom. To do so was its hereditary craft.
In general, Muscovite legislation was devoted, more or less, to the defining and apportioning of State obligations, and not to the formulating or
securing of rights, whether personal or corporate. In practice, the position
in the State of the individual or the class was defined by his or its duties
to the State. What in such legislation seems to resemble corporate
rights was only a series of personal exemptions which served as mere
auxiliary means to a just performance of duties. Such exemptions were
granted to classes, not as a whole, but as separate local communities,
according to the special conditions of their position. Given urban or
rural communities sometimes acquired relief in taxation or certain exemptions from legal liability: yet of any demand for the establishment
of corporate rights of the urban or rural population at large legislation, as
yet, shows few traces. Even the local corporate autonomy, with its
elective authorities, of which I have spoken was based upon the same
principle of State liability and, consequently, responsibility—whether
personal responsibility, *i.e.* of the individual, or public responsibility, *i.e.*
of local communities as a whole. Such autonomy was only the pliant
instrument of centralisation. Rights secure the private interests of
persons or classes. In the Muscovite State order, however, the pre-
valence of the principle of liability to the State left insufficient room for
those private interests, whether personal or class, and sacrificed them to
demands of State. Consequently, in the Muscovite Empire no incumbent
correspondence existed between rights and obligations, whether personal
or corporate; and though it is true that men put up with this grievous
system (under pressure of external perils, and for the reason that personality and public spirit were, as yet, but feebly developed), the reign
of Ivan IV. had the effect of rendering the community increasingly conscious of the main fault in the structure of the State. The Tsar's freewill

(as manifested in gratuitous executions, bannings from court, and confiscations of property) evoked murmuring, not only among the higher classes, but also among the masses of the people (" Anguish and hatred did arise against the Tsar throughout all the world "); with the result that at length there came upon the Russian community the epoch known as the Period of Troubles, which brought with it tentative demands for a legal warranting of persons and property against the unfettered discretion and caprice of the supreme power.

Yet these demands, added to a general sense of the oppressiveness of the State system, could not of themselves have led to such a profound agitation of the State, had not the dynasty which built the Empire come to a sudden end. That dynasty had been the crown of the Imperial arch, and its disappearance sundered the tie which had hitherto held all political relations together. What men had borne patiently so long as they had been called upon to submit to the will of an accustomed master seemed unbearable as soon as that master was gone. In the memoirs of a *diak* or State clerk named Timotheev we find a striking parable concerning the childless widow of a rich and powerful husband whose house was plundered by her domestics after the latter had broken loose " from their station of slaves," and surrendered themselves to anarchy. In the publicist's figure of this helpless woman we see depicted the position of his native land, left without a " born " Tsar and master. Presently all classes in the community rose with their several needs and aspirations, in the hope of bettering their position in the State. Only at the summit of the community did that rising proceed otherwise than in the case of the *strata* below it ; since, whereas the upper classes strove by legislative methods to consolidate and extend their corporate rights at the expense of the lower classes, we can detect no sign in the latter either of a cherishing of corporate interests or of any desire to acquire rights or to lighten the burdens which fell upon the several sections of the community. In this movement each class acted for itself, in its haste to escape from the grievous position entailed upon it by the rigours and irregular apportionment of liability to the State. Each class strove to pass to another and more exempt condition, and, in doing so, to filch something from a wealthier class. Observant contemporaries emphasise the point that the most striking characteristic of the Troubled Period was the desire of the social depths to rise to the surface, and thence to attain the heights. One such chronicler, the monk Palitsin, writes that in those days every man wished to better his station. Slaves sought to become masters, non-free persons strove to attain freedom, and the military man strained every nerve to issue as a boyar; while persons of better sense gave way to these aspirants, and were afraid to say a word to offend them. The clashing of these conflicting aspirations insensibly led to a keen dissension of classes; which dissension was the second derivative cause of the Period of Troubles, and was evoked by the second of the Period's *fundamental* causes. The initiative in this crumbling of the social system is attributed by contemporary observers to the leaders of the community—*i.e.* to the upper classes, and, most of all, to the new, non-hereditary wielders of the supreme power (to whom Ivan IV. and his *Oprichnina* had already set an encouraging example in this respect). While severely reproaching Tsar Boris for his tardiness in seeking to reorganise the territorial system and reform the administration of the State, these observers also blame him for rewarding slanderers, and for promoting to superior posts low-born men who, in addition to being unused to statecraft, were so illiterate as scarcely to be able to append a shaky, inexpert signature to an official document. This policy of his inspired abler and more experienced State-workers with jealousy; and other pseudo-Tsars who followed him acted in similar fashion. Also, in censuring Boris for his conduct, contemporary writers regretfully recall the " born " Tsars of an earlier day, who knew to what type of man, and in reward for what services, to apportion honour, no matter how low-born the recipient might be. Still greater disorder did Boris Godunov introduce into the community by organising a system of espionage which led to slaves rising against their boyar masters, and then, on those masters falling into disgrace at court, to being turned out into the street, and so forced to become roving freebooters. Tsar Shuiski, again, sowed social discord with both hands when, confirming, with one *ukaz*, the serfdom of the peasantry, he, with a second *ukaz*, restricted the powers of masters over their slaves. In this work of augmenting the popular unrest the upper classes had a share. According to Palitsin, Theodor's reign saw the great lords—particularly such of them as were kinsmen or adherents of Boris Godunov (then head of the administration)—possessed with a furious passion for enslavement, an insistent desire to make bondsmen of everyone whom they came across: and their example was followed by others in the State. From the years 1601 to 1604, however, there ensued a period of famine, when, through the fact that many of the masters were unable or unwilling to feed the slaves whom they had impressed, such dependents were turned away at short notice, and, if they took service with other masters, were prosecuted by their former owners for desertion and theft.

Combined with the first, the dynastic, cause of the Period of Troubles, this — the second, the socio-political — afforded great, though indirect, support to the unrest by the fact that it intensified the action of the first cause, as expressed in the success of the various pretenders. For that reason we may take pretendership to have been the third derivative cause of the Period—a cause which arose out of the joint action of the two fundamental causes named. The question of how the idea of pretendership ever came to permeate the community offers no very great popular-psychological difficulty. The mystery with which the death of the Tsarevitch Dmitri was surrounded gave birth to conflicting rumours, of which the popular imagination selected the most congenial, since the consummation desiderated by the majority of the nation was that the Tsarevitch should one day reappear among the living, and dissipate the gloomy uncertainty in which the future was wrapped. As always happens in such cases, men were disposed to believe that villainy had failed, and that once again Providence had acted as the guardian of mundane equity, and forestalled the villains. In the eyes of the harassed nation the terrible fate of Boris Godunov and his family was a striking manifestation of the eternal justice of God, and helped, more than anything else, to bring about the success of the pretenders. Moral feeling found support in a political instinct which was as irresponsible as, owing to that irresponsibility, it was also intelligible to the masses of the people. Pretendership was the most convenient way of escape from the war of irreconcilable interests aroused by the cutting off of the old dynasty. It mechanically, yet forcefully, united under a familiar, though counterfeit, form of authority those elements in the tottering community for which organic, voluntary agreement was impossible.

That is how the origin of the Period of Troubles must be explained. The soil on which it flourished was the taxatory organisation of the nation, added to a general feeling of discontent which, derived from the reign of Ivan IV., was further strengthened by the rule of Boris Godunov. As immediate circumstances which led up to the upheaval we see the conclusion of the old dynasty and the subsequent attempts to re-establish the Imperial line in the person of various pretenders. As the root causes of the Troubled Period we see, firstly, the popular view of the relation of the old dynasty to the Muscovite Empire—a view which hindered the nation from easily assimilating the idea of an elected Tsar; and, secondly, the structure of the State, with its oppressive taxatory basis and an unequal distribution of State dues which gave rise to social discord. The former cause evoked and maintained such a demand for a resuscitation of the fallen Imperial house as assured the success of the pretenders, while the latter converted a dynastic intrigue into sheer socio-political anarchy. There were other circumstances which contributed to the unrest. Among them may be named the form of policy of the administrators who governed the State from the reign of Theodor onwards; the constitutional aspirations of the boyars, which cut across the character of the Muscovite supreme power and the popular view of that power; the low level of public morality, as depicted by contemporary observers; sentences of court banishment upon boyars; a famine and a pestilence which occurred during Boris's reign; provincial agitation; and the interference of the Cossacks. Yet none of these were so much causes as either symptoms, fostering (though not causative) conditions, or consequences of the Troubled Period. That Period stands on the border-line between two contiguous epochs of our history, and is connected with the former of them by its causes, and with the latter by its effects. The first immediate effect of the Period was to put an end to the duration of unrest by giving rise to the accession of a Tsar who became the founder of a new dynasty.

At the close of 1611 the Muscovite Empire presented a spectacle of universal and complete disruption. The Poles had taken Smolensk; a second Polish force had burnt Moscow and entrenched itself within the surviving walls of the Kremlin and the Kitaigorod; the Swedes had occupied Novgorod, and put forward one of their princes as a candidate for the Muscovite throne; the murdered second false Dmitri had been succeeded, in Pskov, by a third pretender, a man named Sidorka; and the first expeditionary force of provincial *dvoriané* had, on the death of Liapunov, been broken up near Moscow. Meanwhile the country lacked an administration. The *Boyarskaia Duma*, which had assumed the lead on the downfall of Tsar Shuiski, effaced itself when the Poles took the Kremlin, and was succeeded by a small band of boyars, headed by Prince Mstislavski. Its centre lost, the Empire began once more to dissolve into its constituent portions, since each town now acted practically alone, or only in conjunction with other towns. Thus the State became formed into a sort of amorphous, coagulated federation. At length proclamations issued from the Troitski Monastery by the Archimandrite Dionysius and the Abbot Abraham aroused the people of Nizhni Novgorod to combine under their *starosta* or prefect, a butcher named Minin; and to their call, again, responded the State servitors, urban *dvoriané*, and "sons of boyars" of the district—men who, for the most part, had lost, in the general disturbance, both their posts, their emoluments, and, in many cases, their *pomiestia*. For this section Minin found a leader in the person of Prince Dmitri Michaelovitch Pozharski, and thus the second expeditionary force of *dvoriané* was formed. In warlike qualities it in no way excelled the first, though it was well equipped with funds collected by the burghers of Nizhni Novgorod and certain allied towns, at some sacrifice to themselves. After four months spent in preparation it advanced upon Moscow, and was reinforced *en route* by additional bands of State servitors, who begged to be taken on, in the hope of receiving future grants of land. Before Moscow there was also posted a body of Cossacks, under Prince Trubetskoi, which represented a remnant of the first expeditionary force. Yet to the provincial *dvoriané* these troopers seemed stranger individuals even than the Poles: with the result that when Trubetskoi sent the *dvoriané* an offer of co-operation they returned him the answer, "Of a surety we stand not with thy Cossacks!" Soon, however, it became manifest that without Cossack support nothing could be done; and, true enough, throughout a three months' investment of Moscow, nothing whatever of importance issued as the result. Although Pozharski's force comprised in its ranks over forty prominent officers of good service names, only two of his subordinates distinguished themselves, and they were not State servitors at all. The two referred to were the monk Palitsin and the butcher Minin. At Pozharski's request the former of these persuaded the Cossacks to lend their support, at a decisive moment, to the Russian *dvoriané*: while the latter distinguished himself by begging of Pozharski some three or four companies, and then, with their aid, effecting a successful attack upon a small detachment of Poles which, under a *hettman* named Chotkeivitch, was making for the Kremlin with supplies for its beleaguered compatriots. Minin's daring exploit put some heart into the *dvoriané* of the expedition, and encouraged them to force Chotkeivitch to retire, after the Cossacks had duly prepared the way. Next, in October, 1612, the Cossacks took the Kitaigorod by storm; but, for their part, the *dvoriané* could not make up their minds to attack the Kremlin, and it fell only through the fact that at length the handful of Poles who were in possession of it were compelled by hunger—hunger which had brought them to the pitch of cannibalism—to surrender of their own accord. Again, it was Cossack *atamans*, not Muscovite *voievodi*, who repelled King Sigismund from Volokolamsk when he was making for Moscow in order to restore the city to Polish hands, and forced him to return home. In short, we see this expeditionary force of provincial *dvoriané* giving yet a second proof during the Period of Troubles that this class was incapable of the very work which was at once its professional calling and its State obligation.

Next, the two generalissimos of the composite provincial-Russian-Cossack force, the Princes Pozharski and Trubetskoi, sent to every town within the Empire a circular inviting the ecclesiastical authorities and a certain number of elected representatives of the *tchini* or service ranks to participate in a territorial council and State electoral convention, to be held later in the capital; and early in 1613 the members began to arrive in Moscow from all parts of the country. Presently we shall see that this was indisputably the first Council of its kind to be constituted of all classes in the community, as well as that it was participated in by provincial-suburban, and even rural, dwellers. When the members had assembled a three days' fast was held, to the end that the representatives of the Russian land might purge themselves of the sins of the Troubled Period before proceeding to transact the important business in hand. On the conclusion of the fast the meetings of the Council began. The first question set before the body—namely, whether or not a Tsar should be chosen from among the royal houses of other countries —was decided in the negative; the Council decreeing that neither from the Polish nor from the Swedish courts should a prince be elected to the Empire of Moscow, nor a member of any of the German faiths, nor a person hailing from any non-Orthodox country, nor "the son of Marina." [1] Although this decree upset the plans of the adherents of the Polish candidate, Vladislav, to find a "born" Russian Tsar was yet no easy task. Indeed, memorials of the day paint the course of the affair in the Council in very gloomy colours. At first unanimity was wholly absent, and in its place there reigned only dissension. Every man wanted his own way, and every man advocated his own particular views. Some proposed this, some that, and all differed from one another. Puzzled to agree upon a suitable nominee, they kept running over a list of eminent names, yet could not come to a decision upon any one of them. Thus much time was wasted. Many of the leading members, and even some of lesser degree, were for bribing their fellows, and plied them with gifts

[1] The infant child of Marina, widow of the second false Dmitri, who had taken refuge with the Cossacks at Astrakhan.

and promises; but in the end the deputies came to terms, and Michael Romanov was elected. This welter of intrigues, manœuvres, and bickerings was due to the fact that the Council had before it a number of highly-born candidates; among whom annals of later date name the Princes Golitzin, Mstislavski, Vorotinski, Trubetskoi, and Michael Romanov. It is even said that Prince Pozharski—a man of humble birth and retiring character—was an aspirant to the throne, and that he spent much money on the quest. The most likely candidate, in point of talents and personal qualities—namely, Prince Golitzin—was in a Polish prison, while eventually Prince Mstislavski retired from the contest. Of the remainder none could possibly be elected, for the Muscovite Empire had issued from the terrible Period of Troubles with no guerdon of heroes, despite the fact that many brave, but mediocre, men had helped to extricate it from its position. Pozharski was not a Boris Godunov, nor Michael Romanov a Skopin Shuiski. As for the Cossacks, on perceiving the weakness of their *dvorianin* allies, they had taken to running amok in the capital which they had cleared of the Poles, and to doing whatsoever they liked in it without reference to the temporary Government represented by Trubetskoi, Pozharski, and Minin. Yet in the matter of the election of a new Tsar they showed themselves true patriots, and, protesting stoutly against the proposal to choose a Tsar from foreign parts, voted for the Russian candidates proper, the infant son of the second false Dmitri and Michael Romanov (whose father—Philaret—had been chaplain to the two Pretenders, and had received from the first false Dmitri the office of Metropolitan, and, from the second, an invitation to be Patriarch in his, the Pretender's, camp near Moscow). In fact, the Cossacks were the mainstay of pretendership, since, naturally enough, they wished to see the Muscovite throne occupied either by a son of their Tsar of Tushina or by a son of that Tsar's Patriarch. At the same time, the Second Pretender's son was not started as a serious runner, but only to please the Cossacks. Yet the latter forbore to insist upon this candidate of theirs when the *Zemski Sobor* was for rejecting him. Of himself, Michael—then a sixteen-year-old boy of no special distinction—could have had no views to speak of with regard to the throne; yet in his person there met such mutually inimical forces as the *dvoriané* and the Cossacks. Yet this unlooked-for coalescence wavered in the Council itself, for, just when the war of factions was at its height, a *dvorianin* from Galitch (which city had furnished the First Pretender) laid before his fellow councillors a written opinion in which he stated that he who by birth stood nearest to the olden Tsars was Michael Romanov, and that he ought to be elected to the throne. Nevertheless Michael was opposed by a large number of members, in spite of the fact that he had long been regarded as a candidate, and that the Patriarch Hermogen had named him as the proper successor of Tsar Shuiski. The written opinion of the Galitch magnate gave wide offence, and infuriated voices at once cried out, "Who hath brought unto us this writing, and whence?" At this moment a Cossack *ataman* from the Don separated himself from the ranks of his fellow councillors, and, advancing to the throne, deposited there a second parchment. "And what writing hast *thou* lodged there, O *Ataman?*" asked Prince Pozharski. "A writing concerning the born Tsar, Michael Theodor-ovitch," replied the Cossack officer. In fact, the *ataman* practically decided the matter, since a chronicler tells us that "after they had read the writing of the *ataman* the councillors did agree to be at peace and of one mind." So Michael was proclaimed Tsar. Yet this was only a *provisional* election, to demarcate the accepted candidate of the Council. The final decision was left to the independent voice of the country. First of all certain trusty emissaries were sent to every town, for the purpose of ascertaining the feeling of the people concerning the question of whom they wished to be lord of the Muscovite Empire; and since the nation seemed already to have made up its mind, the emissaries soon returned with the report that all men, from small to great, cherished but one thought—namely, that Michael Romanov must be Tsar, and that the people desired none other for the State. This secret police inquiry (combined, it may be, with a certain amount of agitation) was the Coun-cil's method of taking an electoral *plebiscite*. Finally, on February 21st, 1613—the first Sunday in Lent—the decisive elections were held, when each member of the Council presented a written opinion, and every opinion was found to contain but one name—that of Michael Romanov. Thereupon two or three of the spiritual members, accompanied by a boyar, were dispatched to the Red Square; where they had hardly time to request the populace, assembled in its thousands, to signify whom it wished to be Tsar, before the assembly cried out with one voice, 'Michael Theodorovitch!"

Thus the election of Michael by the Council was both engineered and confirmed in the Council and among the people by a series of subsidiary methods, by preliminary agitation with the help of the numerous Romanov family, by pressure from a Cossack force, by secret inquisition among the masses, and by the acclamations of a metropolitan mob in the Red Square. Yet these electoral devices proved successful only because they were supported by the relation of the community to one great house in particular. Michael attained victory, not through personal or propagandist, but through purely family, popularity. He belonged to a boyar stock which was one of the most beloved of the Muscovite public—the Romanovs being a recent offshoot of the old boyar house of the Koshkins. As early as the reign of Ivan Kalita [1] there arrived in Moscow from what the *Rodoslovetz* calls "the Land of Prus" a noble who, in the Muscovite capital, subsequently became known as Andrei Ivanovitch Kobuila. He later rose to be a leading boyar at the Muscovite court, and from his fifth son, Theodor Koshka, there sprang the clan of the Koshkins, who flourished at the Muscovite court throughout the fourteenth and fifteenth centuries. They constituted the only non-titled boyar family to remain non-submerged by the stream of new titled servitors which flooded Moscow from the middle of the fifteenth century onwards; yet even among such men as the Princes Shuiski, Vorotinski and Mstislavski the Koshkins still maintained their place in the front rank of boyardom. Now, at the beginning of the sixteenth century a boyar named Roman Yurievitch Zacharin (who was descended from a grandson of the original Koshka, named Zachariah) was occupying a leading position at court: and it was he who became the founder of the new branch of that family—the branch of the Romanovs. Of his sons, again, Nikita (own brother to the Tsaritsa Anastasia [2]) is remarkable for having been the only Muscovite boyar of the sixteenth century to leave behind him a grateful memory among the people. Indeed, we find his name commemorated in a popular *bilina*, or folksong, of the time of Ivan IV., which depicts him as acting as a sort of benevolent intermediary between the nation and its choleric Tsar. Finally, of Nikita's six sons the most prominent was the eldest, Theodor, who was a gentle, kind-hearted boyar, a dandy, and a great lover of learning. The Englishman Horsey, then resident in Moscow, relates in his memoirs that Theodor was very desirous of acquiring the Latin language, and that, at his request, Horsey compiled for him a Latin grammar in which the Latin words were written in Russian characters. To the popularity of the Romanovs, due to their personal qualities, the persecution which the Nikitisches suffered under the suspicious Godunov [3] undoubtedly contributed. Palitsin even goes so far as to place this persecution among the three sins for which God punished the Russian land

---

[1] 1328–1340.   [2] First wife of Ivan IV.   [3] See p. 27.

during the Period of Troubles. Also, their feud with Tsar Shuiski and their connections with Tushino obtained for the Romanovs the protection of the second false Dmitri, and also popularity in the Cossack camps: whence the family's equivocal bearing during the Period of Troubles won for Michael a double amount of support, both in the provinces and among the Cossacks. What most assisted him, however, in the election in Council was the blood tie which existed between the Romanovs and the old dynasty. During the Troubled Period the Russian nation so often erred in its choice of new Tsars that at length it came to look upon no election as lasting which did not fall upon a person connected—no matter how—with the pristine house of Tsars. Consequently in Michael the nation beheld, not the chosen candidate of the Council, but a nephew of Tsar Theodor, who himself had been a "born" or hereditary Tsar. Indeed, an annalist of the day says that men desiderated Michael for the throne "by reason of his union of kindred with the magnificent Tsars." Again, Palitsin calls Michael "the chosen of God before birth," while Timotheev places him in an unbroken line of hereditary Tsars, and next to Theodor (thus ignoring Godunov, Shuiski, and the various pretenders). Moreover, Michael himself, in his memoirs, calls Ivan IV. his grandfather. Finally, it is a moot question whether Michael was not helped to election by a current rumour that, when dying, Tsar Theodor orally bequeathed the throne to his cousin Theodor, Michael's father. At all events the boyars (who supervised the elections in Council) may well have been inclined in Michael's favour by another recommendation—a recommendation which they could not afford to disregard. An item exists that a certain Sheremetev wrote to Prince Golitzin, in Poland, the words: " Our Michael is as yet; but young, and hath not come unto understanding : yet is he such a one as will be familiar unto us." This can only mean that, though Sheremetev knew that the throne would not deprive Michael of the power of maturing, or render his youth a permanent condition, other qualities in the lad presaged the fact that the nephew would resemble the uncle[1] in point of mental and physical debility, and would thus develop into a gentle, kind-hearted Tsar under whom the trials endured by the boyars during the reigns of Ivan IV. and Boris Godunov would never be repeated. In short, it was not the most *capable*, but the most *convenient*, Tsar that was the need of the hour.

Thus the founder of a new dynasty appeared to put an end to the Period of Troubles.

[1] Tsar Theodor.

CHAPTER IV

Immediate results of the Period of Troubles—New political ideas—Their manifestation during the Period of Troubles—Change in the composition of the ruling class—Reform of the *miestnichestvo*—New setting of the supreme power—Tsar and boyars—The *Boyarskaia Duma* and the *Zemski Sobor*—Simplification of the supreme power—The boyar attempt of 1681—Change in the composition and status of the *Zemski Sobor*—The general ruin entailed by the Period of Troubles—Attitude of the community after that Period.

Now let us turn to the study of those immediate results of the Period of Troubles which went to form the moral and political setting in which the first Tsar of the new dynasty was called upon to act. The fourteen tempestuous years through which the Muscovite Empire had passed had left their traces behind them, and the results which manifested themselves after the opening of Michael's reign were due to two principal changes in the State's position which arose directly out of that upheaval. In the first place, the political tradition, the ancient custom, upon which law and order in the Muscovite Empire of the sixteenth century had hitherto been based had become broken through; while, in the second place, the Troubled Period had placed the State in a relation to its neighbours which called for even greater tension of the popular forces in external warfare than had been the case during the century just named. These two changes also gave rise both to a series of new political ideas which established themselves firmly in Muscovite minds and to a series of new political factors which form the fundamental material of our history during the seventeenth century. Let us study both the one and the other.

To begin with, the unrest experienced during the Period of Troubles led to the inhabitants of the Muscovite Empire gaining a stock of new political ideas which had been altogether unknown to their fathers, the men of the seventeenth century. Yet this was not an altogether unmixed blessing. The new ideas, while destructive to peace and contentment, inspired, in their place, a tendency to experiment and to theorise. Just as, in a tempest, the trees toss their leaves upwards, so that the background is revealed, so, in the Troubled Period, the cataclysm shattered the portals of the national life, and, disclosing what lay without them, caused men who had hitherto been accustomed to note only the personal aspect of existence to reflect, and to begin to have an inkling that hitherto their purview had been but limited in its scope. Everywhere this is the first principle in political thought; whereof the best—though also the sternest—school is popular revolution. Through its means the everyday phenomenon witnessed in increased activity of political thought during and immediately after a popular upheaval becomes intelligible. The ideas with which the Period of Troubles enriched Muscovite minds wrought a profound change in the agelong, stereotyped view which the Muscovite community had hitherto held of its Tsar and the State. With that view we are already familiar. The Muscovites of the sixteenth century saw in their Sovereign, not so much a guardian of the popular welfare, as the proprietor of the State's territory; while upon themselves they looked as mere temporary sojourners in that territory—mere political accidents. The personal will of the Sovereign (they considered) was the one mainspring of the State's life, and only the personal or dynastic interest of that Sovereign could communicate to the State's life a *raison d'être*. In short, beyond the Sovereign, neither the State nor a nation existed. But to this time-honoured view the Period of Troubles administered a rude shock, for, during those troublous years, not only did the people of the Muscovite Empire occasionally unite to choose a Tsar for themselves, but also, in certain years, the State was left without a Sovereign at all—the community found itself abandoned to its own devices. In short, the early seventeenth century saw the Muscovite population experience vicissitudes and witness phenomena which would have been accounted impossible—nay, unthinkable—in their fathers' time. The Muscovite population witnessed the downfall of Tsars who had no nation at their back; it saw the State, though left without a Tsar at all, not only escape disruption, but gather to itself fresh strength, and select a new ruler. To the men of the sixteenth century such vicissitudes and phenomena would have seemed, as I say, unthinkable. Formerly, in the popular consciousness, the State had figured *as such* only when a Tsar was actually in being. It had been incarnate in his person, and had been wholly wrapped up with him. But during the Period of Troubles, when the course of events resulted in the absence of a Tsar, or at least in complete ignorance of his identity, ideas hitherto inseparable began to stand apart. In State documents of the Troubled Period the phrase " The State of Moscow " presents itself as an expression that was intelligible to all men, that was something beyond a mere abstraction, that was an existent reality even in default of a Tsar. Ideas were beginning to look beyond the person, and the conception of the State was not only in course of becoming separated from the conception of the Sovereign, but also in course of becoming fused with the conception of *the nation*. Also, these documents present numerous instances wherein the *formula* "Lord Tsar and Great Prince of All Rus" gives place to the expression "Men of the Muscovite State." How difficult it was for Muscovite intellects to assimilate the idea of an elected Tsar we have already seen. The reason of this lay in the absence of the customary theory that, if need be, the will of a people may be competent to act as the source of all legal and supreme authority: and the difficulty of comprehending this axiom arose from the fact that, as yet, the people were not regarded as a political force. The relation of subjects to their Sovereign caused the former to be accounted either his slaves or his domestics or "orphaned" folk who, in default of other kindred or shelter, chanced to be resident on his territory. How, indeed, could a power of political will attach to slaves and to "orphans," or serve as the source of the divinely appointed authority of the Lord's Anointed? To this established political convention the Period of Troubles administered a first, but a very profound, shock, through the fact that that epoch inspired a painful sense of the extent to which the intellectual forces of the nation stood divorced from the tasks which, with menacing suddenness, kept arising out of the elementary course of the national life. During the Period in question the community was thrown back upon itself, and so learnt to act consciously and independently. There gradually dawned upon it the thought that it—the community, the nation—was not the political accident which Muscovites had hitherto conceived it to be, nor yet an aggregate of immigrants into, or of temporary sojourners in, some indefinite State. On the contrary, the political accident in the question was realised to be the dynasty, for the reason that, during the fifteen years which ensued upon the death of Tsar Theodor, no fewer than four unsuccessful attempts were made to found a new line of Tsars, and that it was not until the fifth attempt had been entered upon that the venture proved successful. Side by side with the will of the Sovereign, and sometimes instead of it, there became established another political force which the Period of Troubles called into action—namely, the will of the nation, as expressed in the decrees of the *Zemski Sobor*, in the Muscovite popular assemblage which acclaimed Tsar Shuiski in the Red Square,[1] and in the gatherings of

[1] See p. 32.

chosen representatives of the towns which rose against the brigand of Tushino[1] and the Poles. Thanks to this circumstance, the idea of a proprietor-Tsar gradually receded in Muscovite minds, even if it did not actually become complicated with a new political idea—namely, with the idea of having a Tsar elected by the people themselves. Thus the fundamental elements of a State order began to find their proper level in the Muscovite political consciousness, and to stand in a new correlation to one another. The elements referred to were the Sovereign, the State, and the Nation. Just as, formerly, no State or nation existed apart from the Tsar, and men could more easily imagine a Sovereign devoid of a people than a State devoid of a Sovereign, so experience now showed that, though (for a time at all events) a State could exist without a Sovereign, neither a Sovereign nor a State could exist for a moment without a nation. The same order of ideas was reached—though from another, the negative, side—by certain contemporary publicists who wrote of the Period of Troubles. I refer to Palitsin, Timotheev, and other—though unknown— chroniclers. These writers discerned the root of the evil in a lack of virile self-assurance on the part of the community—in a lack of ability to unite together against the powers who were infringing law and order. When Boris Godunov had completed the tale of his breaches of legality, and had ruined the great capital by which the land had been consolidated ; when "men of birth" had ceased to raise their voices in protest, and had become as mute as fish—even then no strong man arose in Israel to tell the wielders of power, to their faces, the truth. For this public fatuity, for this "senseless silence of all the world" (to quote Palitsin), the country duly paid the penalty.

Even at the Council of 1613 there prevailed, amid all the confusion and quarrelling, the old stereotyped idea of a "born" Tsar—the idea, indeed, to which Michael owed his election. That retrograde movement was a sign of the fact that the popular mind, as represented in the Council by elected delegates, failed to adjust itself to the new position, and preferred, rather, to hark back to antiquity, to the old "senseless silence of all the world." (Hereafter we shall see how, on more than one occasion, the turbid stream of elements in the national life suffused with mire the silent depths of the social consciousness.) Yet in more than one section of the community the idea of the necessity of active, properly-regulated provincial participation in the affairs of the land remained operative throughout the Period of Troubles—and sometimes markedly so. If we

---

[1] *i.e.* the second false Dmitri.

penetrate to the true essence and meaning of that idea, and recall with
what difficulty men's minds assimilate new political notions, we shall
easily see that such a break in customary modes of thought as that which
I have described could not well have taken place without leaving some
traces behind it.   Indeed, traces of its action are to be discerned in more
than one phenomenon of the Period of Troubles.   In 1609 Sounbulov,
a rebel *dvorianin* of Riazan, gathered together a crowd in the Red Square
of Moscow, and demanded of the boyars that Shuiski should be
dethroned.   Yet in the same crowd there were certain individuals who
at once cried out to the malcontents: "What though the Tsar hath
offended you, are ye able to debase him without the great boyars and
a council of all the people?"   Hence it follows that a pan-national council,
with the boyars at its head, was accounted the one institution which had
power to decide an important matter of this kind: and subsequent
Governments recognised and supported this view that the popular will
was competent to decide fundamental political questions.   The same idea
which the more thoughtful citizens expressed to the mob in the Red Square
was expressed also by Shuiski himself, on an occasion when Sounbulov
and his associates were attacking the palace, and Shuiski met them with the
words: "Wherefore, O accursed ones, come ye unto me with such
shouting and offence?   If ye will to slay me, then am I ready to die.
If ye will to debase me from the throne, then is it not lawful for you to
do so until there be gathered together the great boyars and the men of
all ranks.   Nevertheless, whatsoever covenant shall be established by all
the land, unto the same will I yield myself."   Thus frequent invitations
to the community to participate in the decision of important questions of
State gave rise also to the idea that a pan-territorial council, if properly
constituted, had the right not only to elect a Tzar, but also, if occasion
arose, to condemn him.   Indeed, this idea was even *officially* voiced by
Shuiski's Government, when, at the beginning of that ruler's reign, a Prince
Gregory Volkonski was sent to Poland to demand the extermination of
the First Pretender and his Polish adherents.   Acting on the official
instructions given him, the Prince informed the Polish King and
magnates that the people of the Muscovite Empire "do judge with true
judgement," and that they enjoyed the right of punishing evil and
sacrilegious acts on the part of any such Tsar as the false Dmitri.   A
still more daring step was taken by Prince Volkonski when, in further
development of his views concerning punishment, he added that, however
much the true Tsarevitch Dmitri was the direct, the "born," Tsar of

Moscow, he would never have attained the throne "save that he had been *willed* thereunto." Truly Prince Andrew Kurbski, the liberal thinker of the sixteenth century, would have felt his hair stand on end to hear such heresy!

The events of the Period of Troubles not only rooted new political ideas in men's mind, but also brought about a change in the composition of the ruling class with whose help the Tsars of the old dynasty had acted. This change largely contributed to the growth of the ideas to which I have referred. The old Muscovite Tsars had always governed their Empire with the aid of their boyars, who had been a well-organised body, permeated with the aristocratic spirit, and thoroughly inured to power. True, the political status of that body had rested on no direct legal warranty, but on agelong custom; yet such custom, in its turn, had had two indirect supports to maintain it. On the one hand, an article of the *Sudebnik* of 1550 had secured a certain amount of legislative authority to the *Boyarskaia Duma* (in which assembly the leading place belonged to the boyars); while, on the other hand, the *miestnichestvo* had consistently subordinated service posts to genealogical relations, and so given a strong upward impetus to the boyar order. The first of these two supports upheld the status of the boyars as the chief administrative *institution*, while the other one upheld their status as the chief administrative *class*. In Michael's reign a leading representative of that class, Prince I. M. Vorotinski, defined the bygone governmental position of his fellow boyars as follows: "What though the ancient Tsars did sometime lay upon us their ban, yet did they never take from us the ordering of the State. Rights of every sort did we hold throughout the State, and we were dishonoured not by low-born men." By these words Vorotinski meant that, though individual boyars had been wont to suffer from the caprice of bygone Sovereigns, the class as a whole had never lost its governmental standing, nor yet been made to give way to men of mean birth. In short, Vorotinski was formulating a not inapt definition both of the administrative strength of his class as a whole and of the political weakness of its isolated members. Yet, despite the fact that they had always held "rights of every sort throughout the State," the beginning of the Period of Troubles saw the boyars begin to split into two sections. The initial impetus to this movement emanated from Ivan the Terrible. In proportion as the strict *miestnichestvo* ranks of the boyar order gradually grew thinner and thinner, there stepped into the resultant vacancies new families of obscure origin who were both unused to power and lacking in family traditions and political aptitude. Consequently we cease to see the new Tsars surrounded by unbroken ranks of the old aristocratic families who had formerly stood at the head of the community. Under Tsars Michael and Alexis neither the Kurbskis nor the Cholmskis nor the Mikulinskis nor the Penkovis make an appearance; soon afterwards the Mstislavskis and the Vorotinskis leave the scene; and in a list of boyars and *dumnie liudi* for 1627 we encounter the last member of the Shuiskis and no Prince Golitzin at all. In the same way, we see at the head of society none of the families which, though non-titled, came of the original boyar stocks of Moscow. That is to say, we see no Tuchkovis, Tcheliadnins, Saburovs or Godunovs, but, in their place, only men of new houses concerning which little or nothing is known during the sixteenth century—such men as the Strieshnevs, the Narishkins, the Miloslavskis, the Lopukhins, the Boborikins, the Yazikovs, the Tchaadaevs, the Tchirikovs, the Tolstois, the Chitris, and so on. Of titled princely families there may be mentioned the Prozorovskis, the Mosalkis, the Dolgorukis, and the Urussovs; while, in the case of certain other old families, only the weaker branches still remained intact. This change in the composition of the ruling class was remarked both by that class itself and by foreigners; since, early in Michael's reign, we find the remnant of the original Muscovite boyars complaining that the Period of Troubles had brought to the surface many "low-born men"—peasant-traders and youthful "sons of boyars" (*i.e.* provincial *dvoriané* of insignificant extraction)—whom successive chance Tsars and would-be Tsars had promoted to high service rank by creating them *okolnichi*, *dumnie dvoriané*, and *dumnie diaki;* while in 1615 the Polish commissaries who were negotiating with Moscow's representatives taunted the Muscovite boyars with the reproach that Moscow had been so visited for her sins that she was now forced to see plain peasantry and sons of clergy and rude butchers indecently advanced over the heads of princely and boyar scions, and awarded great offices under the State and in the provincial administration. Under the new dynasty these political novices pushed themselves more and more daringly upwards, until they had penetrated to the *Boyarskaia Duma* itself, which steadily decreased in numbers, and became less and less a boyar assembly. *Parvenus* of this description were the predecessors and precursors of those State officials of the eighteenth century whom contemporary writers so aptly termed "occasional men"—*i.e.* men appointed according as occasion might require.

Thus, whereas the Tsars of the old dynasty ruled with the help of the whole of the administrative class, the Tsars of the seventeenth century began to rule only with the help of such individuals as chanced to make their way to the top : and these newcomers, being free from administrative traditions, became upholders and exponents of the new political ideas which first began to permeate Muscovite intellects during the Period of Troubles. This promotion of a throng of *parvenus* to educated and governing circles had the effect of causing still further complications in calculations of *miestnichestvo*. We have seen that the *miestnichestvo* linked the boyar order into a close-locked chain of individuals and families which expanded, during *miestnichestvo* disputes, into a complex tangle of professional and genealogical relations. Usually two competitors for an official post who chanced to be in doubt concerning their mutual standing towards one another defined their relative *miestnichestvo* status by including in their calculations a third, a fourth, or even a fifth party ; and if one of the rivals in question committed a mathematical error — whether through indulgence or through misadventure — he was regarded as 'impinging upon the family honour of the added party or parties, who straightway had to interfere and clear himself or themselves of the extraneous attack which had been made upon his or their family dignity. For instance, on one occasion a Prince D. Pozharski was appointed to a post at a grade lower than was a Prince B. Saltikov ; and in this case the *Duma's* mode of reckoning was as follows. Since Pozharski was the kinsman and equal of a certain Prince Romanovski, and both of them came of the Princes of Starodub, whereas Prince Romanovski had been the inferior of a former Michael Saltikov, and this same Michael Saltikov had been (in his own family) the inferior of the B. Saltikov concerned,—*therefore* Prince Pozharski was the inferior of B. Saltikov. However, the newcomers to the service of whom I have spoken broke the chain by entering into it extraneously to its links ; since usually they gained their place in the ranks of the old *élite* either by direct service to their country or by what at least passed for such. But the *miestnichestvo* took no cognisance of *personal* efforts. What had it to do with service to fatherland ? All that it recognised was founders of genealogical trees and certain lists of service officials. A fatherland, true, the *miestnichestvo* had—but it was a fatherland only of family reputation. On the other hand, the "new men" referred to would not abate an inch of their services and their merits ; wherefore no epoch in the history of the Muscovite Empire proved so productive of *miestnichestvo* feuds as did the reign of Michael. The brunt of the resultant collisions fell upon Prince Pozharski, the most distinguished of the service *parvenus*. It was to no purpose that he cleared the Empire of Cossack brigands and traitorous Poles; it was to no purpose that he rose from the ranks of the inferior *stolniki* (gentlemen-in-waiting) to be a boyar and to acquire "great *otchini*." On the contrary, the boyars seized every possible occasion to pick a quarrel with him, on the oft-repeated grounds that the Pozharskis were not *razriadnie liudi*, nor persons entered on the accredited service lists;[1] that they had never occupied any post more important than that of a city prefect; and that they had never so much as acted as *gubnie starosti*.[2] Nevertheless, when awarded precedence after Prince B. Saltikov, Pozharski said nothing, but simply disregarded both the Imperial *ukaz* and the boyars' decree; wherefore Saltikov entered suit against him for involving his (Saltikov's) honour in contumacy, and the saviour of his country was forced to yield to his insignificant, but better-born, rival, degraded to a rank of no importance, and made to perform a solemn, but ignominious, progress on foot from the Tsar's palace to the house of his competitor. Thereafter a certain Prince Tatistchev, who appeared to have treated Pozharski with too much deference, was flogged to death, and his head dispatched to Pozharski's address. Thus the decay of the *miestnichestvo*, which began with a pitting of birth against efficiency, advanced to a total denial of birth as the basis of service standing. Yet efficiency and high rank that had been won by ability did not in themselves confer gentility, since the basic rule of the *miestnichestvo* was that for meritorious service the Tsar could bestow only money and estates (*pomiestia*), not *otechestvo* (ancestral dignity). When, however, *miestnichestvo* litigation began to wax fiercer and fiercer, and few appointments to posts came to be accepted without disputes or disloyalty, the Government cast about for some means of obviating the harm that was being done to the service thereby. To posts hitherto allotted only to persons who were inscribed in the *Rodoslovetz*[3] it now began to appoint men among whom calculations concerning "places"[4] did not rule. Unfortunately, these officials, on attaining distinguished posts, at once took it into their heads that they had attained also the pages of the *Rodoslovetz*, and fell to engaging in *miestnichestvo* calculations even more than did the aristocracy proper—in many cases, actually with members of that aristocracy. For this pre-

---

[1] See vol. ii. p. 47.   [2] See vol. ii. p. 273.
[3] See vol. ii. p. 45.   [4] See vol. ii. p. 48.

sumption numbers of them were deprived of rank, thrown into prison, or chastised with the *knut*. Yet still they persisted in their conduct—to such an extent, indeed, that, on one occasion, before the very *Boyarskaia Duma* itself, a *diak* and a boyar of the *Duma* who had been incensed beyond measure by having to engage in ceaseless and vexatious examination of trumpery *miestnichestvo* claims administered to a low-born, but vociferous, claimant a good thrashing, with the words : " Thou dost not make petition unto us according unto the matter in hand. Know thou, therefore, thy deserts." Yet these tricks on the part of servitors of mean birth were due, rather, to the circumstances of the time. That is to say, the Period of Troubles gave rise to a great reshuffling of service families —some of whom it raised, and others of whom it degraded. Although service rank, in itself, signified little in the *miestnichestvo*, and conferred upon the recipient no aristocratic standing, a man of birth was usually promoted to high service rank as a means of testifying to his aristocratic origin ; while, on the other hand, lesser men who had won their way to high service rank during the Period of Troubles attempted to convert this sign of eminent birth into its source, by conceiving the idea that, in rewarding a commoner with an exalted *tchin* or service rank, the Tsar conferred upon him also gentility. This supposition, though negative of the very basis of the *miestnichestvo*, belonged to the new order of political ideas which had arisen during the Disturbed Period, and was concisely expressed by a poor State servitor when, in the course of a dispute on the subject of "places," he said to a highly-born rival : "Verily both small and great do live by favour of the Tsar." In 1682 the same idea led to the final abolition of the *miestnichestvo ;* and in 1722 it was taken by Peter the Great to form the basis of his "Table of Ranks," where it helped still further to complete the absorption of the old boyar aristocracy into the newer bureaucracy of *dvoriané* or *tchinovniki*.

The new political ideas which had dawned in men's minds during the Period of Troubles exercised a direct and notable influence upon the State order under the new dynasty—especially upon the setting of the supreme power as regards its conduct of the higher administration. At the same time, the change produced in this respect was only a continuation, a conservation, of the tendencies manifested *during* the Period. I have said, more than once, that hitherto the mutual relations of Tsar and boyars had been based upon practice or custom, not upon law—that their relations had depended either upon accident or the Imperial freewill, and that between the Muscovite Tsar-Proprietor and his boyar servitors there had held good, in the Imperial *ménage*, only conditions of service, not conditions of rule. When the old dynasty came to an end, however, those domestic relations inevitably underwent a transference to a political basis. Whether in the case of a native or a foreign Tsar, the Empire could no longer be looked upon as the Tsar's private *otchina* or ancestral patrimony; wherefore the boyar officials of State set themselves to seek a share in its administration. Even before the Disturbed Period comes to an end we see them (in company with the superior *dvoriané*) making more than one attempt to establish a State order that was founded upon a written agreement with the Tsar—*i.e.* upon a formal limitation of the supreme power. These attempts (to be precise) we witness on the accession of Shuiski and in the negotiations for the Saltikov treaty of February 4th, 1610. They were the outcome of the break in Muscovite political tradition which had arisen out of the cessation of the old dynasty; nor, upon the conclusion of the Period of Troubles, did the boyars desist from their ambitions. On the contrary, the political incitement which they owed to the times of Ivan IV. and Boris Godunov led them to increase their aspirations to the pitch of an insistent demand. Consequently we find the Metropolitan Philaret, Michael's father, writing from a Polish prison (after learning that summonses had been issued for the holding of an electoral council in Moscow) that to re-establish the authority of the olden Tsars would mean the risk of ultimate ruin to the country, and that he, for one, would rather die in a Polish gaol than, as a free man, witness such a calamity. Evidently he had not an inkling that, on his return to his native land (where, later, he was to be associated with his son in the title and status of Tsar), he would have to recast his constitutional views. As it was, the accession of Michael was accompanied by an incident which chimed with Philaret's original opinion; and to it we derive testimony from more than one source. For example, a writer of Pskov who composed a very passable account of the Period of Troubles, as well as of Michael's election, relates with some disapproval that, at the time of the last-mentioned event, the boyars were masters of the Russian land, and that they neither elected a Tsar for any real purpose nor feared him when elected. Then the chronicler goes on to say that, on Michael acceding to the throne, the boyars compelled him, as their nominee, to swear that for no offence whatsoever would he visit any member of a boyar or aristocratic house with death, but only with a period of incarceration. A more detailed account of the matter is given by a writer of later date—

namely, by Gregory Kotoshikhin, who, at one time a clerk in the *Posolski Prikaz*,[1] fled (in 1664) from Russia to Sweden, and there indited a work descriptive of the Muscovite Empire. The fact that he left Moscow so long as nineteen years after the accession of the second Tsar of the new dynasty would enable him to recall—either on the strength of personal recollection or in virtue of recent tradition—the whole of Michael's reign. At all events he ranges that Sovereign with the Tsars who, on the close of the old dynasty, ascended the throne, not by right of hereditary succession, but by way of popular election. According to his account of the matter, these elected Sovereigns acceded to the throne with limitations placed upon their power, and the obligations which they assumed—the obligations " unto which" (to quote Kotoshikhin's own expression) "they were named in virtue of their proper writing"—consisted of an undertaking that "they should ever be merciful and constrained, and that without judgement and without default they should slay no man, and that in all things they should take thought with the boyars and the men of the *Duma*, and that without the counsel of such men they should do nought, whether openly or in secret." Of Tsar Michael Kotoshikhin adds that, though he styled himself "Autocrat," he could take no steps without the advice of his boyars. The same point is borne out by an item which comes to us from the eighteenth century—namely, from the historian Tatistchev, who had the benefit of historical documents which have since become lost to the world. In 1730 this writer composed a small historico-political treatise on the subject of Sovereigns, in which he says of Michael that, although the election of that Tsar to the throne was " made in proper order of all the people," with it there went a demand for identically the same charter as had been exacted from Tsar Shuiski. Under this charter Michael was to do nothing on his own initiative, but " alway to be fain to rest in abeyance" (*i.e.* to be willing to resign all matters of administration to the boyars). Yet when, in another of his works, Tatistchev is examining a statement on the subject by the Swede Strahlenberg (who resided in Russia during the times of Peter the Great) the Russian historian expresses decided doubts as to the making of any such charter; saying that he knows of no evidence, whether written or oral, on the point. On the other hand, in his description of Russia (which was published in 1730), Strahlenberg seems to have been drawing upon recollections and tales of the seventeenth century which would still be fresh in the minds of the Russian

---

[1] Office of Ambassadors—*i.e.* Foreign Office.

public. It is upon them that he must have based a statement that, on acceding to the throne, Michael gave both a documentary and a sworn undertaking that he would safeguard and cherish the Orthodox faith, forego old family differences and scores, make no new laws nor change the old ones, declare no war nor conclude any peace on his own initiative, try all important legal cases in consonance with law and the established order, and, finally, either bequeath his family estates to his posterity or unite them to the Crown lands. Of this sworn charter of Michael's, however, we know nothing, nor do official documents of the period reveal the slightest trace of the obligations which he assumed therein. Yet in the lengthy *Utverzhennaia Gramota*, or "Established Charter," wherewith the *Zemski Sobor* confirmed Michael's election, as well as in the treaty wherein that body swore an oath of allegiance to him, we discern three points which will help us to estimate the authority of the new Tsar. Those three points are (1) the fact that Michael was elected to the Tsarship for the reason that he proved himself to be a nephew of the last Tsar of the old dynasty (Theodor); (2) the fact that the *Sobor* swore allegiance, not only to the Tsar which it itself had elected, but also to the future Tsaritsa and that Tsar's possible children, for the reason that it saw in its nominee, if not a hereditary, at all events a *potentially* hereditary, Sovereign; and (3) the fact that the official class promised to act " without contrary speaking in all affairs of State " so long only as he admitted the members of that class to his service. Though some might doubt the fact of Michael's power having been subjected to any such limitation, at least the tradition that it was so subjected emanated from his own contemporaries, and held its ground for more than a century. Probably certain obscure hints in the literature of the period will best enable us to arrive at the truth of the matter ; for which purpose our most trustworthy source is a Pskovian chronicle which gives the matter in the shape which it would naturally have borne when, as yet, flying rumours had not become crystallised into a concrete tale, a political legend. During the first five years of Michael's reign, and before the return of his father from a Polish prison, the leaders at Michael's court were the Romanovs, the Saltikovs, the Tcherkasskis, the Sitskis, the Likovs, and the Sheremetevs. Yet there still remained intact also the great boyar houses of the Golitzins, the Kurakins, and the Vorotinskis, who had concluded the accession agreement with their co-boyar, Tsar Vassilii Shuiski, and who, later, with Prince Mstislavski at their head, had recognised as Tsar the son of the Polish King, Vladislav. These great clans were still sufficiently dangerous opponents of the Romanov faction to have stirred up a new Period of Troubles had they been denied a share of the spoil; and even Michael's adherents might have found supreme power which had been obtained by chance or intrigue a bone of contention over which they, the Michaelite section, would have come to loggerheads. Consequently the common interest of both parties was to guard against any repetition of the feuds which had been experienced in the days when the reigning Tsar or pseudo-Tsar had been accustomed to treat his boyars as slaves; and to this end there was concluded behind the scenes of the *Zemski Sobor* a secret agreement which closely resembled the one which had been broken by Godunov and afterwards respected by Shuiski. The chief object of the transaction in question was to safeguard the personal security of the boyars against the freewill of the Sovereign. But to bind the weak-kneed Michael with a compact of this kind would have been of little avail—more especially in view of the help which he was receiving from his mother, the Abbess Martha (a confirmed intriguer, and a woman whose dominion over her son was absolute). Therefore the only difficulty for us now to decide is whether or not any *written* charter was exacted from Michael. Though the Pskovian chronicle to which I have referred makes no mention of such an instrument, but only of the verbal swearing of an oath, the early years of Michael's rule seem to justify the supposition that a formal convention of *some* kind was made, since throughout those years we read of the governing class lording it, high and low, over the country, and "abhorring" its Tsar, who had no choice but to wink at the doings of his subordinates. This enables us to understand why the Tsar's accession proclamation was never made public—if it ever existed. From Shuiski's time onwards the elected Tsar, with his limited power, would be looked upon as a mere partisan monarch, a mere instrument in the hands of the boyar oligarchy. Consequently now, when, in addition to the *Duma*, the *Zemski Sobor* was taking a hand in the matter, it would have been a particularly awkward thing for a violently *ex parte* document of State to have been published; whereas a *secret* limitation of that power would have acted as no impediment either to Michael's holding the title of Autocrat or to his being the first to use the new Imperial stamp which had been designed for the purpose.

Hitherto the supreme administrative organ of the ruling class had been the *Boyarskaia Duma;* but during Michael's reign this body did not constitute the only institution of its kind, seeing that along with it we frequently encounter another administrative organ, in the shape of the

Zemski Sobor. Presently we shall see how the composition of the latter became altered, and to what extent it issued as a really representative assembly. Michael's reign was a time of strenuous work on the part of the Government in conjunction with the *Sobor.* Never before nor after that time do we see so many delegates of all ranks assembled in the Muscovite capital for deliberative purposes. In fact, almost every important question of foreign and domestic policy led the Government to resort to the country for help; with the result that, during Michael's reign, it convened, in all, as many as ten sessions of the *Sobor.* An even more important point is that the *Zemski Sobor* of that day seems to have possessed far more extensive powers than it had hitherto enjoyed, or even than it had been awarded by Saltikov's convention. Henceforth we see it superintending affairs which until now had been the exclusive province of the *Boyarskaia Duma—i.e.* superintending such current matters of State as those questions of taxation which, by Saltikov's treaty, had been set apart for the joint decision of the Tsar and the *Duma.* In other words, we see the *Sobor* beginning to participate directly in the *Duma's* field of action. From the very commencement of Michael's reign the *Sobor* stood to him in a special relation. Previous to the newly elected Sovereign's arrival in Moscow, the body referred to acted as a temporary Government, with the boyars at its head; and in that capacity it exercised jurisdiction over every soul within the Empire. Yet it was not the *Sobor* which propounded terms to its own nominated Tsar, but *vice versâ,* since negotiations between the two parties show us Michael (or, rather, his advisers) sounding, with ever-increasing insistency, the imperious, rather than the submissive, note : " We, the Tsar, have been appointed of your desire, and not of our own freewill. Ye have chosen us to be ruler over all the State, and have kissed the cross unto us of your own accord, and are bounden now to serve, and to uphold, and to be at one with us. Since, therefore, there be everywhere slayings and robbings and all manner of evil-doing (which do offend us), do ye straightway remove from before our face these offences, and see that all things be set in order." Sometimes speeches of this kind were delivered to the *Sobor's* emissaries " with great anger, and with tears." " You who have asked me to be Tsar, do you now grant me the wherewithal to rule, nor trouble me with overmuch advice,"—such was the tone which the Tsar infused into his communications. Thus the council's relation to him converted the *Sobor* (as represented by the elective gathering of 1613) into an executive institution which was responsible to the very man whom it had dowered with his authority. Therefore, comparing these sundry *data* with one another, we may safely assert that Michael's authority was limited by obligations analogous to those which had been imposed upon Tsar Shuiski. That is to say, Michael's authority was limited by that of the *Boyarskaia Duma*. But after the Period of Troubles, when it had become necessary to re-establish the State order, the *Duma* found itself confronted with numerous difficulties which it could not cope with unaided. Hence it was forced to turn for co-operation to the *Zemski Sobor*. Yet the direct share in administrative work which, during the Period of Troubles, had belonged to the country at large could not well come to an immediate end with that Period's close; the very fact that the Tsar had been elected by the popular will, by a pan-territorial convention, compelled him to continue ruling with the help of the people, acting through its representatives on the *Sobor*. If, therefore, the *Boyarskaia Duma* restricted the Tsar's authority, at least the *Zemski Sobor*, as the *Duma's* assistant, acted as a check upon, a counterpoise to, the latter. In this fashion the action of the political ideas and demands which owed their origin to the Period of Troubles—ideas and demands which continued to exist also after the close of that epoch—conferred upon the Sovereign's power a very complicated and conditional construction. That is to say, in origin and in composition it was twofold, and of dual significance. Though derived from election by council, it issued from that source under cover of a political fiction which maintained that the Sovereign's power was likewise hereditary by right of birth. Also, though by tacit consent it was linked on to the superior administrative class (which governed through the *Boyarskaia Duma*), publicly, before the eyes of the people, it figured in State documents as autocratic in the same vague, titular rather than juridical, sense which had not hindered even Tsar Shuiski from styling himself, in important deeds of State, *Samoderzetz*.[1] In this way the power of the new Tsar came to consist of two parallel ambiguities. In origin it was hereditary-elective; in composition it was limited-autocratic.

Yet such a setting of the supreme power could scarcely remain lasting and conclusive. It could only hold good until the mutually opposing interests and relations which had been evoked and thrown into confusion by the Period of Troubles had become reconciled. Consequently in this position of affairs we see a mere fortuitous episode in the history of the Muscovite Empire. But gradually the supreme power became consoli-

---

[1] Autocrat.

dated, and the heterogeneous elements which went to compose it either became assimilated with or absorbed into one another. Yet the political obligations which Michael had assumed remained operative (so far as we can judge) throughout his reign ; for though, when his father had returned from a foreign prison, and had been promoted to the double office of Patriarch and of second Tsar, he (Philaret) set himself steadfastly to steer the ship of State, and did not always, in the doing of it, consult the boyar *personnel*, yet to the very end of Philaret's life the Government was carried on by the joint efforts of the two Tsars, aided by the *Boyarskaia Duma* and the *Zemski Sobor*. This dual authority was really a compromise between family ideas and political considerations. On the one hand, it was no easy matter for the father to become subject to his own son, while, on the other hand, the son had need of a permanent regency—and it was the most natural thing in the world for him to intrust it, together with the title of Second Tsar, to his parent. This idea of dividing, yet not dividing, the supreme power was envisaged only with the aid of dialectics. During one *miestnichestvo* dispute, for instance, we find the question as to which of the two Tsars was the greater or the less decided in this fashion : " Whatsoever the Tsar be, the same will the sire of the Tsar be : for their majesty of State is indivisible." Michael died intestate ; nor could he have done otherwise, for the following reason. Under the new dynasty the State had ceased to be only the *otchina* of the Sovereign ; the old juridical method of transmitting the sovereign power—namely, bequeathal—had lost its force. Yet still there existed no law of succession, and therefore both Alexis and his father had to accede to the throne through a method which differed from that by which the Tsars of the old dynasty had succeeded one another. Alexis, for his part, assumed his authority through two juridical titles—namely, through succession without bequeathal and through election by council. In 1613 the country had sworn allegiance to Michael *and his future issue ;* wherefore Alexis ascended the throne as the successor of his father, and contemporary historians refer to him as the " born " (*i.e.* hereditary) Tsar. On the other hand, the *Zemski Sobor* had thrice been convened for the election of a Tsar (of Theodor, Boris, and Michael) ; wherefore election by a council, as the successor of bequeathal, had become the recognised precedent, and there was no reason why, even for the fourth time, recourse should not be had to the same means of converting an accident into a rule, a system, and so of ensuring that election by council should uphold the legal succession which had been established by the sworn agreement of the *Sobor* of 1613. Contemporary native writers all testify that, on the death of Michael, a *Zemski Sobor* was convened which in due order elected to the throne Michael's sixteen-year-old son, and took an oath of allegiance to the same; while a foreign writer—Olearius, the Ambassador from Holstein—also writes (in his description of the Muscovite Empire) that Alexis acceded to the throne by the unanimous vote of all the boyars, leading men of the country, and people at large. Again, Kotoshikhin is clear as to the assembling of a council for the election of Alexis, since he says that, on the death of Michael, the clergy, boyars, *dvoriané*, "sons of boyars," *gosti* (leading merchants), commercial men of all ranks, and *tchern* (probably the populace of the capital—once more forced to make public petition in the Red Square, as had been the case in 1613)[1] "did choose his [2] son unto the Tsarship." But the obligations which Michael had assumed were not repeated by the son, for, in another passage, Kotoshikhin remarks : " What though they did choose this Tsar unto the Tsarship, yet did he of himself give no such charter as former Tsars had given, nor yet was any demand made unto him for the same, seeing that he was reputed to be of very peaceable habit. For this reason doth he now write himself down Autocrat, and rule his State according unto his will." Yet it was not for the *Zemski Sobor* to limit the supreme power : only the boyars could " demand " of Alexis " a charter." Hence, though it is clear that a repetition of the secret agreement of 1613 was thought to be feasible even in 1645, it was not also looked upon as necessary. Alexis justified the confidence of the boyars in their desire not to bind him with accessional undertakings by refraining from using his power to the full, and living in perfect amity with the boyar class; while, as regards the younger generation of boyars with whom he was brought in contact, they were fast losing those political tendencies of the Period of Troubles which had necessitated the transaction of 1613. Accordingly, since the last traces of the political obligations under which the new dynasty had been forced to begin its work were now disappearing, Alexis made an attempt to convert election by council into a symbolical form and no more. A year and a half previous to his death, he (on September 1st,[3] 1674) carried out a solemn public presentation of his eldest son and heir to the people ; which ceremony was performed in the Red Square of Moscow, in the presence of the higher clergy, the *dumnïe liudi*, and the foreign representatives then accredited to Moscow. In this solemn presentation of the Imperial heir to the people we see the form in which the Tsar transmitted

---

[1] See p. 23.   [2] *i.e.* Michael's.   [3] Then New Year's Day.

his authority to his son, as well as the act—the only one—which imparted
to the accession of Theodor [1] (to whom, as to Michael's *grandson*, the
decree of the council of 1613 did not extend [2]) legal shape. Yet this
spectacular mode of transmitting the supreme power in the presence of
the people and with their tacit consent did not prove a lasting one, since
the fact that Theodor died childless [3] once more necessitated election
pure and simple—though this time in a more durable, as well as a more
exact and truncated, form. As soon as ever Theodor's eyes were closed
in death (April 1682), the Patriarch, archbishops, and those of the boyars
who had assembled at the palace to take leave of their late Sovereign
repaired to another chamber of the building, where they debated which
of Alexis' two surviving sons was to be Tsar. Eventually it was decided
that the question should be left to the people at large, without distinction
of rank; whereupon the assembled Patriarch, archbishops, and boyars
issued orders for persons of every degree to repair to the courtyard of the
palace. This done, the Patriarch went out into the portico, and delivered
therefrom an explanatory speech. Although the answering vote was by
no means unanimous, the younger of the two Tsarevitches—Peter, then
a boy of ten—was chosen Tsar; and, on the Patriarch next putting the
question to the clergy and boyars who were standing beside him in the
portico, they too voted for Peter. Finally the Patriarch went to the
boy himself, and formally blessed him to the Tsarship. I have adduced
these details in order to show how simply, in those days, such an
important matter was transacted in Moscow. This convention of a
day seems to have comprised neither elected representatives nor any
set debate—the question being decided merely by a throng of individuals
who chanced to have been drawn to the palace by the event of the Tsar's
demise. Also, it is clear that the men who, on this occasion, decided
the fate of the Empire at the instance of the Patriarch had no real idea
in their minds either of the equity of the case or of constituting a council
or of the very existence of the State. Or, possibly, they may have
considered such ideas to be superfluous on such an occasion. On the
other hand, the *Strieltsi*, instigated by the party of the Tsarevna Sophia,
responded to the action of the authorities by rising in revolt (on May 15th,
1682), and hastily organising a parody of a council which elected to the

---

[1] Alexis' eldest son, Theodor II. of the new dynasty (the first Theodor having been
Michael's father, Philaret).

[2] See p. 76.

[3] He reigned but six years, and died at the age of twenty-two.

throne *both* Peter and his brother Ivan. In the decree issued by this secondary, revolutionary convention we read that "all ranks of the State did make petition that, for the due appeasement of the people, the two brethren be ordained Tsars upon the throne, and both of them do rule as Autocrats."

We have now traced the manner in which the setting of the supreme power underwent certain changes during the first three reigns of the new dynasty, as also the results to which, after the death of the third Tsar, those changes gave rise. The century which had begun with strenuous efforts on the part of the ruling classes to evolve fundamental laws and to organise the higher administration on a constitutional basis ended in the country being left without any fundamental laws at all, any regular administration in its higher departments, or any law of succession to the throne. Not feeling competent to evolve such a law, men had recourse to court intrigue, to symbolical ritual, to counterfeit *Zemskïe Sobori*, and, finally, to armed turbulence. Yet the boyars never wholly abandoned their political tradition. At the close of 1681, when the question of the abolition of the *miestnichestvo—i.e.* the question of the destruction of one of the main bases of the boyars' political status—arose, boyardom made another attempt to retrieve its position. Perceiving its last hopes for the State to be crumbling at the centre of Government, it tried to consolidate itself in the provinces. For this purpose there was drawn up a plan for dividing the Empire into a number of large historical areas which, though become part of the Empire, had formerly been independent States. To these areas there were to be appointed, from among the surviving representatives of the Muscovite aristocracy, certain permanent, non-removable, life *namiestniki* or viceroys, who were to be plenipotentiary local governors —"*namiestniki* of princely and boyaral estate"—of such units as the State of Kazan, the State of Siberia, and so forth. Indeed, Theodor had already accorded his assent to this scheme for an aristocratic decentralisation of the administrative power when the Patriarch, on the scheme being submitted to him for his blessing, blew the project to shreds by pointing out some of the dangers which it threatened to the Empire.

The change in the composition and importance of the *Zemski Sobor* which I have described constitutes one of the most important results of the Period of Troubles. To the *Sobor* of the sixteenth century there had been summoned only official personages, as the instruments of the central and local administrations; but at the *Sobori* of 1598 and 1605 we note the presence of delegates also of the "plain men" or common people. Next, the Troubled Period gave rise to conditions which conferred upon the representative element a decided numerical preponderance over the official; which circumstance eventually communicated to the *Zemski Sobor* the character of a truly representative gathering. Circumstances compelled the community to take a more direct part in public affairs, and the Government itself admitted it to participation therein, and urged and entreated the public both to co-operate with the directorate and to make a bold stand for the Orthodox faith. For this purpose there were solemnly read to the people, in the Metropolitan Cathedral, certain pamphlets which, though seasoned with a religious alloy, related mostly to current events; and thus the hitherto unfamiliar *formulæ,* "Council of all the land," "Common council of the land," "Gathering of all the people," "United Council of all the *miri* (local communities)," and so forth, became current expressions for the new ideas which were beginning to fill the public consciousness. Of these ideas, the one which bit most deeply into the popular fancy was the notion of electing a Tsar "by consent of all the land." Gradually spreading, the idea ended by embracing all departments of public business; so that for every local affair it was considered necessary to appoint "a common council,"—the towns organising, for the purpose, conventions which chose from among themselves a number of *liuchshïe liudi,* or "best men," of every rank. Next, when the country began to be torn asunder between the rival Tsars, Vassilii and the second false Dmitri, there awoke in the nation also a notion of the unity and integrity of the State: for men remembered the miseries of the appanage epoch. Without elected representatives of all grades no important step could be taken. As an example, the mission which, in 1610, was conducted by the Metropolitan Philaret and Prince V. V. Golitzin to the court of Sigismund was accompanied by a train which comprised over a thousand representatives of the several grades of the population. Again, during his advance upon Moscow, Prince Pozharski sent writs to every town, with invitations to select delegates of all grades to wait upon him at his camp. In short, the general desire was that, at every transaction of State import, there should be present (so far as was possible) the country at large, in the person of its representatives, and that by that presence it should then and there testify that the matter in hand had been transacted openly and directly, and not by some secret, tortuous negotiation which contravened the people's will (as had been the course pursued by Maliuta Skuratov, Boris Godunov, and Tsar Shuiski himself, but which form of action was everywhere now recognised to have been the root of all the evils which had visited the Russian land). Hence by tentative experiments the elective composition of the *Zemski Sobor* developed in the public consciousness even before the electoral *Sobor* of 1613—the first authentic essay in true popular representation — was convened. Next, after clearing Moscow of the Poles, the boyars and generals of the Second Contingent summoned, for the election of a Tsar, a pan-territorial council which consisted of certain selected " best men "—" men steadfast and of prudence "—of every rank, including representatives of the suburban and cantonal populations (*i.e.* the industrial inhabitants of the provincial towns) and of the peasantry : which two classes we have seen to have been quite unrepresented on the *Zemskie Sobori* of the sixteenth century. Evidently the leaders of the contingent wished to realise the idea of which the thin end had been inserted by the Period of Troubles— namely, the idea of a pan-popular, a " universal " or " general communal " (to quote a State deed of the period), council. This change in the composition of the *Sobor* was accompanied by a change in the status of that institution. During the sixteenth century the Government con-vened an official *Sobor* for the purpose of selecting therefrom certain responsible executors both of the *Sobor's* own decrees and of the Tsar's *ukazi ;* while, in their circular letter to the towns, the leaders of the Second Contingent wrote that, without a Sovereign, never could the State be set in order. Now, we have seen that, as soon as it had transacted its institutional business, the electoral *Sobor* of 1613 elected a Sovereign to the throne, and then converted itself into a commission of management which, in pursuance of the orders and requirements of the new Sovereign, adopted a number of preliminary measures for reorganising the country until a permanent Government should have been formed. That accom-plished, the *Sobor* acquired a different function. In 1619 orders were issued that, for the due reorganisation of the land, there should be summoned to Moscow certain chosen delegates (men described as " good and prudent ") from every town and of every rank, who should furnish reports concerning the several wrongs and injuries which their local communities had suffered ; and that, after hearing their petitions concerning all local needs, straits, damages, and shortcomings of every kind, the Tsar should take counsel with "his father the Patriarch," "to the end that everything may be ordered as shall seem unto us best." Thus we see these new delegates to the *Sobor* entrusted with a certain initiative in legislative measures, in the form of a right to lay petitions, while the supreme administration reserved to itself the right of finally deciding the questions raised. In other words, from being the bearer of the public will, the *Zemski Sobor* became the mouthpiece of public grievances and aspirations : which two functions, of course, are by no means the same. Hereafter, in studying the phenomena of the seventeenth century, we shall see that it was on the basis of these two changes which I have expounded that there subsequently became determined the organisation, activity, and fortunes of the *Zemski Sobor*.

These various results of the Period of Troubles, together with the new political ideas originated by that Period, a new and revivified composition of the administrative class, a new setting of the supreme power, and a new character imparted to the *Zemski Sobor*, might have seemed to promise fruitful development to the State and to the community, and to have conferred upon the new dynasty a store of means of action, spiritual and political, such as the old dynasty had never possessed. But, unfortunately, sudden breaks in men's minds and ways of life always bear within themselves one particular danger—namely, the danger that, though men may use such breaks to the best advantage, they also may create of the new resources at their disposal a number of new difficulties for themselves. In the results of the Period of Troubles which I have described we discern that a sharp cleavage had taken place in old political tradition, that a sharp rupture had come about in old customs of State; and, however much men may acquire a stock of ideas corresponding to a given break, they still will walk unsteadily until the ideas which have divorced them from ancient custom have become hardened into assured habit. The revolution which, towards the close of the sixteenth century, had taken place in the setting of the supreme power makes it clear that the danger to which I have referred threatened grave menace to the Muscovite Empire ; as also that it was added to by another, and a most unfavourable, series of results of the Troubled Period. This was owing to the fact that the storms of that Period had done immense harm both to the industrial position of the nation and to the moral attitude of the Russian community. In fact, the country was in a state of utter ruin. Certain foreigners who visited Moscow soon after the accession of Michael (to be precise, in 1615), have bequeathed to us a terrible picture of burned and wasted *sela* and *derevni* wherein the deserted huts were choked with corpses which had not yet been removed, and from which the stench compelled even travellers in the winter time to spend the night in the open air. Everywhere persons who had survived the Period of Troubles were wandering about; the whole civil order had been thrown out of gear, and all human relations were now plunged in confusion. Consequently it took a prolonged series of efforts to re-establish order, to collect the wanderers, to resettle them in their old habitations, and to restart them in the daily routine from which they had been ousted by the upheaval. Also, from Michael's day there have come down to us not a few cantonal lists or "tenth books" and agrarian registers or "writers' books" which give us a clear picture of the then industrial position of the service-landowning and peasant sections of the population, since in those records we find particulars of the economic reconstruction of the Muscovite Empire and nation during the first reign of the new dynasty. First of all we note a change in the com-position of the rural peasant population, which served as the principal source of the State's income. Registers of the sixteenth century indicate that amount of substance divided the peasantry into two classes—namely, *krestiané* and *bobili*. *Bobili* were much the same as *krestiané*, except either that they possessed less means and cultivated smaller plots than did *krestiané* or that they held no arable land at all, but merely home-steads. During the sixteenth century the number of *krestiané* consider-ably exceeded that of *bobili*, but from agrarian registers of Michael's day we see that, after the Period of Troubles, quite a different relation became established, and that in some places the proportion of *krestiané* to *bobili* even came to be reversed—the latter either rising to numerical equality with the former or coming to constitute an actual majority over them (thus, in the cantons of Bielaev, Mtzensk, and Elets the cantonal estates of the local State servitors had come, in 1622, to comprise 1187 *krestiané* and 2563 *bobili*). Hence it follows that the Period of Troubles forced an immense number of *krestiané* either to abandon altogether their tillage plots or to curtail the extent of those plots. Also, the increase in the number of *bobili* means that there took place also an increase in *pustota* or waste land; nor can it be regarded as an exceptional instance that a register of the period tells us that, in one district of the canton of Riazan, the local *pomiestia* or service estates contained, in 1616, twenty-two times as much waste land as cultivated. Again, in the works of the monk Palitsin—an excellent monasterial landlord, and a man who was thoroughly acquainted with the industrial position of his country—we find a curious confirmation of this wholesale abandonment of land; for he writes that, during a three years' failure of the harvest in Boris' reign, many persons nevertheless had enormous quantities of stale grain stored in their barns, that threshing-floors were filled to overflowing with straw and hay, and that on these accumulations of old stocks the writer and others subsisted throughout the fourteen years of the Troubled Period, when "to plough and to sow and to reap men did forbear, for the reason that the sword did for ever lie over them." This item testifies both to the great development of agriculture before the Troubled Period and to the decline of that industry during the epoch in question. The re-casting of rural industry, coupled with the change in the industrial com-position of the rural population of which I have been speaking, must have told heavily upon private landownership, more especially in the matter of the industrial position of the provincial *dvoriané*. Let me cite a few *data* which I have culled at random from certain cantonal "tenth books" for the year 1622, when the traces of destruction had become obliterated. The fitness for service of the military class depended upon the productiveness of that class's property and the number and com-parative affluence of the *krestiané* who had settled its *otchini* and *pomiestia*. Nevertheless few cantonal *dvoriané* possessed *otchini;* the great majority of them lived upon incomes which they derived from their *pomiestia*. Thus, in the canton of Bielaev, *otchini* constituted $\frac{1}{4}$ of all the estates be-longing to *dvoriané* in that district; in the canton of Tula they constituted rather more than $\frac{1}{6}$; in the canton of Mtzesk, $\frac{1}{17}$; in the canton of Elets, $\frac{1}{157}$; and in the canton of Tver—even among the *vibor* (the wealthiest *stratum* of provincial *dvoriané*)—$\frac{1}{4}$. The *pomiestia* of cantonal *dvoriané* were also, for the most part, very small, and but sparsely settled with peasantry. For instance, an average-sized *pomiestie* in the canton of Tula comprised only 135 *dessiatini* of arable land; in that of Elets, only 124; in that of Bielaev, only 150; and in that of Mtzesk, only 68. Also, in the four cantons just named the number of taxpaying agriculturists (both *krestiané* and *bobili*) averaged only two souls to every 120 *dessiatini* of *pomiestie* land; or one to every 60. Yet it must not be supposed that all this tillage was actually worked by *krestiané* or *bobili*. Only a small portion of it was so worked, and even of that not all was actually in cultivation. Thus, in the canton of Tver we find the estate of a wealthy *dvorianin*-councillor—an estate made up of 900 *dessiatini* of *otchina* and *pomiestie* land—being worked only to the extent of 95 *dessiatini;* whereof the owner himself cultivated 20 *dessiatini* with his domestic staff, while the remaining 75 *dessiatini* were leased to 28 *krestiané* and *bobili*, who resided in 19 homesteads. Thus each such homestead had attached to it, in round figures, 4.6 *dessiatini*. Indeed, peasant tillage on anything of a large scale was a very rare phenomenon indeed. On the other hand, Elets and certain other cantons of the South contained not only many *dvoriané* who, owning no land at all, possessed (as *odnodvortsi* or "one-homesteaders") but a manor-house to which there were neither *krestiané* nor *bobili* attached as tenants, but also many *pusto-pomiestnïe* (owners of waste *pomiestia*) who could not boast even of an establishment of that kind. Thus, among the 878 *dvoriané* and "sons of boyars" registered in the canton of Elets we note there to have been 133 landless proprietors and 296 "one-homesteaders" and proprietors of waste *pomiestia*. Indeed, it was not an uncommon thing for a *dvorianin* altogether to abandon his *otchina* or *pomiestïe*, and then either to join the Cossacks, to become a bond-slave or servant in some boyaral or monastic establishment, or (if I may quote the phrase employed by a "tenth book") to "fall to wallowing in taverns." The greater became the decline in service landownership, the greater became the necessity of increasing the allotments of monetary salaries to State servitors, if the service efficiency of that class was ever to be restored. Again, increase of salaries led to an increase in the agrarian taxation which fell upon the peasantry alone: and since such taxation was assessed according to area of tillage, the *krestianin* soon found himself unable to bear the ever-growing weight of his imposts, and forced to curtail his arable plot until it had come to pay less. Of this the consequence was that the Treasury found itself in a circle from which there was no escape.

Finally, the Government's internal difficulties were augmented by a profound change in the moral attitude of the nation. The new dynasty was called upon to deal with quite a different community to the one which the olden Tsars had ruled. The alarms of the Troubled Period had exercised such a disruptive effect upon the political adjustment of the people that, from the accession of the new dynasty until the close of the seventeenth century, we see each several class engaged in ceaseless complaints concerning its misfortunes, its growing impoverishment and ruin, and the abuses of the powers that were—engaged in complaints, that is to say, concerning grievances which it had always suffered, yet against which it had never before protested. This dissatisfaction grew until, by the close of the century, it had come to be the dominant note in the attitude of the masses. From the storms of the Troubled Period the nation issued more impressed with and irate with its lot than it had ever been before. It had lost that political long-suffering which had made such an impression upon foreign observers of the sixteenth century; it was anything but the resigned, obedient instrument in the hands of the Government which it had formerly been. This change found expression in a phenomenon which until now we have not remarked in the life of the Muscovite Empire— namely, in the phenomenon that the seventeenth century constitutes, in our history, a period of popular uprisings. It is all the more unlooked-for a phenomenon in that it manifested itself under Tsars who, to judge from their personal qualities and the form of their policy, seem the less to have justified it.

CHAPTER V

HAVING described the results of the Period of Troubles, as disclosed in the internal life of the State and the community, let me turn to another series of phenomena which arose from the same source. By this I mean those external relations of the State which became established after the Period of Troubles had come to an end.

Under the influence of that Period the external, the international position of the Empire underwent a radical change. That is to say, it became incomparably worse than it had been before. For a century and a half the old dynasty had directed its foreign policy unswervingly in one direction —namely, towards the aggressive. Slowly, but surely, it had extended the territories of the State by combining together the various scattered portions of the Russian land. But as soon as the political consolidation of Great Rus had become an accomplished fact, further problems of foreign policy rose to view. Ivan III., in the process of gathering to himself the last purely Russian units to preserve their independence, made it clear—but more especially during his struggle with Poland—that United Great Rus would never abandon her arms until she had not only regained those portions of the Russian land which had been ravished from her by her neighbours, but also had absorbed their several nationalities. Next, his grandson, Ivan the Terrible, strove to extend the territories of the Russian Empire to the natural, the geographical boundaries of the Russian plain, which then lay in the possession of hostile aliens. Thus there arose, in sequence to one another, two problems of foreign policy —namely, the completion of the political consolidation of the Russian nationality and the extension of the Empire's territory to the boundaries of the Russian plain. Although the old dynasty had succeeded in resolving neither of these problems (the national and the territorial), it had attained something in that direction. Between them, Ivan the Terrible's father and grandfather had regained possession of the provinces of Smolensk and Novgorod Sieverski, and so had penetrated to the Dnieper; while Ivan himself turned his attention to the other side of the river, and, making himself master of the regions of the Middle and Lower Volga, extended the State's eastern frontiers to the River Ural and the Caspian Sea. His subsequent movements in the West were less successful; for though, in that direction, he attempted to gain possession of Livonia, for the purpose of advancing the Empire's frontiers to the eastern shores of the Baltic as the natural boundary of the Russian plain, he never succeeded in acquiring the entire course of the Western Dvina. In fact, his struggle with Batory caused him to lose certain Russian towns on the Gulf of Finland and Lake Ladoga which had hitherto been Russian property. Nevertheless, a second war with Sweden (1590-1595) enabled Ivan's son, Theodor, to make good his father's losses, and to establish a firm foothold on the Gulf of Finland (namely, in the district which had formerly constituted the Novgorodian *piatina* of Voti [1]). For the second time the Period of Troubles deprived the Muscovite Empire of those western positions which it had occupied in the sixteenth century. In the first place, the Poles despoiled Moscow of the provinces of Smolensk and Novgorod Sieverski—thus once more severing the Muscovite Empire from the Dnieper; while, in the second place, the Swedes succeeded in ousting Moscow from the shores of the Baltic. That is to say, in 1617 the Treaty of Stolbovo forced the first Tsar of the new dynasty to surrender the Baltic town and the fortress of Orieshek (Schlusselberg) to Sweden, while in 1618 the Treaty of Deulino obliged him to restore Smolensk and Novgorod Sieverski to Poland. Thus once again Moscow found herself divorced from her pristine frontiers on the west. The new dynasty began badly, for not only did it undo the national work of the old dynasty, but also it lost much of what that dynasty had bequeathed. Already, by the entry of the Period of Troubles, the external position of the Empire was undergoing steady deterioration; the reason for which was the contempt in which it (the Empire) had come to stand among its neighbours. In 1612 we find the boyars of Moscow writing, in their circular letter to the towns, that "on all sides is the State of Moscow now torn by foes; in the eyes of all rulers round about are we now fallen into contumely and reproach." The result was that the new dynasty was compelled to put the nation's forces to an even greater degree of tension than had been the case under

[1] See vol. i. p. 321.

the old dynasty. To recover what had been lost was only its national duty—the prime condition of its establishment upon the throne; wherefore, from its very inception, the new dynasty engaged in a series of wars which had for their purpose either the consolidation of what Moscow already held or the recovery of what had been seized by her neighbours. These national efforts were further increased by the fact that, though, in their origin, defensive, such wars gradually—despite the will of Muscovite politicians themselves—became wars of aggression, a direct continuation of the consolidatory policy of the old dynasty, a struggle for portions of the Russian land of which the Muscovite Empire had never before been mistress. Yet, even after her first unsuccessful efforts, international relations in Eastern Europe gave Moscow little or no time to recover her breath, nor to prepare for further attempts, since, in 1654, by rising against Poland and placing herself under the protection of the Muscovite Tsar, Little Rus plunged Moscow into a renewed struggle with Poland, and gave rise to a new problem, the Little Russian question. This helped still further to complicate the tangled accounts which had long been outstanding between Moscow and the *Rietch Pospolitaia*.[1] The Little Russian question was incidentally an outcome of the Moscovite foreign policy of the later seventeenth century, and deflects us to the history of Western Rus. Yet I will touch upon it to no further an extent than will suffice to elucidate for us the conditions of that question's origin. The conditions referred to first revealed themselves at the commencement of the episode which gave rise to the question itself. In 1648 Bogdan Kmelnitski, a *sotnik* (commander) of a Polish *reestrovöe voisko* or "registered" (regular) regiment, headed a rising of the Zaporozhki Cossacks against the *Rietch Pospolitaia*, and received support from the peasantry of Little Rus, who were only too eager to rise against their masters, the Polish and Polonised Russian magnates. On the "registered" Cossacks also seceding to his side, he found himself possessed of a force with which, within five or six months, he succeeded in getting into his hands almost the whole of Little Rus. But properly to understand the roots of the Little Russian movement of 1648 we must first of all determine precisely the nature of the *Rietch Pospolitaia*, the place which Little Rus occupied in the same, the status of the Polish *pani* or magnates in the region just named, the manner in which the Little Russian Cossacks came into being, and the reason why, in this revolt, the Cossacks of Little Rus were joined by the peasantry of the Ukraine.

[1] A Polish translation of the Latin term *Res Publica*.

During the seventeenth century the most difficult question which Moscow had to face in her foreign policy was that of recruiting Western Rus to the Muscovite Empire.   It was a question which comprised several onerous problems—problems which owed their gradual growth in Western Rus to a political transaction which had taken place between the Polish magnates and Jagiello, Grand Duke of Lithuania, at the close of the fourteenth century.   By this transaction the Grand Duke of Lithuania had acquired both the hand of the Polish Princess Jadviga and the Polish crown.[1]   In fact, the agreement was based upon respective calculations of the two contracting parties.   On the one hand, Jagiello hoped that, by becoming King and, with all his people, accepting Catholicism, he would gain the support both of Poland and the Pope against the dangerous Teutonic Order of Knights; while the Poles, in their turn, hoped that, through Jagiello, they would succeed in obtaining control of the forces and resources of Livonia,—more particularly of those of Western Rus, Volhynia, Podolia, and the Ukraine.   Thus the two neighbouring States of Lithuania and Poland became united by a dynastic bond. Nevertheless it was a mechanical union of two alien, and even hostile, States (it might even be said, a dynastic intrigue that was based upon calculations of mutual misunderstandings) rather than a political act which had its basis in unity of mutual interests.   In any case, the transaction brought about some important changes in the position of Western Rus.   To begin with, the subjection of that Rus to the Grand Dukes of Lithuania was accompanied by the subjection of Lithuania to Russian influence.   Consequently the opening of the fifteenth century saw the Russian provinces which had become part of the Lithuanian Principality—namely, the provinces of Podolia, Volhynia, Kiev, Novgorod Sieverski, and certain others—come greatly to exceed, both in area and population, the State of Lithuania which was holding them in subjection. Indeed, both by racial and by cultural composition the Russo-Lithuanian Principality was now a Russian, rather than a Lithuanian State, and for the next hundred years the Russian language and Russian law, Russian morals and the Russian Orthodox faith, spread themselves over the length and breadth of pagan and semi-barbarous Lithuania.   Such progress did this cultural approximation of the two united nationalities, under the dominating influence of the most developed Russian members of the union, make that only some two or three further generations would have been needed to cause the opening of the sixteenth century to witness a

[1] See vol. ii. p. 7.

complete fusion of Lithuania with Western Rus. From the time of the union of Lithuania with Poland, however, Russian influence in the Lithuanian Principality began to be ousted by Polish, which penetrated thither by several different channels. One of those channels was the series of *seimi* or diets by which the common public affairs of the two States were directed. At such gatherings Lithuanian-Russian magnates rubbed shoulders with Polish *pani*, and became familiar both with the political ideas of the latter and with the system which prevailed in Poland. Likewise, Polish influence reached Lithuanian Rus through the medium of charters granted by the King to the Lithuanian princes—documents which, known as *privilii*, established in Lithuania the same order of administration, and the same rights and relations of the several classes, as obtained in Poland. These channels led Polish influence to penetrate also to those Russian provinces which had now become part of the Lithuanian Principality, and to work therein a profound change both in the structure of their government and in the adjustment of the community.

Like their forefathers of the eleventh and twelfth centuries, the Russian princes of the western provinces had hitherto held their principalities by family right of succession; but under the terms of their newly-imposed subjection to the Grand Duke of Lithuania they were bound to serve him faithfully, and to pay him *dan* from their dominions, while, in return, he conferred upon them their provinces as *otchini*, to be held either on hereditary tenure or merely " during the season of his sovereign will." [1] Of course this made a break in the old family right of tenure which these princes had hitherto enjoyed : with the result that by the opening of the sixteenth century they had become simply *sluzhilie votchinniki*, or owners of their provinces under a condition of service to the Prince of Lithuania, and a caste which, with the principal Russian boyars and Lithuanian magnates of the Principality, formed an agrarian aristocracy which closely resembled that of Poland, except that it exercised an even greater influence. Of its members (who were known as *pani* or magnates) was formed also the administrative council, or *riada*, of the Grand Duke of Lithuania —an assembly, be it said, which acted as a strong break upon his power. For instance, a *privilei* issued by the Grand Duke Alexander in the year 1492 stipulated that the Lithuanian ruler must first of all obtain the consent of his *riada* before engaging in any dealings with foreign potentates, before promulgating any new law or altering any old one, before disposing of the State's budget, or before making any appointment to an official

---

[1] See vol. i. p. 79.

post. Also, the Lithuanian Sovereign was to recognise all resolutions passed by the *riada* as binding also upon himself, and, though he might not agree with them, to apply them, nevertheless, "to the good of his *riada* and of the people." Also, Lithuania followed Poland's example by adopting the Polish system of higher administrative posts or *uriadi*, which in time came to be posts held by the occupant for life. These comprised the office of *hettman* or commander-in-chief, that of *kantsler* or keeper of the Great Seal of State, that of *podskarbi* or finance minister (this office was held in duplicate), that of *zemski* or superintendent of the public revenues and outgoings, and that of *nadvorni* or court chamberlain. Governors of provinces which had formerly been ruled by Russian princes in agreement with the *vietcha*, or popular assemblies, of their capital towns were called *voievodi*, and had under them, as their assistants, a number of *kashteliani* (prefects of towns) and *starosti povietov* (wardens of the districts into which each *voievodstvo* or governor's command was divided). Thus both the central and the provincial administrations of Lithuanian Rus came closely to approximate to those of Poland, and acquired an aristocratic stamp.

The *privilii* of which I have spoken—namely, general or pan-territorial *privilii* (conferred upon a whole principality) and local and district *privilii*—established class rights and relations which closely resembled those existing in Poland. At a diet held at Grodno in 1413, which confirmed the union of Lithuania with Poland, there was published a *privilei* by which those of the Lithuanian boyars who had accepted Catholicism were accorded equal rights and privileges with the Polish *shliachta* or *dvorianin* class; while by a *privilei* granted by Casimir in 1447 those rights were extended to include the Orthodox *dvoriané*. Under these charters the Lithuanian-Russian landowners were placed on an equal footing with the Polish as regards rights of possession of *otchini* and conferred properties, as well as were exempted from all tolls and taxes, save a few unimportant dues which had less of a financial than of a symbolical importance, as constituting a mark of subjection. Moreover, these documents took the seigniorial peasantry out of the legal jurisdiction of the Grand Duke's governmental officials or *uriadniki* (*see above*), and placed them under that of their masters. Above all things, Casimir's *privilei* forbade the passage of *krestiané* from the lands of private landowners to those of the Grand Duke, or *vice versa*. In fact, these ordinances laid the foundation of peasant enserfment in Lithuania, even as had been done in Poland, where serf law first became established during the fourteenth century. Together, general and local *privilii* brought about a gradual equalisation of the Lithuanian-Russian *dvoriané*, in the matter of rights and liberties, with the Polish *shliachta* or *dvorianin* class. To the former they communicated the status of the ruling class in the Principality, together with wide authority over the peasant population which dwelt upon its lands, and an influential share in legislation, the dispensation of justice, and general administration. During the sixteenth century the position of the Lithuanian-Russian *shliachta* was still further strengthened by the code known as "The Lithuanian Statute." Of this code the foundation had been laid by Sigismund I. when he published a similar statute in 1529; which preliminary version was revised and augmented to conform with Polish legislation until it had become largely a reflection of Polish jurisprudence, mingled with certain old Russian juridical customs which had survived in Lithuanian Rus from the times of the *Russkaia Pravda*. In its final shape the Lithuanian Statute appeared in the Russian language in the year 1588, when Sigismund III. was ruler of Poland. Under this, the Second, Statute (which was confirmed by a diet held at Vilna in 1566) there became introduced into the Lithuanian Principality a number of diet-councillors belonging to the provincial *shliachta* class (*starosti povietov*, or wardens of country districts), of a type similar to those existing in Poland. These *seimiki* or diet-councillors held periodical meetings in each *poivet* or canton, for the purpose both of selecting local judges to form a *shliachta* class tribunal and of choosing *zemskïe posli*, or representatives of the *shliachta* on the General Diet (two representatives for each *poviet* or canton). Originally the Lithuanian Diet, as established by the Treaty of Grodno, had consisted only of Lithuanian princes and boyars, but the ascendancy over the Orthodox Russian *dvoriané* which the instrument in question conferred upon the Lithuanian aristocracy (who were mostly Catholic by faith) at length incited those Russian provinces which had become united to Lithuania to seize an occasion when, on the death of Vitovt (in 1430), a new feud had sprung up among the descendants of Guedemin to rise against the Lithuanian Government. The result of this was that the Russian princes and boyars won for themselves the rights of Lithuanian magnates; and about the middle of the fifteenth century they acquired also entry to the Diet, which thenceforth became a general one. Yet still the Diet continued to preserve its aristocratic character, for there came to it, from the Russian provinces, none but princes and *pani*, who received personal summonses thereto, and had the deciding voice in its counsels. Next, during the first half of the sixteenth century, when Sigismund I. was ruler of Poland, the Russo-Lithuanian *shliachta* plunged into a violent struggle with their own native aristocracy, and, in the same manner, won for themselves the right of receiving summonses to general diets. Consequently we find the Statute of 1566 organising regular representation of this (the Russo-Lithuanian *shliachta*) class at diets, on the model of the Polish *shliachetski seim* or diet of the Polish *shliachta*. In the matter of the continuance of the Lithuanian-Polish union the Russian-Lithuanian *shliachta* were in favour of the tie with Poland remaining permanent; until, finally, fusion of the Russo-Lithuanian Diet with the Polish, in conformity with resolutions passed by the Diet of Lublin of 1569, placed this class completely on an equality, as regards political rights, with the Polish *shliachta*.

This increase of the *dvorianin* class in the Lithuanian Principality was accompanied by a decline of the ancient towns of Western Rus. In old Kievan Rus the various districts and their *volost* towns had constituted self-contained provinces which had been subject only to resolutions passed by the *vietcha* of their respective capitals; but now the introduction of the system of allotting official posts to members of the aristocracy caused the provincial capital to become divorced from its province, and the place of the local *vietché* to be taken by a *voievoda* or governor appointed of the Grand Duke, with a staff of assistant *starosti*, *kasteliani*, and other subordinates. Thus to provincial-town administration there succeeded Crown administration. Moreover, those urban lands which had hitherto been devoted to the public uses of the capital towns now began to be bestowed by the Grand Dukes upon private owners, in return for an obligation of military service; which service caused such landowners—boyars and what were known as *zemiané*—to cease to be members of the urban communities in question, and to become differentiated, through their privileged position as members of the *shliachta*, from the *miestchané* or commercial-industrial burghers of the capital towns (*miesto*, in Polish, means a town or suburb). Consequently they took to leaving the towns in order to settle upon their *otchini* and *vislugi* (lands granted in reward for good service); wherefore the old Russian town-provinces which had hitherto been governed by *vietcha* gradually became divided up into hereditary estates of princes and *pani*, while the capital towns themselves, shorn of their strength, found themselves stranded as solitary units amid a ring of alien and frequently hostile landed proprietors, who, now that the voice of the local *vietché* carried no further than the walls of its local capital, proceeded to plunder that local capital's ancient province. Meanwhile the Grand Duke's *voievodi*, *kasteliani*, and *starosti* squeezed the citizens themselves ; until, to arrest the decline of such communities, the Polish-Lithuanian Sovereign conferred upon them the German system of urban self-government, the *Jus Magdeburgicum* (Law of Magdeburg). The *Jus Magdeburgicum* first reached Poland during the thirteenth and fourteenth centuries, in company with the flood of German colonists which, at that period, had poured into most of the Polish cities. During the fourteenth century the system was introduced also into the towns of Galicia (which province was added to Poland, in 1340, by Casimir the Great), and next, after the middle of the fifteenth century, into the towns of the remainder of Western Rus. Under it the *miestchané*, or commercial-industrial burghers, not only acquired certain trading privileges and exemptions in the matter of the fulfilment of fiscal obligations, but also became independent of the legal jurisdiction of *voievodi* and other such governmental *uriadniki* or aristocratic office-holders. Also, under this system each town was administered by two councils or boards, which consisted of (1) what was known as the *lava*, the members of which—the *lavniki* or assessors—sat under the presidency of a representative of the King (this representative was known as the *voit* [German *Vogt*]) for the purpose of dealing out justice to the citizens, and (2) the *rada,* the members of which—the *raditsi*—were chosen from the burgher population at large, and, headed by a *burmistrer* (*Bürgermeister* or burghermaster), superintended all matters of industry, commerce, and public order and decorum.

Through this approximation of the Lithuanian-Russian order of State to the Polish the political influence of Poland upon Lithuania helped, during the fifteenth and early sixteenth centuries, to maintain the dynastic union between the two States which, though now united under a single authority, had formerly possessed separate sovereigns. During the sixteenth century, however, there became compounded a new combination of circumstances which not only confirmed the Polish-Lithuanian union, but also communicated to the united States greater solidarity in other directions. With this combination of circumstances went some extremely important consequences for Eastern Europe, but more especially for South-Western Rus. I refer to the great Church schism which arose in Western Europe during the sixteenth century—*i.e.* to the Reformation. Although it would hardly have been thought that Eastern Europe could have had much to do with the fact that, in 1517, one Martin Luther, a

German doctor of divinity, started a dispute over what constituted true sources of inspiration, salvation by faith, and other theological subjects, the Church revolution in the West entailed certain results also upon Eastern Europe; which, though not actually touched by the religious consequences of the Reformation, was at least grazed by them in the rebound. At all events certain freethinking movements in the Russian Church community of the sixteenth century had a more or less direct connection with the Reformation, and rested upon ideas which emanated from the Protestant West. Yet it would be difficult to state whether the Reformation reacted the more strongly upon international relations in Western or in Eastern Europe. In the latter region, at least, it figures as a factor in the history of the Russian Empire so unimportant that, on the whole, I should say—though with all reserve—that ancient Rus must have dwelt in complete detachment from the West, that it ignored and was ignored by the latter, and that it neither exercised any influence upon that quarter nor received any influence from the same. In short, Western Europe seems to have known ancient Rus about as little as it knows the modern Russia of to-day. Yet though, as now, the Rus of four centuries ago may not have had such a complete knowledge of the course of affairs in the West as it ought to have done, at least it suffered from the consequences of those affairs to a greater extent than might have been looked for. Such, at all events, was the case in the sixteenth century. To make permanent the dynastic bond between Poland and Lithuania the Polish Government, headed by the clergy, undertook a vigorous Catholic propaganda among the Orthodox population of Lithuanian Rus. This propaganda was carried on with particular keenness during the times of Casimir III. (the middle fifteenth century), but met with strong resistance on the part of the Orthodox Lithuanian population; which led, at the close of the fifteenth century, to the Principality entering upon a decline, for the reason that most of the Orthodox Russian and Lithuanian princes left the country, and took service under the Tsar of Moscow. Also, the Reformation brought about a marked change in European relations. In Poland Protestant teaching found a receptive soil which had been prepared for it by close cultural ties with Germany, where many Polish youths had been educated, whether at Wittenberg University or at some other educational establishment. But in 1520, three years after the great feud of Wittenberg, the Polish clergy met in session at Petrokov, and forbade Polish subjects henceforth to read German Protestant works. This shows how rapid and successful had been the diffusion of such works. In support of the clergy, the Polish Government published (at a convention held at Torun in the same year) a decree whereby confiscation of property and perpetual banishment were threatened to anyone who should import, sell, or distribute in Poland the works of Martin Luther or any other Protestant writer. These strict prohibitions grew with time, until, in a few years, the threat of confiscation of property was succeeded by a threat of capital punishment. Yet all was of no avail. Protestantism had laid too firm a hold upon the Polish community, and we find even Pats, Bishop of Kiev, openly preaching Lutheran forms of doctrine. From Poland and its neighbours Protestantism spread to Lithuania; with the result that by the middle of the sixteenth century some 700 Catholic parishes had come to contain a proportion of but one Catholic parishioner to about a thousand Protestant converts. Next, in 1525, the Teutonic Order of Knights, headed by Albert, their *Hertzog* or Grand Master, seceded from the Roman Church, and mention is made of some of their number translating Protestant works into the Lithuanian tongue. The chief actor in this diffusion of Protestantism in Lithuania was a Lithuanian named Abraham Kulva, who had studied in North Germany, and taken the degree of doctor. To him there succeeded a German pastor named Winkler, and these two may be looked upon as the prime apostles of the reformed faith. Even greater strides were made by Calvinism, which gained the support of, among others, a leading Lithuanian magnate named Nicholas Radziwill Tcherni—twin brother to Queen Barbara (originally the secret, and, thereafter, the professed, wife of Sigismund Augustus). Next, the middle of the sixteenth century saw an immense number of Catholic *dvoriané* adopt Protestantism, and take with them a portion of the Lithuanian-Russian Orthodox aristocracy, in the shape of such families as the Vishnevetskis, the Chodkievitches, and so on. The final result of this triumphal progress of Protestantism was to bring about (in 1569) the Union of Lublin. Protestant influence had so weakened the force of the Catholic propaganda in Lithuanian Rus that the last two sovereigns of the line of Jagiello (Sigismund I. and Sigismund Augustus) had come to display complete indifference to the religious struggle which was raging within their united Empire. In particular, Sigismund Augustus—an easygoing, empty-headed man who had been brought up amid advanced influences—went so far as secretly to protect the new doctrine by circulating Protestant works from his palace library and allowing his court preachers to deliver sermons of a wholly Protestant tenour. In fact, when leaving the palace for divine worship on festival days, he did not greatly care whether it were a Roman or a Lutheran church that he attended. At the same time, while thus extending his protection to Protestants, he favoured also his Orthodox subjects, and in 1563 issued such an interpretation of the edict of the Diet of Grodno (against the holding of State and public offices by adherents of the Orthodox faith) that the interpretation constituted practically an annulment. This weakening of the Catholic propaganda which had been supported by the Kings of Poland caused the Orthodox population of Lithuania no longer to fear, nor even to show hostility to, the Polish Government: which revolution in the popular attitude rendered possible a continuance of the political union between Poland and Lithuania. On the childless death of Sigismund Augustus, there expired also the Jagiello dynasty, and, with it, the dynastic bond between the two countries. So long as the Catholic propaganda had enjoyed the protection of the Polish Government, and had exerted anything of a vigorous influence in Lithuania, the Orthodox Lithuanian - Russian population had been unwilling to continue the union, and had raised the awkward question of the future relations of Lithuania with Poland ; but, latterly, the tolerance or the benevolent indifference of Sigismund Augustus had caused such Orthodox believers to cease to trouble their heads at all in this connection. In fact, opposition to a continuance of the union was threatened only by the Lithuanian magnates, who were afraid lest the Polish *shliachta* or *dvorianin* class should crush them out. On the other hand, the Lithu-anian-Russian *dvoriané* were all in favour of the union remaining per-manent, and, in January, 1569, a great diet was convened at Lublin for a final settlement of the question. Though, as said, some opposition to the continuance of the union was dispayed by the Lithuanian aristo-cracy, the King contrived to win to his side two influential magnates of South-Western Rus—namely, a member of the line of Rurik named Prince Constantine Ostrozhki, who was *voievoda* of Kiev, and a descend-ant of Guedemin named Prince Alexander Tchartoriski, who was *voievoda* of Volhynia. These two magnates stood at the head of the Orthodox Russian-Lithuanian *dvoriané*, and might, under other circumstances, have caused the King a good deal of trouble. In particular, Prince Ostrozhki was a large cantonal landowner who barely deigned even to recognise the King as his sovereign, seeing that he was both wealthier and more influential than the latter, and had at his disposal estates which embraced not only the whole of the modern government of Volhynia, but also a notable portion of the modern governments of Podolia and Kiev. Indeed, in these regions he owned 35 towns and more than 700 *sela;* all of which brought him in an income of 10,000,000 *zloti* or Polish florins.[1] With them these two magnates carried over the whole of the Russian *dvoriané* of the South-West, who had already undergone sufficient provocation at the hands of the Polish *shliachta;* and, in turn, these South-Western *dvoriané* were followed by the Lithuanian *dvoriané.* This finally decided the question of the union, and the Diet of Lublin saw the political tie between the two States recognised as permanent and unbreakable, despite the fact that the dynasty of the Jagiellos had now come to an end. Simultaneously the Polish-Lithuanian Empire acquired a final type of organisation which united the two States on an equal basis, as the two halves of one realm. Of these halves the first was called the Kingdom, and the second the Principality, while, together, they were known as the *Rietch Pospolitaia* (a Polish translation of the Latin term *Res Publica*). In short the form of administration adopted was an elective monarchy, organised on the lines of a republic. At the head of the Government stood the King, who was chosen to his office by a common Diet, representative of the Kingdom and of the Principality alike, while the legislative power belonged to the Diet (a body constituted of *zemskie posli*, or deputies of the *shliachta*) and to the Senate (a body constituted of the higher officials, lay and spiritual, of the two portions of the joint State). Yet, though possessed of a common supreme administration whereof the three organs were the Diet, the Senate, and the King, the two constituent portions of the *Rietch Pospolitaia* still retained also their separate administrations, their separate ministers, their separate armies, and their separate laws. The most important factor in the history of the South-Western Rus was the series of decrees whereby the Diet of Lublin made over to the Kingdom certain provinces of South-Western Rus which had hitherto belonged to the Principality. Those provinces were Podliachia (which covered what is now the western portion of the government of Grodno), Volhynia, and the Ukraine (which covered what are now the governments of Kiev and Poltava, together with certain portions of the governments of Podolia and Tchernigov). Thus the year 1569 saw the Union of Lublin finally established. With it went some very important results, political and national-religious, for South-Western Rus in particular and for the whole of Eastern Europe in general.

---

[1] Equivalent to over £1,000,000 sterling.

For Western Rus the decrees of the Diet of Lublin were a triumph for Guedemin's descendants—a triumph, that is to say, for the Polish influence which they wielded in the region just named. By those decrees the Poles obtained what they had been desiring for close upon two hundred years—namely, the permanent union of their State with Lithuania and a direct linking of the rich and attractive provinces of South-Western Rus to Poland. Polish influence also enabled the house of Guedemin to break through many ancient customs in the part of Rus over which they had gained the mastery, and to import into its life and organisation much that was new. In old Kievan Rus the various provinces had been administered by members of the princely house of Rurik, in agreement with the old *vietché*-governed capitals of their provinces ; but the development of private landownership had prevented that house from possessing any durable social and economic ties with the provinces which it governed. Consequently, under the rule of Guedemin's posterity, it became displaced by a more settled aristocracy of great landowners who comprised the Russian and Lithuanian princes of the region and their boyar retinues. Again, through the consolidation of dietal-administrative institutions this aristocracy was made to yield pride of place to a class of small military landowners—the class of the *shliachta* or *dvoriané ;* and thus the old provinces or cantons of Kievan Rus which had formerly centred around their respective capitals, as their political *points d'appui,* became split up, in Lithuanian Rus, into a number of administrative areas which were directed by governors appointed of the Grand Duke, and united, not by several centres of local administration, but by one common centre of government. Finally the senior capitals of provinces— the capitals which, through their *vietcha,* had hitherto represented their respective provinces in the relations of the latter with the Grand Duke— now became sundered, through the action of Grand-Ducal administration and private landownership, from their respective units, and converted, owing to the abrogation of *vietché* government in favour of the *Jus Magdeburgicum,* into a number of strictly class communities of *miestchané* which, hemmed within a narrow circle by the force of urban inertia, soon lost both provincial importance of any sort and any power of participation in the political life of the country. Thus overlordship of the *shliachta ;* government posts which, though usually conferred for life, were, in places, made hereditary ; the *Jus Magdeburgicum,*—such were the three innovations which Polish influence imported into Lithuanian Rus. The results of the Union of Lublin also called into action a fourth innovation for which already the way had been prepared by Polish influence. That fourth innovation was serf law. From the middle of the sixteenth century onwards we notice in progress a resettlement of the long-deserted region of the Middle Dnieper. The fact that its Steppes lay conveniently near to hand was, in itself, a sufficient reason why settlers should be attracted thither; and this current of migration was further maintained and increased by the rapid spread of serf law throughout Lithuania. Already the beginning of the sixteenth century had seen several different categories of peasant-agricultural population arise in that Steppe region. Such categories were distinguished from one another by their degree of dependency upon the landowners, and ranged from perambulant *krestiané* (who, known as *zasiadlie* or *nezasiadlie* according as they settled with or without the aid of a loan from their landlords, retained, in either case, their right of removal) to *tcheliad nevolnaia*, or serfs of a domestic-agricultural type. During the times of the first and second Lithuanian Statutes (1529–1566) the political growth of the *shliachta* caused these several classes of peasantry to stand more and more on a level with one another as regards the gradual diminution of their freedom; and this movement was further hastened by the Union of 1569. Under the elective kings of the *Rietch Pospolitaia*, legislation, as also the whole bent of the political life of the country, came under the direct influence of the Polish-Lithuanian *shliachta*, the ruling class in the State, which did not fail to use its political predominance to oppress the peasant population, which lay at its mercy. With the addition to the Kingdom of the Russian provinces on either side of the Middle Dnieper, Polish administration began to penetrate thither also, and to oust the native Russian *régime*; while, under cover of the former, the Polish *shliachta* likewise pushed themselves to the front, and, acquiring lands in the locality, introduced thereto Polish serf law, which by now had assumed certain marked features. Of these neighbours from the regions of the Vistula and the Western Bug the native Lithuanian-Russian *dvoriané* soon adopted the landed-proprietorial ideas and customs. If, in the interests of the treasury, the law and the Government took thought at all for the agrarian and taxatory relations of the *krestianin* to his landlord, certain it is that it handed over his personality into the full power of the new squire. That is to say, the *shliachta* were permitted to assume absolute rights of life and death over their *krestiané*. To kill a *kholop*, a peasant slave, was, in the eyes of a *shliachtich*, about the same thing as to kill a dog. That we have on the authority of Polish writers of the day. To escape such serfdom, which was being drawn, like an ever-tightening noose, around the peasantry, the rural population began to pour from the Kingdom and the Principality into the boundless Steppes of the Ukraine, where it wandered lower and lower down the courses of the Dnieper and the Eastern Bug until it had arrived at regions whither it hoped that the *shliachta* could not penetrate. But in time agrarian speculation began to avail itself of this movement also, and to communicate to it a new force. For instance, *pani* and members of the *shliachta* would solicit life-offices as *starosti* of frontier towns in the Ukraine which had extensive tracts of waste lands attached; whereafter these speculators would either further petition for or simply grab large areas of the illimitable Steppe, and hasten to settle these new estates of theirs by the method of offering attractive exemptions from taxation to such poor *miestchané* and *krestiané* as they could lay their hands upon. In fact, the system adopted with regard to the Steppes of the Ukraine was much the same as was done in the more recent case of the Bashkirs' lands and grazing rights on the eastern shores of the Black Sea. Men of the highest birth and position, such as the Princes Ostrozhki and Vishnevetski and the *pani* Pototski and Zamoiski and others, never tired nor grew ashamed of taking part in this scramble for waste fiscal lands on the Dnieper and its Steppe tributaries, both to right and to left. Yet, even so, the agrarian speculators of that day acted with a better sense of their responsibilities than did their modern imitators of the Urals and the Caucasus. Under the former, the Ukraine swiftly came to life again; swiftly there arose in it scores of new townships, together with hamlets and agricultural settlements by the hundred and the thousand. With this process of colonisation went a process of fortifying the Steppes; without which expedient the former of the two processes would have been simply impossible. That is to say, in front of the chain of old-established towns of the frontier—Braslav, Korsuni, Kanevo, and Periaslav—there were thrown out lines of new forts, to protect the townships and *sela* which were rapidly springing up under their shadow; and the fact that these fortified posts arose amid a constant struggle with the Tartars caused them to become military communities which, in some ways, remind one of those "gates of heroes" with which the Steppe frontiers of Kievan Rus of the tenth and eleventh centuries were encircled. Finally, from these communities there arose the Cossacks of Little Rus.

Cossacks or *kozaki*, in the original meaning of the term, constituted a *stratum* of the Russian community which at one time covered the entire country. In the sixteenth century the term *kozak* was applied to casual labourers who hired themselves out for rough work on peasant homesteads—to men who possessed neither a definite avocation nor a settled domicile. Such was the *original* meaning of the term *kozak*. Later on, however, this vagabond, homeless class acquired, in Muscovite Rus, the name of *volnie guliastchie liudi* ("free, wandering men"), or, more simply, of *volnitsi* ("free men"). The southern regions contiguous to the Steppes constituted a peculiarly favourable soil for the growth of this class, and communicated to it a peculiar character. When the danger of Tartar invasion was beginning to diminish a little there arose a constant sporadic struggle between the dwellers of the border and such Tartar bands as still infested the Steppes. Of this struggle the starting points and bases of support were the fortified towns of the frontier, where there sprang up a class of men whose trade was to go out into the Steppes, with arms in their hands, and there engage in the industries of hunting and fishing. At once daring and lacking in this world's goods, these armed hunters and fishermen of the Steppes must have acquired the means for their dangerous occupation from the local traders to whom they made over their catches; and if so, we see them still retaining their character of labourers who worked for a master. Also, as warriors who were inured to Steppe warfare, they may have received certain subsidies from the Governments of their respective principalities; while the fact that they were constantly engaged in collisions with the Tartar brigands of the desert earned for them the Tartar name of *kozaki*. Later on this term spread also to Northern Rus, where it connoted an unattached or homeless day-labourer of any sort. In the eastern strip of the Southern Steppes collisions between *kozaki* and Tartars began earlier than they did elsewhere; which is why, in my opinion, our oldest information concerning Cossackdom may be taken to be an item which speaks of some *kozaki* of Riazan showing good service to their town in a Tartar affray of 1444. In the sixteenth and seventeenth centuries, also, certain phenomena were repeated in Muscovite Rus which can only be ascribed to a great increase in the number of *kozaki*. Thus sixteenth century "tenth books" of certain of the Steppe cantons contain notes to the effect that such and such an impoverished "son of a boyar" "did go into the Steppe, and there did join himself unto the *kozaki*." This does not mean that he actually entered any permanent community of the class mentioned (the Cossacks of the Don, for instance), but simply that he fell in with some chance companions, and, forsaking alike his service and his *pomiestie*, took to roaming the Steppes at will, and to engaging temporarily in the free pursuits of that region, more especially in fighting the Tartars. That done, he would return to his native place, and re-establish himself in his old position. Indeed, another " tenth book " of Elets (dated 1622) records an item of a whole party of local *pomiestchiki* abandoning their lands and " joining themselves unto the *kozaki*"; after which they entered the service of certain boyars and monasteries as slaves or servitors. The original home of Cossackdom may be demarcated by drawing a line through the frontier towns of the Middle Volga, and Riazan and Tula, and then bending the line sharply southward, and thereafter extending it to the Dnieper *viâ* Putivl and Periaslav. Soon Cossackdom took another step forward into the desert. This was when, owing to the fact that the Tartars were weakening and the Horde was beginning to break up, certain parties (*arteli*) of *kozaki* from the frontier towns, but more especially from Riazan, went and settled in the open Steppes which lay around the course of the Upper Don. These Cossacks of the Don may be looked upon as practically the original form of Steppe Cossackdom, since, during the second half of the sixteenth century, when the Zaporozhski Cossacks had only just begun to organise their military republic, we find the Don Cossacks already an organised body, with, among its members, a number of Christianised Tartars. In fact, there is still to be seen preserved the petition of a converted Tartar of the Crimea who, as stated earlier,[1] left his native region for the Don in the year 1589, and there, for a space of fifteen years, served the Muscovite Tsar against his (the Tartar's) compatriots,—finally retiring to, and settling at, Putivl, whence he forwarded a petition to the effect that his establishment might be exempted from taxation, and he himself commissioned for military service on the same footing as were the local gentry.

Items concerning the Cossacks of the Dnieper occur later than is the case with items concerning the Cossacks of Riazan, for they begin only with the close of the fifteenth century. Both the origin and the original social differentiation of these Cossacks were as simple as in other localities. That is to say, from the towns of Kiev, Podolia, and Volhynia, as also from the region of the Upper Dnieper, parties of adventurers began to go out into the wild Steppe country—there to engage in the industries of bee-, fish-, game-, and Tartar-hunting. In spring and summer these emigrants would carry on their trade on the Dnieper and its Steppe

---

[1] See vol. ii. p. 109.

tributaries, and in winter time they would rally, with their booty, to the Cis-Dnieperian towns, more particularly to Kaluga and Tcherkassi, which were the earliest and principal haunts of Cossackdom, and where some of these Cossacks (as was the case in Northern Rus) hired out their labour to *miestchané* and landowners. With regard to the Cossacks of the Ukraine, however, local geographical and political conditions rendered their fortunes more complex than those of the Dnieperian Cossacks. Here Cossackdom became involved in the vortex of international complications which kept arising between Rus, Lithuania, Poland, Turkey, and the Crimea; and this fact caused the *rôle* which local Cossackdom was called upon to play to acquire a certain historical importance. I have said that the growth of the colonisation of the Dnieper region augmented also the growth of local Cossack population. The latter, though a necessity both to the district and to the State as a whole, were a restless class who were forever creating difficulties for the Polish Government—a class which, despite the fact that its familiarity with the art of fighting rendered it the best defence that the country had to offer against the incursions of the Tartars, constituted a very double-edged weapon. One of its pursuits—in fact, its chief one—was to carry out retaliatory raids upon Tartar and Turkish territory, both by land and by sea; and at the beginning of the seventeenth century we find lightly built Cossack galleys ravaging the northern, western, and southern shores of the Black Sea, and penetrating even to Constantinople itself. In return the Turks threatened Poland, which feared them more than it did all its other enemies. As early as the beginning of the sixteenth century Warsaw drew up a plan for rendering the Cossacks harmless without at the same time diminishing their utility. This plan was to separate the more reputable portion of the disorderly and universally increasing Cossack population from its fellows, and to take that selected portion into the salaried service of the State under an obligation to defend the Ukraine against the country's foes; after which, on retirement, these picked Cossacks were to be permitted to revert to their old mode of life. Also, as early as the beginning of the sixteenth century, we encounter signs of Cossack contingents being enrolled for frontier " watch and post service."[1] Probably this was only one of several fleeting attempts to shape these armed adventurers into a corps of frontier guards for the Steppes, for it was not until 1570 that a permanent force of 300 "listed" (registered) Cossacks was constituted, which Stephen Batory subsequently augmented to 500,

---

[1] See vol. ii. p. 117.

and, later still (*i.e.* in 1625), to 6000. Yet the growth of this corps of "listed" Cossacks did little to diminish the mass of non-registered or supernumerary Cossacks. These outlawed adventurers (who came mostly of the *krestianin* class) local governors and *pani* strove their utmost to reconvert into peasants, and to reawaken to a sense of the obligations which they had cast aside. But men who had once tasted of the sweets of Cossack freedom not unnaturally proved recalcitrant, and considered that they had a right to disobey when all the time the very Government which had placed them, as peasants, under the yoke of the *pani* was only too eager to enlist their help in time of war, and to summon them to its standard, not by registered detachments, but by tens of thousands. Thus the double-faced policy of the Government implanted irritation in the breasts of the non-registered Cossacks, and formed of them an explosive body which easily burst into flame as soon as ever there arose among them an energetic leader. Meanwhile on the Lower Dnieper there became formed a Cossack *läger* which served as a refuge and support for the dissatisfaction which, among the Cossacks of the Ukraine, was so rife that it was gradually being worked up into open rebellion. The stronghold in question was what was known as the *Zaporozhie*, or republic of the Zaporozhski[1] Cossacks.

This institution arose insensibly out of the industrial "cossacking" ("cossacking afield") which became engaged in in the Steppes at times when the Cossack inhabitants of the frontier towns of the Ukraine had followed the course of the Dnieper downwards until they had passed the *porogi* or cataracts.[1] Professor Lubavski too has expressed the opinion that the germ of the *Zaporozhski Sietch*, or military republic of the Zaporozhski Cossacks, was a large *artel* or association of Cossacks who had succeeded in pursuing their industries beyond the cataracts until they had reached the immediate neighbourhood of the Tartar camps : and the first traces of these pioneers he finds at the close of the fifteenth century. When the Cossacks of the towns began to be subjected to pressure by the Polish Government they took flight beyond the cataracts to spots with which they were already acquainted, and to which neither Polish commissaries nor Polish expeditionary corps could penetrate. There, on islands formed by the Dnieper at the point where it issues from the narrows into the open Steppe and expands into a broad, open current, the fugitives built fortified *sietchi* or camps. The chief stronghold of these Zaporozhski Cossacks arose in the sixteenth century, on the Island of

---

[1] From *za*, beyond, and *porogi*, cataracts.   [2] See vol. i. p. 85.

Chortitsa (which lay nearest to the rapids), and was what constituted the once-famous *Zaporozhskaia Sietch*. Later on it was removed to other islands below the cataracts. In form it was a fortified camp around which there were built ramparts of tree-trunks, to represent a *zasieka* or *abattis*. Also, it possessed artillery of a kind, in the shape of small cannons which had been captured from Tartar and Turkish forts. In it these irresponsible and multi-racial emigrants organised a military-industrial association which grandiosely styled itself "The Knighthood of the Zaporozhski Host." Its members lived in huts of brushwood, covered over with horse-hide, and were distinguished from one another by their avocations —some acting as free-lances pure and simple, and subsisting on booty of war, and others acting as hunters of fish and game, and ministering to the requirements of the former class. Women were not admitted to the *Sietch*; married Cossacks lived apart, in winter huts, where it was their duty to cultivate grain for the support of their fellow inhabitants. Up to the close of the sixteenth century the *Zaporozhïe* remained a mobile community, and possessed a mutable composition. In winter it dispersed to the towns of the Ukraine, and left only a few hundred men to take care of the *Sietch's* artillery and other republican property; but in summer time the *personnel* of the establishment totalled some 3000 persons, who were subject to increase at times when the peasantry of the Ukraine had been more than usually provoked by the Tartars or the Lechs, or when some conspiracy was afoot in the Ukraine. At such times every malcontent, ruined man, or victim of oppression betook himself beyond the cataracts for refuge. No one who repaired to the *Sietch* was asked any questions as to his identity, his domicile, his faith, or his family belongings. Everyone was received who seemed likely to make a desirable comrade. At the end of the sixteenth century we note signs of a regular military organisation among these Cossacks—though an unsettled one which attained a firmer standing later. The military fraternity of the place—the *Kosh*—were commanded by a *hettman* or *ataman*, who was chosen by the military council of the *Sietch* to serve, with his elected lieutenant, judges, and "writer," as the *Sietch's* government or directorate. Above all things the *Sietch* valued brotherly equality, and every question which arose was decided by the circle, *rada*, or Cossack *kolo* (board of management) of the *Sietch*. The *kolo* treated the directorate with complete lack of ceremony in the matter of the election of or changes in the same; while undesirables it punished by immersing them to their armpits in the sand of the river. In 1581 there arrived at the *Sietch* a *pan* of Galicia

—a ne'er-do-weel adventurer—named Zborovski, for the purpose of enlisting Cossacks to take part in an expedition against Moscow. Weary of inaction, as also of lack of funds, the "Knighthood" gladly welcomed the *pan*, and at once elected him *hettman*. On the march towards Moscow the Cossacks plied him with questions whether, in the event of their returning safe and sound from Moscow, he would be able to find them other work to do which they could profitably exploit; and on his proceeding to "cry off" Moscow, and to propose, instead, an expedition to Persia, they came very near to killing him during the violent controversy which arose. This quest of employment on expeditions—or, rather, this quest of booty and rapine—increased in proportion as, towards the end of the sixteenth century, Cossackdom became overcrowded. Unable any longer to satisfy their wants by mere hunting and fishing, the Cossacks took to wandering in thousands over the Trans-Dnieperian Ukraine, and to despoiling its inhabitants. Nowhere could the local authorities get rid of these unemployed nomads, and even the freebooters themselves did not know where next to turn, but readily followed any leader who summoned them to attack Moldavia or the Crimea. At length, when the Period of Troubles began, gangs of vagabonds collected who spread themselves over the whole length and breadth of the Muscovite Empire. In those days the Ukraine was accustomed to dub raids upon neighbouring countries "Cossack forays"; and, indeed, no other resource remained open to such vagabonds. Thus to a speech of Sborovski's concerning the duty of submitting to King and fatherland we find them replying with the popular saying, "While men live they must be,"—meaning that, so long as men had to exist, it behoved them to feed themselves. But the Cossacks did not always stop at raids upon foreign countries, for in the sixteenth century the turn of their own fatherland came, and, its complement filled to overflowing, the *Zaporozhïe* became an incubator wherein risings against the *Rietch Pospolitaia* itself were hatched.

Thus the Union of Lublin entailed upon South-Western Rus three results between which there existed an intimate connection—namely, serf law, increase of peasant colonisation of the Ukraine, and conversion of the *Zaporozhïe* into an insurrectionary refuge for the oppressed population of Rus.

CHAPTER VI

The moral character of the Little Russian Cossacks—The stand which they made for faith and nationality—Differences in Cossackdom—The Little Russian question—The Baltic and Eastern questions—European relations of the Muscovite Empire—The importance of Moscow's foreign policy during the seventeenth century.

WE have now followed, in its general features, the history of the Little Russian Cossacks, in connection with the fortunes of Lithuanian Rus, down to the beginning of the seventeenth century, when there took place in the position of those Cossacks a sharp break. We have seen how the character of Cossackdom underwent a change—how gangs of industrial workers of the Steppes became formed into individual military associations which lived by raiding neighbouring countries and were at times enlisted by the Government as guardsmen for the frontiers of the State. These categories of Cossacks looked, in each case, to the Steppes for their maintenance, and, in so doing, helped, more or less, to protect the constantly threatened south-eastern outskirts. But with the accomplishment of the Union of Lublin Little Russian Cossackdom turned against the State which it had hitherto defended, since the international position of Little Rus had demoralised this vagrant rabble, and strangled in it the growth of any civic feeling. Upon neighbouring countries—upon Turkey, the Crimea, Moldavia, and even Moscow herself—the Cossacks were accustomed to look as so many objects of plunder or "Cossack foraging"; and this view they gradually extended to their own State, from the time when landownership by *pani* or *shliachtichi*, with its concomitant of serf law, first began to penetrate to the outlying portions of the *Rietch*. Then, since the Little Russian Cossacks found themselves confronted with a foe more cruel even than Turkey and the Crimea themselves, it was with redoubled virulence that they hurled their forces upon the new adversary, and became divorced from fatherland and faith—the two indissolubly connected bases upon which, at that period, the whole moral world of the inhabitant of Eastern Europe rested, but which, in neither case, did the *Rietch Pospolitaia* permit Cossackdom to retain. Indeed, for the Cossack the thought that he was an Orthodox believer was a mere reminiscence of his boyhood, an abstract idea which neither bound him nor served any useful purpose in his life. During times of war he treated the Russians and their churches no better than he did the Tartars and their places of worship, and much worse than the Tartars themselves would have done. Thus in 1636 we find an Orthodox Russian *pan* named Adam Kissel —a government commissary of Cossacks who knew his charges well— writing that the latter were strongly attached to the Greek Church and clergy, but, in all spiritual relations, resembled the Tartars rather than the Christians. Thus the Cossack had no real moral support left him. Indeed, in no other class in the *Rietch Pospolitaia* was the level of moral and civic development quite so low as in his. Perhaps only the hierarchy of the Little Russian Church before the time of the Union was able to vie with Cossackdom in backwardness. The Cossack's rude standards of thought forbade him even to recognise the Ukraine of his adoption as his fatherland; and to this disability the exceedingly heterogeneous composition of Cossackdom contributed. For instance, among the band of 500 "registered" or enlisted Cossacks which was enrolled by Stephen Batory there were included troopers from no less than 74 towns and rural districts of Western Rus and Lithuania—towns so far removed from one another as Vilna and Polotsk; from 7 Polish towns—*i.e.* Poznana, Cracow, and others; and from Moscow, Riazan, and various districts on the Volga. Also, the contingent numbered within its ranks Scandinavians, Serbs, Germans, and Tartars of the Crimea. What possible bond could unite such a medley throng? Upon its neck sat the *pan* or local magnate, and by its side hung the sword. To rob and to murder the *pan*, and to lease the sword for gain—therein lay the whole political outlook of the Cossack, the whole sociological curriculum which he heard expounded at the *Sietch*, the Cossack academy, the higher school of prowess for every good freebooter, the "nesting-place of treason" as the Poles called it. For money we see the Cossacks giving their military services to the German Emperor against the Turks, to the Polish (their own) Government against Moscow and the Crimea, and to Moscow and the Crimea against their own Government. The early risings of the Cossacks against the *Rietch Pospolitaia* partook of a purely social, democratic character that was devoid of any national-religious tinge; nor is it necessary to state that they emanated from the *Zaporozhie*. Yet the first of those risings had for its leader an alien, a member of a rival Cossack community, in the shape of a ruined *shliachtich* named Christopher Kosinski, who had abandoned his country and his class. Joining the

Zaporozhki Cossacks, he first of all leased himself, with a band of his companions, to the King of Poland, and then, in 1501, for the mere reason that he and his mercenaries had not received their stipulated reward, headed the whole of the *Zaporozhki* Cossacks in burning and razing the towns of the Ukraine, with the farms and country houses of the local *shliachtichi* and *pani*, more especially of the Princes Ostrozhki, the richest landowners in the region. Eventually Prince K. Ostrozhki worsted him in a fight, and threw him into gaol, but subsequently pardoned him and his followers, and forced them to swear to settle peaceably on his lands beyond the cataracts. Only two months later Kosinski raised a new rebellion, swore fealty to the Tsar of Moscow, and, with Turkish and Tartar help, started to turn the Ukraine upside down, to murder the local *shliachtichi*, and to besiege the town of Tcherkassi with the intention of exterminating its inhabitants and their *starosta* (a Prince Vishnevetski, who had sent for assistance to the above-mentioned Prince Ostrozhki). Finally, the freebooter yielded his life in single combat with that *starosta*, but his work was carried on by two leaders named Loboda and Nalivaiko, who, in 1595, ravaged the whole of the Ukraine westward of the Dnieper. Thus the mercenary sword of the Cossacks — a sword divorced from God and country—came to serve as the standard of the national-religious flag of Poland, and to fill the lofty *rôle* of defender of Western-Russian Orthodoxy.

This unlooked-for *rôle* had been prepared for Cossackdom by another, a *Church*, union, which came about some 27 years after the political one. In passing let me enumerate the principal circumstances which led up to that event. The Catholic propaganda which recommenced with the appearance of the Jesuits in Lithuania in 1569 soon overcame the Protestantism of the region, and proceeded to attack Orthodoxy. In this enterprise it met, at first, with stout resistance from the Orthodox magnates, headed by Prince K. Ostrozhki; while, later, it encountered opposition from the urban populations, organised in guilds. Then it was that among the despised, oppressed, demoralised Orthodox hierarchy there again arose the idea of a union with the Church of Rome; and at a convention held at Brest in 1596 the Russian Church community became split into two hostile sections—namely, an Orthodox and a Uniate. The Orthodox community ceased to be the legal Church recognised of the State ; while the Orthodox parish clergy, having lost the only two of their bishops who had refused to accept the union, found themselves left with no prelates at all. On the other hand, the growing secession of

Orthodox gentry to Catholicism and Uniacy caused the Russian *miest-chanstvo*, or commercial class, also to become deprived of their chief political mainstay. Consequently one support, and one only, now remained for the ordinary clergy and the *miestchanstvo*—namely, the Cossacks and their reserve, the ordinary Russian peasantry. Of these four classes the interests were in each case different; yet, in the face of the common foe, those differences completely disappeared. Without actually uniting the four classes, the Church union communicated to their joint struggle a new stimulus, and helped them to a better understanding of one another; while, as regards the Cossack and the *kholop*, they could easily be made to believe that the Church union was only an alliance between the Polish King, the *pan*, the Catholic priest, and the common agent of all three, the Jew, against the Russian God whom every Russian was bound to defend. To tell the driven slave or the free Cossack—both of whom were eager to see the downfall of the *pan* on whose lands they lived—that that downfall would strike a blow for the offended God of the Russians meant a lightening and a heartening of their consciences if those organs chanced to be oppressed with an inward feeling that, come what might, murder was a sin. We have seen that the early Cossack risings at the close of the sixteenth century were devoid of any national-religious character; but from the beginning of the seventeenth century Cossack-dom began gradually to be absorbed into the ranks of the Orthodox Opposition. Thus in 1620 a Zaporozhkian Cossack *hettman* named Sagaidachni enrolled himself and his followers in one of the many Ortho-dox guilds of Kiev, and voluntarily, and without any authority from his Government, joined the Patriarch of Jerusalem in establishing an Ortho-dox hierarchy which should act under Cossack protection. Later (in 1625) the head of this newly-established hierarchy, the Metropolitan of Kiev, summoned the Cossacks of the *Zaporozhie* to defend his Orthodox charges; and, in response, those Cossacks came and put to death the city prefect who had been ill-treating the True Believers.

In this manner Cossackdom acquired a standard on the personal side of which was inscribed a summons to fight for faith and the Russian nation, and, on the reverse side, a summons to exterminate or expel every *pan* and *shliachtich* from the Ukraine. Yet it was a standard which failed to unite Cossackdom as a whole, since, as early as the sixteenth century, there opened in that body an economic rift. Cossacks who had settled in the frontier towns, and lived by the solitary pursuits of the Steppes, began to remove to such industrial sites as they found suitable, and to engage in agriculture and stock raising; until, by the beginning of the seventeenth century, certain of the frontier districts—notably that of Kaniev—had come to be full of Cossack farmers whose industry (as usually happens in such cases) was based upon the leasehold system. Of the presence of this body of agriculturists the Polish Government took advantage to enroll a corps of registered and paid frontier guards; and in time this corps became further subdivided into a number of territorial *otriadi* or regiments, according to the towns which served as the administrative centres of the various districts which were tenanted by the Cossacks. Next, by a convention concluded between the King's *hettman* of Southern Poland and the Cossacks, the contingent of the latter was, in 1625, fixed at 6000 men, divided into six regiments (those of Bielotserkov, Korsun, Kaniev, Tcherkassi, Tchigirin, and Periaslav); while, under Bogdan Khmelnitski, the number of those regiments was further increased to sixteen, and comprised over 230 *sotni* or squadrons. The initiation of this system of division into regiments may be ascribed to the days of the *hettman* Sagaidachni (*circa* 1622), who is usually represented as the prime organiser of Little Russian Cossackdom. In the policy of this *hettman* we see the key to the cleavage which lurked in the Cossack *ménage*. Sagaidachni attempted to draw a distinction between the registered Cossacks, as a privileged class, and those of the plain peasantry of the *Rietch Pospolitaia* who had thrown in their lot with Cossackdom; which gave rise to complaints that in this he was unfair to the peasants in question. Himself a *shliachtich* by origin, he carried with him into Cossackdom the ideas of his class; which caused the struggle between Cossackdom and the *shliachta* of the Ukraine to acquire a special character, since its aim was, not to clear the Ukraine of the immigrant class of alien nobility, but to replace the latter with a native privileged class which in time should come to form a *shliachta* of purely Cossack origin. But the real strength of Cossackdom did not lie in its registered section. Even when constituted of 6000 men, registered Cossackdom absorbed, at the most, but a tenth part of the persons who had joined themselves to the Cossack body, and acquired Cossack rights. In general, such persons were poor and homeless individuals who dwelt on the estates of *pani* and *shliachtichi*—persons who, as free Cossacks, declined to perform identical obligations with the plain peasantry of the *Rietch Pospolitaia*. On the other hand, the Polish governors and *pani* were reluctant to admit the freedom of such persons, and endeavoured by every means to convert them into subjects of the *Rietch*. Whenever the Polish Government needed Cossack military help it enrolled in its Cossack contingent both registered and non-registered Cossacks, and, according as the need for their services became less pressing, eliminated or "wrote out" the superfluous members of the force, with a view to restoring them to their former condition. But these *vipishtchiki*, or "written out men," conceiving themselves to stand in danger of enserfment, would proceed to betake themselves to their stronghold, the *Zaporozhïe*, and there to organise rebellions ; whence it came about that the fourteen years from 1624 saw many such Cossack risings, under the leadership of Zhmail, Tarass Bulba, Suleim, Pavlink, Ostranin, and Guna. Meanwhile, the registered section of the Cossacks generally either split into two sides or took service *en masse* with the Poles. Yet none of these risings proved successful ; they merely ended (in 1638) in the Cossacks losing the most important of their rights. The registered section underwent reorganisation, and was placed under the command of Polish *shliachtichi ;* the post of *hettman* was conferred upon a Government commissary ; the Cossack settlers were deprived of their hereditary lands ; and the non-registered Cossacks were relegated to serfdom under the *pani* of the country. Thus free Cossackdom became extinct ; according to a Little Russian chronicler, every vestige of freedom was taken from the Cossacks, hitherto unprecedented taxes were imposed upon them, and their churches, as well as posts in connection with the serving of those churches, were sold to the Jews.

Poles and Russians, Russians and Jews, Catholics and Uniates, Uniates and Orthodox, guilds and hierarchs, the *shliachta* and the *plebs* of the *Rietch Pospolitaia*, the *plebs* and Cossackdom, Cossackdom and the *miestchantsvo* (commercial class), registered Cossacks and the free Cossack settlers, the Cossacks of the towns and the Cossacks of the *Zaporozhïe*, the Cossack *starshina* (district elder) and the Cossack hind, the Cossack *hettman* and the Cossack *starshina*,—all these social forces, set as they were in opposing and tangled relations to one another, contended in pairs, and allowed their mutual differences, open or latent, to press upon the life of Little Rus with such weight and complexity that there became formed a tangled skein whereof not all the skill of the Government, in Warsaw or in Kiev, could unravel the ends. Bogdan Khmelnitski's rising was an attempt to cut the tangle with the swords of his Cossacks. Whether or no Moscow had foreseen this rebellion, and the necessity of her participating in it, it is difficult to say, since in that quarter all eyes were fixed upon the provinces of Smolensk and Novgorod Sieversski, and the abortive war of 1632–34 was being followed by quiet preparations for retrieving that failure. Little Rus still lay beyond the horizon of Muscovite politics, and the remembrance of the Tcherkassi of Lissovski and Sapiega was still fresh in Muscovite minds. True, intimations had come from Kiev that the Kievan folk were ready to serve the Orthodox Tsar of Moscow, as well as humble petitions that he would take Little Rus under his mighty protection, since the Orthodox people of the region could not get on without a Tsar; but from Moscow merely a guarded reply had been returned that, if ever the day should come when the Poles proved intolerant of the Orthodox faith, the Muscovite Tsar would consider the question of rescuing that faith from the heretics. From the inception of Khmelnitski's rising, ambiguous relations established themselves between Moscow and Little Rus. To begin with, Bogdan's success exceeded his wildest expectations, for never at any time had he contemplated invading the *Rietch Pospolitaia*, but merely stampeding the insolent *pani* out of the Ukraine. Yet, when no more than three victories had placed nearly the whole of Little Rus in his hands, he himself recognised that he had done more than could have been looked for, and his head began to turn, especially after dinner. At such times he had visions of a Ukrainian Principality which should comprise the whole of the Vistula region, and be ruled by a Grand Duke Bogdan. Also, he styled himself "Monarch and Autocrat of Rus," threatened to lay the Poles by the heels, to drive the *shliachta* class across the Vistula, and so on. Also, he conceived a grudge against the Tsar of Moscow for having failed to help him, at the beginning of the affair, by moving against Poland. Angrily, at a banquet, he told some Muscovite ambassadors a few unpleasant truths, and, towards the end of the meal, threatened to come and attack Moscow, and to join issue as to who should rule on the Moskva. This sincere braggadocio was succeeded by grovelling, yet far from sincere, repentance; which changeableness of attitude had its origin not only in Bogdan's personal temperament, but also in a consciousness that he stood in a false position. He could not get even with Poland with the mere help of his Cossacks; so, seeing that no extraneous help came from Moscow, he was forced to have recourse to the Khan of the Crimea. True, after his early successes we see him hinting that he would be prepared to serve the Muscovite Tsar if the latter would but come and assist his Cossacks; but the Muscovite Government procrastinated and held back, like a man who has no settled plan of his own, but looks for inspiration from the course of events. The Muscovite Government scarcely knew how to take the rebellious *hettman*—whether to admit him to fealty, or only to support him covertly against the Poles. It was clear that, as a subject, he would be of less use than as an undeclared ally, since a subject needs to be protected, and an ally may be thrown over immediately that his usefulness diminishes. Meanwhile open support of the Cossacks could only lead to a war with Poland—to a plunging of the whole of Little Russian relations into confusion; whereas to take no part at all in the struggle would mean handing over the Orthodox population of the Ukraine to its foes, and converting Bogdan into a declared enemy of Moscow, seeing that he had threatened that, should he receive no support from the quarter in question, he would proceed thither with the Crimean Tartars, and, in case of failure to conquer the Poles, would make his peace with the latter, and then turn with them against the Tsar of Moscow himself. However, soon after the Treaty of Zborov, Bogdan, recognising that a new war with Poland was inevitable, told the Tsar's commissioner that, should he fail in the struggle, he would be glad to pass, with his Zaporozhian army, into Muscovite territory; and, a year and a half later, on the collapse of Khmelnitski's second campaign against Poland, and the loss of almost all the advantages which he had gained in the first expedition, it was at length acknowledged in the Muscovite capital that Bogdan's idea was the best way out of the difficulty. Hence proposals were made to the Cossack *hettman* that he and his men should settle in the rich and extensive regions which bordered upon the Don; the idea being that such a settlement would not involve trouble with Poland, would avoid driving the Cossacks into allegiance to the Sultan of Turkey, and would give Moscow a splendid advance guard towards the Steppes. However, events did not bear out the forecasts of Muscovite statesmen, for Khmelnitski, finding himself faced with a third contest with Poland under unfavourable circumstances, besought the Tsar to receive him into vassalage, and so obviate his being forced to accept the long-proffered suzerainty of the Sultan and the Khan of the Crimea. Accordingly, early in 1653 Moscow decided to take Little Rus into the Empire, and to declare war upon Poland. Yet even then the matter dragged on for something like a year, since, during the autumn following upon the summer when Moscow's decision was announced to Khmelnitski, a convention of the *Zemski Sobor* was held, for the decision to be ratified; after which the *hettman* suffered yet another defeat near Zhvanetz, through his being a second time betrayed by his ally the Khan. Consequently, it was only in January, 1654, that the Cossacks were finally received into Muscovite allegiance. After the capitulation of Smolensk in 1634 Moscow had waited for thir-

teen years to wipe out that disgrace; and though in 1648 the Little
Russian Cossacks rose, and Poland was now at a low ebb, while, on the
other hand, the Ukraine was begging Moscow to help it to rid itself of the
treacherous Tartars, and to take the country under Muscovite protection,
Moscow did not move, since she was afraid to break the peace with
Poland. Consequently for six years she stood looking on while Bogdan,
defeated by the Tartars at Zborov and Berestechko, was going from bad
to worse, and Little Rus was being ravaged by internecine feuds and her
Tartar allies. Finally, when the country lay *completely* at Moscow's mercy,
she decided to take it under her powerful wing—though by so doing she
only converted the local ruling classes from Polish rebels into mutinous
Muscovite subjects. Such a situation must have been due to mutual
misunderstandings on both sides. Moscow was for getting into her hands
the Cossacks of the Ukraine, either with or without their territory; but
if this was to be accomplished with the Cossack towns, then essentially it
must be on the condition that those towns should be manned with Muscovite governors and officials. Bogdan Khmelnitski, however, reckoned to
become Regent of Tchigirin, or something of the sort—a person who was
to have authority over the whole of Little Rus, under the remote suzerainty of the Tsar of Moscow, and assisted by the Cossack aristocracy,
military commanders, and other notables. Yet, at once ignorant of and
distrustful of one another, both parties, in their mutual relations with one
another, spoke otherwise than as they thought, and acted otherwise than
as they wished. Bogdan expected Moscow to declare an open breach
with Poland, and to deal that State a blow from the East, with the object
of freeing Little Rus from the *Rietch*, and taking it under her protection;
while Muscovite diplomacy, without actually breaking with Poland, waited
with subtle cunning for the Cossacks to weaken the Poles with their
onslaughts, and then force them to retire from the insurgent area; after
which, in legal fashion, and with no infringement of the ancient peace
with Poland, Little Rus was to be united to Great Rus. A note of cruel
mockery can be detected in Moscow's answer to Bogdan when, some
two months before the affair of Zborov which sealed the fates of
Poland and Little Rus, he petitioned the Tsar "to consecrate his (the
Tsar's) army against" the common foe, while he (Bogdan) would, in
God's good time, also fall upon that foe from the Ukraine, to the end
that a just and Orthodox Tsar should rule as Lord and Autocrat over the
country. To this manifestly sincere petition Moscow returned the reply:
"The olden peace with the men of Poland may not be broken; but if

the King of Poland shall be willing to free the *hettman* and all his army of the *Zaporozhie* from his dominion, then will the Tsar recompense that *hettman* and the army of the same, and command that they be taken under his mighty hand." This mutual misunderstanding and distrust of the two parties caused them to err grievously in matters of foresight. Though a redoubtable Cossack warrior, and a skilful diplomatist, Bogdan was not exactly a political genius, and on one occasion we find him expounding the basis of his domestic policy to the Polish commissioners in the following tipsy fashion : " If a prince be at fault, then shall his head be cut off; and if a Cossack be at fault, then shall the same be fitting for him also." His rising he looked upon as a struggle between the Cossacks and the *shliachtichi* who were oppressing them " as the lowliest of slaves " (to quote his own expression). Indeed, he openly confessed that he and his troopers hated *pani* and *shliachtichi* alike. Yet he did nothing to remove, nor even to lessen, the fatal social cleavage which he perceived to be latent in the midst of the Cossack community—a cleavage which, existent before his time, came still more sharply into prominence after he was gone. The social cleavage referred to was the hostility which raged between the Cossack magnates and the Cossack rank and file — " the common people of the towns and the *Zaporozhie*," as they were called in the Ukraine ; which hostility gave rise to an endless series of disturbances in Little Rus, and led to the western portion of the Ukraine falling into the hands of the Turks, and being converted into a wilderness. Yet Moscow reaped the fruits of her cautious and subtle diplomacy. By Muscovites the annexation of Little Rus was regarded (politically speaking) from the traditional point of view, as a continuation of Moscow's territorial ingathering of the Russian land, a wresting of a large slice of Rus from her enemy, Poland, in order to add it to the *otchina* of the Muscovite Tsars ; and on the conquest of White Rus and Lithuania taking place in 1655, no time was lost in aggrandising the Imperial title with the words, " Autocrat of Great Rus and Little Rus and White Rus and Lithuania and Volhynia and Podolia." Yet Moscow knew little of the internal social relations of the Ukraine, and cared less, since it looked upon them as unimportant. Consequently certain Muscovite boyars could not understand why the commissioners of a *hettman* named Vigovski should contemptuously refer to the people of the *Zaporozhie* as drunkards and wastrels, while at the same time they dubbed Cossackdom at large, including its *hettman*, " the Zaporozhian Host." Indeed, curiosity at length moved these boyars to enquire of the commissioners where the *hettmans* of old had lived—whether in the *Zaporozhie* or in the towns, and from whom they were selected, and whence Bogdan Khmelnitski himself derived his title. Though the Muscovite Government had annexed Little Rus, it is clear that it looked upon local relations as a trackless forest. For several decades the Little Russian question—a question so crookedly raised by both parties—continued to weary and exhaust Muscovite foreign policy by plunging it into the hopeless tangle of Little Russian bickerings, wasting its forces in a struggle with Poland, obliging it to retire from Lithuania, White Rus, Volhynia, and Podolia, and making it difficult for Moscow to hold Kiev and the Eastern Ukraine. After such losses Moscow might well repeat of herself the words which Bogdan Khmelnitski once tearfully uttered when reproaching her for withholding her timely assistance : "That it should have been thus was not my will, nor should it have so befallen."

The Little Russian question served directly or indirectly to complicate Moscow's foreign policy. In 1654, on the outbreak of the Polish War for the possession of Little Rus, Alexis swiftly conquered White Rus and a notable portion of Lithuania, including Vilna, Kovno, and Grodno. Next, while Moscow was engaged in gathering to herself the eastern portion of the *Rietch Pospolitaia*, there fell upon Poland from the North another foeman, in the shape of the Swedish King, Charles X., who as swiftly conquered the whole of Great and Little Poland (including Cracow and Warsaw), and, expelling King John Casimir, proclaimed himself King of Poland, and attempted to wrest Lithuania from Alexis. Thus we see two foes who had assailed Poland from different directions meeting and wrangling over the spoil. Alexis next called to mind Ivan IV.'s idea concerning the Baltic seaboard and Livonia ; with the result that in 1656 the struggle with Poland was interrupted for a war with Sweden, and there again arose the question of extending the territories of the Muscovite Empire to their natural boundary, the Baltic Sea. Yet the question never reached a decision, for Rus failed to take Riga, and the Tsar found himself forced (in 1661) to conclude a hasty peace with Sweden, and to return her all his conquests. However fruitless, and even harmful, for Moscow this war may have been, in that it helped Poland to right herself after the Swedish harrying, it nevertheless prevented a single king[1] from uniting under his authority two States which, though both hostile to Moscow, never ceased to waste their forces in mutual hostility to one another.

[1] Charles X. of Sweden.

Across the path of friends and enemies alike—across the path both of the State which he had deserted and of the State to which he had sworn allegiance—stood the declining Bogdan. Alarmed at the *rapprochement* between Moscow and Poland, he entered into an agreement with the Swedish King (Charles X.) and the Prince of Transylvania (Ragotsa) that among the three of them there should be drawn up a scheme for sharing out the *Rietch Pospolitaia.* A true representative of Cossackdom (which was accustomed to serve towards every quarter of the compass), Bogdan could be servant or ally or betrayer of any one of his ruler-neighbours —of the King of Poland, of the Tsar of Moscow, of the Khan of the Crimea, of the Sultan of Turkey, of the Prince of Moldavia, of the Prince of Transylvania. At last he ended by scheming to become a sort of free Appanage Prince of Little Rus, under a Polish-Swedish King—the kind of sovereign which Charles X. aspired to be; and it was owing to these intrigues wherein Bogdan engaged shortly before his death that Alexis found himself forced to put an end to the Swedish war by any means, no matter what. Also, Little Rus involved Moscow in her first direct collision with Turkey: as follows. After Bogdan's death an open struggle began between the Cossack aristocracy and the common people of that race. Bogdan's successor, Vigovski, went over to the King of Poland, and, with a Tartar force under Konotop, annihilated a picked body which, in 1659, Tsar Alexis sent against him. Encouraged by this success, the Poles declined to surrender to Moscow any of her conquests, despite the fact that it was to Muscovite assistance that Poland owed her riddance of the Swedes; whereupon there began a second war with Poland, which brought upon Moscow two terrible disasters, in the shape of the defeat of Prince Chovanski in White Rus and the surrender of Sheremetev at Tchudnov in Volhynia in consequence of the desertion of Sheremetev's Cossack allies. Thus Lithuania and White Rus became lost to Moscow, and, on Vigovski's successors—Yuri, son of Bogdan, and Teteria—also transferring their allegiance to Poland, the Ukraine became divided, according to the line of the Dnieper, into two hostile halves, whereof the eastern half was Muscovite and the western Polish. Thus almost the whole of Little Rus fell into the hands of the Polish King. Yet the two parties had now reached a state of utter exhaustion. Moscow had nothing to pay her soldiers with, and the issue of copper coins at the value of silver called forth, in 1662, a rebellion; while, as regards her enemy, Great Poland, under a leader named Liubomirski, had risen in revolt against the King. Just when Moscow and Poland seemed about to drain the last drop of their blood, they were extricated from their position by an enemy of both, in the shape of a Cossack *hettman* named Doroshenko, who, with the Western Ukraine, had entered the service of the Sultan of Turkey (1666). In the presence of this terrible common foe, Moscow and Poland ended, by the Treaty of Andrusovo, their differences — Moscow retaining the provinces of Smolensk, Novgorod Sieversski, and Kiev, and gaining the long frontier of the Dnieper, from its sources to the *Zaporozhie;* which, true to its historical nature, remained in the half-and-half position of owing allegiance both to the Polish State and to the Muscovite. Thus the new dynasty atoned for its errors at Stolbovo, Deulino, and in Poland. Also, the Treaty of Andrusovo produced a sharp break in Moscow's foreign policy. In directing that policy the cautious, short-sighted B. I. Morozov was succeeded by the man who was primarily responsible for the treaty in question—namely, A. L. Ordin-Nastchokin, who was fully capable of foreseeing the future. This states-man elaborated a new political combination. Although Poland had now ceased to be dangerous, and the old struggle with her had fallen into abeyance for the space of a century, it was a struggle which had compli-cated the Little Russian question with fresh problems relating to Livonia (*i.e.* Sweden) and Turkey; and for dealing with these foemen an alliance with the Poland which both of them were threatening was necessary. The idea of this alliance Ordin-Nashtchokin developed into a whole system. In a report furnished to the Tsar before the Treaty of Andru-sovo he proved, by three considerations, the necessity of a bond with Poland. Only by such a bond could protection be given to the Orthodox population in Poland; only by a close union with Poland could the Cossacks be restrained from making war upon Great Rus at the instiga-tion of the Khan and Sweden; only by an alliance with Poland could the Moldavians and the Wallachians—then severed from Orthodox Rus by hostile Poland—be detached from the Turks, and enabled, by joining Podolia, Red Rus, Volhynia, Little Rus, and Great Rus, to form a great Christian nation which, born of a common mother, the Orthodox Church, should stretch from the Dvina to the furthest confines of the Dnieperian region. The last-named consideration was bound to enlist the Tsar's sympathy, since the thought of the Turkish Christians had long been present to his mind. At Eastertide, 1656, when greeting some Greek merchants then resident in Moscow, he asked them whether they would like to be freed from Turkish serfdom; and, on their making the inevit-able reply, he continued: "When ye shall return unto your own country, ask of your bishops and priests and monks that they do pray for me; for according unto their prayers shall my sword be strong to cut the throat of my enemies." Then, bursting into tears, he added to his boyars that his heart ached for the enslavement of these poor people by unbelievers; that he prayed that God might visit it upon him on the Day of Judgement if, having the power to save them, he neglected to do so and bound not himself to devote his whole army to the sacrifice, and his treasury, and his very blood, for their deliverance. The Greek merchants themselves afterwards related the story. In a treaty concluded in 1672, not long before the Sultan's invasion of Poland, the Tsar undertook to help the Polish King in case of an attack from the Turks, as well as previously to send to the Sultan and the Khan to dissuade them from making war upon Poland. Yet the views of these unwonted allies by no means coincided, since Poland's chief care was to safeguard her external security, whereas Moscow added the question of her co-religionists. Also, there was a double question to be considered—namely, for Moscow, the question of the Turkish Christians, and, for Turkey, that of the Russian Mahomedans. In this manner religious relations in the European East became, during the sixteenth century, extremely complicated. Ivan IV. had conquered two Mahomedan States—namely, those of Kazan and Astrakhan; yet it was to their spiritual head, the successor of the Caliphs, the Sultan of Turkey, that the conquered Mahomedans now turned with a prayer that he would deliver them from the Christian yoke. Again, there lived in the Balkan Peninsula a numerous population which was subject to the Sultan, but of like faith and race with the Russian people; and it was to the Muscovite Tsar, the protector of the Orthodox East, that this population turned for emancipation of the Turkish Christians from Mahomedan supremacy. The idea of a struggle with the Turks with the aid of Moscow was at that time actively spreading among the Balkan Christians; and when, in conformity with treaty obligations, some Muscovite ambassadors journeyed to Constantinople to dissuade the Sultan from making war upon the *Rietch Pospolitaia*, the emissaries of Moscow returned thence with some notable tidings—namely, that, throughout their passage through Moldavia and Wallachia, they had heard the people saying, " Oh that God would grant unto us Christians a victory over the Turks! Then should we begin to surpass them." On the other hand, in Constantinople itself the Muscovite emissaries gleaned the fact that, not long before their visit, there had arrived thither ambassadors from the Tartars of Kazan and Astrakhan, as well as from the Bashkirs, to pray the Sultan that he would accept the States of Kazan and Astrakhan into fealty, since the men of Moscow, hating their (the States') faith, had beaten many of the inhabitants to death, and were forever plundering them. To this (so the Russian emissaries were informed) the Sultan had replied that his petitioners must yet be patient a little; after which he had consoled them with gifts of clothing.

Thus the Little Russian question came to involve two other questions —namely, a Baltic question (concerning the acquisition of the Baltic seaboard) and an Eastern question (concerning the relations of the Balkan Christians to Turkey). The latter, as an idea, was in mere process of being put through its paces in the benevolent minds of Alexis and Ordin-Nastchokin, since in those days it did not lie within the power of the Russian Empire to attack the question directly and practically; for the time being it only led to the Muscovite Government engaging in struggles with the foe which barred the road to Turkey—namely, with the Crimea. This foeman sat like a cataract in the eye of Muscovite diplomacy, and formed a vexing element in every international combination which that diplomacy devised. At the beginning of Alexis' reign, Moscow, finding herself unable to meet her liabilities to Poland, joined the latter in an offensive alliance against the Crimea; and after the peace established by the Andrusovo treaty had, in 1686, become converted into a lasting *rapprochement*, and the Muscovite Empire had made its first entry into a European coalition, and had joined a fourfold alliance of Poland, of the German Empire, and of Venice against Turkey, Moscow took upon herself, in this enterprise, the most difficult part—namely, to enter upon a struggle with the Tartars, to deliver an assault upon the Crimea. Thus with each step the foreign policy of the Muscovite Empire increased in complexity—the Government either mending or re-establishing its broken ties with the many States of which it stood in need in its relations with its hostile neighbours, or to which the Muscovite Government itself was necessary in their (those States') European relations. And even in those days the Muscovite Empire was not wholly a nonentity in Europe; even at the time of its lowest international debasement, when the Period of Troubles had but recently come to an end, it never lost a certain weight in diplomatic circles. International relations in the West happened to be in favourable conjunction for Moscow, for the Thirty Years' War was just beginning, and the relations of the various States were in a condition of uncertainty— each State seeking for itself some external support, and dreading isolation. On the other hand, though politically weak, the Muscovite Empire was strong in its geographical position and ecclesiastical importance. Indeed, it was not merely out of Gallic politeness that Courmenant, the first French ambassador to be accredited to Moscow, called Tsar Michael the arbiter both of the East and of the Greek faith. Moscow happened to lie at the rear of every State between the Baltic and Adriatic Seas; and when international relations in those quarters became entangled, and dissension arose which embraced the whole of the Continental West, each such State hastened to secure its rear to the eastward by concluding an alliance, an estoppage of hostility, with Moscow. That is why, from the accession of the new dynasty onwards, the area of Moscow's external relations gradually widened without any effort on the part of the Muscovite Government—why it continued to be increasingly drawn into the various political and economic combinations which at that time became formed in Europe. We see England and Holland helping Michael to become reconciled to his enemies, Poland and Sweden, for the reason that Muscovy was a valuable market for the former, and also a convenient road to the East— to Persia, and even to India. Again, we see the French King proposing to conclude an alliance with Michael, in order to meet the commercial interests of France in the East, where she was the rival both of the English and of the Dutch. Even the Sultan challenged Michael, rather than Poland, to war, while the Swedish Monarch, Gustavus Adolphus, who had despoiled Moscow by means of the Treaty of Stolbovo, but possessed, in the shape of Poland and Austria, common enemies with Moscow, suggested to the Muscovite diplomatists the idea of an anti-Catholic union, flattered them with the notion of making their modest fatherland an organic and influential member of the European political world, called the victorious Swedish army which was acting in Germany an advance guard to fight for the Muscovite Empire, and took the initiative in appointing a permanent Resident to Moscow. The Empire of Tsar Michael was weaker than the Empire of Tsars Ivan [1] and Theodor, but far less isolated in Europe. The same may, in large degree, be said of the Empire of Tsar Alexis, since at that period the arrival of a foreign embassy was a customary phenomenon in the capital. Muscovite ambassadors also visited every court in Europe, including even the courts of Spain and Tuscany—though in those quarters it was for the first time that Muscovite diplomacy embarked upon so wide a field. On the other hand, now losing, now acquiring, territory on its western borders, the Empire steadily progressed eastwards. Russian colonisation, which, during the

[1] Ivan IV.

sixteenth century, had passed the Urals, spread, during the seventeenth, into the remotest parts of Siberia, until it had reached the borders even of China. By this process—if we can at all apply a geometric measure to Moscow's acquisitions in the regions named—Muscovite territory had, by the middle of the seventeenth century, increased by at least 70,000 square miles. One result of this colonisation was to bring the Muscovite Empire into touch with China.

In this manner the foreign relations of the State became increasingly complicated and onerous, as well as bound to exercise a varied effect upon the domestic life of the State. The growing frequency of wars caused Moscow more and more to feel the shortcomings of her internal institutions, and the need of taking hints from those of her neighbours; while, on the other hand, the ever-increasing appointment of embassies to the Muscovite court served to multiply opportunities for gaining such hints. Closer acquaintance with the Western European world had the result of educating administrative circles in Rus beyond the prejudiced, high-and-dry circle of Muscovite ideas. But the chief effect of her various wars, and of her observation of her neighbours' institutions, was to render Moscow more than ever sensible of the poverty of her own material resources, the prehistoric deficiencies of her own armed preparedness, the insignificant productivity of her own popular labour, and the rough-and-ready way in which that labour was applied. Every new war, every new blow, entailed upon the Government new tasks and cares, and upon the people new burdens. In short, the State's foreign policy necessitated an ever-growing tension of the popular forces. Even a brief summary of the wars waged by the first three Tsars of the new dynasty will show us the measure of that tension. Under Michael, two wars were waged with Poland, and one with Sweden; all of which ended unsuccessfully for Moscow. Under Michael's successor, two wars, again, were waged with Poland for Little Rus, and one with Sweden; two of which three contests ended unsuccessfully for Moscow. Under Theodor, a grievous war with Turkey which had been begun by his father in the year 1673 ended, in 1681, with the fruitless peace of Bakhtchi Sarai, whereby the Western Ukraine was abandoned to the Turks. If, therefore, the total duration of these wars be calculated, it will be seen that, of the seventy years 1613–1682, some thirty were devoted to wars—wars sometimes waged simultaneously, and with more than one opponent at a time.

CHAPTER VII

Fluctuations in the internal life of the Muscovite Empire—Two sets of innovations therein—
Tendencies of the legislation of the day, and the need for a new compendium of laws—
The Muscovite insurrection of 1648, and its relation to the *Ulozhenïe*—The warrant of
July 16th, 1648, for drawing up the *Ulozhenïe*—The fulfilment of that convention—
Written sources of the *Ulozhenïe*—The part taken in its composition by the deputies of
the *Sobor*—The conditions under which it was composed—Its importance—New ideas
therein—New statutory articles in the same.

LET us now return to the domestic life of the Muscovite Empire. From a
survey of the immediate results of the Period of Troubles, as well as of the
foreign policy of the State, we have seen that the Government of the new
dynasty found itself confronted with external tasks which it sadly lacked
the means, whether moral or material, to cope with. Where it was to seek
those means, and how it was to find them, constitutes the question which
we are about to study.

To answer the question, let us examine the most outstanding phenomena of the internal life of Rus of the period. They are exceedingly
complex, and proceed in different, and frequently opposing or intersecting,
currents. Yet in all of them we can discern one common source—namely,
the profound break which was produced by the Period of Troubles in the
minds and relations of men; a break to which I have already pointed
when speaking of the Period's immediate results. The break consisted of
the fact that the ancient customs upon which the State order had rested
under the old dynasty were tottering—that the traditions which had guided
the creators and guardians of that order had now become broken through.
When men cease to act by custom, and drop the threads of tradition, they
begin seriously and anxiously to reflect; and such reflection causes them
to grow resentful and hesitant, until they are forced to make timid trial of
one and another means of action. The same timidity marked the Muscovite statesmen of the seventeenth century. In them a rich store of new
ideas—the fruits of much arduous experiment and tense thought—was
accompanied by vacillation of political procedure and fluctuation of bent ;
a sure sign that those statesmen were feeling uneasy in their position.
Recognising the disproportion of the means at hand to the ends which they

desired, they at first sought new means in old domestic and national sources—in straining the forces of the people, and in repairing, finishing, or re-establishing the system bequeathed to them by their fathers and grandfathers. Then, when they perceived that those domestic resources were clearly becoming exhausted, they began to look abroad, and to summon to their aid foreign forces. Then again they fell into fits of timid irresolution as to whether they had not strayed too far from native antiquity, whether they could not make domestic resources suffice without the help of alien. These ever-changing tendencies occupied, during the latter half of the seventeenth century, a considerable space of time, and, towards the close of the century, came into collision with one another, and produced a series of political and ecclesiastical upheavals. Thereafter they passed into the eighteenth century, and became fused with Peter's reforms, which impelled them into a single channel, and directed them towards a single end. These were the general lines upon which the domestic life of the Muscovite Empire proceeded from the close of the Period of Troubles to the opening of the eighteenth century. Of that process let us study the individual stages.

However much the new dynasty might strive to act in the old spirit, in order to force men to forget that it (the dynasty) was new, and therefore something less than legal, it could not dispense with innovations. So much of what was old had been shattered by the Period of Troubles that the very restoration of what had been destroyed inevitably acquired the character of a complete reconstruction or reformation. The innovations referred to stretch in a more or less broken series from the first reign of the new dynasty to the close of the century, and paved the way for the reforms of Peter the Great. Bearing in mind the dual tendency in the life of the Muscovite Empire to which I have made reference, we can distinguish in the current of the preliminary innovations of which I am speaking two runlets of different character and origin, yet runlets which at times approach, and even mingle with, one another. The reforms of the first series were carried through with the help of native resources, independently of the alien, and in consonance with the dictates of indigenous knowledge and experience. But since native resources consisted merely of extending the governmental power at the expense of the public freedom, and in restricting private interest in the name of the State's demands, every reform of the species entailed upon the welfare and freedom of the public a heavy sacrifice. The affairs of men contain an inward balance of their own which is subject to the purview of the

persons who engage in them.   This balance is usually known as the
force of things.   From the very inception of those reforms there began
to be automatically felt the deficiency or comparative failure of the
scheme; and in proportion as that feeling grew, the more insistently did
it become penetrated with the thought that, come what might, the State
must look to the alien for hints, and borrow ideas from the outside world.

The very aim of these innovations, directed as they were towards
preserving or re-establishing the system which the Period of Troubles had
shattered, led them to be marked with Muscovite caution and lack of
completeness, since, though they introduced new forms and new conditions
of action, they avoided the introduction of any new principles.   Indeed,
the general tendency of this restorative activity might be defined by saying
that it proposed revisions of, yet never revolutions in, the State order—
partial repairs, yet never a thorough reconstruction.   The first thing needful was to regulate the relations of man with man which the Period
of Troubles had thrown into confusion—to arrange them on fixed
lines, and according to a set of exact rules.   In this respect the Government of Tsar Michael had to contend with a multitude of difficulties, since
it had to re-establish *everything*—practically to remake the State anew, so
shattered was the mechanism of the latter.   The author of a Pskovian
account of the Period of Troubles to which I have referred already says
that, under Michael, "the State again began to be set in order."   Indeed,
Michael's reign was a season of great legislative activity on the part of the
Government.   This activity touched the most varied aspects of State life,
and caused the beginning of the reign of Michael's successor to see
accumulated a rich store of new laws which called for classification.
Under the established system of Muscovite law-making new laws were
promulgated in response to questions which had been raised by one or
another *prikaz* (government department) in connection with the judicial-
administrative practice of each, and were referred, for revision or for execution, to the particular *prikaz* whose jurisdiction they concerned.   There,
agreeably with an article of the *Sudebnik* of 1550, the new law was added
to the main digest.   Hence the fundamental code in question had come
to resemble the trunk of a tree in so far as that it sprouted branches in
every one of the various *prikazi*.   These continuations of the *Sudebnik*
were known as the *ukaznia knigi* (registers of *ukazi*) of the *prikazi*, and
in time it became necessary to add to the *Sudebnik* the whole of
these departmental *addenda*, and to combine them into a single digest,
if repetitions of an occurrence—one that was practically unique—which

befell during the reign of Ivan the Terrible were to be avoided. This was when Adashev forwarded to the *Duma*, from his *Tchelobitni Prikaz* (Office for the consideration of Petitions to the Throne), a legislative project which had been decided already, on the application of the *Kazenni Prikaz* (Treasury). The *Duma*, apparently forgetful of the recent expression of its own will, actually commanded the Treasury scribes to add the law in question (which, of course, had been registered by those officials in its proper place) to their *ukaznia knigi!* Similarly it would happen that a *prikaz* would search the registers of other *prikazi* for a law which it had long ago entered in its own books! Consequently we can imagine to what a degree a stupid clerk might make a mess of matters, or to what a degree a clever one could twist and turn them about. This need for a codification—a need that was greatly strengthened by departmental abuses—may be looked upon as having constituted the prime motive which inspired the creation of the new Digest, and even, in part, determined its character. Other conditions which influenced the character of the new Compendium can, if not be stated, at all events be conjectured. The unusual position in which the State was placed after the close of the Period of Troubles was bound to give rise to fresh requirements, and to confront the Government with some unfamiliar problems ; and these requirements of the State, rather than the new political ideas introduced by the Period of Troubles, it was that gave an added impetus to legislation, and communicated to it a fresh bent, despite the best efforts of the new dynasty to hold on to antiquity. Up to the seventeenth century, Muscovite legislation partook solely of a casual nature, as designed only to return answers to current questions which happened to be raised by administrative practice, independently of the actual bases of the State order. In this connection ancient custom served as a substitute for law, as a thing known to and recognised by all ; but as soon as ever the State order began to depart from the beaten rut of tradition, at once there arose a need for abolition of custom in favour of exact jurisprudence. That is why the legislation of the new dynasty acquired an organic character, and, freeing itself from limitation by a mass of individual, concrete *casus* which had been raised by State administration, approached nearer and nearer to the bases of the State order, in an attempt—though an unsuccessful one—to explain, and to express, that order's principles.

A more difficult point confronts us when we try to determine the relation of the *Ulozhenïe*[1] to the Muscovite rebellion of 1648, which took

---

[1] The general digest of laws referred to, in this chapter, as about to be made.

place a month and a half before the Tsar issued his warrant to the *Duma* for a new compendium of laws to be made. In this rebellion we see the position of the new dynasty. The first two of its Tsars failed to enjoy the respect of the people, since, despite its elective origin, the dynasty took on the ways of the old one, and began to look upon the State as its *otchina*, and to rule it seigniorially, with an utter neglect of the "estate" which it was supposed to "form." In short, it imitated all the defects of the old dynasty—though possibly this was because there was nothing else which it could imitate. In the first place, of the sorry fragments of shattered boyardom (alloyed with an admixture of newcomers who in no way surpassed the boyars whom they had replaced) there became constituted a court ring which strove hard to convert itself into the ruling class. An influential section of this ring consisted of the Tsar's—and, still more, of the Tsaritsa's—relatives and favourites. Indeed, for many a long day the throne of the new dynasty stood surrounded with the atmosphere of favouritism, and throughout three reigns the names of court minions stretch out in a long line of Saltikovs, Repnins, Morozovs, Milioslavskis, Nikons, Chitrovos, Zazikovs, and Lichatchevs. Even in the Patriarch Philaret there lurked, under the title of Second Tsar, a most ordinary type of timeserver—a type which in no way resembled the eminent boyar whom Philaret had formerly been—a type which nominated itself to the Patriarchate in succession to a man whose only merit had been that he was a court noble, but, in reality, Philaret's slave. As of set purpose the first three Tsars of the dynasty ascended the throne during their minority, —the first two when but sixteen years of age, and the third when he was fourteen; whereupon, availing themselves of the Tsars' youth, as well as, later on, of their lack of character, governing circles began to assume an independent line in administration, added to a love of gain which the needy State clerks of the period of Ivan IV. might have envied, even though they were officials who maintained their Tsar with one-half of the Treasury's income, and annexed the rest for themselves. Such administrative abuses derived additional encouragement from the privileged non-liability to punishment which was enjoyed by their perpetrators—Tsar Michael having bound himself (as we have already seen) to punish no man belonging to a noble house with death, but only with incarceration, while, under Tsar Alexis, there were occasions when for one and the same offence men of high rank were subjected only to Imperial displeasure or dismissal, while clerks, attorneys, and simple folk of that kind were made to suffer amputation of the hands and feet. These secret and unpublished undertakings between Tsars and boyars were what constituted the root fault in the position of the new dynasty, and communicated to the accession of that dynasty the appearance of a boyar-Tsar conspiracy against the people. To Kotoshikhin's characteristic remark concerning Michael that, " though he did write himself down Autocrat, he could do naught without the boyar council," we can add Tatistchev's statement that Michael "was fain to rest in peace" (*i.e.* to hand over the whole of the administration to his boyars). The people, with their elementary instincts, speedily detected the fault : with the result that after the accession of the new dynasty there ensued an era of popular uprisings. In particular the reign of Alexis was "a season of rioting." Also, appropriate to the times, there arose among the Muscovite community and governing circles a type of "strong man" or "timeserver" (to quote terms then current), who, an exemption-subsidised landowner, clerical or lay, or else an administrator in high favour at court, was strong in his belief in his immunity from punishment, and sufficiently devoid of conscience ever to be ready, with the help of his position and the general disorder of the times, to use his strength against unprotected folk, whom he " did oppress and offend with many offences." This type was one of the most characteristic and outstanding productions of the domestic policy of the new dynasty, and a production which owed its growth in Muscovite governing circles to the idea that the Tsar was in their hands, and could not get on without them. For such "timeservers," however, the populace felt the most cordial hatred, and the Muscovite rising of June, 1648 (which awoke an echo in many other towns) was a clear expression of that sentiment. The populace of the capital lay especially under the thumb of "strong men," both clerical and lay (the former category in no way lagging behind the latter—examples were the Patriarch, the bishops, and the monks). These men seized the common pasture-lands of the city, occupied them up to the suburbs, laid out country-houses and market-gardens on those lands, and ploughed up the roads which led from the city to the forest, so that the plain Muscovite citizen had nowhere to graze a single animal, nor yet to cut firewood, as had been his perpetual right under the olden Tsars. The rebellion of June, 1648, was a rising of the " black " or common people against the "strong men"; when the people "did launch themselves upon the boyars," started pillaging their establishments, as well as those of the *dvoriané* and the *diaki,* and put to death the more obnoxious of their administrators. This menace had a great effect upon the authorities. The court stood panic-stricken ; bribes were hastily distributed among the army and the populace of the capital; the *Strieltsi* were, by the Tsar's orders, plied with drink; for several days in succession the Tsar's father-in-law gave banquets to a select circle of Muscovite taxpayers; and the Tsar seized the occasion of a Procession of the Cross to make a self-exculpatory speech to the people, "the while with tears he did beseech the common folk" to spare his son-in-law and favourite, Morozov. Of promises, indeed, there was no end. At last the authorities began to fear also for the rural communities, so the word was passed round that the Tsar had become gracious, and had banished his "strong men" from the Empire, and had put some of them to death with stones and staves. Never, under the old dynasty, had Moscow experienced such turbulent manifestations of the popular resentment against the ruling classes; never had it witnessed such a swift change from contempt of the people to subservience to the mob; never had it heard such unseemly speeches about the Tsar as were uttered after the rising had begun. "The Tsar is a fool. He looketh at things from the faces of Morozov and Miloslavski, who do rule us all. Yea, the Tsar knoweth all these things, yet doth keep silence, in that the devil hath taken away his understanding." This rising, though it found an echo in other cities, did not actually inspire the idea of the *Ulozhenïe* (there were other causes for this); yet it none the less roused the Government to invite territorial representatives to participate in the work, since the Government looked upon the *Zemski Sobor* which was convened on September 1st of the same year (to hear read, and also to sign, the Digest) as a means of pacifying the people. On the whole, the Patriarch Nikon may be trusted, who wrote (as of a matter known to all men) that the *Sobor* in question was convened, not willingly, but "for the sake of the boyars, and because of the strife come of the common folk, rather than for a just reason." Hence there can be no doubt that these riotings were less the original cause of the codificatory work being undertaken than phenomena which occurred during its progress, which the Government was afraid to mar.

The idea of compiling an *Ulozhenïe* or General Legal Code—the initiative in the undertaking of such a work—emanated from the Tsar and his confidential council, which consisted of the Holy Synod and the *Boyarskaia Duma*. Proclamations distributed in the provinces during the summer of 1648 stated that, in accordance with a decree of the boyars, and in response to a petition from the *stolniki*, the *striaptchi*,[1] and "all ranks of men," the Tsar and the Patriarch[2] had issued commands for the

[1] Court officials of various grades.

[2] Philaret.

inscription of an *Ulozhennaia Kniga* or Book of Ordinances. Yet it is difficult to conjecture how or when such a petition was presented to the Government, even if it was presented at all. It was the custom of the Muscovite Governments which succeeded one another after the close of the old dynasty to speak in the name of the country as a whole, and the phrase "a petition of all ranks of men" had come to be the stereotyped formula for justifying any important administrative act which did not lend itself to exact phraseology. It sufficed merely that any chance group of officials should approach the throne with a petition, and at once the Tsar issued a *ukaz* "in pursuance of the prayer of all ranks of men." Thus the supposed subservience of the *prikazi* to the popular will had degenerated into a kind of political fiction which was kept only for certain occasions, as a species of survival to which a purely conditional importance attached. Probably the truth is that, on July 16th, 1648, the Tsar, the *Boyarskaia Duma*, and the Holy Synod issued orders for a number of "articles fitting unto the affairs of the State and of the land" to be selected from the Apostolic and Patristic writings and the laws of the Greek Emperors; that, in addition, the *ukazi* of bygone Tsars of Rus, together with the former decrees of the boyars, should be collated, and compared with previous *Sudebniki*; and, lastly, that wherever, in such *Sudebniki*, no *ukaz* had been issued by the Tsar, nor any decree made by the boyars, new articles should be drawn up, and the whole completed "in common council." The composition of this draft *Ulozhenie* was entrusted to a special codificatory Committee, consisting of five members—the Princes Odoievski, Prozorovski, and Volkhonski, with a couple of *diaki* named Leontiev and Griboiedov. None of them were men of any particular standing or influence, either in court or official circles; while, as regards Prince Odoievski in particular, the Tsar expressed himself in terms of actual contempt—thus sharing the general opinion of Moscow. Only the *diak* Griboiedov has left his mark behind him, in a treatise which he, our first historical tutor, composed at a later date for the Imperial children, and in which he derives the new dynasty, through the Tsaritsa Anastasia, from the son of a fictitious "Lord of the Prussian Land," who is represented as a Romanov and a kinsman of Augustus, Emperor of Rome. The three principal members of the Committee were members also of the *Duma*; wherefore we may look upon this "*prikaz* of the Prince Odoievski, with his fellows" (as it is called in official documents) as having constituted a Committee of the Boyar Council. The Committee selected articles from the sources indicated to it in its copy of instructions, and drew up new ones; all of which were combined "into one report," and presented to the Tsar and the *Duma* for their revision. Meanwhile, on September 1st, 1648, representatives of all ranks of the official and commercial classes of the towns were summoned to Moscow; although to representatives of the rural or cantonal inhabitants, as constituting a separate "house of parliament," no summonses were issued. On the following October 3rd the Tsar, the Holy Synod, and the *Duma* gave audience to the draft *Ulozhenïe* which had been framed by the Committee, and then ordered it to be read to the deputies who had been convened from Moscow and other towns, to ensure, "in general council, that from henceforth all the *Ulozhenïe* do abide fixed and immoveable." Next, the Tsar commanded the Hierarchy, the Duma, and the deputies to ratify the script of the *Ulozhenïe* with their signatures; after which the document, with these signs-manual, was printed (in 1649), and, finally, distributed to all the Muscovite *prikazi* and chancellories of the provincial governors, "to the end that all things be done according unto this same *Ulozhenïe.*"

Such was the outward history of the "Memorial" (as it is called in the preface which is to be found prefixed thereto). To the Committee there were entrusted two tasks. The first task was not only to collect, examine, and elaborate into a complete digest the existing laws (most of which differed in period, purport, and departmental application), but also to provide for *casus* not foreseen by such laws. The second task was more difficult, in that the members of the Committee could not very well depend solely upon their own juridical prevision and sense of equity to establish *casus*, or to discover norms for defining such *casus*. Consequently the Committee had to make itself cognisant of the social needs and relations of the day, to study the equitable instincts of the people, and to examine the practice which was observed by judicial and administrative institutions. At all events that is how we moderns should face a similar problem. As regards the former of these tasks, the Committee may have been assisted with advice from the deputies; while, as regards the second task, examination must have been made of the procedure of all the chancellories of the day, in order that precedents—"occasions of instance," as they were called—should be discovered to show how provincial governors, the central *prikazi*, and the Tsar had been accustomed to decide questions not foreseen by the law. Truly it was a labour of great scope, a labour that would take years to fulfil, which confronted the Committee. However, the matter never reached the actual proportions which I have imagined, since the Government decided to have the

Ulozhenie composed by short-cut methods, and in accordance with a simplified plan of procedure. For this purpose the Code was divided into 25 chapters, of 967 articles; of which chapters the first 12—*i.e.* nearly half the digest—were ready for "report" (*i.e.* for revision by the Tsar and the *Duma*) by the 3rd of October; while by the close of the following January the remaining 13 chapters had been duly composed, revised, and ratified in the *Duma*, and the labours of the Committee and of the General Council had come to an end, and the *Ulozhenie* was embodied in manuscript form. Hence this very voluminous compendium was composed in a little over six months. To explain such expeditious legislative work we must remember that the *Ulozhenie* was begun amid alarming rumours concerning the popular risings which, in Solvitchegodsk, Koslovo, Talitsk, Ustug, and other towns, followed the Muscovite rising of June 1648; as also that the Code was finished under the influence of a report that a new upheaval was about to occur in the capital. Thus the matter was hurried on, in order that, at the earliest possible moment, the deputies might return to their towns with tidings both of the fresh course adopted by the Muscovite Government and of the *Ulozhenie* which henceforth was to extend to all men "equal" (*i.e.* equitable) justice.

Certainly the *Ulozhenie* was composed in a great hurry; traces of this hurry appear in its very contents. Without plunging into a study of the mass of departmental material to hand, the Committee limited itself to the fundamental sources which had been indicated to it in the warrant of July 16th. Those sources were the *Kormtchaia* (more especially the second portion of it, which included the codes and laws of the Greek Emperors); previous Muscovite *Sudebniki*, more especially that of Ivan IV.; *ukazi* supplementary to the same; and former boyar decrees,—the last two classes forming, collectively, the *ukaznia knigi* to which I have already referred. Indeed, *ukaznia knigi* constituted the *Ulozhenie's* richest source, since, with the help of *verbatim* or paraphrased extracts from them, a whole series of chapters was compiled. For instance, the two chapters concerning *pomiestia* and *otchini* were borrowed from a register belonging to the *Pomiestni Prikaz*; a chapter "concerning the judging of slaves" was borrowed from a register belonging to the *Kholopi Prikaz*; and a fourth chapter concerning matters of brigandage and theft was extracted from a register belonging to the *Razboini Prikaz*. In addition to these fundamental sources, the Committee utilised certain auxiliary sources—in particular, the Lithuanian Statute of 1588.[1] In the long roll

[1] See p. 97.

of the *Ulozhenïe* which is still to be seen preserved we meet with constant citations from this source, since the authors of the *Ulozhenïe* not only used the Statute, but also followed it (more especially when framing the first few chapters of the Code) in their arrangement of subjects, in their order of articles, in their lists of *casus* and relations which called for legislative definition, and in their exposition of legal questions. Nevertheless the Committee invariably sought its answers to those questions in native jurisprudence, and took its formulæ from native norms and juridical positions—though only from such as were common to, or uniform with, both codes; while everything that was superfluous to or alien to equity and to the Muscovite legal system they removed—in most cases also improving upon all that they borrowed. Thus the Lithuanian Statute served less as a legal source of the *Ulozhenïe* than as an aid to its authors in the work of codification, since it gave them a ready-made programme.

It also befell the Committee to draw upon a source which was all the more important in that it was a *living* source, not an archivial. I refer to the Council itself—more strictly speaking, to the elected deputies who had been summoned to Moscow to hear read, and afterwards to subscribe their names to, the *Ulozhenïe*. We have seen how the Digest was composed: that the initiative emanated from the Tsar and the *Boyarskaia Duma;* that the framework of the Code was first worked out, on the chancellorial system, by a Committee of the *Duma*, aided by the *prikazi* (which furnished guidance and material); that the draft was then examined, revised, and confirmed by the *Duma;* that it was next read aloud to the elected deputies; that, lastly, it was handed to the latter for them to append to it their attestations and signatures. But the representatives on the Council were hardly likely to remain passive auditors at the reading of the Digest, even if it was prepared without their help. True, we have nothing to show that, at the reading of the *Ulozhenïe*, its articles were judged by the deputies—that, according as article after article was read aloud, the deputies were called upon to pronounce their assent or dissent thereto; yet there can be no doubt that they were given a considerable share in the work, and a share which assumed various forms. The warrant of July 16th had not contemplated a *new* codex; it had only charged the Committee to collect, and to co-ordinate, the existing stock of legislation, and "to make true with the olden *Sudebniki* former *ukazi* of the Tsars and former decrees of the boyars." Consequently the new articles which were drawn up by the Committee served merely to fill up blanks in the existing laws. Also, the warrant had stated that the Committee was to perform its labours "in common council with" certain deputies summoned to Moscow "that they may work for the State and for the land in company with the boyars of the Tsar" (*i.e.* with Prince Odoievski and his colleagues) ; wherefore these territorial representatives must either have formed an addition to the Committee of Codifiers or at least have held their sittings in the Committee's presence, where, according as the deputies grew better acquainted with the scheme in hand, they would be able, as men of knowledge, to point out to the codifiers what points in the Digest called for alteration or enlargement, and also to mention such requirements of their own as the Committee could formulate as statements or suggestions, and then forward, as provincial petitions, to the *Duma*. In the latter debates would be held concerning these petitions, and decisions come to ; which decisions would be reported to the deputies, in the form of laws, and duly incorporated in the *Ulozhenie*. Thus the deputies must have taken a direct part in the framing of the Code. Nevertheless it is not easy to determine the exact procedure at sessions of the Council—whether at general sessions (290 of which were held) or at sessions by groups. We only know that, on October 30th, 1648, some deputies of the official and urban-commercial classes presented the Committee with two separate petitions concerning the taxing of suburban properties, town mansions, and town trading establishments which belonged to non-taxpaying landowners, and that the Committee combined these two petitions into one, and forwarded them to the *Duma* as a general presentment "from all the land." Also, we know that the various petitions, reports, notes or corrections, and decrees of the *Duma* concerning the same, were worked up into a complete estimate both of the properties held by such urban communities and of the relation in which they stood towards outside persons who were engaged in urban commerce—this estimate eventually going to form Chapter XIX ("Concerning the People of the Towns") of the *Ulozhenie*. Thus advice offered to the Committee of Codifiers by the elected deputies to the Council ; presentation of petitions to the *Duma* through that Committee,—such were the two forms wherein the deputies had a share in the drawing up of the *Ulozhenie*. Yet there was a third form, and the most important form of all, since it brought the deputies into direct relations, no longer with the Committee, but with the State *Duma* itself. This was when the Tsar in Council appeared among the deputies, and, with them, pronounced a decree on any question which had been raised. The *Ulozhenie* refers to at least one such occasion, and as a matter of fact, it was not the only instance of its kind. It seems that the elected deputies of all ranks had presented the Tsar with a petition "from all the land" that such Church estates as had passed into the hands of the clergy, in violation of the law of 1580, should be restored to their former owners. Consequently into Chapter VII of the *Ulozhenïe*—the chapter "Concerning Lands"—we see interpolated an article (No. 42) which says that the Tsar, on the advice of the Holy Synod, and after consultation with the representatives of the service class, "hath laid it upon the Council" to forbid the alienation, in any form, of hereditary lands to the Church. Here we find the deputies enjoying a direct share in the legislative power; yet not *all* of them, but only the service deputies, as representative of the landowners, whom the matter chiefly concerned, even though the petition had come "from all the land" (*i.e.* from all ranks of the people). Consequently the supreme power seems to have stood upon a lower level of political consciousness than did the territorial deputies, since the latter at least understood the interest of the country as a whole, whereas the former understood that only of a class. From documents, also, we learn of two decrees which, though not directly indicated in the *Ulozhenïe*, were issued with the co-operation of the deputies. On the petition of the service deputies, the Tsar, with the *Duma* and the petitioners themselves, charged the Council to abolish what were known as "days of term"—*i.e.* the time-limit for the return of absconding peasantry; which decree is to be found set forth in the opening articles of Chapter XI of the *Ulozhenïe* (that "Concerning Peasants"). The other of my two instances is seen in Chapter VIII ("Concerning the Redeeming of Captives"), which establishes a household tax for the ransoming of prisoners of war, and also a scale of the ransom. This chapter was borrowed from a decree made collectively by the Tsar, by the *Duma*, and by "all ranks of the chosen men"; whence, in this case, we see the whole body of deputies wielding the legislative power. Lastly, an instance occurs which will give us a good idea of the relation of the deputies to the work of framing the *Ulozhenïe*, and also of the relation of the Government to provincial petitions. When returning homeward after the conclusion of the Council, a certain deputy for the *dvoriané* of Koursk, named Malishev, begged to be given an Imperial safe-conduct, as a protection against—whom, would it be thought?—against his own electors! It seems that for two reasons he had suffered every possible maltreatment at his electors' hands—namely, for the reason that he had failed to make due and full presentation of the "needs" of his constituents to the Council, and for the reason that he had been so inordinately vain of his piety as to present to the Tsar a special petition, wherein he had "spoken all manner of evil" by accusing his electors of laxity in the observance of Sundays and Holy Days. In his request, therefore, for a safe-conduct the deputy exonerates himself from the first charge—the charge that "I have not fulfilled their (the electors') wills unto the *Ulozhenie*"; while, touching the second point, he imposes the responsibility upon the Government and the Tsar, in that, though the *Ulozhenie* has named the hours of labour and trading on Holy Days (see Chapter X, Article 25), it has left unspecified (despite representations from the petitioner) all prohibition of or penalties for improper behaviour on festivals. The Tsar so far respected the prayer of this troublesome moralist as to issue rescripts concerning the proper keeping of festivals, "together with a great forbidding." Yet no supplement on the point is to be found added to the *Ulozhenie* itself.

We can now determine the manner in which the Code was composed. It was a process of a complex nature, since in it there are to be distinguished codification, advice, revision, legislative settlement, and ratification by signature (the "strengthening by hand" referred to in the warrant of the 16th July). These various stages were apportioned among the constituent parts of the Council—namely, the *Boyarskaia Duma* and the Holy Synod, headed by the Tsar, the Committee of Five under Prince Odoievski, and the deputies (who sat with the Committee, not with the *Duma*). In the aggregate, then, these various parts constituted the Council of 1648. The codificatory portion of the work was carried out by Prince Odoievski's Committee, and consisted of selection and co-ordination of enactments derived from specified sources, as also of revisal of deputies' petitions; while the advisory stage consisted of the part taken by the deputies in the work of the Committee—a part expressed, as we have seen, in petitions which served as debates. Indeed, one occasion is known when a petition of deputies acquired the character of a direct expression of opinion, and led to the abrogation or emendation of the Imperial *ukaz* against which it was directed. This was when (as mentioned already) some deputies presented a petition that suburban properties which belonged to private landowners should be subjected to taxation. As the result of the request an *ukaz* was framed whereby such properties were commanded forthwith to be conveyed to the Tsar for purposes of assessment, and a census to be taken of the places of origin and dates of settlement of the inhabitants of those properties, provided that such inhabitants had arrived thither not earlier than the year 1613. To escape the customary procrastination of the Muscovite *prikazi*, and also the usual inquisitorial abuses, the deputies then presented a second petition that the properties referred to should be conveyed to the Tsar "without years, and without questions concerning the place wherein each man doth dwell"; and on this request also being laid before the Sovereign, he granted it in full. As for the revisory and legislative stages of the *Ulozhenie*, they belonged to the Tsar and the *Duma*. Revision consisted of examination of existing laws, as co-ordinated by the Committee in their preliminary draft. The warrant of July 16th seems to have suspended the action of those laws, and given them the quality merely of temporary regulations until they should have been accorded new legislative confirmation. Nevertheless, although deprived of the force of legal norms, those old laws retained, during the composition of the *Ulozhenie*, the status of sources of jurisprudence, since we find the *Duma* amending their texts, or scrutinising their contents, or altering or abolishing their norms (though more frequently the Committee's rough draft was supplemented by an established *ukaz* which the Committee had previously submitted to the *Duma*, or else by some new law-making which supplied norms for unforeseen *casus*). Thus with revision there went editorial work. Of this let me confine myself to a single example to be noted in the *Ulozhenie*—namely, the example that, at the beginning of Chapter XVII ("Concerning Lands"), the Committee inserted *ukazi* of Tsars Michael and Philaret relative to the order in which heirs should be invited to succeed to family or "gained" (granted for meritorious service) *otchini*. To these articles in the rough draft the *Duma* assented, but at the same time added to them a regulation as to occasions when mothers and childless widows were to have their support secured upon "gained" properties. Revision was carried out by the *Duma* as a whole; but when giving a *legislative* decision, that body assumed (according to the nature of the question to be decided) a varying composition, and shared its legislative authority with other sections of the Council. Sometimes a decree was pronounced by the Tsar and the *Duma* alone; at other times it was pronounced by them in company with the Holy Synod; at other times it was pronounced by all three sections in association with a few invited deputies of different ranks; at yet other (though rarer) times it was pronounced by the Council as a whole, "the chosen men of all ranks" included. Thus, though the general desire was that "all the *Ulozhenie* do abide fixed and immoveable," the Council worked it out through a sessional system which lacked both fixity and immobility. The Council's general, most serious task—the task for which, in particular, it had been convened—was the ratification of the Digest with the signatures of all the mem bers, *ex officio* and elected alike; which act, on the part both of the official section and of the representatives of the people, must have signified that they recognised the *Ulozhenie* as at once regular and a full satisfaction of their needs; as also that henceforth "all things (shall) be done according unto the same this *Ulozhenie*." The Patriarch Nikon was not speaking fairly when he contemptuously referred to the Digest as "an accursed book and a law of the devil"; for if he really thought it so, why did he keep silence when, in the year 1649, he heard that same "accursed book" read aloud, and appended to it his signature in his capacity of Archimandrite of the Novospassk Monastery?

According to the idea which we may assume to have lain at the basis of the *Ulozhenie*, the Code was designed to stand as the last word in Muscovite jurisprudence—as a full and complete compendium of the stock of legislation which, up to the middle of the seventeenth century, had accumulated in the Muscovite chancellories. This idea glimmers in the *Ulozhenie*, yet is not preserved with complete success, since, in technical respects, and as an example of codification, the *Ulozhenie* must yield pride of place to the older *Sudebniki*. Judging by its disposition of subjects suitable for legislation, it would seem to have wished to build the State order downwards—downwards from the Church, the Tsar, and the Court to the Cossacks and the taverns (the latter of which occupy its two closing chapters). Also, it needs some little effort to collate the various chapters of the Code under the separate headings of State law, legal organisation, judicial procedure, and property and criminal law. For the codifiers these groupings were mere fits and starts in the direction of a system, since the codifiers only drew upon their sources partially and in any order. Also, they took articles from different sources, and articles which did not agree with one another. Occasionally they even failed to fit in their excerpts at all, and let them accumulate in a heap rather than fall into their proper places. If, therefore, the *Ulozhenie* remained operative in Russia during the two centuries which preceded the *Svod Zakonov*[1] of 1833, the fact speaks less for the merits of Alexis' Digest than for Russia's long-sustained ability to dispense with a satisfactory code. Yet, as a legislative

---

[1] Compendium of Laws.

memorial, the *Ulozhenïe* took a notable step forward, as compared with the *Sudebniki*, since it was more than a practical guide to the judge and the administrator—it was a guide which set forth ways and means for re-establishing the law when once infringed, though not the law itself. Yet, like the *Sudebniki*, it allots the largest place to formal law—its third chapter ("Concerning Tribunals") being the longest in the Code, and, in number of articles, forming well-nigh a third of the whole *Ulozhenïe*. Also, the Code leaves many important, though intelligible, blanks in the department of material law. For instance, it contains no fundamental laws at all, for at that time such things were not understood in Moscow, which still remained satisfied with the will of the Tsar and the pressure of circumstances. Also, we note the absence of any systematic exposition of family law, although the latter was a department closely bound up with ecclesiastical and "custom" law. Probably the reason why the authorities decided to touch neither custom nor the clergy was that the former was too shadowy and inert a thing, and the latter were persons too ticklish and jealous of their spiritual monopolies. Yet the *Ulozhenïe* ranged over a far wider field of legislation than did the *Sudebniki*, since it attempted to penetrate to the composition of the community, to define the position and mutual relations of the different classes in it, and to speak both of servitors, service landowners, peasantry, suburban residents, slaves, *Strieltsi*, and Cossacks. Of course, its chief attention is given to the *dvoriané*, as constituting the ruling military-official and landowning class. Indeed, more than half its articles directly or indirectly concern the interests and relations of that class; although on these points, as on all others, the Code strives to remain grounded on reality.

Yet, for all its, in general, conservative character, the *Ulozhenïe* could not refrain from indulging in two liberal tendencies which clearly show in what direction the ultimate bent of the community was turned, or was destined to be turned. One of those tendencies is directly stated in the warrant of July 16th, as constituting the task which confronted the Codificatory Committee; the latter being instructed to draw up a draft *Ulozhenïe* such as should be "equal in judgement and equity for men of all ranks, from the greatest to the least, and in all matters whatsoever." This was not to be an equality before the law which should exclude any difference of rights: it was to be an equality of "judgement and equity" which should take no account of privileged non-liabilities, nor of departmental differences, nor of the class exemptions and immunities which then existed in Muscovite legal dispensation. Yes, the warrant had in view tribunals which should be no respecters of persons, whether boyars or commoners; tribunals which should be of identical competence and procedure, even if not of identical powers to punish; tribunals which should judge all men—even immigrant foreigners—with one and the same equitable judgement, "and be ashamed not before the strong man, and deliver the offended man out of the hand of the unjust." So runs Chapter X. of the *Ulozhenïe*, at the point where an attempt is made to sketch such a universal and equal system of legal trial and dispensation. The idea of a system of this kind arose out of the *Ulozhenïe's* general rule to bring about the abolition of every kind of privileged status and relation which should work detrimentally to the interests of the State, more particularly of the Treasury. The other tendency which I have mentioned arose from the same source, and is stated in the chapter on classes, where it voices a new view of the relation of the free individual to the State. To understand it properly we must to a certain extent renounce our modern ideas of personal freedom. For us moderns, personal freedom is independence of one's fellow-man. It is more than an unquestionable right to which the law can put limits: it is an obligation demanded by morality itself. None of us are willing or able to contract ourselves into formal slavery, since no court of law would support such a contract. But we must not forget that it is the Russian community of the seventeenth century—the slave-owning community in which personal bondage, as expressed in different forms of slavery, still remained operative—that we are now studying; as also that to those forms (as presently we shall see) there was about to be added, at the time of the *Ulozhenïe*, yet another form of dependence, in the shape of peasant serfdom. In those days it was part of the right of the free individual to be at liberty to make temporary or permanent surrender of his freedom to another man without at the same time possessing the right to put a summary term to that dependence: and it was upon this right that the various forms of old Russian slavery were based. Up to the time of the *Ulozhenïe*, however, there existed in Rus a personal dependence, of a non-bonded character, which owed its rise to the system of *zaklad* or "pledging." For a man to pledge himself meant that, as security for a loan, or in return for service of any kind (for example, exemption from imposts or legal immunity), he was at liberty to place his personality and his labour at the disposal of another man, yet still to retain the right of putting a summary termination, at discretion, to that dependence—presumably on liquidation of the "pledge" obligations which had been undertaken on his behalf. Such dependents were known, during the appanage epoch, as *zakladnïe*, while, during the Muscovite era, they were called *zakladchiki*. Borrowing on the security of his labour was, for the poor man of ancient Rus, the most convenient method of earning a living. Yet, though distinct from slavery, the *zaklad* system soon began to assume the exemptions of slavery, and immunity from the payment of State taxes; which constituted an abuse that now moved the law to take measures against *zakladchiki* and their receivers alike. In returning such *zakladchiki* " into *tiaglo* " (*i.e.* restoring them to liability to pay State taxes), the *Ulozhenïe* (see Chapter XIX., Article 13) threatens them, in case of frequent " self-pledgings," with " grievous punishment," in the shape of the *knut* and banishment to Siberia beyond the Lena ; while their receivers it threatens with a prospect of "great despoilment," added to confiscation of the lands whereon the *zakladchiki* had dwelt. Nevertheless, for many a poor man, in ancient Rus, slavery, and, still more, " self-pledging," constituted means of escape from his industrial straits, since the then cheapness in which personal freedom was held, added to the general lack of equity of the day, caused the exemptions and the protection—the " defending "—of a powerful receiver to represent assets of considerable value. Hence the abolition of the system of " self-pledging " struck a heavy blow at the class of *zakladchiki ;* with the result that, in 1649, they hatched, in Moscow, a new rebellion, and loaded the Tsar with every kind of unseemly abuse. This attitude is intelligible, even if we cannot share it. The free individual, whether of the official, the non-taxpaying, class or of the class of renderers of *tiaglo*, became, on entering into slavery or into *zakladnichestvo*, a person lost to the State. Consequently the *Ulozhenïe*, in restricting or forbidding such passage, was merely voicing the general norm which prohibits any free individual who is under an obligation either of State tax-liability or of State service from resigning his freedom through a voluntary sloughing of the State obligations which lie incumbent upon all free persons. He still must belong to, and must serve, the State alone ; he cannot become the private property of another man. " It is commanded that unto no man shall any Christian man sell himself " (*Ulozhenïe*, Chapter XX., Article 97). Consequently personal freedom had become obligatory, and was supported by the *knut*. But a right whereof the enjoyment is compulsory also becomes an impost. It is true that we moderns do not feel the burden of this impost, since the State, in forbidding us to become slaves, or even semi-slaves, also secures to us, in our human individuality, our most valuable possession, and our whole moral and civic being supports that restriction of our will by the State—supports the impost which is dearer to us than any right in the world. But in the Russian community of the seventeenth century this impost was supported neither by personal consciousness nor by public morality, although it was an impost which is the common due of mankind. That blessing which, for ourselves, transcends all possible value had, for the Russian hind of the seventeenth century, no value whatever. Even the State, though it forbade the individual to enter into a personal dependency, was not seeking to preserve in him the human being, nor the citizen, but the soldier and the taxpayer. Consequently the *Ulozhenie* did not abolish personal bondage in the name of freedom : it converted personal freedom into bondage in the name of the interests of the State. Yet this strict prohibition of "self-pledging" had in view an object which causes us to look upon *zakladchiki* in rather a different light. In reality the measure was a partial expression of the *Ulozhenie's* general desire to regulate social grouping by arranging the population in hermetically-sealed, corporate cells, and welding the popular labour, through compression, into the narrow framework of the State's requirements while also enslaving its private interests. The truth was that, at an earlier period than the rest of the population, the *zakladchiki* began to feel the burden which was incumbent upon all classes. That burden represented a general popular sacrifice which the State's position had rendered necessary. This we shall see later on, when studying the structure of administration and the classes after the Period of Troubles was over.

In placing its crown upon the legislative labour of previous ages, the *Ulozhenie* served as a transitional stage from that labour to later legislative activity. But its shortcomings began to make themselves felt very soon after it had come into operation; wherefore, here and there, it was supplemented and corrected with "newly-ordained articles." These articles served as its direct continuation, and examples of them are to be seen in the articles of 1669 concerning cases of stolen property, brigandage, and murder, as well as in the articles of 1676–1777 concerning *pomiestia* and *otchini*. This finicking, partial, and piecemeal revision of the *Ulozhenie's* articles—a revision which wavered between addition to, abolition of, and restriction of different enactments of the Digest of 1649 —is exceedingly interesting, since it expresses the stage in Muscovite State life when Moscow's directors began to feel doubts as to the merits of the legal norms and conditions of administration in the good qualities of which they had hitherto believed—the stage when, in their confusion and perplexity, they began to conceive that something new, something not "home grown," something "European," was called for.

CHAPTER VIII

THE *Ulozhenïe* of 1649 put the finishing touch upon the series of processes of Russian domestic life which began with the Period of Troubles and, under the influence of that Period, added legal confirmation to the position of the State which those processes had, by the middle of the seventeenth century, created. We have seen that, under the new dynasty, new ideas arose in men's minds, and that new men joined the administration. Also, we have seen that the supreme power became established in a new setting, and that the *Zemski Sobor* assumed a new composition. All these innovations arose directly or indirectly out of one fatal source—namely, out of the profound and general break in Russian life which was brought about by the Period of Troubles, and shattered both the forces of the people and the tottering external position of the State. Upon that the Government of the new dynasty found itself confronted with the question of how best to escape from the difficulties which surrounded it. We have studied the chief memorial of Russian legislation of the seventeenth century, in order to discern in what direction the Government moved, and in what quarters, and by what means, it sought an issue from the grievous dilemma in which it found itself placed. Again, we have noted that, after proclaiming the abolition of every sort of legal exemption and the prohibition of all further extension of non-free statuses which emancipated themselves from the payment of State dues, the Government set itself to gather into its hands the available forces of the nation. In short, it collected together everything which had survived the general destruction and might be of use to it—namely, the money which it lacked, the people who had gone into hiding, the payers of taxes, the soldiers, the members of the *Sobor* whose counsel it needed, and, finally, the laws of the country themselves.

In its struggle with its difficulties the Muscovite Government strove, before all things, to rally its own forces, since it felt the need of acquiring greater unity of will, and greater energy in action. With this aim in view, it set out, after the Period of Troubles, to centralise the administration, and to gather into its hands the working of the whole of the administrative power, central and local. At the same time, in the Moscow of that day centralisation had a meaning of its own. That is to say, it did not so much denote departmental subordination of local organs to a single central administration as the union in a single individual or a single institution of the various heterogeneous subjects which touch one another in daily life; just as, in a village shop, under the same signboard, we may see gathered together the most varied of goods to suit local demands, but not goods which are designed to be displayed according to their respective specialities. The inhabitants of Rus took the same view as the Government, since their one desire was to have to deal with a single institution in the matter of their requirements. Indeed, on more than one occasion we see them explaining to the Government that the *prikazi* wearied them beyond measure, since each of those *prikazi* dealt with them on separate affairs, and it would be far better for everything to be done in one *prikaz* alone, "to the end that there be not vain offendings and loss." It was by this practical consideration of expediency that the authorities, under Tsar Michael, were guided in their reconstruction of local government. The old dynasty had left provincial administration in a state of utter disruption. Ivan's provincial reforms had broken up the province, the canton, into a few departments and a multitude of local corporate communities, urban and rural, which consisted only of State servitors and State taxpayers. Each such local community acted alone, and possessed its own elective administration. Yet there had been no local tie to bind them all together, except the one tie of an occasional pan-corporate or pan-cantonal election of a *gubni starosta*.[1] Consequently each of those local communities maintained (through its elected officers) independent relations with the central institutions, the *prikazi*. Only in the frontier towns, where there was a need for a strong military authority, had the sixteenth century seen introduced a number of *voievodi* or military governors, who concentrated in their hands the management of whole districts in all but spiritual matters.

[1] See vol. ii. pp. 272 *et seq.*

This diffuse system of elective provincial administration could act only in times of peace—and for a long while after the close of the old dynasty such times grew scarcer and scarcer. During the Period of Troubles the provinces—including even the inner ones—lay exposed to the risk of hostile attack; wherefore *voievodi* soon began to make their appearance also in the cantons of the interior. A document has come down to us which was composed about 1628. It consists of a list of 32 towns wherein, at one time, there used to be no *voievodi*, but in which such functionaries materialised soon after the "coming of the *Raztriga*"[1] *i.e.* after the opening of the reign of the First Pretender in 1605. These towns were the central ones of Vladimir, Periaslavl, Rostov, Bielozersk, and others; and their number makes it clear to us that the reign of Michael saw the post of *voievoda* become a universal institution. A *voievoda* had under his authority a whole canton, together with its various social classes and its affairs of every kind; and his authority covered both the cantonal capital and the rural communities of the canton, whether in legal and financial matters or in those of police and war. Externally the introduction of *voievodi* would seem to have been an improvement in local government, since it united isolated local corporations under a single authority, and caused the canton to become an integral adminis-trative unit, and local government to become directed by a representative of the central power—by an official who was nominated by the *prikazi*, and not by the local electors. Regarded from this point of view, therefore, administration by *voievodi* was a progression from the territorial principle which Ivan IV. had placed at the basis of his local institutions and bureaucratic system of local government. A *voievoda* was appointed to supervise his canton, not for his own benefit, as were the old *kormlent-shiki*,[2] but for that of the Tsar, as the real power of the Crown. For this reason the *kormi* and *poshlini*[2] which, under the *ustavnia gramoti* or "charters of conferment" of which I have spoken, had formerly gone to the *namiestnik*, or local civil governor, had nothing to do with the *voievoda*. Naturally the central *prikazi* of Moscow found government by *voievodi* a boon, since for them to have to deal with a single general administrator of each canton—especially with a nominee of their own— was a much handier matter than for them to have to deal with innumer-able elective cantonal authorities. For the local population, however, government by *voievodi* was not only a reversion to, but a change for the

---

[1] Unfrocked Priest—meaning the supposed Gregory Otrepiev, the First Pretender.
[2] See vol. ii. pp. 248, 249.

worse from, government by *namiestniki,* since the *voievodi* of the seventeenth century were the sons or the grandsons of the *namiestniki* of the sixteenth, and, though one or two generations may suffice to change institutions, they cannot bring about an alteration in manners and customs. True, the *voievoda* did not collect *kormi* and *poshlini* to the degree which we find indicated in *ustavnia gramoti,* but he was not forbidden to receive dues offered *voluntarily* and "for the sake of respect"; he might, though not armed with an *ustavnaia gramota,* receive as many of these dues as his hand could accommodate. Accordingly we see applicants for posts of *voievoda* frankly requesting to be appointed to such and such a town, "where there be gathering of sustenance." In short, contrary to its own idea, government by *voievodi* degenerated into a continuation of government by *namiestniki.* The latter, though theoretically an administrative emolument in return for military service, represented, in practice, an administrative service under the guise of a subsidy for military liability (since the *namiestnik* both administered and judged); whereas the post of *voievoda* was a post which the authorities sought to make carry with it no sort of emolument at all. The result was that, in practice, it became a non-assessed emolument masquerading under the guise of an administrative service. To these abuses the vague scope of the *voievoda's* authority gave added encouragement, since the laboriously-detailed instructions with which the *prikaz* which appointed him always loaded a *voievoda* prescribed that, in the last resort, he should act "as shall seem unto him expedient, having regard both unto matters in that region and unto God's will." That is to say, such instructions gave him, in practice, full discretion; whence we can understand why it was that the provincials of the seventeenth century came to regret the days when *voievodi* had not come into existence at all. Naturally, such a combination of "red tape" with freewill was bound to cause vagueness of rights and duties—to bring about an abuse of the former and a contempt for the latter; with the result that we see government by *voievodi* alternately exceeding and neglecting its powers.

A *voievoda* administered justice and affairs in a building known as the *siezhaia izba,* or *prikaznaia izba,* which corresponded to our modern provincial government offices; and in his administration of the canton he was assisted by a second organ of the central power, in the shape of a specially appointed *gubni starosta,* whose office or chancellory was known as the *gubnaia izba* (some cantons, it may be said, had two, or even more, *gubnie starosti*). This supreme judicial-police authority in the canton arose, as we have seen, during the sixteenth century, and had a composite character, since he was provincial as regards the source of his powers and central-departmental as regards his jurisdiction. Though elected at a local public convention, it was not local or provincial, but general matters of State—the trial of important criminal cases—that he superintended. During the seventeenth century his jurisdiction also became extended to cover, not only cases of murder and theft, but cases of homicide, arson, secession from Orthodoxy, contumely of parental authority, and so forth. The influence of the Government's general tendency in domestic policy is seen in the fact that the central-departmental element in the duties of a *gubni starosta* soon acquired a decided preponderance over the provincial, and caused his post to approximate closely to that of a *voievoda*. But this tendency did not connote any particular scheme; it constituted, rather, an administrative impulse, not a set programme : which fact is expressed in the endless fluctuations which marked the mutual relations of the two posts. In some localities the duties of the *gubni starosta* were entrusted to the local *voievoda*, whereas, in other localities, the duties of the *voievoda* were performed by the *gubni starosta*. Also, at the request of the townsmen, the *gubni starosta* could replace the *voievoda ;* and if the former eventually proved unsuitable, the *voievoda* could be reinstated, as well as take over the *gubni starosta's* functions. Thus the *gubni starosta* acted sometimes independently of, and sometimes in subordination to, the *voievoda*.

But what of the system of purely provincial local government which, at one time, administered the taxpaying population? With the universal introduction of *voievodi*, that system did not wholly disappear, but only became restricted and subordinated to the *voievoda,* and had its sphere of action contracted. Also, with the passage of the judicial authority to the *voievoda*, the legal colleges of selected *golovi* (mayors) and *tsielovalniki* (assessors) came to an end. Only on Courtlands and in purely peasant *volosti*, as well as in the maritime cantons of the North—*i.e.* in the present-day governments of Archangel, Olonetz, Viatka, and Perm—did locally-elected communal justices survive. Elsewhere there were left to elective local administrations only financial matters (to wit, the collection of State taxes, and matters which related to local industry). As before, the ingathering of indirect taxes, of customs and excise duties, and the like, was carried out by *viernïe liudi* or " trusted men " (mayors and their assessors), while the collection of direct imposts, together with the management of local industrial affairs, urban and rural, was entrusted to local *starosti* and their assessors. Industrial affairs of this kind consisted of the collection of dues for local commercial requirements, the apportionment of communal lands, the selection of officials for various posts connected with local administration, and the appointment of parish priests and their servers. The *zemski starosta*, or local *starosta*, carried on business in what was known as the *zemskaia izba*, or local prefecture, which, whether that of an urban or of a rural district, always stood within the limits of a township, and close to the walls of the town's citadel, in which the offices of the local *voievoda* and the local *gubni starosta* were situated. The immediate supervision of what went on in the *zemskaia izba* belonged to *sovietnïe liudi*, or elected councillors of the cantonal population, urban and rural. With the introduction of *voievodi* into local government a new and heavy burden fell upon the local communities in that they were now called upon to support both the local *voievoda* and his staff—an outgoing which, more than all other things put together, helped to drain the local exchequer. For this purpose the *zemski starosta* kept a book of expenses, in which he entered every item of commercial expenditure, for subsequent audit by the local councillors, the *sovietnïe liudi;* and from these books we see at a glance what the "feeding" of a *voievoda* during the seventeenth century must have meant. Every day the *starosta* jotted down expenses which he had incurred on behalf of the *voievoda* and his staff, through having to provide the *voievoda's* household with every possible domestic and office requisite —meat, fish, pastry, candles, paper, ink, and so on. Also, on festivals or namedays he would have to wait upon the *voievoda*, and offer him his congratulations, and present a gift of *kalachi* (small loaves) or money "on paper"; and similar gifts would have to be offered also to the *voievoda's* wife, to his children, his staff, his household servants, his hangers-on, and even the family *urodivi* or "holy simpleton."[1] Also, these books of communal expenses gives us a good idea of the true status of provincial administration by *voievodi*. The *zemski starosta* and his assessors were only passive instruments in the hands of the central *prikazi;* yet upon them there were imposed all the administrative dirty work with which the *voievoda* and his staff did not care to soil their hands. The *zemstvo*, or local communal administration, transacted its business under the eye of, and in accordance with the instructions of, the *voievoda*. Consequently the *starosta* was forever trotting to and fro between the office of the *voievoda* and his own, and seldom dared to oppose, on behalf

[1] See vol. ii. p. 156.

of his commune, the *voievoda's* commands—though, on rare occasions, certainly, he would frame a protest, and, repairing to his superior's residence, then and there "revile" him (to quote the term current among provincial malcontents of the day). This relation of local administration to administration by *prikazi* gave rise to terrible abuses, since the "feeding" of a *voievoda* frequently led to the utter ruin of a local community. Consequently, to remove, or at all events to lessen, this evil, the Government strove, while avoiding radical measures, to accomplish its end by making the appointment of *voievodi* subject to representations on the part of the local community, as also by allowing local communities to choose for themselves the government staffs which were to act from the central *prikazi*, and by handing over the functions of the local *voievoda* to an elected *gubni starosta*. Also, both in *ukazi* and in the *Ulozhenïe* itself, the Government threatened the gravest of penalties for inequitable justice, as well as gave leave to persons who were wronged to express their distrust of their *voievoda*, and transfer their case to the *voievoda* of a neighbouring canton. Likewise, under Alexis, *dvorïané* were debarred from appointment to posts as *voievodi* in towns where they owned either *otchini* or *pomiestia*; while, under Michael and his successor, *voievodi* were repeatedly forbidden to exact *kormi*, in money or in kind, under penalty of a fine equal to twice what had been exacted. Thus the centralisation of local administration injured local institutions by altering their original character, and depriving them of their independence without also lessening their obligations and responsibilities. This was another sacrifice which the community offered upon the altar of Empire.

The concentration of local government was not limited by the boundaries of the canton, for even under Michael another step forward in the same direction was taken. This was when, at the time of the wars with Poland and Sweden, the Government sought to improve its machinery of external defence by combining the frontier cantons on the western, southern, and south-eastern outskirts of the Empire into a number of large military districts which were called *razriadi*. In these, cantonal *voievodi* were made dependent upon chief *voievodi* of districts, as superior military-civilian administrators and presidents of the military-official class whereof the district corps were constituted. Early in Michael's reign we meet with mention of *razriadi* of Riazan and the Ukraine whereof Tula, Mtzensk, and Novossil formed part; during Alexis' time *razriadi* of Novgorod, Sievski (or Sieverski), Bielgorod, Tambov, and Kazan make their first appearance; and, lastly, under Tsar Theodor it was proposed to unite all the cantons of the interior into military districts by forming *razriadi* of Moscow, Vladimir, and Smolensk. These districts served also as the basis of the division into governments which Peter the Great, later, introduced.

Centralisation also touched—though in a lesser degree—the headquarters administration, where it was even more urgently needed than in the provincial administrations. In speaking of the Muscovite *prikazi* of the sixteenth century I remarked that they were organised on similar lines during the seventeenth century. But the increasing demands and departures of the State now augmented their number to about fifty; nor is it easy to discern in them any kind of system, but only an agglomeration of large and small departments, ministries, offices, and temporary commissions. Also, their number and the varying scope of their several jurisdictions made any control or direction of their activity almost an impossibility. Even the Government found itself at a loss whither to refer one or another extraordinary matter which arose; wherefore, without further reflection, it often proceeded to institute a new *prikaz* for that purpose alone. Hence there arose a need for some co-ordination of this loose machinery of the central administration; which end was accomplished by two methods—namely, by placing groups of *prikazi* of similar jurisdiction under a single director, and by combining groups of *prikazi* into single institutions. In the former case, the groups of *prikazi* acquired a single directorate and a single sphere of action, and in the other case the groups of *prikazi* acquired identical systems of organisation. Thus we see Prince I. D. Miloslavski, the son-in-law of Alexis, head of the *Prikaz Bolshoi Kazni* or Treasury, one of the departments of the Ministry of Finance; but at the same time he was director also of the *prikazi* which managed the new species of military forces which Moscow maintained during the sixteenth and seventeenth centuries. These particular *prikazi* were the Office of Infantry, the Office of Cavalry, and the Office of Foreign Troops; to which latter there was attached also the non-military *Prikaz Aptekarski*, or Office of Apothecaries, for the reason that it comprised the physicians, who themselves were foreigners. Again, the Office of Ambassadors, which superintended foreign affairs, had under it not only nine other *prikazi* by which the affairs of the newly-acquired provinces of Little Rus, Smolensk, Lithuania, and others were managed, but also the *Polonianitchni Prikaz*, or Office for the Ransoming of Prisoners. Through this system of concentration a multitude of small institutions became converted into a few large establishments which served as the precursors of Peter the Great's "Colleges." Also, for purposes of supervision, there arose, under Alexis, two new *prikazi*. One of these, the Office of Accounts, exercised control over finance, and estimated the State's income and expenditure on the basis of books kept by all the other central *prikazi*, as well as by the various provincial institutions. Likewise, it gathered to itself any surplus which happened to be left over current expenses; it consulted its fellow *prikazi* in matters of disbursements to personages like ambassadors and *voievodi* of regiments; and it summoned from the towns, for purposes of audit, the local *tsielovalniki* (assessors), with their books of income and expenditure. In short, it was a department for uniting all the keeping of accounts in one, and arose by at all events the year 1621. The other of the two new *prikazi* was what was known as the "Office of Secret Affairs." Yet its functions were not so strange as its name, since it was no mere department of secret police, but an institution for the management of the Tsar's field sports—of his "beguiling," as the term went. The truth is that Tsar Alexis was a devotee of falconry, and that the "Office of Secret Affairs" had under it the management of 200 falconers and mewsmen, 3000 hawks, falcons, and vultures, and upwards of 100,000 dovecotes for feeding and training the Imperial birds of prey. At the same time, to these falcons and doves the kindly, but parsimonious, Tsar appended a multitude of matters which pertained both to his personal *ménage* and to the State administration. For instance, through the "Office of Secret Affairs" he both transacted his personal correspondence (especially on diplomatic and military subjects) and saw to the industrial working of certain of his properties— mostly salt mines and fisheries. Also, this *prikaz* superintended the conduct of the Tsar's favourite religious establishment, the Savvin Storozhevski Monastery, and also the disposal of his alms, and so forth. Again, it was through this institution that the Tsar issued commands on all possible subjects that were connected with general administration, on occasions when he found it necessary to mingle independently in the conduct of affairs, or to take upon himself the initiative in, or the direction of, any new enterprise which had not hitherto come within the purview of the administration—such enterprises as the mining of ore or the quarrying of granite. In short, it was a *prikaz* which constituted both the Tsar's private chancellory and his particular organ for supervising the administration—an organ which acted independently of the general control that was exercised by the *Boyarskaia Duma*. Of one condition of such supervision we hear from the historian Kotoshikhin, who says that the *personnel* of the *prikaz* consisted only of a *diak* and ten writers (*dumnïe liudi* were expressly excluded from its doors), and that the Tsar attached these writers to embassies which were visiting foreign countries, and to the staffs of generals who were going on campaigns ; in both cases with the object of keeping an eye upon what was said and done. " And the writers," adds Kotoshikhin, " do overlook the ambassadors and the *voievodi*, and, on returning, do make report unto the Tsar." It need hardly be said that the highly-born ambassadors and generals were perfectly awake to the purpose for which these insignificant supernumeraries were attached to their trains, and that they bribed them " in excess of their proper measure" (to quote Kotoshikhin's expression). Consequently, as an organ of secret administrative supervision, as the precursor of Peter's "Institute of Informers," the " Office of Secret Affairs" was not a success. Moreover, it was an exceedingly tactless institution, since Kotoshikhin writes that Alexis organised the *Prikaz* "to the end that all his Imperial thoughts and acts be fulfilled according unto his will," but that "the boyars and the *dumnïe liudi* did take no account thereof, whether of the former or of the latter." Thus the Tsar acted behind the backs of the very executors of his will whom he himself had armed with authority—the very executors with whom he purported to be living " in counsel," while all the while he was conspiring against his own Government ! Though atavism be a fiction, we see the old *Oprichnina* instinct of appanage days repeating itself in a Tsar whose forebears had never been appanage princes at all. However, on the death of the founder of the " Office " no time was lost in closing it.

With the centralisation of the administration there went a concentration of the community. From the reorganising activity of the old dynasty there had issued a community that was as disintegrated as its administration, since it was broken up into a multitude of ranks or *tchini* which, exclusive of the clergy, might be combined under four fundamental classes or statuses. Those classes were—(1) persons of the official class —State servitors, (2) urban payers of *tiaglo* or State taxes, (3) rural taxpayers, and (4) slaves. According to their relation to the State, these four fundamental classes were distinguished from one another by the species of obligations which went with the propertied position of the individual, as well as, in the case of the official class, with the individual's origin ; while the various *tchini* were distinguished from one another by the extent of, or the weight of incidence of, obligations which partook of a similar nature. Thus the peculiar obligation of the service landowners was hereditary military service, with its concomitant, court and administrative service. According to the importance and the responsibility of such service (which, again, was proportioned to the extent of the land tenure and the elevation of birth of the given servitor), the service class was sub-divided into servitors of Duma rank, of metropolitan rank, and of ordinary town rank. The commercial-industrial inhabitants of the towns paid urban *tiaglo* in proportion to stock in hand and nature of trade; and, in proportion as that stock was large and that trade was lucrative, they were divided into *liuchshie liudi, serednïe liudi*, and *molodshie liudi* (literally, "best men," "middle men," and "young men"). A similar system of division marked the class of rural inhabitants or peasantry, who paid agrarian *tiaglo* according to measure of arable land; while slaves—who by law could possess no property to which they had an absolute right, and performed no service to the State—paid no taxes either, but were bound to different forms of bondage in the service of private individuals. Yet neither the various classes nor the various *tchini* were stable, fixed, obligatory statuses, since persons could pass from any one class or any one *tchin* to another one. That is to say, a freeman could, of his own will or of that of the State, either change his avocation or combine it with a second one; and slaves also could do the same, whether of their own will or by process of law. A State servitor could engage in urban trade, or a peasant could enter into slavery, or seek an industrial pursuit in a town. This power of mobility from one fundamental class to another one gave rise to several intermediate, transitional *strata* in the heterogeneous composition of Muscovite society. Thus, between the State servitor class and the slave class there lay a *stratum* of "sons of boyars"—gentry who, possessing only small *pomiestia* or none at all, performed State service from their own or their fathers' *pomiestia*, or entered, as slaves, into the service of boyars and other State servitors of higher rank, and so formed a special category of boyaral retainers. Again, between the State service class and the ordinary urban population stood a class of State servitors "of the lesser *tchini*." These men, who owed their status, not to *otechestvo* or hereditary succession, but to the fact that they were in the hire of the State, consisted of the blacksmiths, carpenters, harness-makers, gunners, and bombardiers attached to fortresses or fortress artillery. The fact that they constituted an appendage to the State service class proper was due to the circumstance that they performed the duties of military artisans. At the same time, they approximated, rather, to the urban population, since it was mostly from the towns (where they could engage in urban trades without having to pay urban *tiaglo*) that they were recruited. Again, around the establishments of the privileged landowners, both clerical and lay, there hovered the class of *zakladchiki* of which I have already spoken. These men also hailed from the towns. Finally, between the slave class and the free classes there wandered a multitudinous, exceedingly mixed class of free or vagrant persons who consisted of the non-taxpaying relatives and hangers-on of taxpayers; of their unattached sons, brothers, and nephews; of lodgers who worked for board and lodging alone; of sons of the clergy who, as yet, had had no parishes assigned them; of "sons of boyars" who had either squandered or been deprived of their estates without subsequently entering private service; of peasants who had left their holdings and not yet made up their minds to adopt another mode of life; and of slaves who had gained their freedom and not reverted to a state of bondage. All persons of this kind were, if they lived in a *selo* (rural settlement), landless persons, and therefore non-payers of agrarian *tiaglo;* while, if they lived in a town, they could engage in industrial pursuits, yet needed not also pay urban taxes.

The extent of this division into *tchini*, added to the presence of these vagrant, intermediate *strata* in the social composition, imparted to the community the appearance of an exceedingly variegated, heterogeneous conglomeration of individuals. Also, although this mobility and heterogeneity of the social composition served to maintain the freedom of popular labour and popular migration, that freedom offered great difficulties to the Government, and thwarted its desire (expressed, later, in the *Ulozhenïe*) to make all men labour for the State, and then to regulate the popular labour strictly in the interests of the Treasury. The two chief obstacles to this were the statuses of *zakladchiki* and of free (vagrant) persons respectively, since they threatened not only a diminution of the sources of military recruitment, but also complete exhaustion of the sources of the State's income. That is to say, through the fact that they enjoyed the right to renounce both their personal freedom and the State obligations with which that freedom was bound up, the two classes in question threatened to become social refuges for persons belonging to the State servitor and State taxpayer classes who desired neither to serve nor to pay taxes. Consequently, to obviate these difficulties and risks, the legislature began, on the accession of Michael, to draw the community closer together, much as we have seen it do in the case of the administration. That is to say, it united such isolated *tchini* as were liable to similar obligations into large, close-locked classes, while to the *tchini* themselves it left complete freedom of mobility *within the limits of* the particular class to which such *tchini* happened to be assigned. Also, it impressed the vagrant *strata* into classes according to (in so far as was possible) similarity of avocations. This social reconstruction the Government effected by two methods—namely, by hereditary attachment of persons to the statuses in which the law which attached them thereto found them situated, and by abrogation of the right of free persons to renounce their personal freedom. Thus the social composition became at once more fixed and more durable. Service and tax-liability according to variations in propertied position and mutations of avocation became converted into fixed obligations by birth ; whence each separate class, having become thus ringed around, became also more compact, and more completely segregated from the rest. Thus, for the first time in the history of our social organisation, the close-locked and obligatory social divisions whereof I am speaking acquired the character of *soslovia* or corporations ; and to the process which brought them into being we may apply the term of " fixation " or " induration " of statuses. Nevertheless, since the process was carried out at the expense of the freedom of popular labour, the results which it attained must be numbered with the other sacrifices which the community was forced to offer upon the altar of Empire.

This fixation and segregation of classes seems to have begun with the State servitor class, which was the most necessary constituent of the Empire, as its fighting force. As early as 1550 the *Sudebnik* of that year allowed only *retired* "sons of boyars" to be received into slavery ; while " sons of boyars " who were still on the active list, with their sons—even if the latter had not yet entered the service—were strictly forbidden to become slaves. True, " sons of boyars " formed the lowest and most needy rank of State servitors ; but that rank was one which contained a vast number of aspirants to boyardom. Consequently by a further law of 1558 it was commanded that only sons of " sons of boyars " who had attained their service majority (the age of fifteen years), and had, as yet, received no nomination to the profession, might become slaves ; while to minors and those who had attained their service majority and become enrolled in the service it entirely prohibited such entry into slavery. Nevertheless necessity and the burden of service often caused these restrictions to be broken through. In Michael's time the *dvoriané* joined the " sons of boyars " in presenting a petition concerning the whole-sale defection of their brethren, sons, and nephews to slavery ; wherefore by an *ukaz* of March 9th, 1642, it was further commanded that such highly-born bondsmen should, if they were owners of *otchini* or *pomiestia*, or had ever been commissioned to the service, be recovered from boyaral households, and restored to the service of the State; while in future it was forbidden to receive into slavery any *dvorianin* or "son of a boyar" whatsoever. This prohibition was inserted into the *Ulozhenie*, and military service became an hereditary, permanent, and corporate obligation appertaining to the State servitor class alone. Likewise there became defined the special corporate rights of that class, as constituting the landowning body. Hitherto the right of landownership had been enjoyed also by retainers of boyaral households, with their parallels, the military retainers of monasteries; and these two categories had been swelled by the addition of State servitors who owned *otchini* or *pomiestia*. But by the *ukaz* of 1642 of which I have spoken the former were restored to the service of the State, and, later, the *Ulozhenie* deprived *both* categories of the right to acquire *otchini*. That is to say, personal landownership, whether of *otchini* or *pomiestia*, became the corporate privilege solely of the State servitor class; even as military service was assigned to it as its special corporate *obligation* : and this privilege and this obligation together caused the various service *tchini* to become united into a single corporation which stood apart from all the other classes.

The same system of segregation of classes was applied also to the urban population. We have seen how the growth of the service-landowning class during the sixteenth century restricted the growth of towns,[1] and how the Period of Troubles ruined and dispersed the payers of urban *tiaglo*. The difficulties encountered by the towns when the new dynasty acceded to power threatened their barely reviving prosperity with renewed misfortune, since, if such urban communities were not to become defaulters as regards the payment of fiscal dues, it was necessary that, being bound together in a circular guarantee for the payment of taxes, they should always have, not only a full complement of burghers, but also a secure market for their labour and their merchandise. Nevertheless the burden of taxpayment kept forcing the weaker townsmen to leave their boroughs, and to sell or pledge their establishments to non-taxpayers—*i.e.* to "white" or exempted persons; while, on the other hand, persons of various *tchini* would settle in the township—*Strieltsi*, peasantry from neighbouring *sela*, Church servants, and sons of priests—and, engaging in local trade and industry, "cut out" the few urban taxpayers who still

[1] See vol. ii. p. 144.

remained, without having to bear any share in the payment of that township's taxes. Even priests and deacons contravened the Church's rules by setting up shops! This avoidance of urban *tiaglo* received influential encouragement from above, for it may be remarked that, every time that the supreme power in Russia has weakened, the ruling classes of the country have hastened to seize the moment to develop a passion for speculation at the expense of the freedom of popular labour. Thus, under Tsar Theodor, son of Ivan IV., we find contemporary writers lamenting the vigorous growth of a bonded servitude in the promotion of which even the chief minister of the State—Boris Godunov himself—and his family took an active share. We see the same thing repeated under Michael in the case of the *zakladchiki*. I have already mentioned this form of private dependency as being distinguished from slavery by the fact that it was not forced, and that it could be put an end to, at any time, by the *zakladchik* himself. The persons who most frequently resorted to this form of hire were the townsmen of the trading and artisan classes; and it was usually to the "strong men"—*i.e.* to the boyars, the Patriarch, the bishops, and the monasteries—that these persons "pledged" themselves. But for their fellow townsmen this was a great misfortune, since, though the principal townships in the Muscovite Empire were girdled about with a ring of suburban settlements in which there lived such Treasury-paid employés as *Strieltsi*, gunners, and "ramparts men," who competed in trade and industry with the townsmen proper, yet shared none of their financial obligations, the *zakladchiki* were even more dangerous rivals, since the "strong men" accepted them wholesale "in pledge," and then settled them upon whole suburbs and suburban properties, whether belonging to themselves (the "strong men") or to the urban authorities at large. In a suburb of Nizhni Novgorod which was the property of the Patriarch there were residing, in 1648, over 600 newly-arrived persons of the trading and artisan classes "who had gathered unto that appurtenance from diverse towns, and had come thither to abide for their trading" (so the townsmen's own representatives worded it in their complaint to the Council of the *Ulozhenie*). This was a new form of "self-pledging," and an illegal one at that, since personal pledging, in its true and simplest shape, had always been a borrowing upon the security of personal labour, under an obligation to work off the debt by service in the household, or on the land, of the receiver; whereas now urban payers of *tiaglo* began to "pledge" themselves without any "borrowing" at all, or with a mere fictitious "borrowing," and usually to the privileged landowners, clerical and lay. For these they performed no household work whatever, but settled on those landowners' tax-free estates, either in scattered homesteads or by whole lots, where they assumed similar agrarian exemptions to those of their landlords, and wilfully avoided payment of urban *tiaglo*, in spite of the fact that they engaged in "all manner of great dealings and barter." In fact, they were capitalists rather than poor household workmen working on a loan; which conditions were an infringement of the law, seeing that in 1550 the *Sudebnik* of that year had forbidden urban trading folk to live on non-taxable Church lands, or to make use of the immunity from *tiaglo* which those lands enjoyed; while, under Michael, the law had strictly differentiated urban taxable or "black" lands from non-taxable or "white." Just as it was forbidden to "white burghers" to "whiten"—*i.e.* to omit paying taxes for—urban homesteads and lands which they had acquired, so it was not permitted to the taxpaying classes, when settling on "white" lands, to "whiten" also themselves on the strength of having done so. "Self-pledging" was a direct abuse, since, though it was not forced slavery (which stood exempt from *tiaglo*), it combined the advantages of forced slavery with the advantage of being able to engage in urban trading without having also to pay urban *tiaglo*. As early as Michael's day we hear of complaints of this evil—though the Government of the new dynasty, true to its adopted custom of preventing nothing and yielding only to force or threats, satisfied individual complaints, yet never clinched the question with a general measure. Thus in 1643 the townsmen of Tobolsk laid a complaint that a mob of *zakladchiki* who had settled on the lands of the local monastery were squeezing and flouting them (the townsmen proper) in all matters of trade, while (so the petitioners took care to represent to the Government) not a single one of the interlopers was performing a State service of any kind, or paying a single tax. Upon this the Tsar gave orders for these *zakladchiki* to be added to the township, and taxed along with the townsmen proper. The insistent complaints of "self-pledging" which continued up to and during the time of the Council of 1648, the suggestive impressions which lingered of the Muscovite insurrection which took place in June of that year, the Muscovite Government's apprehension of the risk which was threatening the Treasury's income, the desire of the same Government to acquire a few thousands of new taxpayers,—all these things led to a capital revision of the composition of the urban population. The various measures which were then adopted are to be found embodied in Chapter XIX. of the *Ulozhenie*—the chapter "Concerning the People of Towns." All suburban properties belonging to private landowners which were situated on urban lands, whether purchased or seized, were now to be estreated to the Tsar, and then returned by him, gratis, to their several towns, for subjection to *tiaglo*, accompanied by the injunction, "Build ye not appurtenances upon the lands of the State, nor buy the lands of the towns." Also, every contract which had been entered into between a *zakladchik* and a receiver was now declared to be inoperative. Suburban *otchini* and *pomiestia* which ran with towns—"homestead unto homestead"—were to be added to those towns, and afterwards exchanged for fiscal *sela* in other localities. Lastly, "self-pledging" was declared henceforth to be illegal, on pain of a heavy fine, while townsmen were attached with such stringency both to their *tiaglo* obligations and to their townships that we find an *ukaz* of February 8th, 1658, threatening death to anyone who should remove from his own town to another one, or even marry outside that town. Thus the payment of urban *tiaglo* which was derived from trade and industry became the corporate obligation of the urban population; while the right of engaging in urban trade and industry became its corporate privilege. Consequently, though peasants might sell "all manner of merchandise" in the country-markets of the towns, they were to do so only from their wains direct— not from shops in the commercial quarter.

CHAPTER IX

WITH the segregation of the State service and urban classes there went a final determination of the position of the rural-agricultural inhabitants. Also, an essential change took place in the fortunes of the peasantry who lived on the estates of private owners and constituted the bulk of the rural population. That change had the effect of differentiating them still more sharply, not only from the other classes in the community, but also from such other categories of the rural population as the "black" or fiscal peasantry, and the peasant-tenants of court lands. I refer to the establishment of serfdom among the seigniorial peasantry. We interrupted our study of the rural classes at the beginning of the seventeenth century, after we had seen that, up to that time, both fiscal and court peasants were attached to the land or to their rural communes. Also, we had seen that the position of the seigniorial peasantry was still indefinite, for the reason that it lay between two opposing interests. Finally I closed my remarks with the statement that at the beginning of the seventeenth century there were already in operation all the economic conditions necessary for the enserfment of the seigniorial peasantry, and that it now remained but to find a judicial norm for converting their practical bondage into a serfdom sanctioned by the law.

In the position of the seigniorial peasantry of the sixteenth century, as a social class, we can distinguish three elements—namely, agrarian *tiaglo*, right of removal, and the need of the *ssuda* or landlord's loan (in other words, a political element, a juridical, and an economic). Each of these elements was hostile to the other two, and the changing course of their struggle produced vacillations in the legislation designed to determine the position of the class in question. The element which evoked that struggle was the economic one. Different causes (causes which we have, in part, studied) led to the middle of the sixteenth century witnessing a great increase in the number of peasantry who needed loans before they could establish or carry on their industry. This need shackled them with debt, and, clashing with their right of removal, extinguished that also, and caused it, without actual abolition by the law, to become a juridical fiction. Again, an element which militated against the peasant's freedom was his agrarian *tiaglo*, since it was an obligation from which serfdom delivered him ; wherefore the legislature of the early seventeenth century strove to prevent the conversion of the *krestianin* into a slave by establishing "perpetuity of peasant estate," or impossibility of escape from his taxpaying status. The combination of these three elements of the peasant's position with the conditions of old Russian personal bondage led to the discovery of the juridical norm whereby the serfdom of the seigniorial peasant became finally established.

By *kriepost*, or "bonding," in old Russian law, was meant the act, symbolical or written, which confirmed a person's authority over a given article ; and the authority which such an act confirmed conferred upon the owner of the article a certain "bonded" right over the same—even over human beings, who also, in ancient Rus, were subjects of "bonded" possession. "Bonded" persons of this kind were known as *kholopi* and *rabi*—the former term, in old Russian juridical diction, being used to denote male serfs or slaves, and the latter female. In ancient documents, however, we never encounter *both* these expressions, since the term *raba* or female slave is only to be met with in ecclesiastical records. *Kholopstvo*, slavery, was the oldest "bonded" status in Rus, for it became established many centuries before the rise of peasant serfdom. Previous to the close of the fifteenth century the only bondage which existed in Rus was what, later, came to be known as "full slavery." This condition was created by seven different methods—namely, (1) by capture in war, (2) by voluntary or parental sale of a free person into slavery, (3) by certain crimes for which a free person was converted into a slave at the bidding of the authorities, (4) by birth into slavery, (5) by culpable insolvency on the part of a merchant, (6) by voluntary entry of a free person into the personal household service of another person without first of all securing a contract warranting the servant's freedom, and (7) by marriage to a slave without securing such a warranty. Not only was a full slave the property of his *hosudar* (as the owner of a *kholop*, in ancient Rus, was called), as well as of his *hosudar's* heirs, but he could hand on his dependent position to his children. Consequently rights over a full slave, as well as the status of the slave himself, were hereditary. The essential feature whereby *kholopstvo* was distinguished from all other "bonded" forms of private dependency was its non-terminableness at the will of the slave. He could leave it only at the will of his owner.

In Muscovite Rus there sprang from full slavery several different forms of mitigated, conditional bondage. Thus from personal servitude —more especially the servitude of a *prikazchik* (clerk), *tiun* (attorney), or *kliuchnik* (steward) in the household of a master—there arose, at the close of the fifteenth century, or else at the beginning of the sixteenth, what was known as *dokladnöe kholopstvo* or "referred slavery"—so-called because the bondage deed had to be accompanied by a *doklad* or "referment" to the local *namiestnik* or civil governor. This form of slavery was distinguished from full slavery by the fact that rights over a "referred" slave varied in their conditions. Sometimes they came to an end with the death of the master; sometimes they passed to that master's children—though not further. Again, I have spoken of *zakladnichestvo* or "self-pledging," which arose at various periods, and was governed by various conditions. Its original and simplest form was a personal "pledging" or hire under an obligation to work for the receiver and to live in his household. Neither the *zakup* of the times of the *Russkaia Pravda*[1] nor the *zakladen* of the appanage period nor the *zakladchik* of the seventeenth century were slaves, since their bondage could terminate at the will of the bonded person, whose debt became extinguished either by its repayment or by the fact of the labour contract having come to an end. "They shall serve their term, and thence go forth, in that they have performed their service for the roubles ; but if they shall serve not their term, they shall render all" (*i.e.* they shall return the whole of the money lent). So runs a decree of the fifteenth century. Other pledge-contracts there were whereby the *zakladchik* was not bound to extinguish his debt by any measure of service, but only to pay the interest in service ("to serve for usury") and, on the expiry of the agreed term, return the *istina* or borrowed capital. Such a "loan contract" was, in ancient Rus, known by the borrowed Jewish name of *kabala ;* and the personal dependency which arose out of an obligation to "serve for usury" was confirmed by a deed which, to distinguish it from the loan *kabala* accompanied by a personal pledging under a contract of labour, was known either as a *sluzhilaia kabala* (service *kabala*) or a *kabala za rost sluzhiti* (a *kabala* of

[1] See vol. i. p. 186.

service as usury [interest]). It is from the close of the fifteenth century that persons figuring as *kabalnïe* first begin to make their appearance. Yet not until long afterwards do we remark in them any signs of actual *kabala* bondage. In those days a *kabala* entered into on the strength of a personal "pledging" was essentially a *zazhivaia kabala*, or a *kabala* which gave the *zakladchik* the right to work off his debt without interest ; whereas a *rostovaia* or *sluzhilaia kabala* ("usury" or service *kabala*) compelled the bondsman to work off the interest in household service, without thereby becoming emancipated from his obligation to return also the capital within the stipulated term. Such, then, were the *kabalnïe* who figure in documents previous to the middle of the sixteenth century, and they were the only *kabalnïe* of whom the *Sudebnik* of 1550—which code fixed fifteen roubles (700 to 800 roubles in modern currency) as the extreme limit of a loan advanced upon such a personal "pledging"—had cognisance. Also, from a law of 1560 it is clear that *kabalnïe* under a *rostovaia* or *sluzhilaia kabala* could be sued for the repayment of their debt : a sure sign that they were not yet become "bonded" persons or serfs, but still remained "pledgers" who possessed the right to redeem themselves if ever they should be able to do so. Also, we learn from the same law that hitherto there had been *kabalnïe* who, if unable to repay their *kabala* loan, were wont to request their master-creditors to take them either into full or into "referred" slavery. The law of which I am speaking forbids this course, and prescribes that, as in former times, insolvent *kabalnïe* shall be handed over to their creditors until they (the *kabalnïe*) shall have repaid or completely worked off their debt. This prohibition; the readiness of *kabalnïe* to enter into full slavery; the evidence given by the English Ambassador Fletcher (who, in 1588, was informed, in Moscow, that the law permitted a creditor to sell the wife and children of a debtor who had been handed over to him for permanent or temporary slavery),—all this shows that *kabalnïe* were drawn in two directions—in the direction of full slavery by their own usage with regard to their masters and domestic servitude, and in the direction of temporary bondage by the law. In this struggle *sakladnichestvo* that was conditional upon service in lieu of interest developed into slavery; yet it did not do so into full slavery—only into that of *kabala*. Nevertheless the usually insolvent condition of persons who thus surrendered themselves to their master led to their being forced practically to work off their debt in perpetuity; whence the *kabala* caused service in lieu of interest to become an extinction of the debt itself, and personal *zakladnichestvo* in return for a loan to become a personal hiring on the receipt of a sum in advance. This combination of "interest" service with the extinction of the debt, added to the personal nature of the *kabala* obligation itself, became the juridical basis of the service *kabala* as a form of bondage. By it also the limit of *kabala* service was fixed. As a personal obligation binding one person to another, *sluzhilaia kabala*, or the service *kabala*, lost its validity on the death of one of the two parties. During the seventeenth century we meet with *kabali* which were accompanied by an obligation on the part of the *kabalni* "to serve his lord in the household until he (the slave) shall die." But in the event of the master predeceasing the slave this condition would have infringed the personal character of the *kabala*, since it would have forced the *kabalni* to serve also the wife and children of the deceased, as though he were an hereditary chattel. In passing it may be said that there were two categories of domestic servants for whom a different event fixed the limit of their service; that event being the death of their master. A law of 1556 ordained that a prisoner of war who had been legally handed over to slavery should serve his master "so long as he (the master) shall live." The other of the two categories consisted of persons who, under like circumstances, entered into personal servitude which included neither a loan nor a hiring. In 1596 we see a service *kabala* concluded whereby a free person bound himself to serve a master without a loan, but merely "upon the substance of the same" until that master should die; after which the servant, with his wife and children, was to be free, and to have left to him and to his children "whatsoever of substance he shall then hold." In this case we see three conditions expressive of the personal nature of the service *kabala*—namely, only *life* possession of the *kabalni* by the master, inalienableness of that possession by the master, and right on the part of the *kabalni* to retain what he should have earned during service. In this case the additional juridical conditions of the *kabala* service were established by agreement, since, up to 1597, we know of no *ukazi* legalising *kabalnie* or prisoners of war to exact them at their own pleasure. With the establishment of *life* duration only of the *sluzhili kabali* this form of service acquired the character of servile bondage, since the *kabalni* agreed to renounce his right of self-redemption, and his bondage was to come to an end only with the death, or at the will, of his master. As early as 1555 an *ukaz* of that year presents the *sluzhilaia kabala* in the light of an act of "bonding" that was equal both to full and to "referred" slavery, while a testament of 1571 uses the phrase "*kabalnïe kholopi* and *rabi*" in place of the hitherto customary expression "*kabalnïe liudi*" (or, more simply, "*kabalnïe*"). At that period there also became established a well-known form of the service *kabala* which lasted, unchanged, for a century. This was the form whereby a freeman—alone, or with his wife and children—borrowed of a given person (usually a member of the State service class) a sum of money for the space precisely of one year, under an understanding that he should "serve for usury in the household of his master all the days of the year, and store up money against the term, and for interest to his master, and serve him daily." This stereotyped formula makes it clear that the norm followed in its composition was that of a terminable "pledging" which had a person, not an article, for its subject, and provided for a possible failure to redeem. Not infrequently, also, *zaklad* contracts of this sort resemble service *kabali* in their conditions, and even in their phraseology. Thus, in 1636, we find a father surrendering his son to a creditor "to the end that he may serve for one year," but under an obligation which required the father, should he fail to repay the money to term, to surrender the son to the creditor as a permanent household bondsman.

It was in this position that an *ukaz* issued to the *Kholopii Prikaz* (Government Office of Slaves) on April 25th, 1597, found *kabala* servitude. The object of the *ukaz* was to regulate slave-ownership by establishing a permanent system of its ratification. Yet it introduced nothing new into the juridical composition of *kabala* bondage—it merely confirmed and formulated its already sufficiently complex relations. After ordaining that only *sluzhilia kabali* should have legal force which stood registered in the *kabala* records of the Muscovite Court of Slaves, and by the town clerks of provincial boroughs, the law commanded that *kabalnïe*, with their wives and such of their children as were named in their *kabala* deeds, should remain in slavery, under the terms alike of those deeds and of deeds of "referment slavery," until the death of their masters ; that where *kabalnïe* proposed to redeem themselves the masters should refuse to accept the money ; and that the Court of Slaves should entertain no petitions from *kholopi* on the subject, but hand them over into servitude, according to the terms of their *kabali*, until the death of their masters. As for the children of a *kabalni* who were named in his deed of contract, or who should be born during his term of slavery, they were to be bound to their father's master until the latter's death. Yet among the regulations of this law there were some new features which at least reveal the covert contempt in which the ruling classes held the people's labour.

Along with *kabalnie* there existed, at that time, certain free-serving men who served their masters without *kabali*, as mere freely-hired domestics —as "willing (*i.e.* voluntary) slaves." Indeed, some of them had served for ten years, or more, without ever desiring to become their masters' *kabalnie*. Consequently they had retained a right which had been recognised by an *ukaz* of 1555—namely, the right of leaving their service whenever they pleased. But now for such free-serving men the above law of 1597 appointed a maximum term of service—namely, half a year. Any man who voluntarily served a master longer than six months was to surrender himself into *kabala* to that master, and the latter was thenceforth to provide him with "food, raiment, and shoes." Karamzin appraises this ordinance aright where he says that it was not only "a law unworthy of the name in respect of its unrighteousness," but also a law which had been published "only that it might please the highly-born *dvoriane*." Yet this restriction of free service was not accomplished without fluctuations of legislation, since, though the Boyar-Tsar, Vassilii Shuiski, had resort to the law of 1555, the *Boyarskaia Duma* fixed half a year as the maximum term of free service, and the *Ulozhenie* shortened this brief term by one-half. In the *ukaz* of 1597 there is another regulation which shows clearly the interests which inspired the authorities under weak Tsar Theodor. I have said that by a law of 1560 which opposed the extension of full slavery insolvent *kabalnie* were forbidden to sell themselves either into full or into "referred" slavery to their master-creditors; but by the above law of 1597 it was decided that absconding *kabalnie*, on apprehension by their masters, might pass into heavier bondage to those masters if they (the absconders) so willed it. Consequently the last-mentioned of these laws weighted, rather than lightened, "bonded" servitude. Abraham Palitsin gives us some further details concerning the legislative tendency, since he tells us that, under Tsar Theodor, the nobles (more especially the kinsmen and adherents of the all-powerful minister, Boris Godunov) and the leading *dvoriane* were infatuated with a lust for enslaving anyone whom they happened to come across; that they enticed men to become slaves by all sorts of kindnesses and gifts; that they constrained them to "inscribe themselves into service" (*i.e.* to bind themselves to become service *kabalnie*) by force and torture; and that some such persons they would even invite to their houses "but to drink wine," and when the unsuspecting guest had drained three or four goblets—well, by that time he had become a slave. After Tsar Theodor was gone, however, and Boris had succeeded him, there followed a period of scarcity when the masters saw that they could not possibly feed such a multitude of menials. Accordingly they bestowed upon some their freedom, and others they dismissed unfreed; while a third section absconded on its own account; with the result that, during the Period of Troubles which followed, all this mass of human wealth—human wealth so heinously acquired, only to be dispersed like dust to the winds of heaven—repaid with interest its former masters!

I have touched upon the history of *kabala* servitude only in so far as is necessary to explain its action upon the fortunes of the seigniorial peasantry. At first sight it is difficult to discern any points of contact between two such different social statuses as that of the slave and that of the peasant, since the one person was a non-taxable individual, and the other a taxable—the one worked in the household of a master, and the other on a master's land. Yet in that master lay the points of contact, since he served as a common knot for all the juridical and industrial relations of the two parties, as well as acted as director of the same. We have seen that, on the accession of the new dynasty, the relations of the peasantry to the land and to the landowners still remained indefinite. A law which Vassilii Shuiski issued in 1607, concerning the personal attachment of peasantry to their landlords by registered lists, lost, during the Period of Troubles, its force, and the *selo* or rural settlement returned to the system which had become established at the beginning of the seventeenth century. Peasant contracts continued to be concluded on the old conditions of voluntary agreement. "He shall do unto me *izdielïe*[1] according unto this writing, even as I will perform unto him this treaty at his pleasure, and inscribe the same in the records,"—so ran the contracts in question. But the passage of properties from hand to hand soon caused peasants who were not bound by long residence, or by any obligations of indebtedness, to be able to remove whither they willed, and incoming landlords had nothing to do with them or their stock, but could only "release them utterly" as the documents express it. At the same time, both *starinnïe krestiané* (old-established peasants who had been born on their lots or had grown up under one and the same landlord) and *starozhiltsi* or "old dwellers"[2] (*krestiané* who had exceeded ten years of settlement) remained where they were, whereas peasantry who had recently settled with the help of a loan from their landlord could be transferred, after he had set them up in business, to any other of his estates. Also, the peasant still worked off the interest on the *ssuda* or

---

[1] See vol. ii. p. 201.   [2] See vol. ii. p. 225.

landlord's loan by *izdielie* or *barstchina* (agreed labour for the landlord); which liquidation of interest by labour gradually caused the *krestianin*-debtor to approximate to the *kabala* bondsman, since the peasant's *izdielie* was personal labour for a master similar to the service of a *kabalni* "for usury," except that the latter performed indoor work, and the latter out-door. "He shall go unto the *dvor*, and shall there do the work of the same"—so it is phrased in contracts. Industrial similarity led also to juridical approximation. As soon as there became legally established the idea that *kabala* obligation extended not only to the acts, but also to the person, of the *kabalni*, and made him a bondsman, the idea began more and more to make its way into the minds of private landowners, and into their relations with their peasantry. It was a notion whereof the general diffusion received an added impetus from the slave quarter, since the move-ment of the peasantry towards slavedom met a contrary movement of slavedom towards peasanthood. Consequently by the side of the peasant-agriculturalist doing work for a seigniorial establishment there appeared the household menial converted into an agriculturalist. The Period of Troubles had swept like a hurricane over the country, and denuded the central provinces of the bulk of their peasant inhabitants; which gave rise to such a crying need for agricultural labour that the private land-owners were forced to turn to an old resource of theirs, and to seek new hands among the slave class. That is to say, they now began to settle their arable estates with household menials, to grant the latter loans in advance, and to fit them out with cots, implements, and plots of land. Also, with those slaves they concluded special agreements which, like the agreements concluded with peasantry, went by the name of *ssudnia zapisi* or "loan contracts"; and in this fashion there arose among slavedom a rural class which came to be known as *zadvornie liudi*, for the reason that such folk lived in special huts behind (*za*) the homestead (*dvor*) of their landlord. It is a class which first figures during the second half of the sixteenth century, since in deeds of 1570–1580 we meet with establish-ments called "*zadvoria*" or "*zadvornia dvorishki*" — *i.e.* cots placed behind the large seigniorial mansions; and throughout the seventeenth century the number of this non-free rural class is seen to be continually on the increase. Thus in agrarian registers for the first half of the century such persons are scarcely noticeable; but during the second half of the century they figure, in many localities, as the customary, as well as the largest, constituent section of the agricultural population. For instance, a register of the canton of Bielozersk for the thirties of the seventeenth century shows us that "peopled" cots belonging to slaves (nor were those slaves by any means constituted solely of *zadvornïe liudi*) formed rather less than nine per cent. of all the *krestiané, bobili* (non-arable-landholding peasants), and slaves residing in special cots on the estates of the service landowners ; whereas by the year 1678 a similar register shows us that the local *zadvornïe liudi* alone numbered twelve per cent. of the whole. In time this class had added to it a section of the seigniorial domestic staffs, known as *dielovïe liudi* or "men of all work." Although we find these menials described in registers as living in the mansions of *pomiestchiki* and *otchinniki*, they were identical, in their industrial and juridical position, with the *zadvornïe liudi*. The latter came of all sections of slavedom, but more especially of the *kabala* bondsmen ; yet their position as slave-homesteaders or holders of cots exercised a certain juridical effect. This was owing to the fact that a law of 1624 made *zadvornïe liudi* themselves responsible for any crimes which they might commit, instead of their masters. Hence, to a certain extent, their substance must have been looked upon as their own, even if not wholly so. Also, *zadvornïe liudi* were attached to the person of their landlord by a special method—namely, by the method that they had to render a "loan contract" to their landlord, not only if settling "from freedom" "behind" the seigniorial mansion, but also if passing thither from the ranks of domestic slavedom. Thus their contracts created a special form of slavery which served as a transitional stage between domestic service and peasant agriculture.

In a register for 1628 we find a *pomiestchik* recording that, on a *pustosh* or area of unoccupied land which he had settled with tenants, he had "set his household *kabalnïe* and old-time folk among the peasantry, and had accorded unto them a loan." This does not mean that he converted his slaves into actual *krestiané*, for such a change in their position would have rendered them freemen, and converted them from non-taxable persons into taxpaying agriculturists—neither of which results would have suited the *pomiestchik*. For a long while past it had been the custom to settle slaves on arable land ; it was a custom which constituted an ordinary condition of private agrarian industry ; but, until now, it had never been said of such slaves that they were settled "among the peasantry." To settle a slave "among the peasantry" was an expression taken, not from jurisprudence, but from the new practice observed in agrarian relations ; and it shows us how nearly the *krestianin* had come to approximate to the *kholop*. At about the same period there appears also in peasant-land-owner contracts a purely *serf* condition, since in a "loan contract" come down to us from the year 1628 a freeman binds himself "to live with my master among the peasantry, and to seek my sustenance, nor to depart thence." This condition of inability of the peasant to remove at will assumed various forms of expression. Formerly the *krestianin*, on settling upon a plot with the aid of a loan from his landlord, wrote, in his "loan contract," that, should he depart without first of all fulfilling the obligations which he had undertaken, the landlord should be free to make him responsible for the loan and a forfeit in compensation both for the landlord's industrial loss and for the landlord's legal expenses in prosecuting the peasant—but not more. Now, however, the peasant's obligation to pay compensation on removal had added it to another condition. "He, my *hosudar*, shall be free to recover me thence unto himself"; "Henceforth I will dwell upon this portion as a *krestianin*, and the holder thereof, and a renderer of *tiaglo*"; "Henceforth I will dwell as a peasant among the peasantry"; "Henceforth, for the loan which he hath accorded me, I will abide alway among the peasantry, and depart not thence." All these forms meant but the one thing—that the peasant renounced, voluntarily and for ever, his right to depart, and thereby converted the forfeit which extinguished his contract obligations into a penalty for desertion which neither restored to him that right nor annulled the contract. Soon this inability to remove at will became the customary concluding condition of a "loan contract"; whence also it came to constitute peasant serfdom ("peasant perpetuity" as it was called in the seventeenth century), and for the first time communicated to the "loan contract" the meaning of an act of enserfment which, though it confirmed the personal dependency of the peasant, failed to give him the right of all dependents to terminate their condition.

The chronological coincidence of peasant enserfment with the settling of slaves "among the peasantry" during the third decade of the seventeenth century was no mere accident, for both processes had a close connection with the great break of the day in State and seigniorial industry. The Period of Troubles had now dislodged from its haunts the great mass of the "old-dwelling" payers of *tiaglo*, both urban and rural, and so had disorganised the old provincial *miri* which had been accustomed to secure the tax-solvency of their members upon the circular guarantee; wherefore one of the first cares of the Government of the new dynasty was to re-establish those communes. Consequently at the *Zemski Sobor* of 1619 it was commanded that all *tiaglo*-paying inhabitants should be registered, and have their circumstances inquired into, while at the same time absconders should be returned to their old domiciles, and *zakladchiki* again be subjected to *tiaglo*. For a time the scheme proved a failure, because of the incompetence of the clerks and inspectors who were appointed to be its executors ; and this non-success, added to the great Muscovite fire of 1626 in which the agrarian registers of the metropolitan *prikazi* were destroyed, obliged the Government to undertake, during the years 1627–28, a new, and this time a general, census on the broadest and most careful lines. The object of the census was police-financial in its nature, since it was intended to ascertain the numbers of, and to attach to their domiciles, such taxpaying forces as the Treasury had at its disposal; and it was with a similar aim that, in later days (*i.e.* beginning with the time of the *Ulozhenie*), the same records were used. That aim was to collect evidence as to the existing relations between the peasantry and the landowners, to put an end to collisions, and to prevent future occasions of quarrel. Yet into those relations the census introduced no new norms, nor did it establish relations where none had previously existed. Rather, it left that task to the voluntary, private agreement of the two parties. Nevertheless this "listing in writing" according to place of domicile afforded a general basis for exercises of agreement, since it regulated them and also indirectly evoked them. The vagrant free agriculturist who was surprised by the census-taker on the seigniorial estate whither he had wandered for temporary "peasant resort," and where he had become registered to its owner, was forced, willy-nilly, to range himself with the rest of the peasantry who had settled there on conditions of voluntary agreement, and by that means to become doubly attached to the person of the owner—both through entry in the returns of the census-taker and through the contract which he (the peasant) had concluded. At this point our attention is caught by agreements which contain direct conditions of *kabala*. Some *krestiané*, before contracting themselves into seigniorial peasanthood, lived several years with their landlords on terms of voluntary agreement—*i.e.* without a contract, as in the case of *kabalnie ;* whereas others contracted to settle without the aid of a loan, and wrote in their agreements that, although from that day forth they would live among the peasantry of their landlord until the decease of the latter, they were to be free, when, by the will of God, the landlord was no longer in the land of the living, to remove whithersoever they willed—which was the fundamental condition of the service *kabala*. One *krestianin* in particular binds himself (as in a previously adduced contract of 1628) "to live among his lord's peasantry" until *his own* death, even as *kabalnïe* undertook to do; but more usually *krestiané* followed old custom by contracting themselves "out of freedom" for a loan, which they bound themselves to repay either in full on a certain date or by instalments at intervals. Most frequently these contracts pass over the point in silence, and merely undertake to repay the loan either in the event of the peasant failing to fulfil his industrial obligations or in the event of his absconding. However various, confused, and complicated the conditions of such peasant contracts may be, we can always discern in them the fundamental threads whereof peasant serfdom was knitted. The threads in question were police attachment to place of residence, loan indebtedness, the action of *kabala* bondage, and voluntary agreement. Of these elements, the first two formed the fundamental sources whence the landowner derived his right to acquire serf authority over his peasantry, while the other two had an official importance, as constituting the means for his actual acquisition of such authority. Also, these peasant contracts would seem to disclose the precise moment of passage from freedom to serfdom, as well as to point to the fact that there existed a connection between that passage and the general census of 1627, since the earliest known contract involving serf obligation may be assigned to the year of the census-taking. In this case certain "olden" (*i.e.* old-established) peasants of a *pomiestchik* concluded with him new agreements which included a condition that they "shall go not out, nor flee, from him, but shall remain bound unto him among his peasantry." As old-established peasants they would stand to him in definite and established relations, while it may also be that, through "old residence" (of more than ten years), they were in any case bound to their plots, and unable to quit themselves of the *ssudi* or loans which at one time or another they had received from him. However, they directly bind themselves, in their new agreements, to be "bonded as of yore unto" their old *pomiestchik*. Hence this new "bonded" condition must have been a juridical confirmation of a practically existing position. This police attachment to *tiaglo*, and to status according to place of domicile gave rise also to the question of attaching the peasant to the person of the landowner on whose estate he (the peasant) happened to have been registered. Yet of ready-made juridical norms for the purpose there were none; wherefore the custom arose of borrowing them, according to similarity of industrial relations, from various quarters—from the service *kabala* and from the *zadvorni's* "loan contract," and of combining in various ways, according to locality, the conditions of peasant *tiaglo* and the conditions of household servitude. To such an intermingling of heterogeneous juridical relations it was chiefly the break which took place (after the Period of Troubles) in the industrial system of the landowning class that led up. Formerly the chief subject of bargaining between the peasant leaser and the landowner had been land which entailed, as a condition of its tenure, an obligation to set apart for the owner either a portion of the products of the soil or a monetary tithe that should be equal in value to the same. In addition, the loan had always taken into account the *barstchina* or personal labour of the tenant for the landlord, as a supplementary rendering for the debt, as well as such of the peasant's property and stock as should be created with the help of that loan; but after the Period of Troubles these conditions of agrarian reckoning underwent yet a further change, since much land had now fallen waste and sunken in value, while both peasant labour and the landlord's loan had risen. The peasant needed the loan even more than he needed land, and the landowner was seeking for labourers rather than for tenants. This dual need explains a contract of 1647—of the period when peasant serfdom had become consolidated, and converted from personal bondage into hereditary—wherein it was not the peasant who gave an undertaking to remain with the *pomiestchik*, but the *pomiestchik* who bound himself not to evict the peasant from his old-established and developed holding: otherwise the peasant should be free to "go forth from" the *pomiestchik* "unto the four quarters of the land." The same dual need, added to the pressure of the general census of 1627, gradually converted peasant contracts from agreements concerning the use of seigniorial land into contracts of obligatory peasant labour; while the right to such labour became the basis for the landlord's assumption of authority over the peasant's personality—over his freedom. Thus (as we shall see later), the census was evoked by the Treasury's need for transferring agrarian tax-incidence from arable land to the tiller of the same; and this new adjustment of industrial relations threw the old juridical statuses into confusion. Slaves now began to enter peasanthood, and *vice versâ;* while household menials betook themselves to the cultivation of peasant land, and agricultural peasants resorted to household service. The total result of the confusion was to create peasant serfdom.

Although the law and the *pomiestchik* seem to have supported one another in this peasant-hunting, the agreement between them was but an external one, since the two parties were pulling in different directions. The State needed sedentary payers of *tiaglo* whom it could always, through its census lists, find settled on given plots, and know to be certain not to weaken their taxpaying capacity with private obligations, while the *pomiestchik* needed agricultural slaves who could not only perform efficiently "their *pomiestie* labour of ploughing and reaping and tending in the household," but also render tithes, and, above all, be ever at hand for sale, or for pledge, or for presentation as a dowry instead of land. To the Government of the first Tsar of the new dynasty—a Tsar who, though elected with the support of the Hierarchy and the *dvoriané*, was under obligations towards the boyars—it befell to have to settle accounts, in this matter of the peasantry, both with the great landowners, boyaral and ecclesiastical, and with the small *dvoriané*. Availing themselves of the grievous position of the taxpaying population when the Period of Troubles was over, the great landowners—*i.e.* the boyars, the prelates, and the monasteries—deprived the Treasury of a multitude of taxpayers by receiving into *zakladnichestvo*, or exempted pledgedom, to themselves, and under their powerful protection, large numbers of *tiaglie liudi* who included a proportion of peasants. Consequently, on July 3rd, 1619, the *Zemski Sobor* ordained that "such *zakladchiki* be as aforetime, wheresoever each of them hath been before the present." That is to say, it commanded that *dokladchiki* should now be re-subjected to *tiaglo*, and returned to their former domiciles. But for thirty years the leading *tchini*, both "black" and "white," repudiated this decree of the "Council of All the Land"; and it was only into the *Ulozhenïe* of 1649 that the deputies of the *dvoriané* and of the towns inserted articles finally ordaining confiscation to boyars and ecclesiastics who should settle their suburban properties with *zakladchiki*. Many other questions with regard to the peasantry still remained to be settled; yet the Government did nothing to expedite matters, for the reason that around Michael—a Tsar who was anything but serious—there stood not a single serious statesman, and the Government tackled current affairs only in desultory fashion, and allowed the course of events to tie such knots as later generations found themselves at a loss to unloose. But with the appearance of serf obligation in peasant contracts the legislature found it necessary to define with an exact landmark the respective spheres of State and private interest. The census list attached the *krestianin* to his status and *tiaglo*, according to his place of domicile; whereas the "loan contract" attached the *krestianin* to the person of his landlord, on the strength of a personal agreement. This duality found expression, in peasant contracts, in variations in the serf formula. In most cases the peasant says vaguely that "according unto this writing will I henceforth be a bondsman among the peasantry of my lord." Yet not infrequently he became attached to the person of his landlord through land tenure generally, not through mere specific definition of his holding; in which case he either binds himself to "live with" his master in such and such a *selo*, or "wheresoever he (the landlord) shall appoint unto me," or he bargains for a plot which "he, my lord, shall grant unto me according to my strength, and where I may prosper." Less often the peasant became attached to his landlord's person "according unto my portion of *tiaglo* land, and according unto this writing"; wherein he combined personal attachment with agrarian— he bound himself to remain permanently on a given *tiaglo*-paying plot, and "never to depart thence." Lastly, even rarer cases occur—indeed, we meet with them only towards the close of the seventeenth century— wherein attachment went by domicile or place of settlement, independently of the person of the landowner. For instance, a "loan contract" of 1688 adds to the customary obligation of the peasant to "live with" the landowner in such and such a *selo* the condition that he (the peasant) shall live "in that *selo*, no matter unto whom it shall, in the future, belong." In the same way, the law did not fix any term for peasant serfdom, nor any measure of the obligations which were entailed by the same, but entrusted the whole to voluntary agreement. In this respect, "loan contracts" were, as we have seen, reinforced by indefinite conditions of service *kabala*. In some localities—to judge by surviving peasant contracts which were concluded in the Zaliesskan half of the Novgorodian *piatina* of Shelon [1] during the years 1642–52—*barstchina* was an exactly defined obligation. That is to say, the *bobil*, or landless peasant, was forced to do work for his boyar master one day a week "afoot," and the *krestianin* the same one day or two days per week "with a horse," or one day the one week, and two the next. But these were mere local customs which grew up independently of the legal normalisation of agrarian relations. The stereotyped and general rule was that the peasant should "do all the work of the *pomiestchik*, and pay such *obrok* (tithe) as he shall lay upon me, and render quit-rent according unto my lot, even as my neighbours do"; or else that the peasant should "serve the *pomiestchik* in all things, and plough his cultivable land, and do his household labour," *et cetera*. Thus the ill-regulated struggle between private interests resulted in the leaving in a state of uncertainty of one of the most important questions in the Muscovite State order—namely, the

[1] See vol. i. p. 321.

question as to how far the landowner was entitled to exploit the labour of his "bonded" peasant. Either this governmental negligence was an oversight, or it was a faint-hearted yielding, on the part of a supreme legislature, to the interests of the *dvoriané*, who, as the stronger party, lost no time in availing themselves of their privilege.

Another governmental concession to the *dvoriané*, in the matter of the peasantry, was the abolition of "years of term"—*i.e.* of the time-limit for suits against absconding *krestiané*. From the beginning of the sixteenth century there had been in operation a five years' term, and in 1607 this had been increased to a term of fifteen years, and lastly, after the close of the Period of Troubles, restored to its old five years' duration. But this term was, in many cases, too brief a one to prevent an absconder from becoming lost to his landlord before the latter could trace and sue him for his desertion; wherefore in 1641 the *dvoriané* begged the Tsar "to render void the years of term." Nevertheless all that was done was to lengthen the time-limit for suits against absconding peasantry for ten years, and the time-limit for suits against *abducted* peasantry[1] to fifteen. In 1645, in response to a second petition from the *dvoriané*, the Government confirmed this *ukaz* of 1641; and finally, in 1646, when undertaking the compiling of a new general census, the Government so far listened to the insistent demands of the *dvoriané* as to promise, in a rescript of that year, that, "even as the *krestiané* and the *bobili* and their homesteads shall be inscribed, so also, in these records, shall the *krestiané* and the *bobili*, with their children and their brethren and their nephews, be bonded without years of term." This promise the Government fulfilled in the *Ulozheníe* of 1649, which legalised the recovery of runaway peasants who stood registered in the census returns of 1620 and the following years, as well as in those of the census of 1646–47, "without years of term." Nevertheless such abolition of the time-limit did not, in itself, change the juridical character of serfdom as a civil obligation of which the infringement was punishable only at the private instance of the complainant. All that it did was to invest the peasantry with another feature in common with slavedom, which stood subject to no time-limit for suits of recovery. But the ordinance which abolished the time-limit attached, not only the individual peasant, but also the entire peasant household—the entire peasant complex family[2] —to the landowner. That is to say, in addition to "listed" assignments to status according to place of domicile, embracing all peasant house-

---

[1] See vol. ii. p. 234. [2] See vol. i. p. 43.

holders, with their portionless descendants and their collateral relatives, it bound them to the *owner of the soil,* who henceforth acquired the right to sue them, like slaves, for desertion, regardless of any time-limit at all. Thus personal attachment was converted into hereditary. Nevertheless we may suppose that such an extension of peasant "bonding" was no more than a confirmation of a position which had long been practically a fact, since it had long been the common rule among the peasantry that a son, when succeeding, in the ordinary way, to his father's homestead and stock, did not conclude a new agreement with the landowner. Only when an unmarried daughter remained as heir did the landowner conclude a special contract with her betrothed, who thereupon could take possession of the daughter-legatee's home "and all her father's living." The ordinance of 1646 found reflection in the peasant contracts of the day, for from that time onwards there begins a succession of deeds which extend the obligations of the contracting peasantry to their families. Indeed, one unmarried *krestianin,* when renouncing his freedom, and bargaining, on terms of a loan, for some land belonging to the Monastery of St. Cyril of Bielozersk, extends the undertakings which he assumes therein to such a future wife and children as "God may grant him on espousal." This hereditary succession of peasant serfdom raised also the question of the relation of the State to the owner of "bonded" peasantry. During the sixteenth century the legislature had secured the Treasury's interests not only by attaching its fiscal peasantry to *tiaglo* according to plots or places of domicile, but also by setting limits to the migratory powers of the seigniorial peasantry; and at the beginning of the seventeenth century it instituted a similar class attachment to cover the other classes of the population. In this we see constituted a general partition of the community according to species of the State imposts to which each was liable; but in the case of the seigniorial peasantry the process was complicated by the fact that between the Treasury (in whose interests the partition was carried out) and the peasant there stood the landowner, who had interests of his own. The law did not interfere in private transactions between the two parties so long as they did not contravene the interests of the Treasury (which is why "bond" obligation was allowed to make its way into peasant contracts—the latter being private engagements with individual peasants, individual householders); but the situation had now changed, since to the person of the landowner there had become attached the entire peasant population of his lands, including even the portionless members of peasant families; wherefore personal attachment by *agreement,* by "*loan contract*," had become converted into hereditary attachment by *law*, by *registration*. That is to say, the peasant's old private and civil obligation had now developed into an obligation of *State*. Also the legislature had hitherto constructed its norms through collection and co-ordination of such relations as owed their origin to dealings between the peasant and the landowner; but in the *ukaz* of 1646 it elaborated a norm of its own—a norm designed to give rise to new relations, both in the industrial and the juridical aspect, while the *Ulozhenie* of 1649 was, in its turn, designed to provide for and to correct those relations.

Following its usual custom, the *Ulozhenie* maintained a superficial— even a false—attitude towards the bonded peasantry. In Article 3, Chapter XI., it ordains that "after this *ukaz* of the Tsar there shall be no forbidding of the State for anyone to take unto himself peasants" (the text is referring to runaway peasants); whereas a previous *ukaz* of 1641 says distinctly that "no man shall take unto himself the *krestiané* and the *bobili* of another man." Also, though Chapter XI. of the *Ulozhenie* is almost wholly taken up with absconding peasantry, it explains neither the essence of peasant serfdom nor the limits of seigniorial authority. Furthermore, though overlaid with additions taken from previous enactments, it draws upon no one source of its own. Yet, in forming an idea what peasant "bonding" meant according to certain casual articles in the *Ulozhenie*, we shall find those previous enactments useful in making good the shortcomings due to the inexactitude of the Code. The law of 1641 distinguished three constituent portions of peasant serfdom—namely, "*krestianstvo*," peasant substance, and peasant possession. Now, since peasant possession meant the right of the landowner to the labour of his bonded *krestianin*, and peasant substance meant the *krestianin's* agricultural stock and implements—all his "instruments of ploughing and the household"—it follows that "*krestianstvo*" must have meant the peasant's act of belonging to the landowner—the latter's actual right to the personality of the former, independently of his industrial position, or of the use which the landowner made of his peasant's labour. That right was chiefly confirmed by registers and census returns, but also by "other bondings" in cases where the *krestianin* or his father stood already registered to the landowner. Of the three constituent portions of peasant serfdom the innocuous use depended upon the degree of exactness and of prevision with which the law defined the conditions of peasant "bonding." According to the *Ulozhenie*, the bonded *krestianin* was hereditarily, and by succession, bound to the person, physical or juridical, to whom he stood registered in the census-roll or similar record. Also, he was bound to that person "according unto his (the *krestianin's*) land "—*i.e.* according to the plot, situated on a *pomiestïe* or an *otchina*, where the census had found him. Lastly, he was bound to the peasant, the *tiaglo*-rendering, status which he possessed through tenure of his plot of land. Yet none of these conditions does the *Ulozhenïe* state consecutively. It forbids the transference of *pomiestïe* peasants to *otchina* estates, since such a course acted to the detriment of the State properties which *pomiestia* represented. Also, it forbids landowners to conclude agreements of service *kabala* with their peasantry, or with the sons of the latter, or to grant *pomiestïe* peasants their freedom, since, in each case, these acts took the peasant out of his *tiaglo*-rendering status, and deprived the Treasury of a taxpayer. At a third point it decides to allow the emancipation of *otchina* peasantry. (See, in turn, Chapter XI., Article 30, of the *Ulozhenïe;* Chapter XX., Article 113; and Chapter XV., Article 3.) Moreover, the *Ulozhenïe* either silently admits or expressly confirms transactions between landowners which had the effect of wresting *krestiané* from their plots, and it admits the alienation of peasants from one landowner to another without occasion given by the peasant, but solely at the instance of the masters themselves. The *dvorianin* who, at a date subsequent to the census, sold his *otchina* and a number of absconded peasantry who were liable to be returned was bound, in lieu of those defaulting *krestiané*, to present the purchaser, from another estate of his, with "the same peasantry," however innocent the latter might be of the trick played upon them by their master. Similarly a *pomiestchik* who unintentionally killed another man's peasant could be mulcted of his "best *krestianin*, together with the family of the same," in favour of the owner of the murdered *krestianin* (Chapter XI., Article 7, and Chapter XXI., Article 71, of the *Ulozhenïe*). Thus the law guarded only the interests of the Treasury and the landowner; the authority of the *pomiestchik* met with a legal barrier only when it clashed with fiscal interest. Of the personal rights of the *krestianin* himself no account was taken; justice merely threw him into its scales, as an industrial detail, when it wished to restore the broken equilibrium of highly-placed interests. For this purpose even the peasant's family could be broken up. A serf girl who ran away and married a widower who was the *krestianin* or the slave of another master was, with her husband, given up to her former owner; but the children of her husband by his first wife always remained with the husband's former proprietor. This anti-ecclesiastical disintegration of the family was permitted by the law to take place equally in the cases of the peasant and of the slave (Chapter XI., Article 13, of the *Ulozhenïe*). One of the *Ulozhenïe's* most disastrous improvidences lay in the fact that it omitted to define the juridical essence of the peasant's *inventar* or stock. Neither the framers of the Code nor its deputy-supplementers (among whom not a single seigniorial peasant was numbered) thought it necessary to establish how much of a peasant's " living" belonged to him, and how much to his landlord. The unintentional murder of another man's *krestianin* paid, if a free man, such a "*kabala* debt" (*i.e.* compensation) for the murder as might have been epistolarily agreed upon (see Chapter XXI., Article 71, of the *Ulozhenïe*); whence the peasant seems to have been looked upon as capable of entering into obligations only in so far as he possessed property. But the peasant who married a runaway peasant girl was given up, together with his wife, to her former owner — but without his goods, which were retained by the owner of the woman's husband (see Chapter XI., Article 12, of the *Ulozhenïe*); whence the peasant's *inventar* or stock was only his industrial belonging as a peasant, and not his rightful property as a person of full rights; and he lost it if he married a runaway girl or even if his landlord so willed.

This duality of the law is explained by the legal practice which we see disclosed in private instruments; wherefrom it is possible to discern the composition and, in certain aspects, the true juridical importance of the peasant's effects. Such effects included agricultural appliances, money, live stock, seed-grain, flour, clothing, and "all manner of household stores." Also, peasant contracts show us that, though a peasant's effects might pass to his children, wife, or daughter in the form of inherited property, as well as to his son-in-law by way of a dowry, this could only take place with the consent, and by the will, of the landowner. Not infrequently a free bachelor *krestianin* who, with empty hands (" with nought pertaining unto him save soul and body "), became, "for a term of years and for living," an inmate of a *pomiestïe* peasant's household ended by marrying his host's daughter, and binding himself to his father-in-law to live in the same homestead with him for a given number of years (*e.g.* eight or ten), and to have the right, on completing the said years, to set up a separate establishment, and to take from his father-in-law (or, after the latter was dead, from his son) a half or a third, not only of the available stock, but also of " what shall lie in the byres and in the land, in the field ploughing and in the gardens." The same process of marriage sometimes took place in the case of peasants' orphaned daughters and widows, through the fact of lodgers going to reside in their cots, and then succeeding to the effects of their late fathers or husbands. Although these effects were "possessed" by the peasants whose daughters or widows the newcomers married, it was from the owner of the estate himself that the bridegrooms received both their goods and their brides, since they became contracted "into the peasantry" of that owner, and were numbered with his "bonded" *krestiané*. This conjunction of two "possessors" in a single property may be explained by the dual origin of the peasant's effects, in that they usually owed their existence to the peasant's labour, aided by the landlord's loan. The *Ulozhenie* has shown us that the husband of a runaway peasant girl lost, when surrendered to the owner of his bride, his goods ; but in peasant contracts of the thirties of the seventeenth century we meet with some even more striking cases—cases not provided for by the *Ulozhenie*. Such documents show us that, though runaway peasants and the wives whom they married after absconding might be given up to their former owners, the property which had been inherited by those wives from their fathers or first husbands was retained by the said wives' masters—the persons who had permitted the unions ! Also, masters seem to have considered that they had a right to alienate the goods of their peasantry by agreement with third parties. In 1640 a freeman, on marrying the foster-daughter of a *krestianin*, contracted himself " into the peasantry " of that *krestianin's* master on right of *kabala* (*i.e.* until the master's death), coupled with a condition that, as soon as he had spent certain agreed years in the house of his father-in-law, he should be free to take either from the latter or from his son one-half of the existing effects, and, with his wife, to " go forth into freedom "—though to the direct detriment both of the peasant *dvor* and the peasant community. Hence it is clear that a peasant's effects were property practical possession of which was distinguished from right of ownership, since the former belonged to the "bonded" peasant, and the latter to the landowner. This rather resembles the *peculium* (private property of a slave) of the Roman law, or the *otaritsa* of ancient Russian jurisprudence. In fact, the seigniorial peasant of the time of the *Ulozhenie* harked back, as regards propertied status, to the position of his social precursor, the *roleini zakup* of the *Russkaia Pravda*.[1] Effects—or *sabini* as they were called during the seventeenth century—could be possessed also by slaves, who, on the strength of the same, could enter into property transactions even with their master. In a service *kabala*-contract of 1596 a slave, in

[1] See vol. i. p. 186.

binding himself to serve a master "for his (the master's) lifetime," also binds that master, on his decease, to give the bondsman both his freedom and licence to depart with all such goods as he, the bondsman, "shall have gained." Legally a slave had no right to property of his own, and could impose such an obligation as the foregoing only in consideration of moral deserts. It is clear that the *Ulozhenïe* looked upon the effects of bonded peasants in the same light that it regarded those of slaves. Not otherwise could it have imposed the debts of *dvoriané* and "sons of boyars" who should be unable to remain solvent on their *otchini* or *pomiestia* equally upon their *kholopi* and *krestiané* (Chapter X., Article 262, of the *Ulozhenïe*). This also explains the "*kabala* debts" of bonded peasantry of which I have spoken. That is to say, a bonded peasant could, on the strength of his effects, enter into certain obligations, and, in case of failure to fulfil them, have his goods distrained upon equally with those of the *zadvorni kholop*. It is worthy of note that the peasant's effects appear with the character of slave property at the very time when the "loan contract" had begun to show traces of bond obligation, since in 1627–28 we meet with pleas entered by *pomiestchiki* that peasants of theirs had absconded and "taken with them *their* goods" (horses and so forth) to the amount of such and such a sum. Serf right had not yet become fully established as a State institution; wherefore the landowners, though calling the effects of peasants the peasants' property, must, in reality, have been suing for property of their own which had been purloined by the run-aways. *Snos*, purloined goods, was a term of slave diction, and meant any property of a master which a runaway slave had carried off either with him or on him (clothes, *et cetera*). Consequently, from the earliest stages of peasant serfdom the *krestianin* found himself in the position of a *tiaglo*-paying slave; and recognition of peasant effects as masters' property, without the *krestianin* having any legally defined juridical share in the same, was not a result, but one of the bases, of the enserfment of the seigniorial peasantry. It was the norm into which their longstanding indebtedness through the *ssuda* had at length become cast.

Attachment by registration and the "loan contract," as the juridical means of hereditary "bonding" of the peasant; the *ssuda*, or landlord's loan, as the economic basis of the master's right to his peasant's effects; *barstchina* in return for a plot of land, as the source of the master's right to discretionary disposal of the bonded person's labour—here we have the three skeins which became drawn into the deadly net which is known to us as peasant serfdom. In drawing that net close the legislature was guided, not by any feeling of equity, nor by any calculations of the public gain, but by consideration of what was possible. Consequently it was not law that it was creating, but a mere temporary position. This view continued throughout the times of Peter the Great, and is forcibly expressed by the peasant writer Pososhkin where, in his book *Poverty and Riches*, he says, that, while the *pomiestchiki* held the peasant but temporarily, "they did hold the Tsar alway." Probably they looked upon their serfs as they did their lands—that is to say, as State properties lent for temporary use to private persons or institutions. But how came the Government so complacently to subordinate to private interest the labour of the bulk of the population which maintained that Government in being? The answer is that, in this respect, the shortsighted Government relied upon an existing position of affairs which had been created, partly by the legislature, partly by the *de facto* relations of former days. For a long time past many landowners had possessed the right to judge their *krestiané* in all matters save such serious criminal cases as sacrilege, murder, and theft with disposal of the stolen goods. Also, we have seen that, during the sixteenth century, the landowner became an intermediary between his peasantry and the Treasury in regard to fiscal payments, and that in certain cases he discharged those payments on their behalf.[1] During the seventeenth century isolated local phenomena of this kind grew into customary, general relations, and when the census of the thirties of that century had been taken there became added to the landowner's judicial authority a right of police supervision over the *krestiané* who stood registered to him. On the other hand, the industrial conditions of the seigniorial peasantry— conditions which were due to loans, exemptions, forced labour, and tithes —became so interwoven with the industry of the landowner that here too it became difficult for the parties to distinguish themselves from one another, and in collisions between a landowner's peasantry and extraneous persons—especially in agrarian disputes—the landowner naturally took the lead of his *krestiané*, as owner of the subject of quarrel. In this connection the *Ulozhenie* merely states it (in Chapter XIII., Article 7) as a common, longstanding, and customary fact of its time that "they, the *dvoriané* and sons of boyars, do make inquiry and give answer for their peasants in all matters save theft and robbery, and the making away of goods, and assaults unto death"; by which is meant that the landowners represented their *krestiané* in all such legal affairs connected with outsiders as they, the landowners, had the right of deciding. Yet, though the

[1] See vol. ii. p. 231.

estate court, the landowner's powers of police supervision, and his competence to interfere in the affairs of his peasantry were the three judicial-administrative departments of authority wherein he replaced the government *tchinovnik*, these functions had the importance of obligations rather than that of rights; and to them, to supplement the shortcomings of the weapons available for the Government, there became added a fourth function which was designed to safeguard the interests of the Treasury. Peasant serfdom was permitted only on condition that the taxable peasant should not, on becoming a serf, cease also to be a competent payer of *tiaglo*. This *tiaglo* he rendered on his taxable plot in return for the right of engaging in agricultural labour on the same, and as soon as ever his labour was handed over to the disposal of his landlord, there passed to the latter also the duty of sustaining him (the peasant) in his ability to pay *tiaglo*, as well as of answering for his tax-solvency. This converted the landowner both into an honorary inspector of peasant labour and into a responsible collector of fiscal dues from his *krestiané;* while at the same time, as regards the peasant, it converted those dues into one of the assets of the seigniorial *tiaglo*, even as the peasant industry which produced those assets formed part of the seigniorial property. For runaway peasants the landowner had to pay taxes until the register had been revised, and the *Ulozhenïe* recognises it as an established rule that "all ingatherings of the State shall be taken, for the peasantry, from their *otchinniki* and *pomiestchiki*," and that for the contributions of runaway peasants one general collection (of ten roubles per year) shall be made of their receivers, both as representing the State's dues and as representing the landowner's income.

This legislative recognition of the responsibility of landowners for the tax-payment of their peasantry was the crowning work in the juridical construction of peasant serfdom, for in this norm there met and became reconciled with one another the interests of the Treasury and the interests of the landowner—interests essentially divergent. Private landownership now became a general police-financial agency for the State Treasury, and from constituting the latter's rival became its assistant. This reconciliation could not but act to the detriment of the peasant's interests. Nevertheless, in the first formation of peasant serfdom to which the *Ulozhenïe* of 1649 gave confirmation, that serfdom was not placed upon a complete level with slave bondage, though it had been constructed according to its norms, since law and judicial practice still continued to draw faint lines of distinction between the two. This is evidenced by the following features.

(1) The bonded peasant still remained a payer of fiscal *tiaglo*, and was allowed to preserve a tinge of civic individuality. (2) As the owner of a person of this kind, his master was bound to fit out the peasant with a plot of land and the stock of an agriculturist. (3) The peasant could not be rendered landless by reception into the household; but he could become landed by bestowal of his freedom. (4) The peasant's effects, though his only as in a state of serfdom, could not be taken from him "by violence" (to use Kotoshikhin's expression). (5) The peasant was free to complain of any levies which might be made of him by his master "with force and with robbery," and could sue for the return of what had been seized. Nevertheless the poorly developed state of the law helped to obliterate these features, and to impel peasant serfdom in the direction of slavery. This we shall see when we come to study peasant industry and the economic results of serf right. Hitherto we have studied but the origin and composition of that right. In conclusion it need only be remarked that, with the establishment of serf right, the Russian Empire entered upon a road which, under cover of a certain external orderliness, and even of a certain prosperity, led to a disorganisation of the popular forces which was accompanied, not only by a general lowering of the nation's life, but also, from time to time, by a series of upheavals.

CHAPTER X

ONE of the results of the segregation of classes or corporations was a new political sacrifice, a new loss for the Russian State order. I refer to the cessation of conventions of the *Zemski Sobor*.

The most mordant element in this mutual alienation of classes was serf right, which was constituted of the bondage of slaves and *krestiané*; and the moral action of that right was wider even than the juridical, since it greatly lowered the already far from high level of Russian civism. In the great blunder of serfdom all classes of the community shared to a greater or a less degree, and directly or indirectly according to its different forms: from the privileged " white " ranks, clerical and lay, with the " loan contracts " which they forced upon their peasantry and the various species of *kabali* which they imposed upon their slaves, to the common people—even to the slaves of boyars—with the " living contracts " which they entered into for various terms of years. But where that right exercised a specially detrimental effect was upon the position and the political education of the landowning classes. Permitted by the law, and upheld by police force, serf right made the " owners of souls "[1] themselves slaves to the powers which went to that upholding, as well as foes to every power which was turned in a different direction. Meanwhile the most energetic, the most vital, of all interests in landowning circles came to be the mean, pettifogging struggle between masters and serfs, and between masters themselves on their serfs' account ; until, gradually developing into a profound social cleavage, the struggle retarded the regular growth of the people's forces, and caused the landowning *dvoriané*, as the ruling class, to impart a warped and monstrous tendency to every form of Russian culture.

---

[1] *i.e.* of serfs and their families.

This effect of serf right disclosed itself, during the seventeenth century, in the clearest possible manner.   During that period the time of the *Kholopii Prikaz* was fully taken up with pleas of masters concerning the abscondings and larcenies of their hirelings and peasantry, and concerning such persons' incitements to, and praise of, mendacity and insinuation and arson and murder and every sort of malfeasance; for the entry of a plea was necessary in order to obviate responsibility for the runaway if, during his absence, he should embark upon a course of theft or assassination. Yet every bondsman of the kind absconded—from the ordinary serf up to the foreman of hands and stores who had served, perhaps, twenty-five years, and now sat "above with writing" by the side of his master.[1]   Runaways also made off with their own chattels—with clothes, live stock, and goods which were directly the property of their masters ; sometimes to as large an amount as, in modern currency, would be equal to two or three thousand roubles.   Especially eager were they to steal their masters' chest of serf indentures, since they could then destroy any evidence which could be used for their capture, or to prevent them from changing their names in their new abode.   But this sort of thing only spurred the masters to greater efforts, and, in the hue and cry for runaways, the former would send out domestic hounds of the chase, which, at sight of their old household acquaintants, when the latter were overtaken, would fawn upon and betray the identity of the quarry, "in that they did know the same." These flights of serfs would be carried out either by single families or by several families banded together.   For instance, from the establishment of a *podiachi*, or lawyer, whose private residence was in Suzdal, a serf absconded with his family and certain of his master's goods, after attempting to fire the house in which his mistress and her children were.   Upon that the lawyer, who happened at the time to be in Moscow on duty, "did set forth thence, to take them who were fleeing"; whereupon, no sooner had he left the capital, than another serf who was in his metropolitan service also absconded, "together with sufficient of his substance,"—the whole affair taking place in Suzdal and Moscow within a space of eight days. Though social statuses and relations, in themselves, had nothing in common with serf right, they became drawn into it, and consequently mutilated.   In 1628, a *diak's* or State clerk's *kabala* bondsman named Vassika absconded with his wife, and, a few years later, returned to the said *diak* as a priest named Vassilii who had been ordained by the Metropolitan

---

[1] *i.e.* working as private secretary in the master's living-rooms, which were ordinarily on an upper floor.

of Kazan and Viatka. (Afterwards the *Ulozhenie* enacted that such or-dained ministers should, if come of the slave class, be forwarded, at the suit of their masters, to the ecclesiastical authorities, for treatment "according unto the rules of the Holy Apostles and of the Fathers." See Chapter XX., Article 67, of the *Ulozhenie*.) In this case the *diak* accepted the priest "Vassilii" as properly appointed; with the result that, before a year was out, "his serving-man, the priest Vassilii, with his wife, did flee from the *diak*, and take unto himself twenty-eight roubles, the monies of the same." The conditions of serf right also served to enslave the work of popular education in its most elementary forms. For the purpose of being taught his letters, a boy would sometimes be handed over to a schoolmaster under a "living contract" that was made out for a term of years, and included an added right, on the part of the preceptor, to cure his pupil of disobedience "with all manner of chastisement." In 1624 the directress of a Muscovite almshouse entrusted her son, for such educational purposes, to the priest of a convent in the city. Also, in company with the pupil's grandmother, who was a pensioner of the same convent, she went bail both for her boy's good behaviour and for the condition that he should live with his tutor, and "do all and sundry the work of the household." Chariton, the tutor in question, taught the boy for four years, but contrived to make out the bond contract for twenty; whereupon the mother and the grandmother, perceiving that Chariton "had made of the boy a man, and had taught him all manner of writing," whereas there still remained sixteen years during which he could retain the boy as his serf, decided, after conference with suitable persons, to steal the lad from the priest, and to let the latter sue for the boy's return. The upshot of the matter we do not know. In reading the adventures of runaway serfs, as we find them in official documents, we almost forget that we have to deal with a Christian community which was armed with every power, ecclesiastical and of police. In one case a runaway household serf who had abandoned his wife and children wandered, with a changed name, from one seigniorial mansion to another, and stated that he was free and a bachelor. At last he contrived to get married on such an estate, and to become registered, under a second *kabala* contract, in the *Kholopii Prikaz*. But his new wife proved "to be not loving unto him"; wherefore he cast her off, and, "calling to mind his fault," returned to his old master, "that he might steal away his (the serf's) wife and daughters." The project, however, proved unsuccessful. It is a story which may be read in a document of 1627, and similar adventures on the part of serfs became so common that the *Ulozhenïe* actually animadverts upon the point in Chapter XX., Article 84, of the Code.

Also, the enserfment of the peasantry entailed upon territorial representation a double injury, political and moral. Hardly had the *Zemski Sobor* begun to settle down as an elective, pan-national, representative council when there became lost to its composition almost the whole of the rural-agricultural population. That is to say, the *Sobor* became deprived of the territorial ground upon which it had hitherto been based, and began to represent only the State services and the urban taxpaying communities, with their narrow corporate interests. Bringing but a *few* of the classes into contact with the Throne, it failed to attract to itself either official attention from above or widespread confidence from below. The petty features of serf life which I have adduced from private documents show, by their very pettiness, the level and the scope of those everyday interests and relations with which the wielder of serf right made his appearance among the people's representatives. In the ruling landowning class, which stood estranged from the rest of the community through its privileges, and was immersed in the sordid details of serf proprietorship, and weakened by unpaid labour, the sense of territorial interest had now grown dim, and the energy of social activity enfeebled. The seigniorial mansion, which oppressed the hamlet and had nothing to do with the town, could not get on even with the metropolitan chancellory, and thus prevented the *Zemski Sobor* from ever acquiring the status of an independent director of the provinces' thought and will.

The *Zemski Sobor*—the Territorial Council or "Council of All the Land"—of the Muscovite Empire of the seventeenth century was constituted of "all ranks of men," or "all sorts of men from all the towns of the Russian *Tsarstvïe*," to quote the Council's own documents. Also, then, as during the sixteenth century, the Council comprised two distinct and unequal sections—namely, an elective section and a non-elective or official section. The latter consisted of the two supreme administrative bodies; which, when attending the Council, did so in their full complement, or even in one increased by the addition of persons who did not usually form part of them. Those two supreme administrative bodies were the *Boyarskaia Duma* (augmented by certain *diaki* from the *prikazi*) and the Holy Synod (consisting of the Patriarch and the bishops, and augmented by certain invited archimandrites, abbots, and archpriests). The elective composition of the *Zemski Sobor* was exceedingly complex.

This fact arose from the non-cohesion and variety of the various electoral units or *statii*, which were, firstly, the superior service *tchini*, or ranks, of the capital (the *stolniki*, the *striaptchïe*, the metropolitan *dvoriané*, and the metropolitan burghers) and, secondly, the superior commercial ranks of the capital (the *gosti*,[1] the members of the *sotnia gostinnaia*, and the members of the *sotnia sukonnaia*—all three being guilds of merchants). Each such rank sent its own deputies to the Council. After the metropolitan *dvoriané* came the provincial-urban *dvoriané*, but in this case the electoral unit was not the *tchin*, but the cantonal class corporation, which consisted of *three tchini*—namely, of the *vibor* (the highest town rank), the local *dvoriané*, and the local "sons of boyars." Only in two provinces—namely, those of Novgorod and Riazan—were the electoral units not whole cantons, but fractions of them ; being, in the former province, fifths or *piatini*, and, in the latter province, portions of eight *stani* or communal districts apiece. *Liudi pribornïe* or "added men" (*i.e.* members of the State service class who did not belong to the hereditary *dvoriané*), with, among their number, the alien members of the class in question, also sent elected deputies of their own to the Council ; the metropolitan members of this category sending deputies from their units of organisation (for instance, *Strieltsi* from the *Strieletski Prikaz*, or from actual regiments of that body), and cantonal members of the same category sending deputies from the various suburban cantonments of *Strieltsi*, Cossacks, and artillery men wherein these folk were settled. As for the representation of the taxpaying population, it was rather simpler, in that, in this case, the territorial electoral unit prevailed, in the shape of the local community or petty provincial *mir,* instead of in that of the college of *tchini* or scattered class corporation. The township—or, more strictly speaking, the townships—of Moscow were divided into "black hundreds" and "black appurtenances," and the latter of these numbered, during the first half of the seventeenth century, thirty-three. Moreover, certain of their titles are still preserved in the street names of Moscow, and serve as indications of the ancient localisation and industrial importance of these guilds. In the case of the provincial townships, boroughs constituted integral districts to themselves. Thus elected deputies were chosen from the *dvoriané* and the commercial circles of the capital according to *tchini ;* from the urban-provincial *dvoriané* according to class corporations ; from the "added" or supernumerary State servitors of the capital according to units of organisation ; and from the "added" State servitors of the pro-

---

[1] See vol. ii. p. 300.

vincial towns, as also from such of the taxpaying portions of the population
as stood represented at the Council (metropolitan and urban-provincial
portions alike), according to *miri*.   Also, at the Council of 1613 we see
the above-mentioned classes headed by deputies of the urban clergy and
of the "cantonal people" (*i.e.* rural population).   Yet it is not altogether
easy to guess the precise system of their election.   To the charter electing
Michael to the throne we see the archpriest of Zaraisk setting his hand
"both for himself and in stead of the chosen priests of his town and the
canton"; yet the manner in which these elected urban and rural ecclesiastics,
headed by their archpriest, acquired their plenipotentiary powers—whether
at a general convention of all the clergy of Zaraisk (as an ecclesiastical
college of the canton) or otherwise—is not clear from the document.
Still more difficult is it to elucidate the representation of the so-called
"cantonal people."   In a canton, more especially in the southern and
south-eastern districts which lay contiguous to the Steppes, there sometimes lived large settlements of "added" State servitors, in the form of
Cossacks.   These, however, were numbered with the urban, not with the
rural-cantonal, inhabitants, and, in signing the charter of 1613, they, like
the other deputies, are to be found set down according to their special
avocation, to their calling of Cossacks.   Consequently we can only
suppose that the term "cantonal people" refers to the peasantry, and
that, like the non-service or taxpaying population, they stand, in this signing of the charter, always alongside the urban provincial residents.   But
the charter shows them as existing in such cantons as those of Kolomna
and Tula, where, as early as the close of the sixteenth century, registers
cease to show the presence of any fiscal peasantry.   Hence the "cantonal
people" of the Council which elected Michael must have been *seigniorial*
peasantry, and in the year 1613 have been looked upon as still free, and
as belonging to the State.   In the maritime towns of the North, where
service landownership was weak or altogether absent, the cantonal
peasantry, both in matters of local industry and in the performance of
their fiscal obligations, were fused into one community with the urban
residents of their townships, and constituted, with them, a single territorial
and cantonal *mir* which repaired to the *zemskaia izba*, or police station of
the townships, "for counsel"—*i.e.* for the drawing up of joint representations to the *Sobor*, if it be that they figured there as "the cantonal
people."   Yet whether, in the year 1613, this was so in the case also
of the southern towns, or whether the local cantonal peasantry formed
electorial *curiæ* distinct from their townships, I cannot say.   At all

events at later *Zemskie Sobori* the deputies of the clergy and of the "cantonal people" disappear, and the Councils lose their pan-corporate composition.

The number of deputies chosen by each electoral unit or *statia* was variable, and had no significance. At the Council of 1619 it was decreed that a new *Sobor* should be convened at Moscow by selecting from every town one ecclesiastic, two *dvoriané* and "sons of boyars," and the same number of burghers; while to the Council of 1642 there were summoned from the "great *statii*," or more populous units, from five to twenty deputies apiece, and "from the people not many in number" from two to five deputies. Again, to the Council of 1648 the *ukaz* summoned from the service ranks of the metropolis and the provincial corporations of the "great towns" two representatives each; from the "lesser towns" one each; from the provincial town districts, the "black hundreds" of the capital, and the metropolitan suburbs one each; from the superior "hundreds" two each; and from the associations of *gosti* (the highest rank of metropolitan merchants) three each. Yet fulness and uniformity of representation were never attained, or were unattainable. At the Council of 1642 we meet with, among its 192 elected members, 44 deputies from the service ranks of the capital (namely, 10 *stolniki*, 22 metropolitan *dvoriané*, and 12 *zhiletsi*); while to the Council of 1648— one of the fullest and most numerous of all these gatherings, since present at it there were no fewer than 290 elected members—there were summoned only 8 representatives of the service ranks of the capital. All the Councils of whose composition we have any knowledge lacked deputies from whole series of corporations of *dvoriané* and provincial-urban residents, for the reason that the preliminary local conventions of *dvoriané* were sparsely attended, and "there were none from whom" to select deputies, while, in the case of the townships, there had happened to be few or no burghers in residence, "and the *voievoda* hath written that the small men of the towns are about thy tax-gathering, O Tsar, and about the collecting of dues in those parts, as thy *tsielovalniki*." Thus the composition of the Council was, in general, very variable, and destitute of any fixed, permanent organisation. Indeed, in this respect it is difficult to pick any two Councils which resembled one another, and at few such Councils do we meet with deputies from *all* ranks and cantons, or from *all* the electoral units. At the Council of 1648 there were present representatives of *dvoriané* and provincial burghers from 117 cantonal towns; whereas at the Council of 1642 there were present only deputies of *dvoriané*—and those but from 42 towns. At hurried conventions of the Council it was thought sufficient if only deputies of such provincial *dvoriané* as happened at the moment to be on rota service in Moscow were present; while at other times the Council consisted of metropolitan members alone. On January 28th, 1634, the Tsar convoked a Council in connection with a new tax-levy for war purposes, and it met next day; yet at it there were present, among its metropolitan members, only "such *dvoriané* as were then in Moscow."

Deputies to the Council were elected at local meetings and conventions, which were held in the cantonal towns at the invitation, and under the supervision, of the urban *voievodi*. *Ukazi* prescribed that there should be elected "such of the best men as shall be good, prudent, and steadfast" (*i.e.* men of substance, equity, and good sense); wherefore the *statii* endeavoured to choose of their best, and the provincial *dvoriané*, in particular, selected deputies from their highest town rank, the *vibor*. Literacy, however, was not an indispensable condition of election. Of the 292 deputies who attended the Council of 1648 we know nothing as to the literacy of 18; but of the remaining 274 members no less than 141—*i.e.* more than half the entire Council—were unlettered. The electoral protocol which was signed by the local electors—the "charter of election given under hands"—was forwarded to the *voievoda*, as a warranty of the fitness of those elected "for the work of the State and of the land"; after which the *voievoda* dispatched the chosen deputies, together with their writ, to the *Razriadni Prikaz* in Moscow, in order that the regularity of their election might be verified. One *voievoda*, however, is found writing to Moscow that he has fulfilled the Imperial *ukaz*, and is sending to the Council (of 1651) two of the "best *dvoriané*" in his canton; but that, with regard to the two "best townsmen," he has come to the conclusion that his town contains at most three available burghers, who are poor men "such as do wander about from house to house," and are quite unfit for the business in hand. Hence, he concludes, he has commissioned a "son of a boyar" and a *pushkar*, or artillery officer, to represent his township at the Council. Upon this the clerk of the *Razriadni Prikaz*—a man zealous for the freedom of provincial elections—dockets the warrant with a strict injunction that it shall be returned, "together with an upbraiding," to the *voievoda*; "for," writes the clerk, "it hath been commanded unto the *dvoriané* that they shall choose men from among themselves, and it is not for him (the *voievoda*) so to choose, and for this he shall be blamed, in that he hath done foolishly as *voievoda*, and, apart from the people of the town, hath sent in their stead a son of a boyar and a *pushkar*." It is not clear whether deputies brought with them any written instructions from their electors. Only in 1613 does the temporary Muscovite Government of the day write, in its writs to the towns for the sending of deputies for the election of a Tsar, that those deputies shall first of all confer with their electors, and then take of them "full covenants" regarding the Imperial election. The reason is that this was an occasion of exceptional importance—an occasion which demanded national unity and an independent mandate from the people; and for the same reason, in 1612, when marching with Minin to relieve Moscow and call a Council there, Prince Pozharski writes that the towns shall send their chosen representatives "with counsel inscribed under hands" (with written and signed instruction from their electors) as to the best manner in which the leaders of the relieving army may make a stand against the common foe, and elect a Tsar. However, none of the official documents of these Councils refer to such written instructions, nor do the deputies themselves ever mention them. Each deputy was given a certain field of action, and at the Council of 1641 a representative of the *dvoriané* of Koursk even went so far as to figure as an accuser of his own townsmen, by presenting to the Tsar a report wherein "he did speak all manner of evil against the churls of the town," in charging them with shameful behaviour on the Church's holy days. Nevertheless this jealousy on behalf of rightness of conduct exceeded the powers of a deputy, and called forth a warm protest from the "churls" referred to, who threatened, in return, "to work all manner of harm unto" their traducer. Even in the absence of formal instructions the very source of his powers bound a deputy to act in agreement with his electors—to be an intercessor "for all such needs of his brethren" as had been laid before him on election; and from the affair of the deputy of Koursk we see that electors considered themselves to have a right to call their representative to account if an *ukaz* should not be issued for the purpose of remedying the needs of local populations, as voiced at the Council. A similar construction was put upon representation by the Government itself, for in 1619 it summoned deputies from the clergy, the *dvoriané*, and the urban populations "who should be able to tell of all offences and all deeds of force and destruction, to the end that the Tsar might know of men's need and oppressions and all manner of lackings, and, having heard their petitions, should be able to think of them, for their welfare." Thus the popular deputy-petitioner

of the *Zemski Sobor* of the seventeenth century replaced the administrative agent of the *Sobor* of the sixteenth, and the petition in council became
the norm of popular representation—the highest means of legislative
interaction between the supreme power and the people.   How far, in
particular, the system helped the wretched departmental draft of the
Ulozhenie of 1649 to be supplemented and improved we have already
seen.

But such a relation of popular representation to authority could not
well contain anything that was peremptory, or binding upon that authority,
or juridical.   The two parties could decide questions in Council only by
means of mutual exchange of their psychological attitudes.   This found
expression in the system whereby those questions were considered.   The
electoral Council of 1613, as an exceptional gathering which had also a
dispositive importance, cannot be taken as a normal instance; but on most
other occasions the *Sobor* was convoked by means of a special Imperial
ukaz.   Once, and once only, did the Holy Synod take upon itself the
official initiative in the matter; which was when Michael's father, on
returning from a Polish prison in the year 1619, consecrated himself to the
Patriarchate, and then, with the spiritual authorities, approached the Tsar
with suggestions concerning various disorders in the Muscovite Empire.
Thereupon the Tsar, with his father, the Holy Synod at large, the boyars,
and "all the men of the Muscovite State," "did make a Council," and
debated the best means of righting matters, and of organising the country.
This instance can be explained by the fact that the Patriarch was not only
president of the Holy Synod, but also Tsar-Coadjutor.   Usually the Tsar,
on a given matter being raised, issued an *ukaz* for "a Council to be made,"
and opened it (either in the Palace Dining-Hall or in the Hall of Angles)
in person—either by "speaking himself in the Council" or commanding
that, in his presence, the chief *diak* of the *Boyarskaia Duma* should read
"unto the hearing of all men a letter"—*i.e.* a Speech from the Throne—
concerning the matters about to be submitted for the Council's consideration.   Thus, at the Sobor of 1634 the Tsar propounded that, for the
continuation of the war with Poland, a new and extraordinary levy would
need to be made, and that, unless it were made, the State Treasury would
"no longer be able to be."   On this occasion, also, the Tsar's speech
ended with a statement to the Council that "the Tsar will ever bear in
mind your aid, and be forgetful of naught; wherefore he deigneth now
to bless you with his Imperial blessing in all measures which shall be
taken."   Thereafter the members of the Council (among whom we notice

the presence of no provincial-urban deputies at all) said, in answer to the Speech from the Throne, that they would "grant the monies, having regard to each man's thrift, and according as every man may be able to give." That was all: the question would seem to have been decided in a single day, at a single general session, and at a single sitting of that session. Six days later the Tsar appointed a special commission (of a boyar, an *okolnich*, the Archimandrite of the Tchudes, and two *diaki*) to collect the levy. But according to an Act of the Council of 1642 a similar question was, on this occasion, submitted to a complex procedure which may have been adopted also at other Councils, and since became fined down in the process of compiling summarised expositions of such of their Acts as have survived to us. In 1737 the Cossacks of the Don seized Azov, repelled the Turkish assaults, and presented the captured fortress to the Tsar; whereupon at a Council at which the Tsar himself was present, with the spiritual authorities and the *Boyarskaia Duma*, the clerk of the latter body declaimed the Imperial *ukaz* which had convened the Council, and then, in the presence only of the *Duma*, read aloud to the assembled deputies a letter wherein the Tsar propounded the double question: Shall Rus go to war with Turkey and the Crimea over Azov? —and if so, where is the money (which will be needed in large quantities) to be obtained? The letter also charged the deputies "to think of this in common, and to state their thoughts in writing unto the Tsar, by letter, to the end that he may know of all things concerning the matter." After the reading of the Imperial rescript it was distributed "to the chosen men of all ranks, for the judging of the same by each man in the presence of the boyars"; while upon the ecclesiastical authorities there was also laid a special charge that, after separate consideration of the matter, they should furnish the Tsar with an epistolary statement of their opinions. As for the clerk of the *Duma*, he acted as interrogator to the deputies when requesting the pronouncement of each one on the matter. Other Councils also there were where the various deputies were "questioned apart," and returned individual answers by "statements" or "memorials." Indeed, this system of "questions apart" was one of the regular forms of pronouncement in Council. Another form is to be met with at the Council of 1621, when to a proposition by the Tsar and the Patriarch that war should be declared against Poland the deputies responded with a petition in favour of that course. The difference between the two forms—*i.e.* between the statement in answer to question and the petition in answer to proposition—lay, so far as we can judge from official documents of these Councils, in the fact that the "memorial" in answer to question set forth the opinion of the members on the matter in hand, but left the ultimate decision to the Tsar; whereas the petition in answer to proposition gave a more decided response to the proposition of the supreme power, and also (it may be) complicated the matter with some cognate proposition on the part of the members—a course allowed also in the "answers to question." The service deputies at the Council of 1642 were divided into three groups, whereof the *stolniki* formed one, the Muscovite *dvoriané*, the chiefs of *Strieltsi*, and the *zhiltsi* another, and the provincial-urban *dvoriané* a third; while over each such group was set a special *diak*—probably for their guidance, but more especially for editing their written opinions. Only to the metropolitan commercial deputies was no *diak* appointed; nor do we see any urban deputies from the cantons at this Council. Yet this grouping did not govern the manner in which the opinions themselves were rendered. On the occasion of which we are speaking eleven written "sayings" or "statements" were presented—namely, from the spiritual authorities, from the *stolniki*, from the metropolitan *dvoriané*, from two members of that class who differed with their fellows and desired to present a special opinion, from the metropolitan *Strieltsi* (although no opinions from the *zhiltsi* are contained in the Council's records), from the urban *dvoriané* of Vladimir, from the *dvoriané* of three other sub-metropolitan (*i.e.* central) towns, from the *dvoriané* of sixteen other central and western towns, from the *dvoriané* of yet another group of twenty-three towns (mostly southern ones), from the *gosti* and other metropolitan guilds, and from the metropolitan "black hundreds" and minor guilds. In this order the protocols are to be found inserted in the Council's Act, after the list of names of the 192 deputies who were present. According to the "statements" of these deputies, representatives of the *dvoriané* were in attendance from forty-three cantonal towns instead of from the forty-two which are to be found specified in the list of names; which discrepancy arose from the fact that in the presentation of protocols no part was taken by the deputies of the *dvoriané* of eight of the towns which are entered in the names-list, while deputies from nine towns not named in that list took part in the presentation. It is difficult to see how this happened, but it may be remarked that not only the deputies of the provincial-urban *dvoriané*, but also such of their constituents as happened to be in service at the time in Moscow, took part in the framing of the protocols. Thus the above-mentioned protocol of three cantonal towns makes mention of "men of Luchi who be here in Moscow":

while in the names-list there is mentioned, as present from the town of Luchi, only one deputy. Furthermore, the deputies of urban *dvoriané* who are to be found set down in the list of names of this Council do not seem to have been summoned thither from their own towns, but chosen in Moscow from among the *dvoriané* who were there on rota service. The *ukaz* whereby the Council was convened was composed on January 3rd, and on January 8th the presentation of the "statements" began. This expedition in procedure explains the absence from the Council of any deputies from the provincial townships. Also, the protocols of deputies at all such gatherings have a certain internal connection among themselves, since some members borrowed opinions, or individual expressions, or whole passages from one another. The deputies would assemble, somewhere and somehow, by groups, and then confer together, exchange ideas, and, according to their "statements," draw up and correct their protocols. For instance, the "statement" of the above twenty-three towns resembles, in many respects, the protocol of the sixteen, while the opinion of the "black hundreds" and the minor guilds must have been composed according to the "statement" of the *gosti* and two superior "hundreds," but with an added class application. Of *general* debates in the Council, however, we can see no sign, nor yet of any general decree by the Council—the main question being decided in the negative by the Tsar and the boyars, for the probable reason that the protocols were couched in such a deprecatory tone. The present of Azov from the Cossacks was declined, and war was not declared upon Turkey and the Crimea, inasmuch as no money was available, nor yet anyone from whom to raise it.

Although these Councils did not invariably proceed on the lines of that of 1642, the detailed general protocol of the year in question helps us to explain the political importance of the *Sobori* of the seventeenth century. Then, as during the sixteenth century, they were convoked on extraordinary occasions for the consideration of graver matters of State organisation and foreign policy, but more especially for the consideration of questions of war and the financial burdens entailed by the latter. The change which took place was not in the powers of the Council, but in the nature and composition of popular representation, since in this connection the Government had to deal, not with its own official agents, but with elected intermediaries on behalf of the needs and "lackings" of electors. The political significance of these gatherings depended upon the part taken in them by the *Boyarskaia Duma*, headed by the Tsar; and, as regards this point, we note the existence of a dual system whereby the *Duma* acted either jointly with the elected representatives or apart from them. In the latter case the Tsar and the boyars were present only at the reading of the list of proposed measures; after which they withdrew without further participating in the work of the deputies. At the same time, that work was limited to conferences in groups and renderings of individual opinions, and never was a general and inclusive session held, or any decree of the whole Council drawn up. Under the system the *Sobor* acquired a mere advisory or informative importance—the Tsar and the boyars taking the opinions expressed by the deputies for their guidance, yet retaining the legislative stage, the ultimate decision of the question, for their own settling. Thus did matters proceed at, for instance, the Council of 1642; and we have seen the same thing done at the Council of the *Ulozhenïe*, held in 1648. The draft *Ulozhenïe* was read to all the deputies together, and then reported to the Tsar and the *Duma*, who were sitting in another chamber, apart from the deputies; the latter having appointed to them also a special committee of three boyars, to act as a kind of *praesidium*. Yet this division of function did not render the *Duma* and the *Sobor* in any way comparable to an upper and a lower chamber of parliament, as they are sometimes called, since the *Duma*, under the Tsar, was not merely one of the legislature's organs—it was a supreme administration which combined within itself the whole complement of legislative power. While listening to the reading of the articles of the draft *Ulozhenïe*, the *Duma* from time to time amended and confirmed them, and so created laws; whereas the *Sobor*, the Council of Deputies, did not stand *alongside* the *Duma* on this occasion, but figured as a body attached to it merely as a codificatory committee; and while hearing the *Ulozhenïe's* articles recited by the reader, it from time to time framed petitions to the Tsar concerning the alteration or augmentation of those articles; which representations were then forwarded, through the committee, to the Tsar and the boyars, who considered these " petitions from all the ranks of the people," and, with the help of the documents in question, pronounced new laws. On other occasions, however, the deputies took a more direct share in the work of lawgiving. This was on occasions when the *Duma*, headed by the Tsar, became an actual part of the *Sobor*, as though fused with it into a single legislative body. At such times the boyars stated their opinions equally with the deputies, and a general decree in Council was framed which received the force of a law, while the *Duma* acted also as the dispositive authority which took measures to execute that law. This is the system to be observed in operation at all the Councils under Michael which followed the electoral Council of 1613—namely, at the Councils of 1618, 1619, 1621, 1632, and 1634. The Council of 1621 is a particularly good instance in point. Turkey, the Crimea, and Sweden had invited Moscow to join them in a coalition against Poland, and to the Muscovite Government this had seemed an excellent opportunity for getting even with the Poles for what they had done during the Period of Troubles. Accordingly, at the Council convened to consider the matter the spiritual authorities bound themselves to pray " for victory, and for the conquering of our enemies"; the boyars and other service ranks undertook to fight valiantly against the Polish King, and to spare no pains in the effort ; and the commercial deputies swore to contribute such means as the substance of each man would permit. In addition, a *general* decree was framed that, allied with the Sultan of Turkey, the Khan of the Crimea, and the King of Sweden, all ranks should withstand the Polish King, while the *dvoriané* and " sons of boyars," in particular, laid before the Tsar a petition that he would enroll them according to towns, in so far as each man was able to serve the State—" to the end that no man be in default" : but the actual *ukaz* for enrolling the *dvoriané* and sending letters to the towns with announcements of the Council's decree and commands that all members of the service class should prepare themselves for the field, and " feed their horses," and " lay up store," was promulgated by the two Tsars (father and son) " after speaking with the boyars"—*i.e.* it was promulgated by a decree of the *Boyarskaia Duma* alone, without any participation of the *Sobor* therein.

This legislative significance the *Sobor* retained until the last few years of Michael's reign—*i.e.* until the Council of 1642. Yet the same significance reappears later, at the Council of 1653, when deputies and boyars spoke on equal terms with one another in the debates ; and though the former were, as in 1642, " questioned apart and by ranks," the ultimate decision to accept Bogdan Khmelnitski into Muscovite allegiance was arrived at by the Tsar on the advice of the Council as a whole, and not merely in accordance with a decree framed by the boyars. Even the purely advisory *rôle* (such as that played by the Council of 1648) was not infrequently interrupted by a legislative interlude, as when, for instance, " the Council was charged " to forbid ecclesiastical institutions thenceforth to acquire, or to " take in pledge," the estates of members of the State service class. Yet the very duality of the Council's voice—now as an advisory, now as a legislative organ—reveals to us the political instability of representation at these gatherings, and how borrowed a light was the Council's legislative authority, seeing that, being secured by no warranty, it served less as a recognition of the claim of the popular will to be a political force than as a gracious, yet fleeting, extension of authority to subjects—an extension which, while detracting nothing from the fulness of that authority, weakened its responsibility in case of mischance. In short, the extension was a grant, not a concession, and enables us at length to explain the various irregularities in the Council. Before us we have elections, electors, and elected. We hear questions put by the Government, and answers returned to them by the representative deputies. We witness a delivering of advice, of opinions, and of decrees. In a word, we have all the procedure of representation. Yet what the precise political limits of the Council may have been we cannot tell, since we can note no establishing of any particular system of action, and no exact defining of dates when the Council should meet, no defining of any uniform composition or competence for the Council, and no defining of set relations which were to subsist between it and the superior governmental institutions. Forms we see without norms, and plenipotentiary powers without rights or guarantees; yet also we see the very circumstances and the very motives which usually give rise to norms and guarantees, though with the circumstances entailing no consequences, and the motives resulting in no sort of action. How active a source of popular representative rights the need of a Government for money has often been in the West we know; we know also the extent to which that need has led to the convoking of all orders in the State, for the purpose of soliciting their help: yet never have those orders helped the Treasury for nothing, —always they have extorted concessions, and with their subsidies bought rights and guarantees. So, too, in Rus of the seventeenth century were such occasions and such motives not lacking. Of all the Russian Councils of that century, with the exception of the Electoral Conventions, only three had no visible connection with finance. The three Councils in question were the gatherings of 1618 (when the King of Poland's son, Vladislav, was in process of moving upon Moscow), of 1648 (the Council of the *Ulozhenie*), and of 1650 (when, in connection with a rebellion at Pskov, the Government was for bringing the Council's moral influence to bear upon the rebels). In short, emptiness of the Treasury was what served as the Government's most frequent and suggestive reminder of the existence of the *Zemski Sobor*. Whenever the balance of the State's ordinary income and expenditure failed to become re-established after a period of disturbance, recourse was had both to extraordinary imposts and to the exaction of loans or non-returnable levies from the capitalists. Without this the Imperial Treasury was powerless to "continue to be." But such ingatherings needed the sanction of the country at large. For instance, in the year 1616 there were requisitioned of the rich Stroganov family 40,000 roubles, over and above the family's assessed annual taxation of 16,000 roubles—the same being set by the Government against the Stroganovs' future payments to the Treasury; and this huge demand—amounting, in all, to over 600,000 roubles in modern currency —was ratified by "a decree of all the *miri* of the *Zemski Sobor.*" When "the supreme power and the men of all the towns" jointly decreed, it was difficult to disobey! For the non-taxpaying classes these requisitions by the Council took the form of voluntary subscriptions offered on behalf of the State's extra needs. In 1632, at the beginning of the Polish war, the *Sobor* made an agreement with the non-taxpaying classes that, for the maintenance of the military operations, "each man should give as he could"; and the spiritual authorities also stated in the Council the exact amounts which they were prepared to grant from their domestic and private funds, while the boyars and the State servitors promised to furnish lists of what each member of those orders could contribute. To voluntary giving of this kind the Council imparted, by decree, the form of an obligatory self-assessment, and thus revealed to the Treasury the quarters whence it could reap the income which, indispensable though it was, was also unattainable unless the *Sobor* should give the necessary permit. Thus in this matter the Treasury was wholly dependent upon the *Sobor.* The electors would take compassion upon the administration, and dower it with money without demanding—yes, even without requesting—any rights in return, since they (the electors) remained satisfied with the gracious, but not necessarily binding, promise of the Throne that "the Tsar will ever bear in mind your aid, and be forgetful of nought; wherefore he deigneth now to bless you with his Imperial blessing in all measures which shall be taken." Clearly, then, the idea of equal representation, joined with political guarantees of such representation, had not yet dawned in the minds of the Government and the community. In fact, the *Sobor* was still looked upon merely as an instrument of the Government. To give advice, when asked by the country, was not the *Sobor's* political right, but an obligation on the part of the territorial councillors of exactly the same sort as the renderings demanded by the Treasury of the taxpayers.

Hence the indifference of the electors to provincial representation. The deputies from provincial towns attended the Council much as they would go on military service, and rendered there their quota of "counsel"; while their electors attended the electoral conventions in the towns in such an unwilling spirit as often to necessitate a second intimation from the *voievoda*. Though possessing no support in its political ideas, the Council found none in the structure of the administration, as then adjusted, nor yet in its composition.

When the Russian community came to be confronted with a series of difficult questions, as a sequel to the Period of Troubles, no single person, no political party, no closelocked ring of administrative officials, found himself or itself able to decide them; wherefore the collective intelligence of the country had to be called in, and the general result, together with what had been attained by the individual intellects of governmental and ordinary-official personages, was collated into the mentality of a single pan-territorial Council, and expressed in decrees or petitions by that Council. We might well have expected that this status of the Council as regards the central administration would have caused the deliberative, the pan-territorial, principle to gain support, and even an increase of strength, in the *provincial* administration also, since popular representation without local self-government is unthinkable, and a free deputy and non-free electors constitute a contradiction in terms. As it was, the epoch of the *Zemski Sobor's* increased activity chanced to coincide with a temporary decline in provincial institutions, and with the subordination of those institutions to the central *prikazi*. This was because the new dynasty's legislative policy was bent in two opposite directions. With one hand the Government of that dynasty destroyed what with the other hand it created. That is to say, at the very time when deputies were being summoned from the provinces to decide questions of higher administration in the company of the boyars and the metropolitan *dvoriané*, the electors of those deputies were being delivered into the power of those boyars and *dvoriané*, and thus the centre, the seat of the *prikazi*, became the last refuge of the territorial-representative principle just at the time when the officials of the *prikazi* in question were making themselves masters of the provincial cantons. This contradiction disclosed itself also in another quarter. Soon after the Council "of the men of all ranks" had become an operative institution, and had created a new dynasty, almost the whole of the rural population (85 per cent. of the whole, or, with the court peasantry, 95 per cent.) was taken out of the composition of the free community, and its deputies ceased to figure at *Zemskïe Sobori*, and deprived those gatherings of all semblance of pan-territorial representation. Finally, with the segregation of classes into corporations, the structure of the individual classes fell to pieces, and their mutual relations sank into disorder. The Council of 1642, for instance, witnessed an utter discord of opinions and interests. To the question of war with Poland the Holy Synod returned its stereotyped answer that, in the matter of military affairs, " the conduct of the same doth belong unto his Imperial Majesty and the boyars of his State, and hath never been customary unto the clergy of the State." Nevertheless it promised, in the event of war, to contribute what it could towards the army. As for the *stolniki* (an order of metropolitan servitors of State) and the metropolitan *dvoriané*, they, as the *élite* of the *dvoriané*, the *garde du corps*, answered tersely that they would leave it to the Tsar to decide the question of war and of obtaining the necessary men and means for the same, so long only as he would command the Cossacks to retain Azov, and send a few volunteers to help them. Yet two *dvoriané* named Bekle-mishev and Zhelabuzhki thought it right to append to their brethren's statement a closely reasoned postscript, wherein they advocated the acceptance of Azov, and also an equal distribution of the burdens of the impending war among all classes, not excepting even the monasteries. But the loudest utterances on the subject came from the lower depths of the community, as represented in the Council. Indeed, two rescripts pre-sented by the provincial-urban *dvoriané* of 39 central and southern cantons constitute a sharp political *critique* of the existing order of things, coupled with a programme of reforms for the future, since they are full of bitter complaints concerning the ruin wrought by non-equalisation of the burdens of State service, and also by the privileged position of the metro-politan *dvoriané*, more especially those in service in the Court Depart-ment. But the gravest beam in the eye of the provincial-urban *dvoriané* was the Muscovite *diaki*, who, said the protestants, grew rich through venality, and built themselves mansions of marble such as had formerly belonged only to nobles of high birth. Consequently these *dvoriané* prayed that the service obligations of the landowners might no longer be apportioned according to estate area, but to the number of peasant homesteads thereon ; wherefore, said the *dvoriané*, let an exact estimate of the number and the ownership of peasantry both on *otchini* and *pomiestia* be made, and the wealth of the clergy looked into, and the "household treasures" lying amassed in the hands of the Patriarch, the bishops, and the monasteries be turned again to the needs of the State. In short, the *dvoriané* were willing to contend against the foe "with their heads, and with their whole souls "—but only so long as men-at-arms were recruited from every *tchin*, and only their (the *dvoriané's*) "bonded folk and peasantry" left exempt.   These complaints and suggestions they capped with a sharp censure of the administration at large.   "Now are we undone, even worse than the Turks and the men of the Crimea did ruin us, both with Muscovite malfeasance and through manifold injustices and unjust judges."   As for the superior merchants of the capital and the men of the metropolitan trades-guilds, they, like the provincial *dvoriané*, were in favour of accepting Azov, and had no fear of war, but stood prepared to make financial sacrifices for its success ; yet they speak more humbly, in a more minor key, and with less speculation concerning the future than the *dvoriané*, though it is with a bitterness equal to the bitterness of the latter that they bewail their impoverishment through taxation, services to the Treasury, and ill-treatment by *voievodi ;* wherefore they beseech the Tsar to "look upon their neediness," and gloomily recall their ruined local independence of administration.   In general, the tone of the "statements" by the deputies of 1642 is very expressive.   To the Tsar's question as to how to order matters some of them reply drily : " As thou dost desire."   Others with loyal complacency say : "Touching the question whence men and money are to be gotten, thou, O Tsar, art free in that matter, and thy boyars, as our lord overseers of olden time, will see to the same"; yet these loyalists also take the opportunity of intimating to their Sovereign that the administration which he maintains is in a bad way, that the institutions which he directs are nowhere in a condition of efficiency, that the services and imposts which he demands of men are beyond men's means to render, that the administrators whom he appoints—the host of *voievodi*, judges, and, worst of all, the *diaki*— have, through their highhandedness and venality, brought the people to utter destitution and wasted the land even worse than did the Tartars, and that the clergy of the State, the spiritual authorities, do seek but to fill their secret coffers with money.   "Such is the thought and the state- ment of us slaves."   This dissatisfaction with the administration was accentuated by class cleavage, since the various social sections all differed in their aims, all felt discontented with their respective positions, and all complained of inequality in financial burdens.   This led the upper classes to strive to impose new exactions upon the lower, the commercial *stratum* to envy the service class for its multitudinous *otchini* and *pomiestia*, the service class to envy the commercial *stratum* for its mercantile wealth, the metropolitan *dvoriané* to sneer at the provincial-urban *dvoriané* for the easy conditions of service which they enjoyed, and the provincial-urban *dvoriané* to reproach the metropolitan corps for the large incomes and lucrative posts and huge perquisites which fell to their lot in the capital, while at the same time not forgetting to remind the Tsar both of the ecclesiastical riches which were gradually becoming lost to the State and of the fact that their own serfs and peasantry must on no account be touched. Indeed, in reading the statements presented to the Council by the deputies of the various classes there represented, we feel that those deputies had nothing to do with one another—that they had no work to perform in common, but that everywhere there was a clashing of interests. Each class thought of itself separately from the rest, and knew but its own immediate needs and the inequitable privileges of its fellows. Hence it is clear that political segregation of the corporate classes had led to a mutual estrangement which had put an effectual end to any joint activity in the Council.

Yet, though languishing in the governmental and privileged sections of the nation, the idea of the *Zemski Sobor* survived a while longer in those small *côteries* of the taxpaying population which had survived the legalised enserfment of the seigniorial peasantry. Thus, in the " statements" presented by the leading Muscovite merchants and the minor trades guilds of the capital (it was upon these latter that most of the dirty work of the administration fell) to the Council of 1642 we see glimmerings of a feature which rendered those sections of the population superior to the "white *tchini*" by whom the reins of authority were held. That feature was the fact that, while expressing their readiness to serve the Tsar " with their heads" (*i.e.* with their lives), these commercial magnates and members of trades-guilds also declared the acceptance of Azov from the Cossacks to be not a class affair, but one which " concerneth all the land of the Empire, and all Christian men," and therefore one in which the whole country, without exception, must bear the necessary burdens, "to the end that no man be in default." Nothing similar do we hear from the service *dvoriané*: those *tchini* merely go on wrangling with one another, and looking into one another's mouths lest a crumb too much should light there, and striving to roll the new service obligations from their own shoulders on to those of other classes. On the other hand, the trading-commercial spokesmen not only knew the purpose for which they were attending the Council, but also understood the interests of the country at large, the true spirit of territorial representation; wherefore those humble seventeenth century guildmen-representatives of the lower depths of the community still cherished some of that sense of civic duty which was fast dying out in the upper *strata* with which their shoulders were burdened. Still more direct and insistent expression do the spokesmen of the lower classes give to the true idea of the *Zemski Sobor* when, a little later, the *Zemski Sobor* has finally passed away. This was as follows. The credit operations in copper coinage which began in the year 1656 led to a rise in prices, and so to a great deal of discontent, since the crisis touched everyone, and could be removed only if the Government and the various classes of the community would consent to join together in friendly co-operation. But the Government's idea of obviating the difficulty was merely to confer with the mercantile magnates of the capital; which duty —the duty of consulting those magnates as to the best measures to be taken—was, in 1662, entrusted to, among others, Ilia Miloslavski, father-in-law of the Tsar, and an utterly unscrupulous boyar whose malfeasance had helped, if anything, to aggravate the mischief. Then, as in 1642, the *gosti* and trades-guildsmen of the capital spoke very much to the point, for in circumstantial language they revealed the economic relations then existing in the country, the ill-adjustment of those relations, and the class antagonism that was latent both between the village and the township and between landowning and mercantile capital. Yes, many a bitter truth did they tell the Government to its face; pointing out to it its ignorance of what was brewing in the country, its inability to maintain the judicial system, and its utter indifference to the voice of the public. With the right of engaging in trade and industry in the towns, said these protestants, there was legally combined the payment of commercial *tiaglo*, in the shape of tolls and dues renderable for the benefit of the Treasury; but now all the best and most extensive trade had, in defiance of the State's regulations, fallen into the hands of the spiritual, military, and legal *tchini*—of the archbishops, the monasteries, the priests, and the State servitors and civil service officials, "who do trade, without tolls, among the *tarchani* (hucksterers), and set the State at nought in many things, and cause great loss of dues and taxes to the Treasury"; while, through being forced to sell their goods at high prices in return for copper money that was debased in value, the commercial community had earned for itself the hatred of all ranks of the public, which was unable properly to understand the situation. To these complaints the Muscovite merchants unanimously appended the statement that to the question of how they could deliver the Government from its straits they had nothing to say, for the reason that "the matter is a great one, and doth appertain unto all the State, and all the land, and all the towns, and all the *tchini*; wherefore we do pray the Tsar that of his goodness he will give commands that to this end there be chosen from among all ranks in Moscow and in the towns the best men who be there, since without such men of the towns can we of ourselves not decide the matter." This prayer for the convocation of another *Zemski Sobor* was really a covert protest against the Government's tendency to replace the "Council of All the Land" with sectional conferences with leaders of classes; a proceeding which the petitioners looked upon as a governmental mistake. In fact, these spokesmen of the Muscovite trading community indicated the same administrative and social fault as, twenty years ago, they had referred to with such bitterness at the Council of 1642. *Then* they had used the Council as a place wherein to protest against that fault; *now* they looked upon the Council as a means for the removal of that fault, despite the fact that the *Zemski Sobor* was composed of the very men who were responsible for the fault—composed of representatives of the very classes which had created it through their mutual antagonism. Hence, since the Muscovite "commercials" recognised the *Sobor* as the only means of reconciling the various disconnected forces and interests of Russian society, this indicated, for territorial representation, a new and added task. Such representation had arisen out of the Period of Troubles, as a means of re-establishing law and order; consequently, now that it would have to organise the very system which law and order, after their re-establishment, had failed to create—now that it would have to reconstruct the community even as, formerly, the Government had reconstructed it—we may well ask ourselves whether this reconstructive task would really have been possible for the *Sobor* when all the time the Government itself was to be the actual factor in that social rebuilding?—whether such an agreement would have been possible when all the time administrative circles and the privileged service classes had no need for it (since they constituted the very classes responsible for the creation of a fault which redounded to their own advantage), and were indifferent to social strife so long only as their own "bonded serfs and peasantry" were not touched, while the Muscovite *gosti* and guildsmen were too light in weight to be able to bring about any rebalancing of social relations? No, the establishment of serf right, added to the insignificant political importance and the faint-hearted civic sense of the clergy, would have caused the needs and interests of the rural taxpaying world to possess only feeble spokesmen in metropolitan merchants and provincial burghers, since, overburdened with class imposts, these men would have had to stand in the presence of a crushing majority of State service officials and members of a boyar-departmental Government. At all events the *Sobor* upon which, in 1662, the said spokesmen of the commercial classes insisted so strongly was never convoked, but, instead, the Government had to deal with a new Muscovite rising, which was raised and suppressed with the usual amount of Muscovite blundering.

The duality of the political character of the *Sobor*; its want of political adjustment; centralisation; serf right; class cleavage; inability of the Government to execute the task which confronted it,—such were the most noticeable conditions of the *Zemski Sobor's* failure to remain in existence; and they explain both the extinction of the *Sobor's* activity and the gradual demise of popular representation. Of the debased level of the political ideas, customs, and demands—political temperature, so to speak—of Moscow of that day I need not speak, since such a level always spells death to any State institution which is designed to stimulate the spirit of freedom. It is a condition which lies, in this case, at the root of all the rest, since it made it possible to introduce the various futile and baneful innovations wherewith the new dynasty began its policy. The action of the above series of conditions is best seen in a gradual disruption of the composition of the *Zemski Sobor*—a disruption which began at a very early period. Even at the Councils following upon the Electoral Council of 1613 that process can be marked by a disappearance of representatives of the clergy and of the rural population, when the Council lost the significance of a pan-territorial, general-class gathering, and became representative only of the State service and of the urban taxpayers, rather than of the country as a whole. Sometimes even this representation—simplified though it was, and torn from its parent soil of pan-nationality—underwent further mutilation, for, in case of need or at its discretion, the Government would omit to call upon the provincial townsmen at all, and summon to the Council only elected deputies of the metropolitan *tchini*, with such provincial-urban *dvoriané* as happened at the moment to be present in Moscow on service; while at the Council of 1634, though it established an extraordinary, pan-territorial levy "from all men," with, among other things, what was known as "fifth money"—a tax which fell mostly upon the provincial-urban populations —we see present no deputies of those populations. Thus the *Zemski Sobor* underwent destruction from below: from it there dropped its in-

ferior, its most radically territorial, elements, in the shape of the deputies
—spiritual, taxpaying (urban and rural), and official—who attended from
the local communities of the provinces; which caused the *Sobor* to lose
its representative significance, and to revert to the old type of the sixteenth century, as an official convention of the metropolitan *tchini* of
service and commerce alone (we have seen that the commercial *tchini*
of the capital combined liability to *tiaglo* with treasury service[1]). The
Council of 1650 also comprised no provincial-urban spokesmen, while
the metropolitan commercial taxpayers were represented only by official
personages, *starosti* and *sotskïe*, as had been the case at Councils of
the sixteenth century. With this curtailment of territorial representation there went a social disintegration of the latter: from the *Zemski
Sobor* the Government turned to a form of conference which was a
direct negation of the *Sobor's* idea. That is to say, to a given question
of State the Government imparted a special departmental or class significance, and then summoned, for its further consideration, either elected
or *ex officio* representatives of the class which, in the view of the government, the question most nearly concerned. Thus in 1617 the English
Government addressed Moscow with proposals for allowing English merchants to use the Volga *en route* to Persia, as well as for arranging certain
trade exemptions and concessions; to which the *Boyarskaia Duma* replied
that "in none of its articles may such a matter be resolved without the
advice of all the State." Yet the "advice of all the State" did not go
beyond questions addressed to the *gosti* and other merchants of the
metropolis. Even at general *Zemskïe Sobori* certain questions were decided sectionally. For instance, the above-mentioned ordinance on the
subject of service *otchini* was adopted by the Tsar and the *Duma* solely
in council with the clergy and service officials—*i.e.* without any participation by deputies of the remaining classes. Between 1654 and the death
of Tsar Theodor (son of Alexis, and stepbrother to Peter the Great) the
Sobor was not convened at all, and during that interval State matters
of more than ordinary importance were decided by the Tsar in company
with the *Boyarskaia Duma* and the Holy Synod. Thus in 1672, when
the Sultan of Turkey was threatening to carry out a disastrous raid upon
Muscovy, special levies of taxation were proclaimed by the Tsar after
conference with the *Duma* and the Hierarchy alone: yet in 1642 a
similar case—and, if anything, a less important one—had necessitated a
convoking of a whole *Zemski Sobor*. Furthermore, during this interval the

[1] See vol. ii. pp. 285 and 299.

Government turned more frequently than ever to the method of class conferences; until the latter had come to be the only form in which the community participated in administrative matters. No fewer than seven such occasions occurred between the year 1660 and the year 1682. In 1681, for the consideration of the question of military reform, only deputies of the service *tchini* were convoked, under the presidency of the boyar V. V. Golitzin; but in the case of the other gatherings (which concerned financial questions) deputies were summoned also from the taxpaying classes. Thus the Government itself destroyed the *Zemski Sobor*, and replaced pan-territorial representation with special conferences with leading men of classes—conferences which committed the Government to nothing, yet converted the general work of the State into the special question of a given class.

Thus the history of the *Zemski Sobor* during the seventeenth century is a history of the *Sobor's* destruction. This is because the *Sobor* owed its origin to the temporary need of a Tsar-less land to emerge from anarchy and disorder, and owed its support to the temporary need of a new Government to strengthen its foothold in the land. Both to the new dynasty and to the classes whereby that dynasty was maintained (namely, to the clergy and the *dvoriané*) the *Zemski Sobor* was a necessity so long as the land failed to recover from the upheaval caused by the Pretenders; but in proportion as peace came about, so did the Government's need of the *Sobor* diminish. Figuring, in 1613, as a pan-corporate[1] gathering which had institutive powers, it created a new dynasty, re-established the shattered order of State, and for two years practically took the place of the Government—thus seeming to be in a fair way to become a permanent institution. Later it acquired an occasional legislative importance—though one which lacked any sort of confirmation; and in this capacity it was convoked, under Michael, ten times (sometimes from year to year), and, under Alexis, five times—though only during the first eight years of his reign. Yet it was gradually merging into deformity, owing to the loss, first of one of its organs, and then of another, until at last it changed from a pan-corporate council into a bi-corporate—nay, even a uni-corporate —gathering that was composed of *dvoriané* alone. Finally it broke up into a series of conferences with class leaders, and, convoked not once under Theodor, and convoked only with a miscellaneous composition on two hurried occasions in 1682, for the purpose of seating upon the monarchical throne the two younger brothers of Theodor, it was in 1698

[1] In the sense of drawn from all classes of the community.

called together for the last time by Peter the Great, for the purpose of
sitting in judgement upon the Tsarina-conspirator Sophia. Not constituting a political force, but only an administrative aid, the *Sobor* never
succeeded in extricating the Government from its difficulties, but, leaving
faint legislative traces of itself in the *Ulozhenïe*, and surviving temporarily
in the political consciousness of the Muscovite merchants,[1] it gradually
sank into oblivion save in the dim historical recollections of the peasantry
of the maritime North, who for a time preserved its memory in a *bilïna*
which relates that, on one occasion, Tsar Alexis—the man who jestingly
wrote that "always unto the speech of the *miri* do I incline mine ear," yet,
with his own hand, suppressed the mouthpiece of those *miri*, the *Zemski
Sobor*—addressed to his subjects, from the *Lobnöe Miesto*, or Place of
Execution, in Moscow, the words:

> " Give aid unto your Tsar, that he may counsel take.
> Together let our counsel be, and not apart."

The elective *Zemski Sobor* entered into the life of the Muscovite Empire as a fortuitous result of the mechanical impetus which the cutting
off of the old dynasty communicated to that life; after which it reappears
episodically, and from time to time. In the *Sobor* the country, the nation,
made its entry upon the administrative stage at a moment when the
Government had ceased to figure there; and it made a re-entry at a later
period when the re-established Government was feeling the need of the
country's, the nation's, help. The misfortunes of the Period of Troubles
had united the last efforts of the Russian community in restoring the
shattered order of State; and it was by that same forced social unanimity
that the representative *Sobor* was created and maintained. Thus, in
Russia, popular representation arose, not for the limitation of authority,
but for the discovery and confirmation of authority: wherein it differed
from representation in Western Europe. Yet, having created and supported the supreme power, the *Sobor* naturally became, for a while, its
partner, and in time might have become, in virtue of long custom, its
permanent coadjutor. What hindered it from so doing was the fact that
the necessities of the re-established State joined with the Government's
schemes for their satisfaction in destroying the social unanimity which
dire misfortune had extorted from the community, and so forced the
latter to become split into a number of isolated corporate classes, and
the majority of the peasantry to sink into a condition of serfdom to the

[1] See above.

landowners. This deprived the *Zemski Sobor* of its territorial character, and made it representative of the upper classes alone, while disuniting those classes politically and morally—politically through inequality of corporate rights and obligations, and morally through antagonism of the corporate interests which flowed from such inequality. On the other hand, neither the experiences of the Period of Troubles nor the increased activity of the *Zemski Sobor* under Tsar Michael served to widen the political sense of the community to a sufficient degree to lead it to make territorial representation its substantial political demand, and to convert the *Sobor* from a temporary auxiliary resource of the Government into a permanent organ of the people's needs and interests. No influential class had arisen in the community for which representation of such a sort could become such a demand. Although, on the establishment of peasant serfdom, the *dvoriané* absorbed boyardom, and became practically the ruling class in the State, they soon found a more convenient road for the furtherance of their interests than the *Zemski Sobor*. That road lay in independent presentation of collective petitions to the supreme power ; and the boyar-*dvorianin* officials who alone formed the bodyguard of the weak Tsars of the day facilitated that road. Meanwhile the metropolitan mercantile community stood isolated, through finding itself unable to abandon the idea of territorial representation which it had adopted, and in 1662 we find its spokesmen complaining of the little which had been accomplished by that means. Thus two separate series of phenomena hindered representation in Council from hardening into a permanent institution during the seventeenth century—namely (1) the fact that, though serving, at first, both as a support for the new dynasty and as an auxiliary organ of the administration, the *Zemski Sobor* grew less and less necessary to the Government in proportion as the dynasty became consolidated and the resources of the administration—more especially the official world of the *prikazi*—greater ; and (2) the fact that the community, disunited as it was by corporate obligations and class variance, found itself unable, in view of the depressed condition of its sense of equity, to convert, by friendly co-operation, the *Sobor* into a permanent legislative institution which should be limited by political guarantees and organically bound up with the order of State. Hence representation in Council fell in consequence at once of the growth of centralisation in the administration and of the State's fixation of corporate classes.

CHAPTER XI

The connection between the various phenomena—War and finance—Assessed, indirect, and direct taxation—"Given money," "tithes money," "posting money," "prisoners' money," and "*Strieltsi* money"—Census returns—Non-assessed levies—Experiments and reforms—The salt tax and the tobacco monopoly—Copper credit tokens, and the Muscovite rising of 1662—The "living" quarter of land—Per-homestead taxation, and the census of 1620 and the following years—Class apportionment of direct taxation—Finance and the local administrative units—Extension of *tiaglo* to *zadvornie liudi*—Distribution of popular labour among the various forces of the State—Extraordinary imposts—The budget statement of 1680.

REPRESENTATION in the *Zemski Sobor* expired later than did local self-administration. The disappearance of the one and the fall of the other were parallel, but not coincident, results of those fundamental changes in the State order which I have described towards the close of the last chapter. The growth of centralisation crushed out local provincial institutions, and the decline of the latter, added to the isolation of classes in compartments, destroyed the *Zemski Sobor* which hitherto had served as the chief means of enabling the local corporate *miri* to take part in the legislation of the country. Both these fundamental changes had their origin in a common source—namely, in the financial difficulties of the State; and, these difficulties also forming the hidden spring by which both the administration and the social measures of the Government were directed, inspired the latter to reorganise the administration and the community, and so forced it to offer many sacrifices at the expense of social order and public prosperity.

The weakest spot, therefore, in the Muscovite State order under the new dynasty was finance, since the demands necessitated by the frequent, costly, and rarely successful wars of the day far outweighed the resources which lay at the disposal of the Government, and left it at a loss to restore the balance. Always, in the end, the army engulfed the Treasury. In 1634, when requesting the *Zemski Sobor* to continue the war with Poland, the Tsar explained that the funds which, during years of peace, he had accumulated "not from the land" (*i.e.* not through direct taxation) had all gone in preparations for war, and that it was impossible to provide for the upkeep of the auxiliary troops without imposing extra taxation, since military losses in conflicts with the Polish and Swedish forces now compelled the Government to take anxious thought concerning the question of improving its military contingents on foreign models. Two documents exist which will give us a good idea of the remodelling of the *dvorianin* militia, as well as of the increase of the cost of its upkeep during a space of fifty years. In a *smietni spissok*, or estimate, for the year 1631 we find set down the numbers of the armed forces which the Treasury maintained at its own cost, and paid for with remuneration which took the form of *pomiestia*, money, and emoluments in kind. The numbers given in the *spissok* total 70,000 men, and consisted of metropolitan and provincial-urban *dvoriané*, artillery men, *Strieltsi* (musketeers), Cossacks, and foreign men-at-arms; while in the provinces representing the old Khanates of Kazan and Siberia a further mixed force of Eastern aliens is reckoned at 15,000 Tartars, Tchuvashes, Tcheremissians, Morduines, and Bashkirs. At the same time, these received no monetary remuneration for their services, but were embodied only on extraordinary occasions when, to quote the *smietni spissok*, "there shall be of all the land full service"—*i.e.* there should be a general mobilisation. In the year 1670 we find a foreigner named Reitenfeldts mentioning an Imperial review of 60,000 *dvoriané*, who must have been drawn, not only from the metropolitan *tchini*, but also from members of the upper *strata* of the provincial *dvoriané* who were efficient for foreign campaigning and able to take with them their proper complements of armed dependents. The same foreign writer declares that his eyes were absolutely dazzled with the glitter of these sumptuous troopers, with their arms and trappings. But in all probability they showed to greater advantage in Moscow—more especially in the eyes of an æsthetically impressionable Tsar—than they did on the battlefields of Lithuania and Little Rus. At all events they meant the sacrifice of an immense proportion of the nation's working strength. Moreover, the military efficiency of this heterogeneous host of *dvoriané*, Cossacks, Tartars, and Tchuvashes—who were first of all mustered to defend the Empire, and then disbanded when campaigns were over—may be estimated from Kotoshikhin's words where he says that "of teaching for war have they none, nor know they how to range themselves." Only the *Strieltsi* (who were embodied in permanent regiments or *prikazi*) had any regular organisation. The recasting of this mass of warlike material was effected as follows. Under the command of foreign (mostly German) colonels and captains, who were posted to *sotni* or companies, there became formed of the provincial-urban *dvoriané* and "sons of boyars" (but more especially of those who possessed but small, poor *pomiestia*, or none at all), as well as of volunteers and recruits from the other classes (even of the peasantry and the slaves), certain regiments or corps of cavalry (*reitari*), infantry (*soldati*), and horse-footmen who were known as *draguni*.[1] For this purpose whole villages in the outlying districts of the South were converted into military settlements, and in 1647 a monasterial *selo* in the Lebedianskaia canton which comprised upwards of 400 peasant homesteads was enrolled to form a corps of *draguni*. Again, in accordance with instructions issued in 1678, all "needy" *dvoriané* who were fit for service were enrolled as infantrymen, at a monthly salary; and by a further *ukaz* of 1680 there became embodied all such *dvoriané* of the three *razriadi* (military districts) of Novgorod Sieversski, Bielgorod, and Tambov as were efficient for the purpose. These, however, were only extraordinary measures. For the normal filling up of the regiments of alien composition there came into action a new and dual method of supplementation, in the form of impressments of *datochnie* ("given men" or unpaid conscripts), either according to the number of peasant homesteads in a village (for instance, from every 100 homesteads there might be taken 100 *reitari* or *soldati*) or according to the family composition of those homesteads (*i.e.* from every two or three unattached sons or brothers there might be enrolled one trooper, or from every four sons or brothers of the same family two troopers, and so on). These conscript levies or *nabori* served substantially to supplement the old method of *pribor* or "adding," and, according to calculations made with regard to the twenty-five years 1654–1679, they subtracted from the sum-total of the working population of the country at least 70,000 men. The new regiments were given a course of drill and musketry, and the results of this tardy reorganisation of the armed forces of the Empire are to be found recorded in a *rospiss ratnim liudam*, or "list of warlike men," for 1681. Under this system the troops were allotted to nine *razriadi* or military districts. Only the army corps of the capital (which consisted of 2624 men of the various metropolitan *tchini*, with contingents of armed slaves and "given men" to the number of 21,830, and 5000 *Strieltsi* added) remained under the old organisation—the organisation of native origin; while the other eight army districts and the sixteen *prikazi* or corps of *Strieltsi* had joined to them

---

[1] Men who could fight either mounted or dismounted, like the old-time dragoons or the modern mounted infantrymen.

twenty-five regiments of foreign cavalry and thirty-eight battalions of foreign infantry, under foreign colonels. Only three of these corps were commanded by Russian subjects, in the capacity of generals. Of the old *dvorianin* militia (according to a list for the year 1631 it numbered some 40,000 men) there were left under the old system only 13,000 men-at-arms—the rest having become part of sixty-three reorganised regiments, of 90,000 men. Yet the army was not strictly a *regular* one, since it was not permanent, and on the conclusion of a campaign the new regiments would be disbanded to their homes, and leave behind them only *cadres* of officers. In all, if we reckon the Cossacks, but exclude 50,000 men-at-arms from Little Rus, the grand total numbered, according to the above list for 1681, 164,000 men; and if we compare (so far as possible) the various homogeneous portions of this host with the lists already referred to (exclusive of the Eastern aliens, who were not entered in the *spissok* for 1681), we find that, between the years 1631 and 1681, the armed forces which the Treasury was compelled to maintain increased $2\frac{1}{2}$ times. Also, the mercenary pay or "monthly sustenance" of the innumerable colonels and captains of foreign origin was very high; and if they remained in Muscovite service this payment became converted into life pensions, whereof one-half descended to their wives and children. Cavalrymen, infantrymen, and dragoons were mostly enlisted from the needy classes, and received a high rate of pay, free armament, military necessaries, and, when actually campaigning, rations at the expense of the Treasury. Thus the cost of the army grew from, in 1631, 3,000,000 (modern) roubles to, in 1680, 10,000,000 roubles. Hence, while the numbers of men increased $2\frac{1}{2}$ times, their cost trebled during that period. Naturally the cost of wars grew in proportion. The abortive expedition of Michael against Smolensk cost from 7,000,000 to 8,000,000 roubles; while Alexis' first two campaigns against Poland (1654–55)— campaigns which effected the subjugation not only of Smolensk, but also of Little Rus and Lithuania—cost from 18,000,000 to 20,000,000 roubles; which total almost equalled the whole capital sum of income received, in 1680, by all the financial institutions of the centre put together!

With the increased cost of the army the national budget kept pace. To elucidate the many attempts of the Government to place its financial resources upon a level with the ever-growing expenses of the State we must picture to ourselves—though on general lines—the financial system which gradually became compounded. The Treasury's ordinary resources consisted of *okladnie dochodi* and *neokladnie dochodi,* or assessed income

and non-assessed income. Assessed income was the name given to
levies for which there was fixed in advance, in the estimates, a definite,
obligatory amount or *oklad;* and it was a source which consisted both of
direct and indirect taxes. In the Muscovite Empire, *podati,* or direct imports, fell either upon communities as a whole or upon individuals, and were
known, in the aggregate, as *tiaglo;* while the persons subject to their incidence were called *tiaglïe liudi,* or, more simply, *tiaglïe.* The chief subjects
of *tiaglo*-imposition were lands and homesteads, while the basis of that
imposition was the *Soshnöe Pismo*—a register of taxable lands and homesteads according to *sochi.*[1] The *socha* was a taxatory unit which comprised
either a given number of taxable urban establishments or a given area of
taxable peasant tillage. On good *pomiestïe* or *otchina* land the *socha*
included 800 *tchetverti;*[2] on good monasterial land it included 600
tchetverti; and on good "black" or fiscal land it included 500 *tchetverti.*
In each such *socha,* of course, the number of *tchetverti* of medium and poor
land was proportionately increased; while the quality of land was defined
by its income-producing properties rather than by the nature of its soil.
On the other hand, the urban *socha* varied greatly in its composition.
For example, in Zaraisk, towards the close of the sixteenth century, 80
establishments of the better, the more affluent, class went to the *socha,*
100 medium establishments, and 120 establishments of the poorer folk;
whereas in Viazma, during the first half of the seventeenth century, there
went to the *socha* 40 superior establishments, 80 medium, and 100 neces-
sitous. Next let us enumerate the chief sources of assessed income;
beginning with the indirect imposts, whereof the two principal were
customs dues and excise dues—in the seventeenth century the two richest
sources upon which the Muscovite Treasury could rely. Customs dues
varied greatly in their amount, and were collected both on the transit of
merchandise and on its sale; while excise dues were derived from the sale
of certain articles which constituted Treasury monopolies. These two
sources of income usually had given rates assigned them by the Government, which either farmed them out or assigned them "on trust"—*na
vieru*—by delegating the collection of customs and the sale of such commodities as liquor to certain "trusted" (sworn) overseers and *tsielovalniki,* whom the payers of *tiaglo* had to select for the purpose from
among themselves, and whose defalcations were recoverable either from
the selected officials themselves, or from the selectors if the latter did not

---

[1] See vol. ii. p. 249.
[2] Quarters. The *tchetvert* was equivalent to 4.29 English acres.

in time discover what was going on, and report the peculations or the irregularities of their officials to the authorities. Overseers and *tsielo-valniki* whom outsiders detected in acts of theft or embezzlement were, by a law of 1637, liable to "punishment by death without mercy." That is to say, the law punished, for their irregularity or their incompetence, the agents of the very Government which laid upon the inhabitants not only the obligation itself, but also the duty of seeing that it was duly fulfilled—though both of these functions came within the Government's province. In 1653 all indirect imports were combined into a single due, and, instead of the innumerable customs-renderings there was introduced what became known as the "rouble toll" (10 *dengi*[1] in the rouble) —an exaction from the vendor of 5 per cent. on the selling value of his goods, and an exaction from the purchaser of 5 *dengi* in the rouble on the amount tendered.

The two fundamental direct imposts were *dengi dannia*, or "given money," and *dengi obrotchnia*, or "tithes money." *Dengi dannia* (or, more simply, *dan*) was the name given to various direct taxes incident upon those of the urban-industrial and rural-agricultural inhabitants who were subject to *tiaglo*, and levied according to the number of *sochi* ascribed by the census registers to a given urban or rural community. On the other hand, *obrotchnia dengi*, or, more simply, *obrok*, had a dual significance, for sometimes the term was applied to a payment to the Government in return for the right of a private individual either to use certain fiscal lands or *ugodia*[2] or to engage in some particular industry ; and in this sense it connoted the fiscal income produced by fisheries, hay-growing lands, hunting grounds, shops, taverns, washhouses, and other industrial undertakings which belonged to the Treasury. In other cases *obrok* denoted a general tax which was laid upon the inhabitants of a given district in place of *several* taxes and dues. For instance, the name was applied to the impost whereby the *kormi* and *poshlini* renderable to *namiestniki* and *volosteli*[3] became replaced on the abolition of those posts during the reign of Ivan the Terrible. Only *obroki* such as these were reckoned to be part of *tiaglo*, and their imposition was regulated by the *Soshnöe Pismo*, or Register of *Sochi*. Also, as general taxes, both *obrok* and *dan* were paid in unvarying amounts and at fixed rates, whereas the rates of all other State imposts were variable, and defined by special Imperial edicts.

[1] Half-kopecks. [2] Grass- and timber-cutting properties.
[3] See vol. ii. pp. 248, 249.

To the State's sources of assessed income we may also assign special taxes which were ordained to meet the State's special needs. These were *yamskia dengi* ("posting money"), *polonianitchnia dengi* ("prisoners' money"), and *strieletskia dengi* ("musketeers' money"). *Yamskia dengi* was devoted to the maintenance of the transport service for ambassadors, couriers, and certain military and official personages; for which purpose *yami* or posting stages were established along the principal roads. The tax was leviable upon townsmen and peasantry alike according to the *Soshnöe Pismo*, and payable to a central institution known as the *Yamskoi Prikaz*, which had to do with the post riders to whom the salaries and fees for the posting service were paid, and upon whom it was a binding obligation that they should always have a certain number of horses ready at each *yama* or posting house. *Polonianitchnia dengi* was a tax levied according to homesteads, not according to *sochi*, and its *raison d'être* was the ransoming of prisoners from the Tartars and the Turks. For a while during Michael's reign the impost was levied only by special instructions of the Government; but, later, it became a permanent due, and the *Ulozhenie* of 1649 ordered it to be collected annually, and "from all men," *tiaglo*-paying and non-*tiaglo*-paying alike—though in proportions which differed according to the status of the individual. Urban dwellers and Church peasantry paid 8 *dengi* (in modern currency, about 60 kopecks) on their homesteads; Court, "black," and *pomiestie* peasantry paid one-half of that amount; and *Strieltsi*, Cossacks, and other members of the inferior ranks of the State service paid 2 *dengi*. Also, Kotoshikhin tells us that, in his time, the total payments of *polonianitchnia dengi* averaged 150,000 roubles (2,000,000 in modern currency), and that, when paid, the tax went to the *Posolski Prikaz*, or Office of Ambassadors (Foreign Office), which had the management of the ransoming of prisoners. *Strieletskia dengi* was appointed for the upkeep of the *Strieltsi*—a permanent infantry corps instituted, during the sixteenth century, by Tsar Vassilii. At first the impost was small enough, and only levied on foodstuffs, but during the seventeenth century it began to be collected both in foodstuffs and money; and, in proportion as the *personnel* of the *Strieltsi* increased, so did the tax grow into one of the most important of direct taxes. Indeed, we know from Kotoshikhin that during Alexis' reign there were stationed in Moscow, even in times of peace, over 20 *prikazi* (regiments) of *Strieltsi*, of which each contained from 800 to 1000 men (the exact total, in 1681, was 22,452), while the provincial-urban corps of *Strieltsi* contained as many again.

All the above-mentioned taxes, except the *polonianitchnia dengi*, were assessed in accordance with the *Soshnöe Pismo*. Upon each *socha* the Government imposed a given sum, an *oklad*, of taxation, and left it to the payers of the sum, the *tiaglie liudi* of the *socha*, to divide the impost among themselves, according to the paying powers of each—"to make it equal among themselves, according unto their goods and their business and their ploughing and all manner of appurtenances." The basis of tax-imposition per *socha* was *pistsovia knigi* or census registers. From time to time the Government compiled returns of all immoveable property which was subject to *tiaglo*, and, for the purpose, sent enumerators into the cantons who, from statements and documents furnished by the inhabitants, took particulars of all the taxable properties in the locality and verified them against former census returns after personal inspection. That is to say, census registers recorded particulars of every town and canton, of their joint population, of their *ugodia* (rights of pasturage and timber-cutting), and of their commercial-industrial establishments, with the dues payable upon the same. In enumerating these urban and cantonal populations, townships, suburbs, and differing types of rural settlements, the register also specified in detail the *tiaglo*-liable dwellings and persons in each inhabited unit, and also the householders who had living with them their children or any of their kinsfolk. Also, it recorded the amount of arable, vacant, pasture, and forest land belonging to each unit, it divided into *sochi* such urban establishments and areas of rural cultivable land as were subject to *tiaglo*, and it used these *sochi* to calculate the amounts of *tiaglo* incident upon the given unit according to the landed property or the industrial pursuits of its inhabitants. In the Muscovite archives of the present Ministry of Justice there are still to be seen preserved many hundreds of census registers of the sixteenth and seventeenth centuries—documents which serve as our fundamental source of the history of the financial organisation and economic life of the Muscovite Empire. Registers of the kind existed even in the earliest days, but it is only with the close of the fifteenth century that they begin to come down to us, in the shape of a few from Novgorod the Great. Their value as at once cadastral surveys and financial records rendered these census registers frequent aids in the making of civil and other dispensations, since, with their help, agrarian disputes underwent settlement, rights of possession of immoveable properties were confirmed, and conscriptions of *datochnie liudi* or "volunteers" could be carried out. When, in 1619, Philaret, Michael's father, returned from Poland, the two Tsars convened the *Zemski Sobor*, and charged it to send enumerators and inspectors into the provinces, for the purpose of compiling returns of the various towns, sorting their inhabitants into sections, and allocating them according to the localities where formerly they had lived and paid *tiaglo*. Next, on the strength of this ordinance, there was undertaken, in the twenties of the seventeenth century, a general census of all the *tiaglo*-paying population in the Empire, with the object of discovering and organising its tax-paying powers; and it was these same registers that the *Ulozhenie* used as a documental basis, both in establishing serf-proprietorship of landowners and in legalising various other forms of bondage. Also, these registers served to decide suits against runaway peasantry; lastly, to introduce the serf condition into peasant loan contracts.

The second category of sources of State income (the non-assessed dues) consisted chiefly of payments made by private persons in return for having sundry requirements of theirs satisfied in one or another governmental institution. Such payments consisted of duties upon various private transactions, upon petitions forwarded by private persons to different administrative or judicial offices, and upon documents granted them in the form of legal decisions, and so forth.

As a basis to this financial system of the seventeenth century, the Treasury carried on certain enterprises of two kinds—namely, enterprises which, in the form of experiments or schemes, had a tendency to abolish the established order, and enterprises which, in the form of innovations, had a tendency to recast that order. First of all the Treasury set itself to collect its scattered taxpayers. The Period of Troubles had removed from their taxable position a great number of *tiaglie liudi* who, on the re-establishment of order, resumed their dutiable avocations, yet not their payments of *tiaglo*. Against such "defaulters" a prolonged legislative and police struggle was begun. After the *Sobor* of 1619 the Government prosecuted as felons any *zakladchiki* who "pledged" themselves to landowners. Next, in conjunction with the *Sobor* of 1848-49, it made a compromise by ordaining, through the *Ulozhenie*, that non-urban persons who were engaged in industry in the towns should either abandon their industry or share in the towns' payment of *tiaglo*. Also, we have seen that, with the object of securing to the Treasury a constant supply of direct or indirect workers, the legislature collated the community into closelocked corporate classes, and, attaching the latter to their obligations, both forbade any voluntary quitting of townships and converted the life bondage of seigniorial peasantry through an agreement into serf dependence through heredity. Yet, however carefully the Government might register and attach to their obligations such of the inhabitants as were competent to pay *tiaglo*, there still remained a large number of "defaulters" who evaded their fiscal payments. Consequently, with a single general measure, as with a great fishing-net, the Government attempted to convert the *whole* of the population into workers for the Treasury—both commoners and privileged persons, adults and minors, men and women. That is to say, at the time when, in the West, politico-economic theorists were insisting that indirect imposts must be substituted for direct, and that articles of consumption ought to be burdened rather than capital and labour, Moscow sought to enter upon the same road at the bidding of no imported theory, but only at that of her own bad native practice (since Muscovite financial policy generally led to indirect taxation triumphing over direct). Especially during the seventeenth century did the Government exhaust this source, in the fond belief that the taxpayer preferred to pay a surplus for his commodities rather than be burdened with a direct imposition, since in return for the surcharge he would get something at least usable, whereas, in the other case, he would get nothing save a receipt, a quittance. Hence, in all probability, it was that there originated the idea—an idea commonly said to have been suggested by an ex-*gost* and acting *diak* named Nazarei Tchisti—of replacing the more important direct imposts with an increased tax on salt, since salt was a necessity to all, and therefore a commodity which would make all men pay in proportion to their use of the same, and allow of no "defaulters." Consequently, up to 1646 the Treasury exacted, per *pood*[1] of salt, 15 kopecks (approximately 60 kopecks, in modern currency) ; but by a law of the same year this impost was raised, by a quarter, to 20 kopecks per *pood*, or half a kopeck per pound. Comparing, therefore, the half-kopeck of those days with 6 kopecks of to-day, we see that the Treasury's duty on salt in the seventeenth century exceeded, by some six times, the present market price per pound of the commodity in question. This measure the *ukaz* justified with a series of naive considerations ; such as that the measure would do away with the taxes for the maintenance of the *Strieltsi* and the posting service (the two heaviest and most unfairly distributed of the direct imposts), that the new salt tax would fall equally upon all men, that it would suffer no "defaulters" to escape, that all would pay the tax of themselves instead of necessitating distraints and harsh prosecutions, and that foreigners

[1] Forty Russian pounds.

resident in Moscow would also pay it (as things were, they rendered nothing whatever to the Treasury). These fine calculations, however, came to naught, for thousands of *poodi* of cheap fish whereon the populace subsisted during seasons of fasting were left to rot on the banks of the Volga, for the reason that the fishermen could not afford to salt their wares. Also, far less salt of the more expensive kinds was sold than had hitherto been the case. Consequently the Treasury suffered great losses, and, early in 1648, it was decided to abolish the new tax. But the tax had so strengthened popular resentment against the Administration that, in the summer of the year just named, there broke out a rebellion, in the course of which the rebels cried out, as they put Nazarei Tchisti to death: "There, traitor! This for thy salting!" The same financial need led a pious Government to bow to a popular-ecclesiastical prejudice in declaring the sale of tobacco—"the God-hated and impious herb"—a Treasury monopoly, even though by a previous *ukaz* of 1634 it (the Government) had threatened any one who used or traded in the "herb" with the penalty of death; after which the Treasury proceeded to sell tobacco for wellnigh its weight in gold—*i.e.* at a price varying from (in terms of modern currency and weight) 3 to 3.6 roubles per ounce! However, after the rebellion of 1648 the tobacco monopoly was, like the salt tax, abolished, and the law of 1634 restored. Thus its perplexity as to the best course to take led the Government to play the sheer fool in its enactments.

Still more lamentable was the end of another financial enterprise. Want of money rendered Muscovite financiers of the seventeenth century extraordinarily inventive, and, after envisaging the idea of replacing direct taxes with indirect, they arrived, in an equally spontaneous manner, at the idea of State credit. In 1656, when the first war with Poland had come to a successful conclusion and Moscow was preparing to make a break with Sweden, the Muscovite Treasury had no silver currency whatever wherewith to pay its troops. Accordingly an intimate of the Tsar's named Rtishtchev (at least so it was commonly said) started the notion of issuing copper coinage at a forced ratio to silver, since the Muscovite market was well-used to monetary tokens of nominal value, and deterioration of the currency would form an auxiliary source of income to which the Treasury could turn in case of need. The Muscovite monetary circulation of the day comprised neither native gold nor any silver coins of large value: the rouble and the half-rouble were the only two units of calculation, and for small change men used kopecks, *dengi* (half-kopecks), and *polushki—*

the latter equal in weight to from a fourth to a sixth part of the kopeck, or even less; and these small, awkward, oval-shaped dies purchasers in the market-place would, for their better security, hold tucked away in the corners of their mouths! Unable to obtain the silver which it needed, the Muscovite Treasury fashioned the money out of imported German coins which came to be known in Russia as *efimki* (dollars or crowns). Nor did the Treasury forget its own interests in the process. On the Muscovite market the *efimok* was worth some 40 or 42 kopecks, but, when melted down, could be reminted to represent 64 kopecks. Consequently the Treasury made a profit on this reminting of from 52 to 60 per cent. Sometimes the operation was limited to placing the Tsar's stamp upon the *efimok*, and turning it from a 40-kopeck coin into a coin of 64: only with the beginning of the first war with Poland did it become necessary to mint silver roubles and quarter-roubles at the normal value of the stamped *efimok*, and also give small copper coins the form and weight of silver ones. At first these tokens made of the baser metal enjoyed the people's confidence, aad circulated on equal terms with coins made of the superior ore, but in time the seductive operation fell into hands which are ever prone to temptation, and artisans of the mint who had not hitherto been rich men suddenly became affluent, and took to squandering money right and left, building themselves splendid houses, decking their wives out like boyar ladies, and buying goods in the shops without haggling over the price. Also, rich merchants, and even *gosti*, of Moscow—though the latter were the appointed supervisors of the issue of copper—purchased that metal for themselves, and, taking it, with some fiscal coinage, to the Mint, had it refashioned into credit currency. Thus the market became flooded with "rogue" money—*i.e.* copper currency which had been filched from the State's credit, and a fault appeared in the circulation which grew until, beginning with 4 kopecks, the difference between silver and copper coins had, by the close of the year 1660, reached the point of 2 copper roubles being given for a single silver one; by the year 1663, 12 copper roubles; and, a little later, 15. Of course goods rose similarly in value, and military men found themselves in a peculiarly difficult position, for the reason that they received their pay in nothing but copper currency. In the end there came to light the fact that the knavery which Muscovite financiers and *gosti* had displayed in making their huge hauls of money had been screened by officials of the central *prikazi*—officials who, in this matter, had shown their usual lack of principle. At their head had stood the Tsar's father-in-law, the boyar Ilia Miloslavski, aided by the Tsar's uncle by marriage, a member of the *Duma* named Matiushkin, and the very man who had been entrusted with the direction of copper coinage; but Miloslavski was looked upon as the person chiefly responsible for the fraud, and from him the Tsar withdrew his favour, while Matiushkin was forced to resign his post. Also, various artisans of the mint, *gosti*, and officials of *prikazi* were found guilty, had their hands and feet cut off, and were sent into exile. But certain of their coadjutors, on perceiving the comparative immunity of the leading spirits in the affair, availed themselves of the general outcry against the enhancement of prices to raise an agitation which had for its object the shaking of the position of the boyars, as had been the case in 1648. Inflammatory notices distributed in Moscow declared Ilia Miloslavski and others to have been guilty of treason, and in July, 1662, when the Tsar was residing in the suburban *selo* of Kolomna, a mob of malcontents, some 5,000 strong, approached Alexis (who had come out to meet them) with a demand that the traitors should be brought to trial; and, while making their request, they held their Sovereign by the buttons of his coat, and forced him to swear by God, as well as to strike hands with one of their number on the oath, that he would prosecute the matter in person. Yet no sooner did another mob which had come out from Moscow join the first one and begin rudely to demand the surrender of the traitors—threatening that, should the Tsar not give them up of himself, they would take them from him by force—than Alexis called upon his *Strieltsi* and court retinue, and there began a wholesale massacre of the unarmed malcontents which was followed up by torture, executions, drownings in the river Moskva, and sentences of perpetual exile to Siberia. Also, these alarms of July so agitated the Tsaritsa that she fell ill for more than a year. In the counterfeiting of the copper coinage, as also in the rebellion, men of different statuses took part—priests, Church servers, monks, commercial magnates, ordinary burghers, peasants, and slaves. Even soldiers and a few military officers joined the rising. Yet, though contemporary writers have reckoned that over 7,000 persons were executed because of the affair, and over 15,000 were punished with amputation of the hands and feet, banishment, and confiscation of their property, the true thieves, the real conspirators, numbered only 200; the rest (the mob which went out to see the Tsar) consisted only of curious sightseers. These dealings in copper coinage completely disorganised the course of trade and industry, and, in its efforts to escape from the *impasse*, the Treasury only added to the disorganisation. We have seen that at the governmental conferences with the Strieshnevs and Ilia Miloslavski concerning the causes of the rise in prices the traders of Moscow put their position very plainly. This was that, with the aim of supplementing its now exhausted stock of imported monetary silver, the Treasury had obliged Russian merchants to become vendors to the Government, for copper money, of such Russian articles of export as furs, hemp, potash, and bullock's grease; after which it had resold those articles to foreigners in return for the latter's *efimki*. Meanwhile Russian merchants had bought imported goods of foreigners for silver, since they (the foreigners) had refused to accept Russian copper money. Yet these goods the merchants of Rus had been forced to resell to their customers for copper, and thus the silver which they had originally put into circulation had never come back to their pockets, and further purchases from the foreigner had become impossible for them, and they had found themselves left without either silver or goods, and had had to declare themselves " men fallen from trading." The utter failure of the scheme led to its forced liquidation, and in this connection the issue of copper credit tokens, as a State non-interest-bearing debt, suggested the possibility of exchanging the tokens in question for real money. Consequently by an *ukaz* of 1663 a return to silver was established, and it was also forbidden either to harbour or to utter copper coinage, all of which was to be melted down into other articles of use, or else to be returned to the Treasury, which, according to Kotoshikhin, paid 10 *dengi* in silver for the copper rouble, and, according to the *ukaz* of 1663, but 2 *dengi*. In other words, the Treasury acted like a bankrupt who pays his creditors from 1 to 5 kopecks in the rouble. The result was that shortly before and after the rising of July the combined *prikazi* had amassed, from the "corner" in export goods engineered by the Treasury at the expense of the Russian merchants, a sum of a little under 1,500,000 (nominal) roubles in copper (in modern currency, 19,000,000). Yet this can only have been a part of the total output of copper issued from the Mint—though rumour of the day placed the total for five years at the incredibly large sum of 20,000,000 roubles (in modern currency, 280,000,000).

Far more serious were the *innovations* which the Government introduced into the administration of its finances. Of them there were three—namely, (1) abolition of the unit of assessment of direct taxation, with a new type of agrarian registration, (2) class apportionment of direct taxes, and (3) a bringing of the local communities of the provinces within the administration's financial system. That is to say, in the system of direct tax-imposition those communities passed from imposition of taxation

according to *sochi* to imposition of taxation according to *dvori* or homesteads. But such passage was not a direct one ; it took place, rather,
through an intermediate stage—through the stage of the " living " (*i.e.* the
inhabited) *tchetvert* (quarter of land [1]). The earliest scholar to investigate this intermediate stage was M. Leppo-Danilevski, in his treatise concerning direct taxation in the Muscovite Empire during the seventeenth
century. Census registers also help us to explain the origin of this unit
of tax-assessment. Never at any time was the rural *socha* a fixed taxatory
dimension, since the peripatetic system of agriculture [2] then in vogue kept
removing worn-out land from tax-liability, and introducing thereto land
which had undergone a rest. Again, the latter half of the sixteenth century
saw the taxatory integrity of the *socha* broken, in the central provinces,
both by the migratory movement towards the outlying districts and by the
shrinkage of peasant tillage. The number of plots long abandoned—
" lots which had been cast void "—constantly increased at the expense of
the area of " living " (*i.e.* occupied and tax-paying) tillage, and from this
passage of land " from livingness to emptiness " (to quote the language of
the census registers) the *Soshnöe Pismo* gained nothing, but, rather, the
reverse. The truth is that the Period of Troubles almost entirely put an
end to agricultural work in the country—so much so that, according to
the evidence of a contemporary writer, ploughing ceased nearly everywhere, and the people subsisted on old stocks of grain. But as soon
as peace was restored the peasantry—*i.e.* such of them as had remained
where they were or returned from flight—saw around them only a multitude of empty homesteads and sites of homesteads which had become nearly
overgrown with bush ; wherefore, on recovering from the upheaval, those
peasantry took to ploughing only small sections of their own tillage land,
and turned their surplus labour to " strange ploughing "—*i.e.* to the till-
ing of neighbouring plots which had been abandoned by their former
holders, and left to fall out of taxation, owing to the fact that those
holders had either been killed or captured, or had disappeared completely
from view. Census registers show us that in one place where, at the close
of the sixteenth century, peasantry were ploughing 4350 *dessiatini* there
remained, in 1616, only 130 *dessiatini* of taxable " living " land, and 650
of non-taxable " strange " land. In particular we meet with a property in
the canton of Riazan where, in 1695, peasant tillage amounted to 1275
dessiatini, but where, in 1616, nine peasant homesteads stood on three
taxable *dessiatini*, and ploughed a further 45 *dessiatini* of " strange " land

---

[1] Equal to 1½ *dessiatini*, or 4.29 English acres.   [2] See vol. i. p. 217.

belonging to homesteads which had been vacated by their neighbours. In other localities we meet with plots so shrunken that six or seven peasant homesteads went to a single "living" quarter of land, although to that they had added from 40 to 60 *dessiatini* of "strange" tillage. Such "visiting" agricultural industry (*i.e.* the working of "strange" plots at a distance) combined, in places, with the extreme diminution of taxable tillage to entail great losses upon the Treasury; wherefore the latter did its best to limit the evil. Undertaking, in the twenties of the century, a general agrarian census, it sought, through a series of *ukazi*, to stock the rural districts with the greatest possible number of homesteads which should be bound to payments of *tiaglo* according to the "living" quarter of land. Yet the Government kept wavering, and correcting itself, and altering its own returns. For instance, in the case of estates belonging to the metropolitan *tchini*, it at first imposed upon the "living" quarter a per-homestead tax at the exceedingly light rate of 12 homesteads of *krestiané* and 8 of *bobili* to the quarter, or else of 16 of *krestiané* alone (since it reckoned one full homestead of a *krestianin* to be equal to two of *bobili*). Next, it increased the *oklad*, or rate, by one-fifth—it ordained that 3 homesteads of *krestiané* should go to the quarter. Lastly, it again eased the rate by fixing that 5 such homesteads should be the numerical complement of the standard area. Of the *tiaglo* incident upon the "living" quarter the per-homestead shares were reckoned according to the number of homesteads imposed by the Government thereupon. That is to say, if 8 homesteads of *krestiané* were imposed upon the quarter, and the *krestianin* himself ploughed an eighth part of the quarter, he paid according to the number of *tchetveriki* (tax-share-units) in his tillage. But with the growth of taxable tillage the "living" quarter gradually lost the significance merely of a fraction of the *socha*, and became the customary unit of calculation in tax-imposition. The *dvor* included in an eight-homestead "living" quarter had assessed to it a payment per *tchetverik* of its tillage even though, in reality, that homestead ploughed from 4 to 5 taxable quarters. Naturally, in proportion as taxable tillage increased, so the per *socha* assessment—the sum of taxation incident upon the "living" quarter (*i.e.* upon the group of homesteads assigned to the quarter)—rose, and became divided according to the number of portions in the quarter which happened to enter into the given calculation. To the *dvor*, therefore, which paid so much per *tchetverik* of its registered tillage there was, if the *oklad* amounted to 2 roubles to the quarter, assessed a payment of 25 kopecks, or a quarter-rouble, irrespective of the total amount which it ploughed. But this was only the computative, not the actual, payment; for, in the assessment of *tiaglo*, the homestead which paid so much per *tchetverik*, per $\frac{3}{16}$ of a *dessiatina* (in three fields) of its registered tillage, yet ploughed, as a matter of fact, a total of 4 taxable *dessiatini*, paid, in reality, a different sum to the *dvor* which, though rated, in the same manner, according to *tchetveriki*, ploughed 8 *dessiatini*. Wherefore assessment of payment according to tillage was the work of the peasant himself, or of his landlord the *pomiestchik*—not of the census-taker, the assessor.

Financial necessity also led to the idea of considering, in fixing agrarian *tiaglo*, not merely the available taxable tillage, but also the available working forces and industrial conditions, of the locality—of attempting to tax not only the tillage, but the tiller himself, and so make him plough more. This consideration also ruled the fixing of the varied, mutable composition of the homestead complement of the "living" quarter, so as to make it coincide in the different cantons. Yet we can easily imagine that a tax-imposition built upon two dissimilar bases—a basis of land and a basis of homesteads—only confused both the payer and the assessor, and so increased the technical inconveniences of the system of the *Soshnöe Pismo*. The difficulty of measuring off exact squares of tillage, and of fitting them into *sochi* without also including already-broken spaces and tillage that was either "strange" (*i.e.* cultivated by peasants from a distance) or bush-grown; the complicated reckoning of portions of *sochi* according to the queer fractional arithmetic of ancient Rus—an arithmetic which reckoned only the numerator as a unit, and denominators as mere ciphers divisible into 2 or 3; the work of calculating good land, medium, and poor; the difficulty of proving both the statements of inhabitants and the errors of assessors, not to mention the difficulty of detecting tricks played for the purpose of avoiding *tiaglo*, or at least of procuring a reduction of the same,—all these things opened to disorder, schemes, and misunderstandings a wide field of action. Certainly tax-imposition according to homesteads was simpler, and, perhaps, more equal in its incidence; wherefore at the *Sobor* of 1642 the provincial-urban *dvoriané* prayed the Government to collect the money for the general upkeep of the army according to the number of peasant home-steads, and not according to the agrarian census registers. Especially did *pomiestchiki* of the smaller type see clearly that, now that the peasantry had become enserfed, the industrial force to be exploited was the labourers (with their goods) who worked the land, and not the land itself. Conse-quently in 1646 there was set on foot a general census of homesteads—a census which, while attaching the peasantry both personally and indefinitely to their landlords, also transferred direct tax-imposition from the *Soshnöe Pismo* to the register of homesteads : and in 1678–79 that census was repeated. In this manner there came into existence assessment lists of a peculiar type—the *perepisnia knigi*, which were distinguished from the older type of registers by the fact that, whereas the latter recorded the available lands, hay- and timber-cutting rights, and occupations—in short, the industrial *resources*—of the country, the *perepisnia knigi* entered in their pages the *working forces*—the taxable homesteads and their inhabitants—which paid the tax. Thus these *perepisnia knigi* came to serve as the basis of a new system of tax-imposition according to homesteads. Yet even this novel unit of assessment left the system of calculating and adjusting direct taxation as before. That is to say, the Government appointed for each taxatory district an average per-homestead rate of taxation, and, according to the number of taxable homesteads contained in the said district, calculated for the latter a general sum of taxatory payments, and left the payers themselves to apportion this sum among the individual homesteads occupied by the taxable community, in the same manner that, in former days, they had apportioned that sum among the homesteads of each *socha*, in proportion to the means of the payers and the "*tiaglo* and workings" of each several homestead.

The passage to per-homestead imposition evoked a demand for a unification of the long-accumulated stock of direct taxes, since it was difficult to apportion them according to so small a unit of assessment as the homestead. Yet, despite the fact that in the unification of indirect taxes which had been carried out in 1653 there lay ready to hand a model for a unification of the direct, there existed this essential difference, that, whereas an indirect impost takes cognisance of the consumer, but not of his economic position, the direct impost is bound to reckon with the latter. Serf right had now split the taxpaying population into two categories—into (1) the free urban and rural dwellers, who paid of their capital and of their labour, and wholly to the State, and (2) the serfs, who divided their labour between the State Treasury and the landowners' estate offices. Between these two categories of taxpayers the unified direct tax had to be assessed proportionately to their very dissimilar liabilities to the payment of fiscal dues. However, another way of escape suggested itself, and this time through the necessities of the Treasury itself. Of all the direct imposts which became permanent during the seventeenth century the tax for the upkeep of the constantly-growing corps of *Strieltsi* had increased the fastest, since, originated in 1630, it, from the year 1663 onwards, multiplied itself nearly nine times over. The inevitable result of this raising of the tax beyond the means of the taxpayers was a host of arrears. Following upon the homestead census of 1678, there were added to the *Strieltsi* tax other direct imposts; after which it was, by an *ukaz* of September 5th, 1679, transferred to the per-homestead register, at varying rates. Nevertheless the arrears still increased, and, after making a list of them, the Government, in 1681, summoned two deputies from every town, and asked them whether they were, or were not, able to pay the *Strieltsi* tax at the present rate of assessment; and if not, why not. To this at once artless and uncivil inquiry the deputies replied that they could *not* pay the tax, owing to the ruin entailed upon their constituents by the various dues and levies; whereupon a committee of Muscovite *gosti* was charged to arrange for an easing of the tax-rate, and the *gosti* thereafter reduced it by 31 per cent. Yet of its incompetence, of its utter ignorance of the position of affairs, the Muscovite Government was not in the least ashamed. Indeed, it even flaunted its shortcomings, as though they were natural and perfectly venial faults which the persons administered were bound to make good, even as they were bound to make good its financial deficits,—both the one and the other, forsooth, being their local obligations. Also, the same *ukaz* of 1679 fused the taxes for prisoners and for the posting service into a single impost; after which these two combined levies were apportioned between the two categories of taxpayers of which I have spoken. Upon the taxpaying urban populations, as well as upon the " black " [1] peasantry of the northern and north-eastern cantons, there was imposed, in lieu of the old direct taxes, a single *Strieltsi* due, divided into ten homestead rates, varying from 2 roubles to 80 kopecks according to the paying powers of taxatory districts; while upon the seigniorial peasantry of the remaining cantons (*i.e.* such of those cantons as contained peasantry of that category) there was imposed, in view of the additional burdens laid upon the *krestiané* by their masters, only a combined prisoners' and posting service tax of 10 kopecks per homestead for the Church peasantry, and of 5 kopecks for the peasantry belonging to the Court and to lay landowners : which two imposts were respectively eight times and sixteen times less than the lowest rate of the *Strieltsi* tax. This shows us what an immense source of income was surrendered by the Treasury to the irresponsible use of the serf-owners, and that even its financial policy followed the general

---

[1] *i.e.* holders of "black" or fiscal lands.

scheme of class differentiation which ruled the adjustment of the social order of Moscow during the seventeenth century.

The abortive ingenuity shown in the search for new financial resources inspired caution in the disposal of those which were already in existence. The tendency to gather every possible species of income into the coffers of the Treasury also found expression in a curtailment of local expenditure—*i.e.* in an annulment of those local posts which required to be supported by *kormi* (tithes or legalised perquisites), and were recognised to be superfluous (posts such as those of town architects, secret police agents, posting masters, grain inspectors, and even *gubnïe starosti*). All matters connected with those posts were now entrusted to the local *voievodi*, in order that the taxpayers might be weighted with no extra burdens of *kormi*, and be able, therefore, the more easily to discharge their fiscal obligations. At the same time, with the object of still further cheapening the cost of the local tax-gathering, the *voievodi*, with their *diaki* and clerks, were relieved of the duty of collecting both the *Strieltsi* tax and the local customs and excise,—the management of these matters being now imposed upon the payers themselves, through their locally elected *starosti*, "trusted men," and *tsielovalniki*, and on the payers' own responsibility. This was a return to the local institutions of the sixteenth century; yet not an establishment of local self-government—merely a transference of fiscal business from interested official agents of the Crown to local, honorary, responsible executors.

For ourselves the passage to per-homestead tax-imposition is doubly important when studying the social adjustment of the Muscovite Empire during the seventeenth century, since it not only widened the limits of tax-imposition—more strictly speaking, it complicated the composition of the taxpaying population—but it also left behind it certain *data* which will enable us to judge of the extent to which the labour-efficiency of the people was distributed among the governing forces of the State. One result of per-homestead tax-imposition was to help the Treasury to discover a large section of new taxpayers. We have seen that *zadvornïe liudi*,[1] though slaves in their juridical status, resembled *krestiané* in their industrial position, as also in their contract relations with their masters ; since they had cots to themselves, enjoyed the use of plots of land, and rendered peasant obligations to their landlords. But on the transference of *tiaglo* from tillage to homesteads these *zadvornïe liudi* began, on the strength of those cots, to undergo assessment for *tiaglo* on the same

[1] See p. 175.

footing as did *krestiané* and *bobili;* and, to judge from indications which M. Miliukov has met with in ancient financial records, that assessment began with the homestead census of 1678. In short, it constituted one of the first stages in the juridical fusion of slaves with seigniorial peasantry into a single class of serfs which reached its consummation in the first Revision of Peter the Great.

In the *perepisnia knigi*, or registers of the homestead census of 1678, we find the sum-total of taxable peasant homesteads which, later, and even in the time of Peter, the Government used in its estimation of tax-imposition. That sum-total enables us to imagine with some clearness the social structure of the Muscovite Empire as it stood compounded towards the closing quarter of the seventeenth century, on the eve of Peter's reforms. Yet, though the total is preserved in different figures in different documents, the largest figure given is the most reliable, since the remaining figures may have been computed from incomplete *data*, and there were reasons for minimising the number of taxable homesteads, but none for exaggerating it. According to the largest sum-total (that given in the census returns of 1678), the number of taxable peasant *dvori*, both urban and rural, was 888,000. Also, Kotoshikhin and certain *ukazi* of 1686 and 1687 furnish figures of the homesteads tenanted by free peasantry, urban and rural, and by Church, Court, and boyaral peasantry—peasantry who belonged to the superior administrative class of the State; where-fore, excluding the homesteads of these various categories from the sum-total given by the census returns of 1678, we obtain also the number of peasant homesteads which belonged to those State servitors, metropolitan and provincial, who constituted the *dvorianstvo* in the proper sense of the term. Thus the distribution of the taxpaying masses may be set down—according to categories of landowners, and in round figures—as follows:

Homesteads belonging to the free peasantry, urban and rural	92,000 (10.4 per cent.)
Homesteads belonging to the Hierarchy and the monasteries	118,000 (13.3 ,,)
Homesteads belonging to the Imperial Court . .	83,000 (9.3 ,,)
,, ,, ,, ,, boyars . .	88,000 (10.0 ,,)
,, ,, ,, ,, *dvoriané* . .	507,000 (57.0 ,,)
	888,000 (100 per cent.)

This division of the people's labour affords some curious evidence. Only a trifle over one-tenth of the taxable aggregate, urban and rural, was still in the enjoyment of its freedom, and placed in an independent relation to the State; considerably more than one-half of the taxable population of the country had been delivered over to the servitors of the State, in return for that class's obligation to defend the country from external foes; one-tenth had been placed at the disposal of the ruling class in return for that class's labour in administering the country; rather less than one-tenth was in the possession of the Imperial Court; a good deal over one-tenth was in the possession of the Church; one-sixth of all the Church peasantry—close upon 20,000 souls—was bound to forced labour for the Hierarchy (*i.e.* for prelates who had renounced the world in order spiritually to direct it); nearly five-sixths of the Church peasantry (exclusive of the peasantry belonging to cathedral and parish church bodies) were bound to forced labour for monasteries (*i.e.* for establishments which had renounced the world in order to pray, at the world's expense, for its sins); and, lastly, nearly nine-tenths of all the taxable population of the country were in serf dependency upon the Church, the Court, or the military servitors of the State. From such a State organism it would have been unfair to expect any desirable growth, whether political, economic, civic, or moral.

Strive as earnestly as it might to increase the tension of taxation, the Government habitually found itself unable to estimate with exactitude what expenditure confronted it, or to strike a just balance with income. Nay, in the very act of making the attempt it would perceive the falsity of its preliminary calculations, and take refuge in extraordinary resources. For instance, at a moment of great difficulty during the early years of Michael's reign, it joined the *Zemski Sobor* in exacting forced loans of such capitalists as the Stroganov family and the Troitski Monastery of St. Sergius. But these occasions were rare, for the Government's usual sources of extraordinary income were *zaprosi voleu* ("appeals to good-will") and *protsentie nalogi*, or "loans at interest." Both the one source and the other had a class significance. The *zapros voleu* was a voluntary subscription list to which the Government, authorised by the *Zemski Sobor*, invited the privileged classes—*i.e.* the landowners, spiritual and of the State service—to contribute, in order to cover any extraordinary war expenditure. For instance, we have seen that, in 1632, at the beginning of the war with Poland, and by the decree of the two Tsars in conjunction with the *Zemski Sobor*, the spiritual and service *tchini* of the *Sobor* stated how much they were prepared to give, while the remaining *tchini* promised to furnish lists of what each one of their members might be able to afford;

and a similar system was resorted to when requesting voluntary help of the *Sobor* of 1634. Also, *zaprosnia dengi* was requisitioned of the non-serf peasantry; though not in the shape of voluntary subscriptions— rather, in that of a loan assessed at the fixed rate of from a rouble to 25 kopecks per homestead (14 to 3 roubles, in modern currency). On the other hand, the *protsentni nalog* or "loan at interest"—also known as "fifth," "tenth," "fifteenth," or "twentieth money" as the case might be —was a financial device invented by the *Sobor* which elected the new dynasty, and was incident upon the commercial members of the community at the rate of 20, 10, 6.66, or 5 per cent. In 1614, the year after Michael's election, we find the *Sobor* which had elected him giving orders that, for the benefit of the troops, a levy "of profits shall be made according unto assessment, and from him who can give of his substance and of his living one hundred roubles shall there be taken a fifth part, and of him who can give whether more or less shall there be taken a toll according unto the same reckoning." Thus, in the same breath, the decree gave three mutually incompatible bases for the imposition of the levy—namely "substance and living" (*i.e.* stock and working capital in conjunction with labour), "profits according unto assessment" (*i.e.* net income according to the valuation of assessment committees), and power to "give whether more or less" (*i.e.* conscientious declaration of means). In other words, this decree, when embodied in the usual proclamation, was worded by the Muscovite *diaki* in much the same manner that persons of that class have always worded their documents—namely, in a manner which admitted of no less than three separate meanings. Yet the intention of the *Sobor* of 1614 was perfectly simple. Why should it have ordained "fifth money" when it might as well have ordained "fourth" money or "sixth"? For the reason that, in the money market of the day, the highest legal rate of interest on a loan, and also the one most customary, was 20 per cent. Yet at this rate of interest the borrower could afford to take the money only if, with the capital borrowed, he could make a great deal *more* than 20 per cent. profit; whence this rate of interest represented, in those days, minimum net produce of capital, and, in the normal order of things, doubled that capital in five years. But the *Sobor's* decree ordaining the taking of "fifth money" from the trading classes demanded that the capital thus put into circulation should surrender to the embarrassed Treasury the first year of its interest, and so work out its own doublement in *six* years, not in five; wherefore the idea of the *protsentni nalog* was, not that it should demand a fifth part of property in general, nor yet a fifth part of any income from property, but that it should mulct commercial working capital and commercial immoveable assets (shops, factories, and so forth) of their minimum net produce per year. Unfortunately the *prikazi* so framed the *Sobor's* decree as to call forth a great deal of misunderstanding, and even many breaches of the peace. In some localities "fifth money" was understood to be a general property tax, and, through the taking of inventories of all local properties, assessors soon evoked opposition on the part of the taxpayers; while in other localities the impost was assessed in precisely the same way as an ordinary tax (for example, such a tax as the *Strieltsi* impost). Where the idea of the tax was best understood it was looked upon as a tax upon the turn-over of trade, a tax which, after the assessors had calculated, through the customs returns, "how many goods, and to the value of how many roubles, have been brought hither and dispatched," took a fifth part of the value of the latter. Such collisions and misunderstandings became frequent when levies of "loans at interest" were made, owing to the want of clarity of the formula "from substance and from living." As a matter of fact, these levies were the same levies of income tax as are referred to by the German writer Reitenfeltz, who visited Moscow in 1670, and who says that taxes existed which fell upon persons of every calling, provided that such persons were in any way connected with trade or industry—whether taxpayers or non-taxpayers, clergy, persons belonging to the "white" (*i.e.* tax-exempt) *tchini* of State servitors, *Strieltsi*, artillerymen, *krestiané*, *bobili*, or slaves (provided that the latter took part in any commercial business). The "fifth money" levied in 1614 was repeated in the following year; and twice during Michael's second war with Poland—namely, in 1633 and in 1644— similar levies were made. Again, in 1637 and 1638, when it became necessary to defend the country from the Crimea, the Government first of all doubled the *Strieltsi* tax, and then requested the *Zemski Sobor* to authorise a conscription from among the Court and the seigniorial peasantry, *and also* a heavy monetary levy of about 20 (modern) roubles per *dvor* upon all trading folk, and of half that amount upon the "black" peasantry. In 1639 this extraordinary monetary requisition was repeated. With these levies went an immense amount of arrears—a sign that the payers were ever growing weaker; and, indeed, we find them complaining that things were, for them, "exceeding hard." If to this we add the forced sales to the Treasury of the more profitable species of goods (for instance, the sale of flax at Pskov at a price which had already been fixed by *ukaz*), we shall be able to understand the bitterness of a Pskovian chronicler where he complains that "value ruleth not according unto will, and purchasings are without gain, and in everything there is great offence, and enmity of which folk do speak not; so that no man in all the land may dare to offer or to sell of himself." Particularly heavy levies of extraordinary taxes took place also under Tsars Alexis and Theodor, when the prolonged and ruinous wars with Poland, Sweden, the Crimea, and Turkey were entailing grievous sacrifices of men and money upon the nation. Indeed, during the twenty-seven years 1654–1680 loans of 5 per cent. and 6.66 per cent. were, in each case, exacted from the trading community once, loans of 10 per cent. five times, and loans of 20 per cent. twice, without counting the annual homestead levies—the levies made at a fixed and uniform rate. Thus these extraneous taxes acquired the character of temporary-permanent imposts, and came though special, non-assessed dues, to be part of the State's ordinary income.

What success, then, did the Government attain with its oppressive, variable, and ill-regulated imposition of taxes? Kotoshikhin, writing of the sixties of the seventeenth century, says that every year there flowed into the Imperial Treasury, from the Empire at large, 1,311,000 roubles, over and above the Siberian Treasury's income in furs, which he declares himself to be unable to value exactly, but estimates roughly at a little over 600,000 roubles. Also, some twenty years later, the French Agent, Neville (who arrived in Moscow in 1689), was told by local informants that the annual income of the Muscovite Treasury was from 7,000,000 to 8,000,000 French *livres;* and since the *livre* of the seventeenth century was worth but a sixth of a Russian rouble, his figure approximately equals that of Kotoshikhin, while it would be difficult to estimate the profit upon the forced sales of Treasury merchandise. However, there exists a statement of income and expenditure for the year 1680 which M. Miliukov first discovered and worked upon when investigating the State housekeeping of Rus in connection with the reforms of Peter the Great. In this document the total income of the State is reckoned at nearly 1,500,000 roubles (in modern currency, 20,000,000), of which the largest item—the indirect taxes, more especially the customs and excise dues—constitute 49 per cent., and the direct taxes 44 per cent. (of these 16 per cent. consisted of extraordinary taxes). Of this grand total nearly one-half was devoted to military requirements (700,000 roubles), and, of the remainder, the Imperial Court absorbed another

15 per cent.   Yet matters touching the social welfare and the organisation of society (such as, for instance, the posting service—the means of
transport) absorbed but a little under 5 per cent. !   At the same time
this budget statement gives us a poor idea of the State *ménage* of those
days, since all that came in did not invariably go to the central *prikazi*,
but was received and spent locally.   True, this budget for 1680 shows
a notable surplus ; yet its real significance is seen in the fact that the
annual dues estimated for by the Treasury were by no means realised in
full, and that the arrears which had been accumulating since 1676
exceeded a million roubles, and had, in this year of the budget, to be
compounded.   Evidently the taxpaying powers of the nation were nearly
at the point of exhaustion.

CHAPTER XII

Dissatisfaction with the position of affairs in the State—The causes of that dissatisfaction—Its principal manifestations—Popular risings—Expressions of dissatisfaction in the literature of the day—Prince J. A. Chvorostinin—The Patriarch Nikon—Gregory Kotoshikhin—Yuri Krizhanitch.

IN re-establishing order after the Period of Troubles the Muscovite Government took no account of the radical break which had occurred in the system, but strove to preserve the system's ancient bases by under-taking only such partial and technical changes as seemed to be amend-ments or improvements. In fact, the Government's attempts to reform the structure of the State administration, with its segregation of corporate classes and its essays in State stewardship, were invariably timid and non-consecutive—they represented no broadly thought-out and practically elaborated plan of action, but seem to have been suggested by chance indications of the moment. Yet those indications had their origin in a common tendency, since, directly or indirectly, they arose from a common source—*i.e.* from the financial difficulties of the Government; and, through the force of physiological necessity, the Government's various experiments in reform were directed solely to removing those diffi-culties. Nevertheless, being of unfortunate origin, the experiments in question proved failures. Its very bent caused the now strictly cen-tralised Administration to become neither less costly nor less inequitable, since it did nothing to remove from the tax-ridden sections of the com-munity their grievous fiscal burdens. Rather, the delimiting of corporate *strata* in the community served to strengthen the cleavage of social interests and mental attitudes, while financial innovations led to exhaustion of the popular forces, and so to bankruptcy and chronic accumulation of taxatory arrears. All this created among the nation a feeling that the position was unbearable; and this feeling the Court, the personality of the new dynasty, and the foreign policy of the latter helped to bring to the pitch of a profound popular dissatisfaction with the course of affairs in the State. During the first three reigns of the new dynasty the Muscovite Government seems to have consisted of men who attained authority through a mere accident, and found themselves engaged in work which was alien to their nature. With three or four exceptions, these statesmen were seething with ambition, yet lacked either the necessary talents to direct it or any administrative experience which might take its place. Worst of all, they lacked any civic feeling. Yet it was a clique which appears to have been helped by at least one chance circumstance —namely, the circumstance that some fatality or other which overhung the new dynasty seemed to bring it about that few of the wielders of the supreme power to whom that dynasty gave birth attained their majority before the time of their accession to the throne. Of the first five Tsars of the Romanovs, three—Michael, Alexis, and Ivan—acceded at the age of sixteen, when scarcely out of their boyhood, while two others attained the Tsarship at an even earlier period in their lives—Theodor when he was but fourteen, and Peter when he was ten. Another family pecu-liarity distinguished this dynasty—namely, that, whereas its daughters usually grew up to be strong, alert, "manly," energetic young women (Sophia [1] is a case in point), most of the Tsarevitches recalled the founder of the dynasty in being feeble, short-lived, and degenerate youths, such as Theodor and Ivan. Even the lively, florid personality of Alexis con-cealed beneath it a frail constitution which could compass but forty-six years of life. As to what Alexis' younger brother Dmitri (who took after his great-grandfather, Ivan the Terrible) might have come to be we do not know; but if Kotoshikhin's testimony is to be believed, some friends of his (the Tsarevitch's) father poisoned the unfortunate boy—and that in such a cunning manner that no one ever guessed how he came by his death. In the same way, Peter the Great we need not take into account, since he was an exception to every rule. The first Tsar of the new dynasty, Michael, found himself surrounded with an administrative en-vironment even before he had acquired the intelligence or the will to know one member of it from another; and it was these early coadjutors of his who gave to his reign the whole of its tendency and colour. It was a mischance which found most poignant expression in his foreign policy, since foreign policy, above all things, created the Government's financial difficulties, and represented pre-eminently the field in which, after the territorial losses entailed by the Period of Troubles, the new dynasty ought to have justified its pan-territorial election. Michael's diplomacy—more especially after the badly-planned and ill-executed

---

[1] Daughter of Alexis by his first wife, Maria Miloslavskaia; sister of Ivan V. and Peter the Great; and Regent during the minority of the latter.

campaign of Smolensk—was distinguished by the usual caution of the beaten; but, under Alexis, the blows sustained by his father were forgotten, and Muscovites who had, against their will and after much hesitation, been led to acquiesce in the struggle for Little Rus found their anxiety relieved by the brilliant campaign of 1654–55, when, simultaneously, there fell not only Smolensk, but also the whole of Little Rus and Lithuania. Muscovite conceit, however, outran Muscovite good sense, for men never stopped to consider the fact that they were beholden for these successes, not to themselves, but to the Swedes, who at the same moment had fallen upon the Poles from the west, and so drawn off the best of Poland's forces. Muscovite policy assumed a grandiose course, and neither money nor men were spared to shatter Poland, to seat the Tsar of Moscow upon the Polish throne, to expel the Swedes from the country, to clear Little Rus of the Crimean Tartars and the Turks, and to get possession not only of both banks of the Dnieper, but also of Galicia, whither, in 1660, Sheremetev set out with an army. Yet so bewildered and weakened did Moscow grow with these complicated schemes that, after an exhausting struggle on three fronts for twenty-one years, and a series of unprecedented defeats, she abandoned Lithuania, White Rus, and the right bank of the Dnieper, and contented herself with the provinces of Smolensk and Novgorod Sieversski, the left bank of the Dnieper, and Kiev. Even the treaty of Bakhtchi Sarai which, in 1681, she concluded with the Tartars of the Crimea did not give her an advantageous frontier towards the Steppes, nor yet abrogation of the humiliating tribute to the Khan, nor yet recognition of Muscovite supremacy over the *Zaporozhie.*

With this feeling of heavy sacrifices made and dire misfortunes suffered there arose a feeling of discontent with the course of affairs. It was a feeling which, falling as it did upon a soil which the Period of Troubles had prepared for general unrest, came to embrace the community from top to bottom, but did not find the same expression among the upper *strata* as among the lower. Among the masses of the people it expressed itself in a series of agitations which communicated to the seventeenth century a restless character which has caused it to become known in our history as the era of popular risings. Without mentioning the intermittent smoulderings which burst into flame under Michael, it will be sufficient but to enumerate the risings during Alexis' reign to see the strength of the public dissatisfaction. In 1648 rebellions took place in Moscow, Oustuga, Koslov, Solvitchegodsk, Tomsk, and other towns.

In 1649 a rising of *zakladchiki* (self-pledgers) was hatched in Moscow, but averted in time. In 1650 riotings took place in Pskov and Great Novgorod. In 1662 another rebellion broke out in Moscow, over the copper coinage. In 1670–71 the great rebellion of Stenka Razin raged in the south-eastern regions of the Volga—a movement which, though originating among the Don Cossacks, acquired a purely social character as soon as ever it became fused with a movement of the general populace against the upper classes. Lastly, the years 1668 to 1676 witnessed the revolt of the Solovetski Monastery against the revised versions of the Church's service-books. During these various ebullitions occasional revelations occur of the relation in which the populace stood to the authority which was bolstered up with so much official ceremonial and ecclesiastical teaching. Not a shadow of reverence for such authority is to be seen, but only rudeness—rudeness not to the Government alone, but also to the wielder of the supreme power himself. As for the upper classes, they displayed their discontent in a different manner. If, among the masses, discontent deranged the nervous system, among the classes it had the result of stimulating thought, and so of inducing increased criticism of the domestic order. Just as, among the one, it was enmity against the heads of society that gave an impetus to the movement, so, among the other, the ruling note among the babel of protesting voices was a consciousness of popular insolvency and impotence. Almost for the first time we meet with expressions of Russian thought in the difficult and slippery field of the publicist, of the critic of surrounding actualities. Manifestations of this character appear at the *Zemski Sobor* of 1642, and, next, at the conference which, in 1662, an administrative committee held with the Muscovite traders concerning the rise of prices. Without altering their political discipline, and without dropping the tone of respect, these merchants nevertheless permitted themselves to speak with great earnestness on the subject of administrative disorder, the unhindered infringement of the law by privileged persons, and the contempt for public opinion which was shown by the Government in that, though ordered by Imperial *ukaz* to take the opinions of the trading classes, it tackled, in accordance with those opinions, only a trifling matter or two. But these were *guarded* statements of the people's needs and thoughts; and it was with much greater energy that other observers of the position of things in the Empire expressed their personal ideas. I will confine myself to a few examples, in order to show how these early attempts at public criticism voiced the state of things in bygone Rus.

The first such attempt of which we have any knowledge was made at the beginning of the seventeenth century, during the Period of Troubles. Undoubtedly it owed its inspiration to the Period. Prince J. A. Chvorostinin was a prominent young man at the court of the First Pretender, and a young man who, having studied Latin, had become versed in Latin literature, infected with Catholic opinions, and accustomed to pay as much respect to Latin *ikoni* (sacred images) as to Orthodox. To correct this he was sent, during the reign of Vassilii, to the monastery of St. Joseph, whence he returned in a reckless and angry frame of mind, and, lapsing into freethought, renounced prayers and the resurrection of the dead, " and did waver in the faith, blaspheme Orthodox truth, and speak impious words concerning the holy means of grace." Meanwhile he kept up his interest in Slavonic ecclesiastical literature until he had made himself an authority on Church history who was accustomed to display the most virulent acrimony in private literary discussions on books, and had come to be distinguished for his accomplished arrogance. " No man did he reckon equal unto himself in skill of learning." Something also of a penman, he, during Michael's reign, indited a passable account of his times, in which he philosophised rather than treated of men or events. The result of this meeting in the same personality of a medley of views and opinions, and of their refusing to combine into an integral, sanely reasoned outlook which did not menace Orthodox-Byzantine traditions and ideas, was to set Prince Chvorostinin at loggerheads with everything native to his own country. The rites of the Russian Church he treated with controversial contempt, and he " kept not fasts nor Christian custom." He even forbade his servants to attend church, remained drunk, "without awakening," during the Passiontide of 1622, and was in a state of intoxication even when he went to break his fast on Easter morning. Also, that day he did not attend to present his congratulations to the Tsar, nor put in an appearance at Matins or at Mass. After thus isolating himself by his behaviour and line of opinions, he bethought him of migrating—even of fleeing—to Lithuania or to Rome, and for this purpose sold his *otchini* and his Muscovite mansion. This led the Imperial *ukaz* which formulated his misdemeanours to pass a particularly warm judgment upon his sins against his compatriots; and, a domiciliary search having been made at his house, there were discovered there some autograph manuscripts which contained productions both in prose and in verse (the latter written in a Polish metre). In these documents, as also in his discourses, he expresses great weariness and despondency at finding himself in "an alien land," and serene contempt for the native order of things and the denizens of the Muscovite Empire, whom he accuses of senseless devotion to idols. He complains that "in Moscow of men there are none, but all are gross, and not to be consorted with. They do sow the earth with rye, and live alway in falsehood." In short, it is impossible for him to hold any communication with them. Finally he falls foul both of his parents and of the inhabitants of Moscow—which latter city he loads with blame and senseless raillery, and refuses even to write the Tsar's title as it ought to be written, since he calls his Sovereign "the Russian Despot," and not "the Tsar," or "the Autocrat." For the second time the Prince was banished to a monastery, but this time to that of St. Cyril, where he repented, and then returned to Moscow, where he regained his place among his fellow *dvoriané*, and was accorded the *entrée* to Court. Dying in 1625, he represents an early, and a curious, phenomenon in Russian intellectual life—but a phenomenon which, later, became far more common. He was not a Russian heretic of the type of the sixteenth century—of the type which, tinged with Protestantism, fed its ideas on dogmatic doubts and debates concerning the ritual of the Church, and represented a remote echo of the Reformation which was raging in the West. Rather, he was an original Russian freethinker, framed on a Catholic lining—a person who, permeated with profound antipathy to the hardness of Byzantine-ecclesiastical formality, and everything in Russian life which that formality nourished, represented a remote, spiritual precursor of Tchadaev.

Next, an unlooked-for phenomenon amid the series of accusers of the irregularities of domestic politics is seen in the supreme overseer of the native ecclesiastical-religious system himself—the Patriarch of All Rus. But he was not merely Patriarch—he was also Patriarch Nikon. It must be remembered that this man raised himself to the patriarchal throne from the peasant class, and then gained immense influence over Tsar Alexis, who dubbed him his "beloved friend." Later the two friends fell out, and in 1658 Nikon abdicated from the Patriarchate, in the hope that the Tsar would humbly beg of him to return. The Tsar, however, did nothing of the sort; wherefore, in a fit of anger and wounded self-esteem, Nikon wrote his Sovereign a letter concerning the position of affairs in the State. On such an occasion the Patriarch's judgement could hardly have been expected to be a passionless one, and the curious colours which he lays so thickly upon his gloomy picture of the situation of the time were all of them derived from the financial difficulties of the Government and the industrial disorder of the nation. Most of all he was incensed with the *Monastivski Prikaz* or *Prikaz* of Monasteries, which was charged with the judging of the clergy in non-spiritual matters, and also managed the huge *otchini* of the Church. This *Prikaz* consisted only of a boyar and a staff of *diaki ;* not a single spiritual person did it contain. Consequently in the year 1661 Nikon wrote the Tsar an accusatory letter on the subject. Hinting at the hated *Prikaz*, he writes, with a play upon certain of his words : " The judges of this world do judge and exercise violence, and therefore thou hast collected against thyself, towards the Day of Judgement, a great council to rail at thy iniquities. Also, though thou dost enjoin upon all men that they shall fast, it is not within knowledge how many men do fast, rather, from lack of bread. Yea, in many places men are fasting even unto death, in that they have naught to eat. There be none who shall be pardoned—whether beggars or the blind or widows or monks or nuns. All are burdened with heavy tribute, and everywhere there is weeping and affliction, and no man doth rejoice." In similarly lurid colours he depicts (in a letter which he sent to the Eastern Patriarchs in 1665, but which was intercepted by agents of Moscow), the financial position of the State. Complaining of the sequestration of Church properties which the Tsar indulged in, he writes that "they do take men for service, and both grain and money do ravish without stint. All the Christian race is burdened by the Tsar with twofold and threefold tribute, or with more. Everything is vain."

The same reign saw begun, under very exceptional circumstances, another Russian attempt to depict the faults of the Muscovite State order. Gregory Kotoshikhin, who served awhile as a clerk in the *Posolski Prikaz* or Ministry for Foreign Affairs, and there performed diplomatic functions of no great importance, was, in 1660, wrongfully accused of misdemeanours, and, for making a mistake in the Tsar's title, was beaten with rods. Next, impressed as a conscript into the army of Prince Yuri Dolgoruki during the second war with Poland, he refused to perform an illegal order of his commanding officer, and, in 1664, fled to Poland : after which he lived for a time in Germany, and, finally, settled in Stockholm. Here, though the dissimilarity existing between foreign institutions and those of his own country had struck him greatly during his wanderings abroad, the fact inspired him, rather, to undertake a description of the condition of the Muscovite Empire. Upon the wits and experience of Selitski (as Kotoshikhin called himself in his new home) the Swedish Chancellor set considerable store, and encouraged him in the work which he had begun upon, and which he performed so well that it has come to represent one of the most important historical memorials of the seventeenth century; but Kotoshikhin came to a bad end, since, after a sojourn of a year and a half in Stockholm, he seceded to Protestantism, became over-friendly with the wife of a man at whose house he was lodging, and, finally, killed the suspicious husband; for which crime he duly paid the penalty on the scaffold. His historical work (whereof the Swedish translator calls the author a man of unbalanced mind) a Russian professor discovered, during the past century, in Upsala, and it was published in 1841. In the thirteen chapters which it is divided into there are described the life of the Muscovite Court, the composition of the Court class, the system of Moscow's diplomatic relations with foreign countries, the structure of the central administration, the army, the urban-trading and rural populations, and the domestic life of the upper circles of Muscovite society. Kotoshikhin gives vent to few opinions of his own, but, for the most part, describes the institutions of his country in clear, simple, exact language. Everywhere it is manifest that of his late country he takes a slighting view; which relation serves the author as a dark background whereon to draw what appears to be an impartial picture of Russian life. At the same time, some direct personal opinions occur in it, and always unfavourable ones which have for the object of their indictment numerous grave faults in the life and morals of the Muscovites. The latter the author judges severely for their " nature which fears not God," their pride, their tendency to cheat, and, most of all, their bad manners. Russian folk, he writes, are " by nature proud and unused to affairs, since in that State they have no instruction in aught which is goodly, but are all for pride and shamelessness and hatred and untruth. Nor do they, for the gaining of learning and usedness with men," (*savoir faire* in society) " send their sons to other States, since they fear that, through learning of the faiths and the customs and the goodly freedom of other States, their sons will put away the faith which is in them, and join themselves unto other folk, and have not the will or the power to return home to their own kinsmen." Then the author draws a caricature-sketch of a sitting of the *Boyarskaia Duma* at which the boyars, " setting in order their beards," return no answers to the Tsar's questions, and cannot give him good advice " for the reason that the Tsar maketh many such to be boyars, not because of their prudence, but out of his greatness of heart, since many of them have no skill in learning, nor have studied aught." Of the family routine of the Russians, too, Kotoshikhin draws a sombre picture. For anyone who holds the idea that, in spite of her numerous political and civic faults, ancient Rus could have elaborated, even with the help of the Church's rules for household management, a juridically and morally strong family, —well, for that man the last chapter of Kotoshikhin's work, " On the life of the boyars, and the *dumnïe liudi*, and the privy councillors, and all other ranks of men," will prove a stumbling-block. In it we see a dispassionate description of the powers exercised by parents over their children, of the cynicism of the marriage relationship and contract, of the indecency of the marriage rite, of the gross cheating of portionless daughters by their parents (with the view of wresting from them their poor little substance), of the lawsuits which arose therefrom, of the beatings and forcible shavings of the head which were awarded to loveless women, of the poisoning of wives by their husbands and of husbands by their wives, and of the unspiritual interference of the ecclesiastical authorities in family quarrels. This murky picture of family conditions frightens even the author himself, and he concludes his simple and frigid narrative with the excited exclamation : " O prudent reader, marvel not at this. Yet is it the truth that in all the world there is no such despoiling of maidens as in the Muscovite State ; for thither never hath the custom been brought which ruleth in other States—to wit, that consent and agreement shall first of all be made with the maidens themselves."

It will be interesting to compare the opinions of this Russian who had forsaken his country with the impressions of a foreign observer who came to Rus in the hope of finding a second fatherland. Yuri Krizhanitch, a Serb and a Catholic father, was a man of many-sided culture—something of a philosopher and a theologian, something of a political economist, a great philologist, and above all things a patriot ; or, rather, an ardent Pan-slavist, since his true fatherland was not any country known to history, but united Slavdom—*i.e.* a purely political fantasy which stood outside of history. Born a subject of the Sultan of Turkey, he was, as a poor orphan, conveyed to Italy, and afterwards received his education at ecclesiastical seminaries in Zagreb (Hungary), Vienna, and Bologna. Lastly he entered the Roman College of St. Athanasius, where the Roman Congregation for the Propagation of the Faith trained special missionaries for work among the schismatics of the Orthodox East. As a Slav, he was appointed thence to Muscovy. He himself felt a leaning towards that far-distant country— he collected all the knowledge that he could about it, and presented to the Congregation carefully thought-out plans for its conversion. Yet he had his own secret schemes the while. For the poor Slavonic student missionary zeal served but as a means for winning material support for himself from the Congregation. He regarded the Muscovites neither as heretics nor schismatics ; and this not out of sophistry, but for the reason that he considered them to be Christians who had lost their way through ignorance and simplicity of soul. Early he began to think about, and to feel deeply ashamed of, the wretched position of enslaved and downtrodden Slavdom; and to the credit of his political sagacity must be assigned the fact that he divined the true road to a unification of the Slavs. If men are to unite with one another they must first of all *understand* one another, and herein the Slavs were hindered by their differences of dialect. Consequently, even during his course at the Roman college, Krizhanitch took care not to forget his native Slavonic language, but studied it carefully, with a view to attaining perfect speech in the same, and was at great pains to clear it of all alloy or local debasement, and to work it up in such a way that it should be understood of Slavs in general ; to which end he thought out and indited grammars, dictionaries, and philological treatises. Another—a still more daring—act of divination must be laid to his credit. This was the fact that he realised that the consolidation of scattered Slavdom must be brought about from some political centre. No such centre was then available; nothing had yet occurred to designate it, or to make it an historical factor, or to cause it to become, as it did later, a beacon to some men and a scarecrow to others. Yet in the end he discovered by instinct the key to the riddle. He, though a Serb and a Catholic, had the sense to seek that future centre of Slavdom neither in Vienna nor in Prague nor in Warsaw, but in Moscow—in Moscow which was Orthodox by faith and, in the opinion of Europe, Tartaric by nationality. How men must have laughed at this in the seventeenth century ! Even yet one may smile at it. Nevertheless, between that age and our own there have occurred moments when it was not easy to over-value the idea. As the future centre of Slavdom, Krizhanitch calls Russia his second fatherland—though he never had a first' one except the land of Turkey. How he came to pitch upon that centre—whether it was through the instinct of ardent patriotism or through consideration of policy—it is difficult to say. In any case he did not settle in Rome, where the Congregation posted him after the polemic with the Greek Schism, but set out of his own accord, in 1559, for Moscow. There the Roman-Apostolic scheme was, it appears, abandoned, for he was forced to keep silence concerning his Roman priesthood, lest he should fail to be admitted into the city. As a matter of fact, he was received there simply as "a strange Serb, by name Yuri Ivanovitch," on the same footing as were other foreigners who arrived thither to enter the service of the State; wherefore, in order to create for himself an assured position in the State's metropolitan service, he proposed various services to the Tsar, and ended by becoming not only a Muscovite-Panslavist publicist, but also the Imperial librarian ; in which capacity he wrote a veracious history of the Muscovite Empire and the Slavonian people at large. Yet all the salary that he received was from $1\frac{1}{2}$ to 3 (modern) roubles *per diem*, in spite of the labour which he had so lovingly bestowed upon his Slavonic grammars and lexicons and of the fact that he had gone to Moscow with a view to carrying out, from that centre, a literary and linguistic consolidation of Slavdom. He himself soon recognised that his idea of a Panslavist language would never effect anything beyond the walls of Moscow, although from boyhood he had given his heart to the work of correcting "our mutilated (nay, even our dead) tongue to the decking of mine own mind and that of all the people." Also, in another of his works he writes : "Men do call me a roamer and a wanderer, but they say this in error, for that I have come unto the Tsar of mine own race, unto mine own people, unto mine own fatherland, unto mine own country, where alone my labours shall be of profit and bring me advantage, and where alone my merchandise—to wit, my dictionaries, my grammars, and my renderings [1]—shall be of value and meet for barter in the market." A little over a year later he was sent, for some reason, to Tobolsk, where he resided a further fifteen years. Exile, however, served to assist him in his literary-scholastic productiveness, and the sufficient salary allowed him in Tobolsk left him an amount of leisure of which even he himself at times grew weary, so that he complained that he had no work to do save to feed well, like a beast in the slaughter-house. In Siberia he wrote much, and also copied out the Slavonic grammar which he had taken such pains over, and upon which, to quote his own words, he had "thought and laboured for twenty-two years." Eventually Tsar Theodor restored him to Moscow, and soon afterwards he asked to be allowed to return "unto his own land,"—no longer concealing his missionership or his canonical orders (the orders "of a shaven priest"—so the term "canonical" was then interpreted in Moscow). Finally, in 1677, he quitted his titular fatherland for ever.

These circumstances of Krizhanitch's life are interesting to us as explaining the opinions on Russia which he voices in the largest of his

[1] Translations.

works—in the work entitled "Political Thoughts" or "Discourses on Politics." This was written in Siberia, and is in three parts. In Part I. he airs his views on the economic resources of the Empire; in Part II. he considers the question of the Empire's warlike resources; and in Part III. he judges of its resources of intellect, and adds thereto certain discourses on extraneous subjects, more especially on subjects of a political nature. Thus the work has the appearance of being a politico-economic treatise. In it the author reveals erudition both in ancient and modern literature, as well as a certain acquaintance with the written records of Rus; but for ourselves the most important point about it is that the author everywhere compares the condition of the States of Western Europe with the system then in vogue in the Muscovite Empire—that he for the first time brings Russia face to face with those States. Let me enumerate the principal views which he expresses. The work is in the form of a series of rough jottings—now in Latin, and now in a peculiar, self-evolved Slavonic dialect, with, as *addenda*, a number of corrections, interpolations, and fragmentary remarks. He expresses a firm belief in the future of Russia and of Slavdom. He thinks that their turn is to come next in the march of successive nations towards culture—to come next in the passage of the arts and sciences from one nation to another: which idea bears a close resemblance to the theory concerning the cycle of civilisation to which, at a later period, both Leibnitz and Peter the Great gave expression. No one can say, writes Krizhanitch in an estimate of the cultural progress of the different nations, that to the Slavs some celestial fatality has not particularly pointed out the road to learning. For his own part he considers the time ripe for the Slavonic race to improve itself. "*Adda i nam treba uchitsia, yako pod tchestitim Tsaria Aleksieia Michaelovitcha vladaniem motch chotchem drevnia divietchini pliesen otert, umietelei sia näuchit, pochvalnie obstchenia natchin priat i blazhenievo stana dotchekat*" ("Now is there need for us to instruct ourselves, in that under the honoured power of Tsar Alexis Michaelovitch it may be given unto us to rub off the old mould of barbarism, and to become wise in learning, and to take unto ourselves the precepts of stronger communion, and to achieve a more fortunate State"). This passage gives us an excellent example of the Panslavonic dialect which Krizhanitch elaborated with such solicitude. Hitherto the consummation desired by the author had been hindered by the two chief misfortunes or faults under which Slavdom laboured; one of which he calls *tchuzebiesïe*, or a mad passion for everything exotic, and the other one *tchuzhevladstvo*, or the foreign yoke under which all the Slavonic peoples had fallen in consequence of that passion. Indeed, on every occasion when he refers to these misfortunes Krizhanitch's utterances sound an angry note, and his imagination is not sparing of the most repellent of images and colours whenever he wishes to give an adequate picture of the hated enslavers, more especially of the Germans. "No people under the sun," writes he, "hath ever been so shamed and wronged by the foreigner as have we Slavs by the Germans. Nay, we are stifled beneath a multitude of aliens; they do fool us, and lead us by the nose; they do sit upon our backs, and ride us like cattle; they do call us swine and dogs, while thinking themselves equal to gods, and ourselves but simpletons. Upon that which is wrung of our tears and sweat, and of the forced fasting of the Russian people, do these foreigners—these Greek merchants and German merchants and officers and Crimean robbers—grow fat. And all this hath arisen of our fondness for the stranger. At everything which is strange we do marvel, and do praise and extol it, while despising everything in our life which is our own." A whole chapter does the author devote to an enumeration of the "shamefulnesses and offences" endured by the Slav peoples at the hands of the foreigner. But, he adds, Russia is destined to deliver Slavdom from the misfortunes under which she, like her fellow Slavs, is suffering. Next he addresses to Tsar Alexis the following appeal : "Upon thee, O most honourable Tsar, hath the lot fallen to take thought for the Slavonic people. Thou alone, O Tsar, hast been given us of God to succour them who do dwell beyond the Duna,[1] the Tsechs and the Lechs, to the end that they may perceive that they are oppressed of the stranger, and living in shame, and that they may begin to cast the German yoke from off their necks." Yet when Krizhanitch looked abroad in Russia, and noted the life of the future saviours of Panslavism, he could not but feel struck with the multitude of irregularities and vices from which those saviours themselves were suffering. Particularly he protested against the conceit of the Russians, their boundless attachment to their customs, and their ignorance—yes, above all things, their ignorance. The latter, he said, was the chief cause of the economic instability of the Russian nation. Russia was a poor country as compared with Western States, since it did not stand on so high a plane of development. In the West the intellects of the nations were shrewd and calculating. Those nations possessed books on agriculture and other industries. Likewise they could boast of harbours; and not only agriculture and the trades flourished in their midst, but also

---

[1] Danube.

maritime commerce.   But of this there was nothing to be seen in Russia. The country was debarred on every side from international trade : on the two sides of the sea by oceans which were difficult to navigate, and on the other two sides by deserts and savage peoples.   Also, it contained few trading towns, and no valuable or indispensable manufactures at all. The nation's intelligence was slow and stupid ; it could think out nothing for itself until it was shown how to do so.   Men were unskilled in trade, in agriculture, or in home industries ; nay, they were too lazy and improvident even to benefit themselves, unless compelled to do so by force.   Of books on husbandry and other industries they had none ; merchants never even learned arithmetic, and were cheated right and left by the foreigner.   Of history or antiquity the average Russian knew nothing, nor could he carry on a conversation on politics.   For this the foreigner again despised him.   The same intellectual sloth expressed itself (said Krizhanitch) in the unlovely cut of the Russian's clothes, in his outward man, in the setting of his home, and in his whole mode of life, since his unkempt hair and beard made him look like a dirty, comical man of the woods, and foreigners were led to despise both his slovenliness and the fact that he held his money in his mouth, never washed his crockery, and so on.   The Russian peasant, remarked Krizhanitch, would offer his guest a jug of water to wash in, yet decline to dip more than a finger of his own into the liquid ; while in foreign journals it was a current saying that " if a Russian merchant do enter a shop, no other man may enter the same until an hour be past, by reason of the stench." Also, the Russian dwelling was a sorry one.   It was low, and the huts contained no chimney at all, so that many persons went blind from the smoke.   Other failings did Krizhanitch observe in the Russian community—such as drunkenness and a lack of animation, of noble pride, of manly spirit, and of personal and national dignity.   Although, in war, the Turks and the Tartars might seek refuge in flight, they never gave themselves up to be slain, but defended themselves to the last breath ; whereas, whenever a Russian warrior fled, he did so without looking back, and could be cut down like a corpse.   But the greatest of the national vices was want of moderation in authority.   The Russian could never put a rein upon himself, nor strike a middle course, but must rush to extremes.   In one part of the country administration would go to rack and ruin, and be carried on in a slovenly way, while in another part of the country its execution would be extraordinarily firm, strict, and oppressive.   No State in the world, said Krizhanitch, is so slovenly and so remiss as the Polish, nor any administration in the world so harsh as that of the famous Russian Empire. Angered by these various short-comings, Krizhanitch could almost have preferred the Tartars and the Turks to the Russians, and holds up the former to the latter as persons to take lessons from in sobriety, in valour, and even in modesty. Clearly Krizhanitch's eyes were so open to the faults of the Russian public that he exaggerated the faults which he observed. Clearly, also, Krizhanitch was a Slav, and therefore devoid of the merit of being able to be moderate, or to look at things in a simple, direct manner. Yet the author does not merely bewail matters; he also ponders, and proposes means for healing the sicknesses which he laments: and those means he works up into an entire programme of reforms which is of far more importance to us than ever could have belonged to the merely clever reflections of a Slavonic immigrant who came to Moscow in the seventeenth century. Four methods of correction does he propose. (1) Enlightenment, learning, and literature, which, though inanimate, are wise and just counsellors. (2) Administrative regulation, operating from above. Krizhanitch believes in the Autocracy. In Russia, he says, there is complete absolutism, and it is always possible for an Imperial edict to rectify or to control what is expedient; whereas in other lands such a course would be impossible. "Thou, O Tsar"—thus he apostrophises Alexis—"dost hold in thy hands the miraculous staff of Moses, with which thou art able to work marvellous wonders in the government. In thy hands there is full autocracy." The author pins great hopes upon this method, despite the fact that he proposes the strangest of means for its application. For instance, if a merchant should be ignorant of arithmetic, his shop was to be closed by *ukaz* until he had mastered the art of numbers! (3) Political freedom. Under the Autocracy, says Krizhanitch, there can be no harshness of administration, nor any burdening of the people with impossible dues and levies—with any what the author calls "*liudoderstvo.*"[1] For this purpose certain "licenses"—*i.e.* political rights and class self-government—are necessary. The merchants must be given the right to choose for themselves *starosti* and a class tribunal; the tradesmen must combine in guilds; commercial folk must be allowed to treat with the Government concerning their needs, as well as concerning their protection from provincial administrators; and the peasantry must have secured to them freedom of labour. Moderate emancipation Krizhanitch looks upon as a curb to restrain administrative officials from "sorry

[1] Approximately, duress of the people.

lustings "—as the one shield which subjects can use to defend themselves from departmental abuses, and by which justice can be safeguarded in the State, since neither interdicts nor penalties will restrain persons in office (*dumniki*—"men of the *Duma*") from schemes of oppression, if there be no freedom. (4) Spread of technical education. For this purpose the State must interfere authoritatively in popular industry, and institute in every town technical schools, and not only establish by *ukaz* women's colleges for teaching the industrial arts and handicrafts, but also impose upon every intending bridegroom an obligation to inquire of his intended what she has learnt from her preceptors. Also, the State ought to emancipate slaves who, after mastering a trade which calls for special technical knowledge, shall be able to translate into the Russian language German works which bear upon commerce and the handicrafts. Lastly, the State ought to invite from abroad, and more especially from Germany, artisans and capitalists who shall be capable of teaching the Russians their (the foreign artisans' and capitalists') skilled trades and methods of business. The author concludes with the observation that all these measures must be directed towards a vigorous and compulsory exploitation of the natural riches of the country, as well as towards wide diffusion of new manufactures, more especially manufactures connected with metallurgy.

Such was the programme of Yuri Krizhanitch. Not only was it an exceedingly complicated one, but also it was one which was not altogether free from a certain internal lack of consistency, seeing that Krizhanitch allowed himself to include in the scheme several contradictions and a modicum of ambiguity. Indeed, it is difficult to understand how he can ever have measured with one another the various methods which he puts forward for correcting the faults of the Russian public—to understand, for instance, what distinctions he can have drawn between governmental regulation, as strengthened by absolutism, and public self-administration, or how his proposed "*gostogonstvo*"—*i.e.* expulsion of the foreigner—could ever be reconciled with the recognised impossibility of doing without the foreign instructor. Yet, in reading Krizhanitch's exceedingly original programme, one is almost involuntarily led to exclaim that it is the programme of Peter the Great, even to the faults and the contradictions of the latter, and to its idyllic belief in the creative force of an *ukaz*, and to the possibility of spreading education and commerce through translation of German books or temporarily closing the shop of a merchant who had never learnt the art of arithmetic. However, these contradictions and this similarity between the programmes lend to Krizhanitch's opinions a special interest. He, a man unique of his kind (as an *immigrant* observer of Russian life), in no way resembled the multitude of foreigners who chanced to visit Moscow, and there recorded their impressions. Such visitors looked upon the phenomena of Russian life as so many oddities of an uncultured people which were interesting for idle curiosity to peruse, but no more; whereas Krizhanitch was both an alien in and a native of Russia—an alien by origin and education, and a native of the land in racial sympathies and political hopes. He had come to Moscow not merely to observe, but also to preach, and to propagate the Panslavist idea, and to issue a battle summons on its behalf. Indeed, this aim is directly stated in the Epilogue to his *Discourses*. "Up ye, and defend ye the nation! Thence do I desire to drive out all foreigners, and to raise the men of the Dnieper—the Lechs, and the Lithuanians, and the Serbs, and all who still do make war among themselves—to fight by my side!" When two parties are about to meet in battle it is necessary to calculate their comparative strength, and then to supplement the shortcomings of one's own side on the models of one's opponent, through a process of looking for and borrowing thence what he possesses in greater measure. Hence originate the favourite conditions of Krizhanitch's method of exposition: he is forever collating and projecting— forever comparing phenomena observed among the Slavs with kindred phenomena to be observed in the hostile West, and then proposing to preserve some particular phenomenon of his country *in statu quo*, and to correct, perhaps, some other phenomenon on Western lines. Hence also arose his manifest inconsistencies : they were contradictions in the life which he was observing, not mistakes on the part of the observer himself. He was forced to borrow of the alien, and to learn at the hands of the foe; and though he looks for, and gladly takes note of, anything in Russian life which seems superior to what is to be found in the life of the foreigner, and defends the life of his countrymen from slanders and false accusations, he refuses to deceive either himself or others. Though he looks for miracles to come of the Autocracy, yet the disruptive effect of harsh Muscovite administration upon the morals, the prosperity, and the external relations of the people is not described by any foreigner with the clearness with which it is to be found depicted in the chapter of Krizhanitch's *Discourses* which treats of the "duress" of the Muscovites. He is no devoted worshipper of authority, but thinks, rather, that, if it were possible to question all rulers on the subject, there are many who would be unable to explain why they exist at all. Authority he values only as a cultural means, while placing a mystical trust in his own Muscovite staff of Moses; though he cannot but have heard of Ivan the Terrible's fearful cudgel,[1] and also of the crutch of the lame Michael. In the main, Krizhanitch's comparative estimate of matters does not issue in favour of his own people, for he recognises the decided superiority, both in intellect, in knowledge, in morals, in orderliness, and in the conditions of life generally, of the foreigner. Consequently he propounds the question: What place are we, the Russians and the Slavs, destined to hold among our fellow nations, and what historical *rôle* has fate ordained us to play on the stage of the world, seeing that our nation stands between the cultured peoples of Europe and the barbarians of the East, and, as such, is ever bound to act as an intermediary between the two? Then from petty observations and detailed projects Krizhanitch's thought rises to broad generalisations. For him the Russian-Slavonic East and the alien West are two separate worlds, two sharply differentiated cultural types. Indeed, in one of the dissertations which he introduces into his main treatise we find a shrewd comparison of the qualities which distinguish Slavs in general, and the Russians in particular, from the nations of the West. The latter he declares to be fair of feature, and therefore proud and overbearing, since comeliness breeds pride and arrogance; whereas the Russians have neither the one nor the other of those qualities, but are a people of moderate exterior. Also, we Russians are not eloquent, and cannot express ourselves clearly; whereas they are loquacious, and " bold in words of upbraiding," and sarcastic. We are devious in thought and simple of heart; whereas they are replete with every species of cunning. We are not parsimonious, but prodigal—we make no estimate of expenditure, but scatter our goods with a lavish hand; whereas they are thrifty and greedy—day and night they think but to pack their moneybags the more. We are slothful both in labour and study; whereas they are industrious, and sleep not a single hour that may bring profit. We are dwellers in a needy land; whereas they are natives of rich and bounteous countries, and lure us with the tempting products of those countries as hunters lure their game. We speak, act, and think in simple fashion—we quarrel and become reconciled; whereas they are secretive, and prone to dissimulation, and rancorous; they remember a word of insult until death, and, having once quarrelled, never become sincerely reconciled,

---

[1] The staff with which, in a fit of rage, Ivan killed his own son.

but, when at peace, still seek an occasion for revenge. In short, there may be assigned to Krizhanitch a special, yet a very clear, place among our historical sources. For over a hundred years we encounter in our literature nothing wholly resembling the observations and judgements which he expresses. While his observations present the student with a new pallet of colours wherewith to paint Russian life during the seventeenth century, his judgements serve the student as a verification of the impressions to which that life gives rise.

Neither Nikon's letters to Alexis nor the compositions of Kotoshikhin and Krizhanitch acquired general notoriety in their own day. Kotoshikhin's work was not read in Russia before the fourth decade of the nineteenth century, when it was discovered in the library of the University of Upsala by a Russian professor; while for many a long day Krizhanitch's great treatise lay "in the upper rooms" of the palace of Tsars Alexis and Theodor—though copies of it were possessed by two influential adherents of the Tsarevna Sophia, the Princes Madviedev and V. Golitzin, who seem to have intended to print it during Theodor's time. Krizhanitch's notions and observations may have served to supplement the stock of revolutionary ideas which arose in the minds of Muscovite administrative circles; yet we cannot deny to *all* the personages of the seventeenth century whose opinions I have quoted in this chapter an important significance for students of the century, since they testify to the attunement of the Russian community. The most outstanding note in that attunement was dissatisfaction with the position of affairs, and in this connection Krizhanitch is especially important, as an observer who describes with evident resentment certain untoward phenomena which he would fain not have encountered in the land which, to him, represented the distant, but all-powerful, stay of Slavdom. And that dissatisfaction is an extremely important turning stage in the Russian life of the seventeenth century, since it was accompanied with numberless consequences which, together, form the essential subject-matter of our later history. Of the most immediate of those consequences the first was the introduction of Western European influence into Russia: and to the origin and earlier manifestations of that influence let me next proceed to call attention.

CHAPTER XIII

IN turning to the beginning of Western influence in Russia, we must first of all define with more exactness what that influence meant. Once upon a time—*i.e.* during the fifteenth and sixteenth centuries—Russia was familiar to Western Europe, and transacted business, both diplomatic and commercial, with the same, borrowed the fruits of its enlightenment, and summoned to her aid its artists, skilled artisans, physicians, and soldiers. But this was not influence: it was intercourse. Influence appears upon the scene when the community by which it is received begins to recognise the superiority of the culture or environment with which it (the community) is being influenced, and also the necessity of studying it, of morally submitting to it, while at the same time borrowing from it not only the amenities of life, but also the very bases of a system of life—views, ideas, and social relations. Only with the seventeenth century did Russia manifest such signs in relation to Western Europe; and it is in this sense that I am speaking when I say that Western influence *began* with the period in question.

But why did that influence—that mental and moral submission—not begin during the sixteenth century? Because its source was Russia's dissatisfaction with life and her own position. And that dissatisfaction arose from one particular difficulty wherewith the Government of the new dynasty found itself confronted—a difficulty which pressed with more or less insistence also upon the whole of the community, and all its classes. The difficulty lay in the impossibility of making the material requirements of the Government square with the stock of domestic resources offered by the Government's system of subsistence. That is to say, the difficulty lay in the recognised necessity of reorganising the Government's system of subsistence in order to provide the means which the State so sorely lacked. It was no mere novelty which had never before been experienced; the necessity of reorganisation was not for the first time being felt among the Muscovite community: yet never before had it led to what was happening now. From the middle of the fifteenth century onwards the Muscovite Government which unified Great Rus began more and more to feel the impossibility of grappling with the new problems propounded by that unification—at all events, of grappling with them with the aid only of the old stock of appanage resources; wherefore at length it applied itself to organising a new State order through means of a slight development of the State order of the appanages. That new order, however, it constructed without outside help, and solely of its own devising, from materials afforded by the life of the people, while at the same time referring to the experiences of and the indications furnished by its own past. Still it believed in the hitherto neglected ability of its native land to become the lasting basis of a new order; wherefore that reorganisation strengthened, if anything, the authority of native antiquity, and maintained in the reorganisers themselves a consciousness of the forces of their own countrymen, and fed a sense of national self-reliance. During the sixteenth century the Russian community also conceived a belief that the Moscow which had unified the Russian land was the centre and bulwark of the whole of the Orthodox East: and this belief continued until the seventeenth century, when the situation changed. The complete break-down of the existing order of things, the failure of all attempts to right it, led to a notion that the very bases of that order were at fault, and forced many persons to think that the nation's creative forces and innate intellect had reached the point of exhaustion—that, antiquity being no valid guide for the present, it ought to be dropped, since now there was no good reason for maintaining it. Then there began a profound break in men's minds. Both among Muscovite administrative circles and in the community at large men became oppressed with doubts as to whether antiquity had bequeathed a sufficient measure of resources for successful existence in the future; men began to lose their old national self-complacency, and to look around them, and to seek guidance and instruction at the hands of the alien of the West, and to feel more and more persuaded both of his superiority and of their own inefficiency. Thus a declining faith in native antiquity and the forces of the people gave way to a despondency, a distrust of the national capacity, which opened wide the door to foreign influence.

It is not easy to say whence this difference in the sequence of phenomena between the sixteenth and the seventeenth centuries arose, nor why the inhabitants of Russia did not earlier recognise their inefficiency, nor why they found themselves unable to repeat the creative efforts of their immediate predecessors. Was it that the Russian of the seventeenth century was weaker in nerve-power, and more deficient in spiritual force, than his grandfather, the Russian of the sixteenth century? Or was it that the religious assurance of the father had shattered the spiritual energy of the son? Most probably the difference arose from the fact that a change had taken place in the relation of Russia to the world of Western Europe. In Western Europe of the sixteenth and seventeenth centuries the ruins of the feudal system gave birth to certain great centralised States; while, simultaneously, popular labour emerged from the confined sphere of feudal agricultural industry to which it had been confined by force, and, taking advantage of the geographical discoveries and technical inventions by which a wide field became opened to its activity, began to work vigorously in new directions, and with new urban or commercial-industrial capital, which, in its turn, entered into successful rivalry with capital of the feudal, seigniorial order. Again, these two factors—*i.e.* political centralisation and urban, bourgeois industrialism—led, on the one hand, to great progress in the development of administrative, financial, and military technique, in the organisation of standing armies, in the redistribution of taxation, and in the growth of the theory of national and State stewardship, and, on the other hand, to great progress in the development of economic technique, in the creation of mercantile marines, in the growth of factorial industry, and in the organisation of commercial routine and credit. Russia, however, took no part in this progress, but spent the whole of her strength and resources in external defence, and in the upkeep of a Court, a Government, and various privileged classes which, including the clergy, did nothing, and could do nothing, for the spiritual and economic growth of the people. For this reason Russia was, during the seventeenth century, more remote from the West even than she had been at the beginning of the sixteenth. Thus the influx of Western influence into Russia arose from a feeling of Russian national impotence; the source of which feeling was a lack of native spiritual and material resources as compared with those of Western Europe—a lack which continued to reveal itself with ever-increasing clearness in Russia's wars, diplomatic relations, and commercial traffic. This had the effect of rendering her painfully conscious of her own inefficiency.

Western influence, in penetrating into Russia, came into contact with the hitherto all-prevalent influence of the East, of Byzantium. Yet between the two we can remark an essential difference, and I will proceed to compare them, with a view to seeing what the one left behind it in Russia, and what the other one brought thither in its train. Greek or Byzantine influence was brought to, and diffused through, Russia by the Church, which directed it to moral and religious ends. Western influence, however, was introduced into Russia by the State, which invoked it to satisfy its material needs, yet did not confine it solely to the sphere of the State, as the Church confined Greek influence to the sphere of religion. Indeed, the latter did not embrace by any means every aspect of Russian life ; for, though it ruled the moral and religious life of the nation, and helped to adorn and to support the native State power, it gave little guidance in the matter of State organisation ; it introduced few norms into civic right (especially as regards family relations) ; it found little expression in the daily routine of existence, and still less in popular industry ; and it regulated the holiday conduct of the people, and the spending of their leisure time, only until Mass on festival days was ended. Also, it did little to increase the stock of positive knowledge. On the contrary, leaving no visible traces upon the weekday ideas and customs of the nation, it left a free hand in such matters to the nation's own initiative and innate grossness of conduct. Yet, while taking no cognisance of the individual, nor yet depriving him of his native and national peculiarities, of his originality, it embraced within its scope the *whole* of the community, and penetrated with equal force into all classes. That is to say, it communicated to the ancient Russian community a complete spiritual wholeness. On the other hand, Western influence penetrated into all spheres of life through the method of modifying certain notions and relations ; of pressing with equal force upon the State order and the social and weekday routine ; of introducing new political ideas, new civic requirements, new forms of associated life, and new provinces of knowledge ; of bringing about various changes in costume, manners, customs, and beliefs ; and of renovating the outward appearance, while reconstructing the inward mental attitude, of the Russian of that day. Yet, though affecting *every* man, both in his personality and as a citizen, it had (as yet, at all events) failed to embrace the community as a whole—its absorbent force had scarcely begun to act upon the subtle, the ceaselessly mobile and sensitive, *stratum* which lay superimposed upon the surface of the Russian community. Thus Greek influence was ecclesiastical, and Western influence was of the State. Greek influence embraced the whole community, but did not affect the individual, and Western influence affected the individual, but did not embrace the community as a whole.

From the encounter and the struggle between these two influences there issued two tendencies in the intellectual life of the Russian community, two views of the cultural position of the Russian nation. Developing and growing more and more complicated, changing their colour, their appellation, and their conditions of action, these two tendencies pass through our history in two parallel streams which, at one time hidden, at another time bursting into the open, refresh, like rivulets in a sandy desert, the arid social life of the people, which, with a few bright intervals, was ruled, up to the middle of the nineteenth century, by a State policy at once vague, futile, and oppressive. We see them first undergo demarcation during the latter half of the seventeenth century, in connection with the question of Transubstantiation of the Elements and the closely allied question of the comparative utility of the Greek and the Latin tongues (in which polemic we may divide the disputants respectively into Hellenists and Latinists). Next, during the latter half of the eighteenth century a second apple of discord was thrown into the Russian community by French progressive literature, as connected with the question of Peter's reforms and the allied question of independent national growth. At first the nationalist upholders of native independence of thought called themselves "Russophils," and dubbed their opponents "Semi-Franks," "Gauls," "Freethinkers," and "Voltairians"; but seventy years ago the adherents of the one view became known as "Westerners," and the supporters of the other as "Slavophils"; and in this latter stage of their development the essence of the two views in question might be expressed as follows:—The "Westerners" taught that though, in the basis of our civilisation, we are European, we are Junior European by historical growth, and therefore bound to traverse the same road as has been traversed by our elder brethren in culture, the Western Europeans, and also to adopt the fruits of their civilisation; whereas the Slavophils taught that we are European, but also Eastern—that we have native principles of life of our own which we must work out through efforts of our own, without entering into any ties with Western Europe. Russia, these Slavophils said, is not the teacher, nor the satellite, nor even the rival, of Europe: she is, rather, its successor. Russia and Europe are two contiguous cosmopolitan-historical stages, two successive phases, in the cultural growth of humanity. Sown with monuments (I am permitting myself faintly to parody the customary, rather stilted style of the Slavophils),—sown with monuments, they say, Western Europe is a vast burying-ground where, sleeping under stately marble memorials, there lie the great dead who are gone ; whereas Russia of the Forest and the Steppe is a rough wooden cradle wherein the world's future lies uneasily tossing and impotently weeping. Europe has nearly lived her life, whereas Russia is only *beginning* to live hers ; and, since she is fated to live when Europe has altogether passed away, she ought to be able to live *without* Europe—to live by her own wits, by her own principles, and with them eventually to supplant the outworn principles of European life, and to flood the world with a new light. Hence, though in our historical youth, we are under an obligation not to imitate, nor yet to borrow, the fruits of alien cultural effort, but to elaborate those principles of our own historical life which lie hidden within the depths of the national soul—principles which have never yet been put into effect by humanity. Thus the two views of which I am speaking not only regard Russia's position in Europe with different eyes, but also point out to her different roads for her future historical progress. However, at this juncture we need not enter into an exact appraisement of these views, nor debate what Russia's historical destiny may be, nor whether she is fated ever to become the light of the East, or only to remain a mere shadow of the West. In passing, it will be sufficient to refer to the more *noticeable* peculiarities of the two trends of opinion. The " Westerners " were remarkable for discipline of thought, love of exact study, and respect for scientific learning; whereas the Slavophils went in for a spreading floridity of ideas, a firm belief in the forces of the nation, and an undulating sort of lyrical dialectic which served as a welcome cover both to the mistakes in their logic and to the gaps in their erudition. Now, though I have outlined the two views in their final form, as complicated by various native and extraneous alloys of the previous two centuries, my real task is to note the moment of their birth and their original, unaffected form. To derive them from Peter's reforms is useless : they sprang to birth in men's minds during the seventeenth century, but more particularly in the minds of men who had lived through the Period of Troubles. Possibly it was the *diak* Ivan Timotheiev who noted the exact moment of their birth when, at the beginning of Michael's reign, he wrote his *Vremennik,* or " Chronicle of the Times," and began it with the reign of Ivan the Terrible. Timotheiev was an exceedingly sagacious observer, for he possessed both principles and ideas. In politics a Conservative, he explained the unhappiness of his age by the abrogation of antiquity and the disruption of the old legal ordinances—a process which, he said, had had the effect of causing men to turn round and round like wheels. Bitterly he laments the absence from the Russian community of any manly determination, as well as the inability of that community to offer to any tentative or illegal innovation a certain friendly resistance. The Russians, he declares, have no confidence in, and turn their backs upon, one another. Some look to the East, and some to the West. Whether this last ought to be taken as a happy chance expression, or whether it ought to be looked upon as a well-aimed remark, I cannot say. At all events, during the second decade of the seventeenth century—the period when Timotheiev wrote—Westernism was a refuge for such individual oddities as Prince Chvorostinin rather than a deliberate public movement. Every community includes within itself certain eccentric persons who, earlier than their fellows, begin to think and to do what, later, will be thought and done by everyone else, yet who fail to recognise the true reason why they have begun so to think and to do ; just as there exist certain persons who, in a given stage of mental weakness, are able to detect a coming change of weather sooner than its approach could possibly have been remarked by a healthy person.

Next, let us familiarise ourselves with the earliest manifestations of Western influence. In so far as it was adopted and utilised by the Government, it developed very consecutively, and with a gradual extension of its field of action ; such consecutiveness being due to the Government's desire —in fact, to its obligation—to make the State's requirements (which conduced towards that influence) harmonise at once with the popular psychology and with the Government's inertia (both of which factors were adverse to the said influence). Beginning by turning to the foreigner for help in the matter of satisfying its most urgent material need—namely, the defence of the country (a point wherein the existing inefficiency was gradually coming to be felt with particular keenness), the Government borrowed, first military, and then other technical, improvements from abroad—yet reluctantly, and without ever looking forward to the possible consequences of its own beginnings, or making any inquiry either as to how the Western European mind had attained its achievements in technique or as to the outlook upon the world and the problems of life which had served to direct the efforts necessary to attain those achievements. The Muscovite State needed guns, muskets, machinery, ships, and skilled labour; wherefore Moscow decided that the articles in question constituted no danger to spiritual salvation, but that even the study of cunning devices of this kind was a harmless, negligible matter from the moral point of view, seeing that, if need be, the ordinances of the Church permitted departures to be made from canonical precepts—at all events as regards the petty details of the daily round. In matters of *conscience*, however—in matters relating to feelings, ideas, and beliefs, where the higher, the dominant, interests of life prevail—it decided not to yield an iota to foreign influence.

To the above cautious concession the Russian army of the seventeenth century was beholden for some important innovations, and Russian manufacturing industry for its first successes. More than once bitter experience had revealed the inefficiency of our ancient *dvorianin* militia when encountering the regular, the properly trained, troops of the West—troops furnished with fire-arms ; wherefore, with the close of the sixteenth century, the Muscovite Government began to supplement its military forces with foreign contingents. At first the idea was to use the military science of the West independently, by hiring alien warriors, and obtaining military equipment from abroad. Early in Michael's reign the Government took to sending out armies which were made up of native and of mercenary troops; and on one occasion the officer in supreme command was an English lord, named Aston. Next, on the supposition that it would be better to learn the military art of foreigners than simply to hire them, the Government began to place its native troops under the instruction of foreign officers, and to raise properly trained and equipped regiments of its own. This passage of the Russian army to a system of regular formation was a passage of great difficulty, and one undertaken about the year 1630, just before the second war with Poland. For the struggle long and anxious preparations were made—made with the care of men who had once been beaten. Of Western volunteers there was, at that time, an ample supply, for those countries which had become directly or indirectly involved in the Thirty Years' War were filled with wandering soldiers of fortune who not only had swords to employ, but also were well aware that the Treaty of Deulino [1] was on the point of expiring, and that war would follow. In 1631 a hired general named Leslie undertook to raise in Sweden a force of 5000 volunteer infantrymen,[2] to purchase for them arms,

---

[1] By this treaty, in 1618, a ourteen years' truce was concluded between Moscow and Poland.

[2] At that period Scotch military adventurers swarmed in Russia.

and to engage German artificers to work the force of artillery which had just been organised in Moscow by a Dutchman named Koet. At about the same time another officer-contractor named Vendome undertook both to hire, in foreign countries, a regiment of 1760 good and trained soldiers and to import some German gunners and experienced instructors to train the Russian men-at-arms in the military art. Yet these foreign military experts cost Moscow a great deal of money. At the outset, Vendome's force cost, in arms and annual upkeep, 1,500,000 roubles in modern currency; while the commander of Leslie's contingent had guaranteed to him a yearly salary of 22,000 roubles (in the same currency). Lastly, in 1632 the force which moved against Smolensk numbered 32,000 men, with 158 guns, and among that force were six foreign infantry regiments which, under the command of hired colonels, comprised 1,500 German mercenaries and nearly 13,000 soldiers of the Russian foreign establishment. Indeed, a Russian chonicler of the period notes with surprise that never before had a Russian army included in its ranks so many infantrymen armed with firearms—more especially Russian infantrymen who had been trained to drill and the art of fighting. Even the failure of the attempt upon Smolensk did not stop that reorganisation of the army of which we know the further course: and for its further consolidation there was composed, in the reign of Michael, an edict by which, in future, Russian soldiers were to be drilled by the foreign military element. Finally, in 1647, when Alexis was Tsar, this document was printed, under the title of "The Teaching and Craft of Our Warlike Establishment of Foot Soldiers."

Naturally the maintenance of a semi-regular army raised also the question of the means for arming it. Armament and artillery equipment were invariably procured from abroad, and before the war of 1634 Colonel Leslie was ordered to purchase, in Sweden, 10,000 muskets, together with the requisite ammunition and 5,000 swords; and after the war had begun, 10,000 additional *poods* of powder and iron cannon balls were ordered (subject to a high tariff) from Holland. All this, however, was expensive and tiresome, and Moscow soon began to think of manufacturing her own munitions of war; which, in turn, led her to bethink herself of the mineral wealth of the country. In those days iron could be procured only from mines in the neighbourhood of Tula and Ustruzhna, where, in local furnaces, it was smelted into nails and other objects of domestic use. Also cannons and matchlocks were manufactured in Tula. Inasmuch, however, as this was not sufficient for the needs of the War Department, and thousands of *poods* of iron had also to be procured from Sweden, it was decided to develop the metallurgical industry on broader lines, and to invoke the aid of foreign experts and capitalists. Next, a vigorous search was begun for mines, and men "skilled in metal" were invited from abroad to act as furnace engineers and artificers. Thus, in 1626, a free passage to Russia was accorded to an English engineer named Bulmer, who "of his craft and of his wisdom did know where to find ores of gold and silver and copper, and likewise precious stones, in that he had good knowledge of those places." Next, with the help of these imported experts, expeditions were fitted out for the purpose of discovering and working mineral veins at Solikamsk, throughout the region of the Northern Dvina, and elsewhere. Again, in 1634, Moscow hired copper smelters from Saxony and Brunswick, on the promise that "in the State of Moscow they should be able to fashion much copper"; which makes it clear that already rich seams of the metal in question had been discovered in Russia. Also, manufacturers were procured, and foreign capitalists. In 1632, just before the war with Poland, a Dutch merchant named Andrew Vinnius was granted a concession to build factories for the making of cast and other iron near Tula, on the understanding that, at the cheapest rates possible, he should manufacture cannons, cannon-balls, musket-barrels, and other articles of the given metal for the Treasury. At Tula, therefore, there arose our first ordnance works—works which subsequently became acquired by the Treasury. Also, to guarantee these works a sufficiency of hands, a Court *volost* was made over to them *en bloc;* and in this manner there became founded the class of factorial peasantry. In 1644 another commercial company of foreigners, headed by a Hamburg merchant named Marselis, was granted a twenty years' concession to build factories along the rivers Vaga, Kostroma, and Sheksna, in addition to factories in other localities, on the same terms. As for Moscow itself, there had been established there, as early as Michael's reign, a factory near the river Neglinna, whereat foreign artisans cast numbers of cannons and church bells and many Russians received an excellent education in the science of metalfounding. Manufacturers had a perpetual obligation laid upon them to teach those Russian subjects who were apprenticed to their works every one of their manufacturing processes, and to conceal from them no single detail of their art. Also, potash, glass, and other factories first became established, and the advent of these metallurgical experts to Moscow attracted thither foreign furriers, weavers of velvet, spinners of wire, clockmakers, water-raisers, lapidaries, iron-casters, and portrait painters. Indeed, it would be difficult to say *what* artisans Moscow did not send for, and always on the condition that "they do teach the men of our State their craft." Even the Western European *savant* was needed, and in 1639 Adam Olearius—a professor of the University of Leipzig who more than once visited Moscow in the capacity of Secretary to the Holsteiner Embassy, and wrote a remarkable account of the Muscovite Empire—received, in the following terms, an invitation to enter the Imperial service : " Unto Us, the Great Tsar, is it known that thou art exceeding learned and skilled in astrology, and in geography, and in the heavenly courses, and in the measuring of the earth, and in many other like masteries and subtleties. Of a wise man of this sort have we need." Along the Moskva the hostile rumour ran that a magician was coming who could foretell the future by the stars ; but Olearius declined the invitation. Also, since, in the West, men and States usually grew rich through an extensive oversea trade which was carried on in fleets of trading vessels, the middle of the seventeenth century saw the Muscovite Government begin to concern itself on the subject of ships, harbours, and maritime commerce generally ; and schemes were mooted for hiring shipwrights in Holland, and sailors to man the ships when built. In particular, the above Vinnius proposed to build a fleet of barges for the Caspian Sea ; wherefore in 1669 there was put together on the Oka, at the village of Diedinovo in the canton of Kolomna, a vessel built by imported Dutch shipwrights, and named the *Orel*. Costing about 9,000 roubles (125,000 roubles in modern currency), she was launched at Astrakhan, but in 1670 was burnt to her keel by the Cossack rebel, Stenka Razin. Likewise, though the Muscovite Empire had harbours at Archangel (on the White Sea) and at Murman (on the Gulf of Kola), these ports were too far from Moscow and the markets of Western Europe, while, in addition, Moscow was cut off from the Baltic by the Swedes. Accordingly there dawned in Moscow the idea of *hiring* foreign harbours for the future Muscovite fleet, and in 1662 a Muscovite emissary who was on his way to England had a long conversation with the Chancellor of Courland as to whether it would be possible to maintain Muscovite ships in the Courlander ports. But to this the Chancellor merely replied that it would be more fitting for the Great Tsar of Moscow to maintain his ships in his own port of Archangel.

Amid this mining and manufacturing excitement there next began to glimmer in the mind of the Muscovite Government an idea which came to it with peculiar difficulty. This was because the Government not only organised its financial system exclusively on a narrow fiscal basis, but also sought its fiscal profit at the expense of thought for the industry of the people. When any new expenditure had to be incurred which was not covered by the income available it resorted to its usual financial arithmetic, and, reckoning up the number of its registered taxpayers, divided the required sum among them according to that number, and ordered the said sum to be collected, on pain of various penalties for its non-provision, in the form either of a *zapros* (forced subscription list) or of a permanent impost, while at the same time leaving it to the taxpayers to apportion the amount among themselves as they pleased, and to get the money from whatsoever quarter they could. Upon this irresponsible financial policy arrears and troublesome complaints of inability to pay served as the only checks, and, while constantly increasing its exactions, the Government did nothing to increase the taxpaying capacity of the people's labour. Nevertheless, observation of the commercial-industrial skill and technical dexterity of the foreigner, added to certain insistent representations from the native traders, gradually drew the financiers of the Government into a circle of popular-industrial ideas and relations which had hitherto been unknown to them. Against their will their administrative outlook became widened, and notions became imposed upon them which it was difficult for their minds to assimilate—such notions as that any raising of the taxes should be preceded by an increase of the productiveness of popular labour; that, for this purpose, labour ought to be directed to new income-producing enterprises—to the discovery and exploitation of the hitherto dormant riches of the country; and that, to this end, skilled workers, knowledge, practice, and business organisation ought to be procured. These notions constituted the first impressions to be produced upon the Muscovite Government by Western influence. In the community also they awoke an echo. In other words the administrative ferment evoked by these notions; the search for mines, forests of shipbuilding timber, sites for saltboiling, and spots for the erection of sawyards; questionings of local inhabitants as to the profitable natural assets which happened to lie within their knowledge,— all these things aroused the population to visions both of new fields for their labour and of Government pay for information to that end. Persons who could point out (for instance) a good mineral seam received a promised reward of 500, 1000, or even more, roubles (the sums being calculated in modern currency). Thus word was brought to Moscow of a great hill of alabaster on the Northern Dvina—and instantly an expedition, headed by a German, was dispatched to survey and to describe the hill, to ascertain from commercial experts the amounts per *pood* for which alabaster could be sold abroad, and to hire workmen for the quarrying of the stone. Everywhere rumours became current concerning the sums likely to be paid for useful novelties which anyone might discover or invent; for when in a community there develops a tendency which corresponds to some necessity of subsistence, that tendency seizes upon men like a fashion or an epidemic,—it inspires the wildest of schemes, and evokes unhealthy exaggeration and a risky spirit of enterprise. From the time when, during the Period of Troubles, the nation underwent losses and humiliations at the hands of the foreigner the question of the re-organisation of the country's external defence, and of what new discoveries and inventions could be designed to strengthen that defence, became living issues. In 1629 a Tveran priest named Nestor forwarded to the Tsar a petition "concerning a great work which never yet hath God revealed unto living man, either among ourselves or in other States, but which He hath revealed unto me, the priest Nestor, to the glory of the Tsar, and to the saving of our distressed land, and to the confusion and amazement of its enemies." What the priest Nestor undertook to do was to build for the Tsar a cheap, portable citadel in which soldiers should be able to take refuge, as though it were a real, an immoveable fortress. In vain the boyars requested the inventor to construct a model or a sketch-plan of the moveable redoubt which he had devised, for the purpose of showing it to the Tsar, but the priest refused to say more than that, not having "beheld the eyes of the Tsar," he would mention not a detail, since he did not trust the boyars. In the end he was dispatched to Kazan, where for three years he was confined in a monastery in chains, for the offence of having said that he could "accomplish a great work" while refusing to explain any details of that work—in short, for acting to men's confusion, and not as though he were in his right mind.

Thus both the Muscovite Government and the Muscovite community came to feel an insistent need for the military and industrial technique of Western Europe, and ended by deciding to study both the one and the other. It may be that at first the needs of the State called for nothing more than that technique; but a social movement, when once initiated by a given impetus, is prone, *en route*, to gather to itself other new motives, which mould its limits of aim.

As said, a vigorous search for skilled labour had the effect of attracting to Moscow a multitude of foreign technical experts, officers, soldiers, physicians, artisans, merchants and manufacturers. As early as the sixteenth century—to be precise, during the reign of Ivan the Terrible—there became formed the German Quarter, which consisted of a colony of Western-European immigrants settled on the River Yauza, near Moscow; and after the accession of Michael, when the influx of foreigners to the capital had increased still more, newcomers settled wherever they could, and, purchasing establishments from the natives, set up breweries and kirks within the walls of the metropolis itself. In time, however, the close juxtaposition of these immigrants with the natives, the feuds and collisions to which such juxtaposition gave rise, and the complaints of the Muscovite clergy concerning the propinquity of German kirks to Russian churches so far alarmed the Muscovite authorities that, during the reign of Tsar Michael, an *ukaz* was issued which forbade Germans to purchase establishments of Muscovites, or to build their kirks within the actual walls of Moscow; and of one of the many incidents which forced the Government to isolate Muscovites and foreigners we have an account from Olearius, as follows :—The wives of some German officers whom the latter had taken from certain alien mercantile families in Moscow saw fit to look down upon the wives of plain merchants, and tried to sit in front of them when attending kirk; but this privilege the wives of the plain merchants would not concede to their rivals, and on one occasion they picked a quarrel with the officers' ladies which developed into an actual riot. The noise of the fracas penetrated even to the street, and attracted the attention of the Patriarch (who, by bad luck, happened at the moment to be passing); with the result that, as soon as he learnt where the trouble lay, he, as the guardian of ecclesiastical law and order even among the adherents of other faiths than his own, ordered the kirk to be pulled down : and the order was carried out that very day. This incident may be referred to the year 1643, when orders were given that all kirks which had been built within the limits of the city should be destroyed, and a site was granted for a new general kirk beyond the Zemliani Rampart, while the numerous Germans scattered about the city were to be evicted from the capital, and settled in a spot on the river Yauza, where, according to ranks and callings, they were to have plots of land where some German homesteads had formerly stood. Thus there arose a new German or Foreign Quarter which quickly developed into a large and well-built suburb, with broad, straight streets and alleys, and handsome wooden mansions. Indeed, according to Olearius, the first few years of its existence saw it comprising upwards of 1000 persons, while another foreign writer, Meierberg, who resided in Moscow in 1660, speaks in vague terms of "a multitude" of foreigners then resident in the Quarter, which contained three Lutheran kirks, one Reformed kirk, and a German school. There a multi-racial, polyglot population of various callings eked out a comfortable, cheerful life, and enjoyed full liberty of native customs and manners. In fact, the Quarter represented a little corner of Western Europe which had come to nestle on the eastern outskirts of Moscow.

In addition, this German settlement came to be the exponent of Western-European culture in departments of Muscovite life where for such culture there was no demand by the State's material needs. The technical experts, capitalists, and military officers whom the Government engaged for external defence or the industrial requirements of Muscovite domestic existence brought with them to Moscow not only their military and industrial skill, but also the comforts, the amenities, and the conveniencies of life as lived in Western Europe, and it is curious to note the eagerness with which the leaders of Muscovite society leapt at foreign luxury and imported delights, though, in so doing, they broke with their own rooted customs, prejudices, and tastes. There can be no doubt that external political relations helped to strengthen this leaning towards alien attractions and amenities—that the frequent diplomatic missions which visited Moscow from abroad at length aroused in the Muscovite Empire a wish to figure in the best possible light before the foreign observer, and to show him that in Russia men knew how to live like gentlemen. Also, we know that at one time Alexis considered himself a candidate for the Polish throne, and that, in that capacity, he strove to organise a Muscovite Court life which should resemble the Court life of the Realm of Poland. Likewise Russian ambassadors who were leaving for foreign countries were always charged by their Government to pay special attention to the setting and gaieties of foreign Courts; nor will it escape notice that Court balls—more particularly, Court spectacles—figure with great prominence in the diplomatic reports of these ambassadors. In 1659 a *dvorianin* named Lichatchev was sent on a mission to the Duke of Tuscany at Florence, where he received an invitation to a Court ball and spectacle; and, in his account of the same, he describes the "sport" or "comedy" with a perfect wealth of minute detail—a sign that such matters aroused the greatest interest in Moscow, and that Muscovites were unwilling to lose a single scene, a single decorative feature, of such pageants. "Then were there set forth pavilions, and beneath the same a pavilion which did stand forth from the rest;[1]

Probably some kind of stage or proscenium.

and of this pavilion were there changes made to the number of six. In
them there was shown a sea tossing with billows, and in the sea fishes,
and, on the fishes, men riding, and, above the pavilion, the heavens,
where other men did ride upon the clouds. And from the heavens there
did launch himself an old man from a cloud, in a chariot, and over against
him, in another chariot, was a beautiful maiden, and the horses of the
chariots were as though they were alive, so did they beat with their
hooves. And the Duke did say unto me that the one of these was
the Sun, and the other one the Moon. And in another change there was
shown a man, with fifty of his fellows—all in armour, and they did begin
to fight with spears and swords, and to shoot at one another from arque-
buses, and, as it were, to kill the man and three of those who were with
him. And, after that, many wondrous youths and maidens in golden
attire did come forth from behind a curtain, and they did dance and do
many marvellous things." Nevertheless, in describing the life of the
upper classes of Moscow, Kotoshikhin remarks that the people of the
Muscovite Empire " do live in houses which are very unseemly," and
that they " do live in houses which have no great orderliness " (*i.e.* no
great amount of comfort or refinement); while in sketches made by the
above-mentioned Meierberg we see the Metropolitan riding in a clumsy
old sledge, and the Tsaritsa doing the same thing in a roughly-covered
cart ! But now, in imitation of foreign example, the Tsar and the boyars
began to take the air in stately German coaches—in vehicles which were
upholstered in velvet, adorned with paintings, and fitted with windows
of crystal. Also, the boyars and richer merchants took to building
themselves mansions of stone in place of their old wretched dwellings of
wood, to ordering their domestic *ménages* on the foreign scale, to lining
the walls of their rooms with " golden leathers " of Belgian make, and to
adorning those rooms with pictures and clocks. Indeed, Tsar Michael—
who, owing to his lameness, had to stay much at home, and therefore was
perennially at a loss for amusement—was so exceedingly fond of clocks
that he simply heaped his chambers with them. Also, he used to have
music performed while he was at dinner, while in the palace of Tsar
Alexis, during the hour of the evening meal, " Germans did play upon
organs, and blow upon trumpets, and beat upon drums." Thus foreign
taste was called upon to correct native coarseness. Also, upon the
boyar B. I. Morozov—at one time Alexis' favourite and tutor, and, subsequently, his brother-in-law—the Tsar conferred a wedding coach which
was upholstered in gold brocade, lined with costly sable, and hooped with

pure silver in place of iron. Even for its massive tyres the more valuable metal was used! Nevertheless, in 1648, when pillaging Morozov's mansion, the rioters smashed this piece of extravagance to atoms. In passing, it may be noted that, during the evening meal and its accompanying German music, the same Tsar would toast his guests (his confessor included) far into the night, until all were in a state of intoxication. Frequently, also, Muscovite ambassadors were ordered to procure for the Tsar's service foreign trumpeters who should be warranted to play dance music in the best possible manner. Again, the Court and the higher circles of Muscovite society developed a passion for "comedy acts"— i.e. theatrical spectacles. Yet it was not without certain religious qualms that this form of entertainment (this "sport of the devil," this "spiritual foulness"—so certain strict guardians of true piety expressed themselves about it) was honoured in Moscow. Indeed, Tsar Alexis owned as much to his father confessor—who, however, decided to allow the Tsar his theatrical spectacles, and justified the decision by the example of diverse Byzantine Emperors. These "comedies" were played at Court by a troupe of actors specially chosen from among sons of foreigners who were engaged in commerce or the State service, and their training was performed by the pastor of the Lutheran church which stood in the German Quarter—one Master Johannes Gottfried Gregory, upon whom, in 1672, the Tsar conferred the appointment as a thank-offering for the birth of the Tsarevitch Peter. For the same purpose there was built in the suburban *selo* of Presbrazhensköe (destined, later, to be the favourite scene of Peter's diversions) a theatre or "hall of comedy." Here, at the close of the year 1672, the Tsar witnessed a comedy produced by the Pastor, and turning on the subject of Esther; which so pleased the Tsar that "for the ordering of the comedy he did recompense" the stage manager with 1,500 roubles-worth (in modern currency) of sables. Also, in addition to "Esther," Gregory produced, at the same theatre, a piece called "Judith," a "comforting" (*i.e.* a diverting) comedy on the subject of Joseph, and a "pitiful" comedy on the subject of Adam and Eve— *i.e.* of the fall and subsequent redemption of man. Yet, despite their Biblical subjects, these pieces were not mediæval mystery plays of a moral and edificatory nature, but translations from the German which might be trusted to strike the beholder with their strange pictures of executions, fighting, and much firing-off of guns. Also (with the exception of the tragedy on Adam and Eve) they had in them a certain alloy of the comic —or, more correctly speaking, of the showbooth—element, in the person of a jester, who was an indispensable personage in such plays, and cracked rude, and often unseemly, jokes. Also, no time was lost in organising the training of native actors. By the year 1673 Gregory had under him, for instruction in the dramatic art, twenty-six young men who had been selected from the " New Quarter of Burgesses " in Moscow. In other words, though Moscow had not yet compassed elementary schools for the teaching of letters, she had succeeded in organising an academy of drama! But before long there succeeded to the comedy on Biblical subjects the ballet. In 1674, at the season when the Tsar and the Tsarina, with their children and the attendant boyars, were celebrating the conclusion of Lent, they witnessed, at Preobrazhensköe, a comedy wherein Artaxerxes had no sooner ordered Haiman to be hanged than some German youths and household menials in the service of Matviev, the Minister for Foreign Affairs—persons who likewise had studied the theatrical art under Gregory—played " viols, organs, and other instruments, and did dance." I repeat, therefore, that these novelties and recreations, though luxuries only of the higher circles of Muscovite society, nourished in the latter new and more refined tastes and demands which had been altogether unknown to the Russian of earlier generations. But was Muscovite society likely to stop at the amusements and amenities which it had thus eagerly borrowed?

In the West the amenities and elegancies of life of that day owed their existence not merely to the fortunate economic position of the wealthy and more pushing classes of the community, nor yet to the whims of pampered taste; for in the creation of those amenities a part was played by prolonged spiritual efforts on the part both of individuals and of entire communities—the external graces of life developed hand in hand with the progress of thought and of sensibility. Man always seeks to fashion for himself an environment which shall correspond to his tastes and his views of life ; yet, duly to accomplish that correspondence, he must think deeply concerning his tastes, as well as concerning life itself. When borrowing the environment of aliens, he usually adopts, insensibly and involuntarily, the tastes and ideas by which that environment was created ; otherwise it would seem to him to be lacking both in the one and in the other. But our forefathers of the seventeenth century thought differently. Originally, when borrowing the amenities of Western Europe, they conceived that they were not bound also to adopt Western European learning and conceptions, or to renounce their own; wherein they perpetuated the ingenuous error into which suspicious and reluctant imitators have ever been prone to fall. Consequently, when, in Moscow of the seventeenth century, men took to seeking after the amenities of the alien, they began also, in vague and gradual fashion, to be alive to the *spiritual* interests and efforts which had created those amenities, and to admire those interests and efforts before they had come properly to realise the relation of the latter to their own native tastes and ideas. That is to say, the Russian of the seventeenth century began by admiring foreign amenities merely as abstractions of life or pleasant exercises in realms of thought into which he had never yet ventured. Thus, while the upper circles of Muscovite society were borrowing of the foreigner his "diverting crafts" and "specious devices," those same circles also developed an intellectual love of knowledge, an interest in scientific erudition, a willingness to think upon subjects which had not yet come within the ordinary purview of the ancient Russian, or within the daily round of his requirements. For instance, at Court in particular there arose an association of influential amateurs of Western European comfort and culture. Alexis' uncle, the kind-hearted and jovial Nikita Romanov—the richest man in the Empire, after the Tsar, and the most popular of all the boyars—became not only a protector and lover of the Germans, but also a devotee of their music and dress (as well as, to a certain extent, a freethinker). Next, the Tsar's tutor and brother-in-law, Morozov, complained bitterly, during his declining years, that in his youth he had never been given a finishing education. Also, he dressed his foster-son, as well as the playfellows of the latter, in German costume. Again, an *okolnichi* (a State councillor of the secondary rank) named Theodor Michael Rtistchev became a jealous amateur of learning and scholastic education; as the head of the Office of Ambassadors we see an erudite *diplomat* named A. L. Ordin-Nastchokin; and his successor, a boyar named A. S. Matviev—the son of a *diak*, and another of the Tsar's favourites—was the first Muscovite to start, in his sumptuously Europeanised mansion, a species of debating society which had for its aim the exchanging of ideas and news not only in the presence of the lady of the house, but also without the accompaniment of liquor. Likewise it was Matviev who organised the Court theatre. In this way the relation of the Russian community to Western Europe underwent an insensible change. Formerly the average Russian had looked upon Western Europe as a workshop for military and other wares which a man might purchase without making any inquiry as to the manner in which they had been fashioned; but now the Russian of the day began to regard that Europe as a school wherein a man might learn, not only the handicrafts, but also the way in which a man ought to live and to think.

Yet even in this respect no alteration took place in the usual guardedness of ancient Rus. She decided not to borrow Western education direct from its native haunts—direct from its actual masters and workmen, but to search out intermediaries who could be trusted to transmit her that education in an innocuous form. Who were those intermediaries to be? Between the ancient Rus of Moscow and Western Europe there lay a country which, though Slavonic, was also Catholic—namely, Poland; and Poland was closely connected, both by ecclesiastical kinship and by geographical propinquity, with the Europe of Rome and Germany, while serf right, in its earliest and most unfettered form, added to complete political freedom of the Polish upper classes, rendered the Polish nobility a peculiarly grateful and receptive soil for Western culture, in spite of the fact that the features of the country, added to those of the national character, communicated to that culture, when borrowed, a distinctively local hue. Confined to a single class which enjoyed exclusive predominance in the State, Polish culture fostered a joyous and animated, yet narrow and lax, outlook upon the world. Nevertheless it was Poland which became the first medium for the permeation of Russia with Western influence, in that the Western European civilisation of the seventeenth century reached Moscow first in the guise of a Polish product, in the guise of the costume of the *shliachta*, or Polish gentry class. At the same time, it was not the *pure* Pole who acted as the first introducer of Western civilisation to Rus. Between a large section of Orthodox Rus and the Polish *Rietch Pospolitaia*, or Monarchical Republic, there existed strong political ties; in addition to which, the national-religious struggle between the Orthodox community of Western Rus and the Polish Empire and Roman Catholicism forced the Russian contestants to apply themselves to the study of arms (though it is true that a large section of them were opposed to this course), to scholarship, to literature, and to the Latin language : in all of which accomplishments Western Rus had, by the middle of the seventeenth century, come greatly to surpass Eastern Rus. Thus it was the Orthodox monk of Western Rus who had studied in the school of Rome, or else in the Russian school which was modelled thereon, that proved to be the first exponent of Western learning whom Moscow called upon to help her.

That call was first issued by the Muscovite Government itself; but in this connection Western influence came into contact with a movement emanating from a totally different quarter. In studying the origin of the great Church Schism we shall see that it was a movement which owed its origin to the straits of the Russian Church, and that, though it was partly directed against Western influence, the two opposing sides combined together in at least one common social interest—namely, in that of the spread of enlightenment, and that they temporarily clasped hands for the purpose of joint action. In those days the written literature of Rus contained not a single full or correct text of the Bible. That is to say, the Russian Hierarchy, which raised an almost worldwide storm over dogmatic questions of Alleluias and the secularisation of monasterial lands, contrived, for centuries and quietly, to do without any complete or reliable version of God's word! However, at the middle of the seventeenth century (*i.e.* in 1649 or 1650) the Muscovite Hierarchy sent for three learned Kievan monks named Epiphany Slavinitski, Arsenius Satanovski, and Damaskin Ptitski (inmates of the local Bratski and Petcherski Monasteries), and charged them to translate the Bible from the Greek into the Slavonic tongue. These Kievan experts it rewarded on a lower scale even than it did its hired German officers, for Epiphany and Arsenius were paid a daily fee only of 4 *altini* (which would amount to about 600 modern roubles a year), awarded free lodgings at the Tchudovoi Monastery, and allowed board and extra liquor from the palace at the rate of 2 *tcharki* (mugs) and 4 *krushki* (tankards) of beer and mead per day. However, after a while the monastery wage was doubled. In addition to executing the chief task which had been entrusted to them, these *savants* who had been imported from Kiev were called upon to satisfy other requirements of the Muscovite Government and community. That is to say, by order either of the Tsar or of the Patriarch, they compiled or translated various educational aids and encyclopædic compendia—geographies, kosmographies, lexicons, and so on; all of which subsequently met with a great demand among the reading public of Moscow in general and at Court, and in the Office of Ambassadors in particular—the originals being procured, through the various Russian ambassadors, from Poland. Epiphany translated a geography, a "Book of Medicine and Anatomy," and a work entitled "Citizenship and the Teaching of Manners unto Children" (a mixed treatise on politics and the education of the young); while Satanovski did the same with regard to a book called "On the Station of a Tsar"— a collection of this, that, and the other which had been compiled from various Greek and Latin writers, pagan and Christian, and which embraced the whole gamut of the sciences as they were then known, from theology and philosophy to zoology, mineralogy, and medicine. In fact, every available literary force was made use of. Also, besides the Kievan *savants*, *German* professors were impressed into the work of translation. For instance, a certain von Delden translated some books from the Latin and the French, while Döorn, Austrian Ambassador to Moscow, translated a short kosmography. In relating these facts, Olearius adds that such books were read by many of the most eager amateurs of knowledge in Moscow. The composition of this new literature was stimulated, not only by purely scientific questions, but also by practical. For example, at about this period translations of books on chemistry began to circulate freely, and in an old "proceedings" of the Office of Ambassadors we find the curious item that in 1623 a Dutchman named van Derhin, who was in the State service of Moscow, submitted, for the approval of the office, an article on "Alchymical Wisdom and Other Matters," and that, later, he again came forward with a treatise on "The Higher Philosophy of Alchemy." Evidently in Moscow much curiosity was existent as to the mysteriously seductive science by which men hoped to discover the art of making gold. Yet, in the main, the contents of works translated or compiled by Slavinetski and Satanovski point to scientific interest having been their leading motive—in so far as scientific interest had yet taken hold upon Muscovite intellects.

Thus the Muscovite community began to feel the need of book-learning and scientific education, and thus the beginnings of scholastic instruction were laid as an indispensable means to the acquisition of such education. The need to which I refer increased in proportion as intercourse with Western States obliged Muscovite diplomacy more and more to study the position and the mutual relations of the States in question ; and not only the Government in Moscow, but also private individuals, did their best towards establishing schools. Among others, the Eastern Greek Hierarchy more than once represented to the Muscovite Tsars the necessity of having a Greek college and printing-press founded in the Muscovite capital; whereupon Moscow began to search high and low for such scholars, and the East furnished them to the best of its power. Yet, somehow, matters did not prosper in this connection. Under Michael not a single one of the desiderated educational establishments came into being; but in 1632 a monk named Joseph visited the Muscovite metropolis with a message from the Patriarch of Alexandria, and was persuaded to remain in Moscow for the purpose not only of translating into Slavonic certain Greek polemical works against the Latin heresies, but also of "instructing, in a hall of learning, young children in the Greek letters and tongue." True, the scheme fell to the ground owing to Joseph's early death; yet the idea of founding a seminary in Moscow which should serve as a nursery of enlightenment for the whole of the Orthodox East was not wholly abandoned, whether in Moscow or in the East. In time there arose near the Patriarch's palace, in the Tchudovoi Monastery, a Greco-Latin college under the direction of a Greek named Arsenius, who originally came to Moscow in 1649, but shortly afterwards, on suspicion of non-Orthodoxy, was banished to Solovki. Also, invitations were sent to Epiphany Slavinetski and Arsenius Satanovski that they should revisit Moscow for the purpose of teaching oratory: but as to whether they obtained any pupils in that art we have no knowledge. Again, in 1665 three secretaries in the "Office of Secret Affairs" and "Office of the Courts" were bidden to submit themselves, for instruction in Latin, to a Western Russian *savant* named Simeon Polotski; and for this purpose there was built in the Spasski Monastery of Moscow a special edifice which is referred to in documents as "the School for the Teaching of Letters." Yet it must not be supposed that these various establishments were genuine, regularly constituted schools which possessed properly elaborated charters, regular schemes and *curricula* of work, a permanent staff of lecturers, and so forth. On the contrary, they represented only fortuitous, temporary commissions to one and another visiting *savant* to give instruction in the Greek or the Latin tongue to young persons whom the Government might send to them, or to persons who might, of their own volition, desire to receive such instruction. Herein we see the original form of the Russian Government school of the seventeenth century—a direct continuation of that older method of teaching letters whereby, in return for a certain agreed payment, the clergy or special masters received children into their homes, and there taught them. In certain places, however, private individuals—or, perhaps, whole communities—erected special buildings for the purpose, and thus evolved the counterpart of the permanent public school. For example, in 1685 there stood near the market-square in Borovski, near the almshouses of the town, a "school for the teaching of children" which had been erected by the local clergy. Also, we may suppose that it was to meet the needs either of home or of school instruction that, at about the middle of the seventeenth century, certain scholastic publications appeared. For instance, in 1648 there was published in Moscow a Slavonic grammar, the work of a Western-Russian *savant* named Meletius Smotritski; while in 1649 a reprint was made of a short Catechism that was originally written, at Kiev, by Peter Mogila, rector of the Kievan Academy and, subsequently, local Metropolitan. Everywhere private individuals vied with the Government in furthering the cause of enlightenment. Yet these zealots for progress belonged mostly to the administrative class, and among the most ardent of them was Tsar Alexis' trusted adviser, the *okolnichi* T. M. Rtistchev. Rtistchev built, near Moscow, a monastery to St. Andrew, and in 1649 summoned thither, at his own expense, from the Petcherski cloister of Kiev and other Little Russian monastic establishments, upwards of thirty learned monks, whose function it was to translate foreign books into the Russian tongue, and also to teach all who wished it the rudiments of the Greek, Latin, and Slavonic languages, the art of rhetoric, the science of philosophy, and various other branches of orally imparted learning. Rtistchev himself became a student at this free school of his, and spent whole nights in study and conversation with the school's professors, who taught him the Greek language. Also, he commissioned Epiphany Slavinetski to compose, for the use of the school, a Greco-Slavonic lexicon. To these visiting scholars from Southern Rus there joined themselves also a number of the more erudite monks and priests of Moscow; and in this way there arose in the capital a brotherhood of learning which represented a sort of free Academy of Sciences. Likewise, availing himself of his position at Court, Rtistchev compelled certain scions of the metropolitan State service to repair to his Monastery of St. Andrew, for instruction in the Latin and Greek tongues by the Monastery's Kievan professors. Again, in 1667 the parishioners of the Muscovite Church of St. John the Divine (which was situated in the Kitaigorod, or Kremlin quarter, of the city) bethought themselves of adding to their church a school, yet not a mere parish educational establishment, but, rather, a *general* educational establishment for the imparting of "cunning in letters, and the Slavonic, Greek, and Latin tongues, and other free teachings." To this end a suitable petition was forwarded to the Tsar, as well as a petition for the appointment of an "honourable and devout man" who should represent the parishioners at Court. Next they besought the blessing of the Patriarch of Moscow, and of some Eastern Patriarchs who happened to be visiting Moscow at the time in connection with the Nikon affair; until, finally, the Muscovite Patriarch—moved, probably, by respect for the importunate prayers of the "devout man," if not by respect for those of Rtistchev, who had suggested the idea of the school—consented to accord his benediction to the scheme, "to the end that students of zeal may have freedom to seek free teachings of wisdom, and to gather together in some common hall for the whetting of their minds through well-skilled teachers." But as to whether the school ever came to be actually opened we have no knowledge.

The members of the upper *stratum* of Muscovite society did their best to lay by the means for educating their children at home through the method of engaging, as resident tutors, both Western-Russian monks and Poles. In this matter Tsar Alexis himself set the example, since, dissatisfied with the elementary education which his eldest sons, Alexis and Theodor, had received from their official Muscovite tutor, he gave orders for them to be taught also Latin and Polish, and appointed, as their finishing tutor, a Western-Russian monk named Simeon Sitiano-vitch Polotski—a pupil of the Kievan Academy, and a man who was familiar also with Polish scholarship. Simeon was a pleasant pedagogue who could present learning in an attractive dress, and in some poetry which he composed we have a versified summary of his *curriculum*. Touching upon politics, he endeavours to develop in his Imperial charges the political sense:

> "How excellent the state of the citizen is
> 'Tis meet that the lords of that citizen should know."

Also he draws for his young pupils a politically idealistic picture of the relation which ought to subsist between a Tsar and his subjects—a picture couched in the form of a parable concerning a good shepherd and his sheep:

> "Thus it doth behove a governor to do:
> To bear the burden of his subjects well,
> Nor yet despise them, nor account them dogs,
> But love them better even than his sons."

Thus the diffusion of the Polish tongue, through the medium of Polish tutors, caused interest in translations from the Polish, as well as in Polish original works, to penetrate both into the palace of the Muscovite Tsar and into the mansions of the Muscovite boyars. I have said that the two eldest sons of Alexis were taught Polish and Latin; and, in addition, the Tsarevitch Theodor learnt the art of versification, and co-operated with his tutor, Polotski, in turning out a versified paraphrase of the Psalter, in which he transposed two of the Psalms. Indeed, it was commonly said of him that his one devotion was science, more especially mathematics. Also, one of the Tsar's daughters, Sophia, learnt Polish, and was able to read Polish books, and to write in Latin. Likewise we learn from Lazarus Baranovitch, Archbishop of Tchernigov, that, in his time, "the Tsar's *sinklit* (Privy Council) abhorred not the Polish tongue, and did read Latin books and tales with delight." Also, other members of the Muscovite community sought to imbibe Western learning from its primal sources, and the more so because such learning was now beginning to be accounted an indispensable aid to success in the service of the State. For instance, Matviev taught his son both Latin and Greek, while Ordin - Nastchokin, his predecessor as director of the Office of Ambassadors, surrounded his son with Polish prisoners of war, who inspired in the boy such a love for the West that at length he succumbed to the temptation to abscond thither. Again, the first Russian Resident in Poland, Tiapkin, sent his son to a Polish school, and in 1675, before dispatching the said son on a diplomatic mission to Moscow, presented him to the Polish King, John Sobieski, in whose presence the son recited a speech of thanks for "the bread, salt, and school instruction" which had been accorded him in Poland. This utterance the boy delivered in the then jargon of the scholastics—a jargon half-Polish and half-Latin; yet, according to the father's account, "his little son did offer his oration so clearly, and with such a presentment, as in no single word to stumble." For so doing the King rewarded the orator with 100 *zloti* (Polish florins) and 15 *arshini* (ells) of red velvet.

Thus Moscow came to feel the necessity of assimilating, firstly, European arts and comforts, and, in later days, European scientific erudition. Beginning with foreign officers and German artillerymen, she ended with German ballets and the Latin Grammar. Yet, though it was evoked by the material needs of the State, Western influence brought in its train, not only what was needed, but also what the State did *not* need, could well have done without, and might have waited for a little longer.

CHAPTER XIV

The beginning of the reaction against Western influence—The protest against the new
learning—The great Church schism—A story concerning its inception—How the two
sides explain its origin—The force of religious rites and texts—The psychological basis
of the schism—Rus and Byzantium—The eclipse of the idea of the Church Universal—
Tradition and the new learning—The national conceit in matters ecclesiastical—State
innovations—The Patriarch Nikon.

DESIRE for the new learning which came from the West conflicted with
the Muscovite public's invincible, agelong antipathy to, and suspicion of,
everything which emanated from the Catholic and Protestant West.
Hardly had Muscovite intellects tasted the fruits of Western learning
when they became seized with grave doubts as to whether such learning
were not dangerous, were not inimical to the purity of faith and morals.
That lack of confidence constitutes the second stage in the mental attitude
of Russia of the seventeenth century, and, owing its origin to dissatisfaction with the position of affairs, entailed some very important consequences. From a fragmentary item which has come down to us from
the year 1650 we can see at a glance whence that lack of confidence arose, .
and what added fuel to the flames. The item in question refers to some
members of the rising youth of Moscow—namely, to Lucian Timotheiev
Golosov (afterwards a *dvorianin* member both of the *Duma* and of the
State Council), one Stepan Aliabiev, a youth named Ivan Zasietski, and
the son of a *diak* of the Holy Synod, named Constantine Ivanov. These
young fellows constituted a band of intimates who were bound together
by similarity of mental outlook. "Here," ran their prime complaint, "is
this Rtistchev learning of his Kievans the Greek letters: yet in those
letters there is heresy." Aliabiev, in particular, is represented as stating
that, when the Greek *savant*, Arsenius, was residing in Moscow, he
(Aliabiev) desired to learn of the professor the Latin tongue, but ceased
his studies as soon as the *savant* was banished to Solovki, and tore up
his horn-book, since Luchka Golosov, Ivan Zasietski, and his relatives all
urged him, "Forbear thou to study the Latin tongue, in that it is evil,"
—though *why* it was evil they do not seem to have specified. Golosov
too, according to the item, had been invited by Rtistchev to study Latin

under the latter's Kievan professors at the Monastery of St. Andrew, but was opposed to such learning, in that he deemed it perilous to faith. Hence we see him saying to the *diak's* son, Ivanov: "Tell thy archpriest" (*i.e.* Stepan Vonifatiev, the father confessor of the Tsar) "that I will learn no longer of the wise men of Kiev, in that they are not pious old men, and that in them I have found naught of good, nor in their teaching aught of the same. What though, until now, I have cozened Rtistchev, through fear of his power, I will henceforth cease to learn of his teachers." To this the young man added, "Whosoever hath studied the Latin tongue, the same hath wandered from the true road." At about the same period (and, again, at Rtistchev's instance) there went to Kiev, to complete their education in the local Academy, two young men of Moscow whose names were Ozerov and Zverkalnikov; but of this departure the *diak's* son and his cronies did not at all approve, since they feared that, as soon as these young men had finished their studies at Kiev and returned to Moscow, they would think too much of themselves; wherefore, if they visited Kiev, it were far better that they should *never* return, seeing that, if they did, they would begin to find fault with everyone, and to make light of the reverend archpriests of Moscow, and to say of them that, "though physicians, they do heal not, and of them is there naught meet to be heard, and unto themselves they do no honour, in that they do but teach what they themselves know not." Also, we read that the same jealous observers of honour whispered of Morozov that he retained a father confessor only "for the wheedling of men," and that, inasmuch as he had taken to retaining Kievans in his pay, it was clear that he paid attention also to their heresies.

We see, then, that one section of the rising generation of Moscow accused the other of conceit through the new learning, as well as of indulgence in presumptuous criticism of the recognised native authorities. This was not conservative distaste for innovations, but an expression of a view of science which had its roots in the profoundest depths of Russia's ecclesiastical sense. In Russia of past times science and art were valued only for their connection with the Church, as means towards an understanding of the Word of God and spiritual salvation; whereas any knowledge, any artistic embellishments of life, which had no such connection with the Church were looked upon merely as the vain curiosity of a shallow mind—as personal, frivolous diversions or "beguilings." In fact, they were looked upon in much the same light as reciters, story-tellers, and buffoons. Although the Church tolerated them in silence, as childish games and recreations, every now and then the stricter sort of preachers would denounce them as dangerous attractions or distractions which could too easily be converted into wiles of the devil. At all events, neither to such knowledge nor to such art did they attribute any formative force, nor did they allow them a place in their educational system, but referred them to a debased order of life as, if not direct vices, at least weaknesses inherent in the addiction of human nature to sin. Nevertheless science and art, as introduced to Russia by Western influence, figured in a more pretentious light than this, for they formed part also of interests of a higher category. That is to say, they figured, not as concessions to men's weakness, but as lawful demands of the human intellect and heart—as necessary conditions of the proper organisation and conception of life in common which found their justification, not in the service of the Church's requirements, but in *themselves*. In ancient Russia the Western artist or *savant* was looked upon, not as a quack, a dealer in forbidden books, but as a respected artificer of stage-plays, or of works on geography, whom the Government itself confessed to be "wholly skilled in many necessary crafts and works of cunning." Thus Western influence—or, more strictly speaking, Western culture— came to us, not as the humble handmaid of the Church, nor as a sinner whom the Church had convicted, but had decided to tolerate, but as the rival—at least, as the coadjutor—of the Church in the work of arranging the welfare of mankind. Old Russian thought, being entangled with tradition, was bound to fight shy of such a coadjutor, and still more so of such a rival; nor is it difficult to understand why closer familiarity with the new culture caused the Muscovite community to ask itself with some anxiety, " Has this culture no peril for the Orthodox Faith, and for right living, and for the lasting stability of the national life?" True, the question first arose at a time when the exponents of that culture in Russia were Orthodox Western-Russian *savants;* but when, as tutors, there appeared also foreigners, Protestant and Catholic alike, the question inevitably entered a more pressing phase, and the doubt which it raised concerning the moral-religious innocuousness both of the new learning and of the Western influence by which that learning had been introduced led to a serious cleavage in Russian Church life. Indeed, the connection of this latter phenomenon with the moral and intellectual movement then in progress among the Muscovite community of the seventeenth century was so intimate as to force me to halt for a moment at the origin of the Great Schism.

By the Great Schism in the Russian Church is meant the separation of a large portion of the Russian Orthodox community from the Russian Orthodox Church. This cleavage in the body ecclesiastical began in the reign of Alexis Michaelovitch, in consequence of certain Church innovations which were introduced by the Patriarch Nikon; and to this day that cleavage continues. Yet the *Raskolniki*—the Old Believers, the Schismatics—consider themselves as much Orthodox Christians as we are. Between ourselves and them, the Primitive Ritualists, there exists no real difference either of dogmatic faith or of the basic teaching of dogma. The reason why the Old Believers splintered off from our Church and ceased to recognise the authority of our Church Government was that they decided to adhere to the "old faith" which had been (so they deemed) discarded by that Government. Hence we regard them, not as heretics, but as schismatics; while they, for their part, call us Churchmen or Nikonians, and term themselves the Old Believers, or the Observers of the Old Faith—of the faith which still holds to the Pre-Nikonian ritual and religion. But if the Old Believers do not differ from us in dogma, or in the bases of dogmatic teaching, the question arises—Whence arose the Church cleavage which placed a notable section of the Russian Church community outside the pale of the dominant Church in Russia? The story of the beginning of that cleavage might be outlined as follows.

Up to the time of the Patriarch Nikon the Church community in Rus was a united flock under a single supreme pastor; but in it there had, at different times, and owing to various causes, arisen and become established certain local Church opinions, customs, and rites which were distinct from those originally adopted by the Greek Church whence Rus had received Christianity. Instances of these local rites, and so on, are the signing of the cross with two fingers, the form of writing the name Jesus as " Issus,' the serving of Mass with six, instead of five, wafers, the passage according to the sun (*i.e.* from left to right according as the altar is faced) during certain acts of the priest (for example, during christenings at the font or marriages at the chancel steps), the special reading of certain passages concerning the Symbol of the Faith, and the doubling of all ejaculations of Alleluia. Yet, inasmuch as some of these rites and peculiar usages were recognised by the Russian Hierarchy at a Church Council of 1551, they had acquired legislative confirmation from the supreme ecclesiastical power. Next, when book-printing came into use in Moscow, these rites and different readings penetrated from the manuscript service-books into printed editions of the same, and so became diffused through Russia. Thus the printing-press not only imparted to them a new value, but also extended their use. In particular, some of them were imported into the new editions by the correctors of certain Church service-books which were printed during the years 1642–1652, while Josephus was Patriarch; and since the text of the majority of Russian manuals still remained in a non-corrected condition, Joseph's successor, the Patriarch Nikon, began his term of ecclesiastical rule with a tentative effort to remove the inaccuracies from such works. At the Church Council of 1654 he brought forward a motion that the Church's books should be re-edited in accordance with the true texts to be found in old Slavonic and Greek parchments: whereupon from the Orthodox East and different corners of Russia there were collected piles of old manuscripts, in Greek and ecclesiastical Slavonic; and the new editions, corrected with the help of these originals, were distributed to the different Russian churches, together with instructions that every uncorrected version, printed or written, should be removed and destroyed. But certain Orthodox Russians stood aghast when they beheld these newly-corrected manuals and found in them neither the bi-digital sign of the cross, nor the name "Issus," nor certain other time-hallowed rites and readings. Rather, they saw in the new editions only a new faith which the Holy Fathers had never known, and cursed them as heretical while continuing to observe the services and prayers prescribed by the older manuals. Upon these recalcitrants the Muscovite Church Council of 1666–67 (at which two of the Eastern Patriarchs were present) imposed its anathema for their opposition to ecclesiastical authority, and cut them off from the Orthodox Church; while, for their part, the excommunicated ceased to recognise as their proper Hierarchy the Church authorities who had thus cut them off. Ever since then the Russian Church community has been divided by schism.

But whence did the schism arise? According to the Old Believers, from the fact that, when correcting the service-books, Nikon, of his own initiative, abolished the bi-digital sign of the cross and certain other Church rites in which there was embodied the tradition of the Holy Fathers and pristine Orthodoxy—the tradition without which it was impossible to be saved; and that when certain men, faithful to the older ritual, made a stand for that tradition, the Russian Hierarchy excommunicated them from their already mutilated Church. But this explanation does not make everything clear. How was it that such rites as the bi-digital sign or the passage according to the sun became, for the Old

Believers, sanctified traditions without which it was impossible to be saved? How was it that a mere Church custom, a mere rite or text, could acquire such an importance as to become a sanctity, a dogma, which was not to be touched? Of this the Orthodox, for their part, give an explanation of more profundity. The schism, they say, originally arose from the grossness of the Schismatics—from their narrow understanding of the Christian religion, and from the fact that they could not distinguish in it the essential from the external, the kernel from the shell. Yet even *this* answer does not fully decide the question. Let us suppose that certain rites, hallowed by tradition or by local antiquity, could acquire such a disproportionate importance of dogma : yet, even then, the authority of the ecclesiastical Hierarchy is equally sanctified by antiquity—and that by a universal, not a local, antiquity the recognition of which is necessary for salvation, and without which the Holy Fathers were not saved, as they were without the bi-digital sign. How was it, then, that the Old Believers decided to sacrifice one Church ordinance for another, and to venture to save themselves without the guidance of the legal Hierarchy whom they had rejected?

When explaining the origin of the schism, it is not unusual for certain people to refer with great emphasis and not a little contempt to the blind attachment of the Old Believers to their rites and texts, to the strict letter of their Law, and to imply that these are matters which have little to do with the working of religion. For my own part, however, I do not share this contemptuous view of religious rights and texts. I am no theologian, and feel conscious of no call to explain the theological meaning of such matters ; but the religious text and the religious rite, like every text and every rite which has a practical, an everyday, effect, possess, in addition to their theological significance, a significance of psychology, and can, from that aspect, as workaday (*i.e.* historical) phenomena, fitly be made the subject of historical study. From this point of view alone, therefore—*i.e.* from the popular-psychological standpoint—I will touch briefly upon the origin of the schism.

Religious rights and texts express the essence, the substance, of religious doctrine ; and doctrine, in its turn, is made up of two kinds of belief—of *verities*, which establish the outlook upon life of the believer, and decide for him the higher questions of creation, and of *exigencies*, which direct the moral acts of the believer, and point out to him the problems of his daily round. These verities and these exigencies transcend not only such means of understanding as lie at the disposal of the logically thinking mind, but also the natural tendencies of the human will ; wherefore both the one and the other are looked upon as worthy of reverence rather than are matters which lie more directly open to the senses. Thinkable, intelligible *formulæ* of religious verities are known as dogmas, while thinkable, intelligible *formulæ* of religious exigencies are known as precepts. But how can the one and the other be assimilated when they are accessible neither to logical thought nor to the natural will? They are to be assimilated only through the gaining of religious knowledge, only through certain processes of religious thought or religious education. Yet let not the student be alarmed at these terms : religious thought or mind-development is as much a method of human mind-exercise—though a method distinct from the use of logic or of reason—as is artistic conception : the only difference between the two is that the former is directed to a higher class of subjects. Not always does man attain his ends through logical lines of thought. Indeed, it may be that on such lines he attains the least possible proportion of what he is seeking. Similarly, in the assimilation of dogmas and precepts, the believer adopts certain religious ideas and moral motives which are as little open to logical dissection as are artistic ideas. For instance, could any intelligible musical *motif* be subjected to a scheme of logic? Religious ideas and motives constitute *beliefs*, and the pedagogic means for their assimilation lie in certain Church activities which, in the aggregate, constitute theology. Again, dogmas and precepts find expression in sacred texts, while Church activities concentrate themselves into rites—although the latter are only the forms of belief, the wrappings of doctrine, not its true essence. But religious apprehension, like artistic apprehension, is distinguished from apprehension based upon logic or upon mathematics by the fact that, in it, an idea or a motive is indissolubly bound up with the form through which it is expressed ; whereas an idea which is *logically* deduced or a theory which is *mathematically* proven can be understood in *any* sort of formulation—in a known or an unknown tongue, in a readily or a non-readily apprehensible style, and even through the medium of a token which is purely conditional. Not so does the religious and æsthetical sense act, for here the law of psychological association causes an idea or a motive to become organically one with the text, the rite, the form, the rhythm, or the sound through which that idea or that motive is expressed. Forget the picture or the musical combination of sounds which has evoked in you a given frame of mind—and instantly you find yourself powerless to reproduce that mental attitude. However splendid be the poem which you translate into prose, its witchery will, in the act of translation, disappear. Similarly, sacred texts and theological rites are compounded historically, and contain in their character no element of unchangeableness or of intangibility. Although we are best able to envisage those texts and those rites which nourish in us the religious feeling, those texts and those rites do not change us in our worser sentiments. When an Orthodox Russian priest ejaculates, in Russian, at the altar, "Lift up your hearts!" the Orthodox believer at once becomes attuned to the customary religious attitude which helps him to lay aside the cares of life; but should the same priest ejaculate, in the words of the Roman missal, "*Sursum corda*," the believer would, though well aware that the ejaculation was the same as before, but couched in the Latin tongue and a more energetic style of phrasement, derive no elevation of soul from the exhortation, for the reason that he is not accustomed to the words. Thus the religious outlook and attitude of every community is inseparably bound up with the texts and the rites by which that outlook and that attitude are nourished.

Yet it may be that such a close connection of religious rites and forms with the essence of doctrine is, in itself, a fault in our religious education, and that the faithful soul can well dispense with the added burdens of rites, and ought to be helped to dispense with them. Yes, it may be that with time, if such additions should ever become superfluous, and the human soul should, through ultimate self-perfection, ever free its religious sense from the influence of external impressions, as well as from the need of them, that soul will be able to pray solely "in spirit and in truth." Then will religious psychology be something wholly unlike to what the practice of hitherto known religions has nourished. Yet never since men first began to be conscious of themselves have they, the centuries through, been able to do without rites, whether in religion or in any of the other relations of life which partake of a moral character. Between the assimilation of truth through consciousness and the assimilation of truth through will-power we must draw a clear distinction. Consciousness needs only a given effort of thought and memory to understand and to lay to heart truth. Yet even this is not enough to make truth the arbitress of the will, the directress of the life, of whole communities, since for that purpose it is necessary to abstract truth into forms, into rites, into a complete organisation which, through a ceaseless flow of superincumbent impressions, shall eventually reduce our thoughts to a given system, shape our senses to a given attitude of mind, soften our rude wills to a given order of volition, and thus, through constant exercise and use, convert the demand for truth into an everyday moral need, an involuntary abstraction of the will. How many glorious truths, enlightening the soul of man, and capable of warming and brightening his life in common, have come to naught so far as he is concerned, for the reason that they have never succeeded in becoming abstracted into such an organisation as that of which I speak, and men have never risen to a sufficiently high level of education through their means! And it is in everything as in religion. However beautiful a musical *motif*, it does not necessarily, in the simple form wherein it was born in the artistic imagination of the composer, produce upon us an artistic *impression*; it needs first to be worked out, to be committed to an instrument or a whole orchestra, to be repeated in a dozen harmonies and variations, and to be played before a whole audience—an audience among whom the small enthusiasm of each separate hearer will communicate itself to his neighbours on either side of him, until from all those miniature personal raptures there becomes born one general, one accumulated impression which each individual hearer can take with him home, and there for many a day preserve inviolate from the cares and mischances of his daily life. The men who first heard the Gospel of Christ died many ages ago, and with them disappeared the impressions which they derived from that Gospel; yet still we feel a portion of those impressions, since the text of the Gospel stands fixed for us in the framework of our theology. Thus the rite or the text is a kind of phonograph; in it there lies dormant a moral moment which may at any time awaken men to good deeds and right sentiments. The men who first heard the Gospel have long been gone, and never since their day has the moment recurred; yet, with the help of the rite or the text wherein it first took refuge from human forgetfulness, we can reproduce that moment according to our desire to do so, and again experience its action according to the measure of our moral enterprise. From those rites, then, and from those customs and conditional relations and conventions into which there have become fitted the thoughts and feelings which direct the existence of man, and serve as his ideals, there has become formed, through a course of vacillation, dissension, conflict, and bloodshed, the life of humanity in association; and though what man will have become a thousand years hence I do not know, at least I know that, deprive the human race of to-day of its hardly earned and hereditarily transmitted stock of rites, customs, and other conditional appurtenances, and it will forget them all, unlearn them all, and be forced to begin anew.

But if the religious psychology of every ecclesiastical community is such that that community cannot dispense with the rite and the text, why is it that nowhere and at no period has there arisen from the rite and the text such a violent quarrel, such a schism, as there arose in Russia during the seventeenth century? To answer that question we must first of all recall certain phenomena which manifested themselves in our Church life *previous* to the seventeenth century.

Up to the fifteenth century the Russian Church was the obedient daughter of Byzantium, her metropolis. Thence she received her Metropolitans and bishops, her ecclesiastical laws, her every function of Church life. For many centuries the authority of Greek Orthodoxy stood unchallenged in Rus, but from the fifteenth century onwards it began to totter, for the reason that, in proportion as the Grand Dukes of Moscow gradually realised their national status, they became unwilling to stand, in Church matters, in dependence upon any extraneous power, whether of the Emperor or of the Patriarch of Byzantium. Hence they originated a custom whereby the appointment and consecration of Metropolitans of All Rus should, in future, be carried out at home, in Moscow, and only from among the ranks of the Russian clergy. To effect this change was the easier a matter in that the Greek Hierarchy was not regarded with any very great respect in Rus. True, upon the *ecclesiastical authority* and the *sanctity* of the Greek East ancient Rus still looked with awe; yet the terms Greek and rogue were considered as synonymous, and we find a chronicler of the twelfth century saying of a certain Greek bishop that "he was deceitful because he was a Greek." The origin of this view was at once early and simple, and lay in the fact that, to establish Christianity in the far-off and barbarous metropolis of Rus, the Patriarchate of Constantinople sent, as a rule, by no means the best members of the Greek Hierarchy. In Moscow, cut off from their flock by differences of tongue, of ideas, and of official ceremonial, these prelates were powerless to acquire a pastoral influence, and had to rest satisfied with their outward setting of ecclesiastical magnificence and the good-will of certain pious Grand Dukes. At the same time they sent home large remittances of Russian money, and in the twelfth century a respected Russian bishop of Novgorod thought it necessary, in a pastoral address to the clergy of his diocese, to issue a hint upon the subject. In fact, every Greek priest who came to Rus to live upon the newly-enlightened natives of the country exacted as much as he could for the benefit of the Greek Hierarchy. Next, in the fifteenth century the Greek Hierarchy further lowered itself in the eyes of Rus by adopting the Florentine Union of 1439—*i.e.* by agreeing to that junction of the Orthodox Church with the Catholic which had been organised at the Council of Florence. Although Rus had strictly defended the Hierarchy in the struggles of the latter with Latinism, the Hierarchy had now surrendered to the Roman Pope, and betrayed Eastern Orthodoxy—the Orthodoxy which had been established by the Apostles, and subsequently confirmed by the Holy Fathers and seven Universal Councils; and if the Tsar Vassilii Vassilie-vitch had not seen fit to impeach his mischievous foe, the "Devil's son," the Greek Metropolitan Isidor, who had first brought the Union to Moscow, that Metropolitan would have Latinised also the Russian Church, and destroyed the ancient piety which had become established in Rus through Saint Vladimir. A few years later Byzantium was overthrown by the Turks; and since, for a long while past, it had been the custom of Rus to look upon the Greeks from a lofty and suspicious point of view, Rus saw in the fall of the walls of Tsargorod before the godless Hagarenes a sign that Greek Orthodoxy also was about to collapse. Listen, for instance, to the confident way in which the Russian Metro-politan, Philip I., explains the connection between the world events of his time. Writing in 1471 to the Novgorodians (who were then in a state of ferment against Moscow), he says: "Ponder ye upon this, my children. Tsargorod did stand unshakeable so long as there did shine in it, like unto the rays of the sun, the spirit of piety; but instantly that it did forsake truth, and join itself unto the Latin Church, in that hour did it fall into the hands of the pagans." Yes, in those days the light of the Orthodox East was burning very dimly in the eyes of Rus, for, even as the first Rome fell through heresies and pride, so the second Rome had fallen through inconstancy—had fallen at the hand of the godless eaters of raw meat. These events produced in Rus a deep, but not wholly ineffaceable, impression. True, the old lights of the Church were now extinguished, and Greek piety had with-drawn behind a cloud,—Orthodox Rus felt lonely and forsaken in the world, for world events had forced her into involuntary opposition to Byzantium; yet Moscow contrived to slough the Hagarene yoke from her neck at very nearly the same moment that that yoke was imposed upon the neck of Byzantium. Though Empires might fall because of their treachery to Orthodoxy, yet would Moscow stand fast and be true to it, since she was the third and final Rome—the last, the one refuge, in all the world, for the Orthodox Faith and true piety. These thoughts at once raised and widened the historical outlook of the Russian thinkers of the seventeenth century, and filled them with anxious reflections concerning the fortunes of Russia. Indeed, in their eyes the fatherland had assumed a high destiny, and a Russian monk named Philothei is seen writing to the Tsar Vassilii, the father of Ivan the Terrible: "Give heed unto this, O pious Tsar. Two Romes have now fallen, and the third one, our Moscow, yet standeth, and a fourth one shall there never be. In thy puissant Empire the Council of our Church doth shine throughout all the world with a light of holiness which is greater even than the light of the sun. In all the world thou alone art the Christian Tsar." In Tsargorod the Orthodox Faith was fallen a victim to the spells of the godless Hagarenes; whereas in Rus it was shining forth the brighter with the teaching of the Holy Fathers. Thus wrote our publicists of the sixteenth century. And this view not only became an article of faith with the educated community of ancient Rus, but penetrated also into the ranks of the masses, and evoked there a string of legends concerning a reputed exodus of holy men and things from the two fallen Romes to the new, the third, Rome, the Muscovite Empire. It was through this that there became concocted in Russia of the fifteenth and sixteenth centuries the stories concerning the voyage of a Roman Abbot named Antonius to Novgorod—a journey performed on a rock, with, as cargo, certain holy relics; concerning the miraculous translation of a wonder-working *ikon* of the Holy Mother from the Byzantine East to Tikhvin in Rus; and so on. Also certain personages who came to Rus from the ravaged Orthodox East, to beg alms or to seek an asylum, helped to confirm in the Russians their national conviction. For instance, during the reign of Theodor, the son of Ivan the Terrible, there arrived in Moscow, to solicit eleemosynary aid, the Patriarch Jeremy of Tsargorod; and, by consecrating to the office of Patriarch of All Rus the Muscovite Metropolitan Job, Jeremy, in 1589, finally confirmed the long-pending hierarchical separation of the Russian Church from the Patriarchate of Constantinople. It would seem as though Jeremy must have got wind of the cherished ideas of the Russians of the sixteenth century, so nearly to the thoughts of the above Philothei did the words which he addressed to the Muscovite Tsar concerning the institution of a Patriarchate in Moscow approximate. "In thee," said he, "there dwelleth the Holy Spirit; and of God is it now given unto thee to remember that ancient Rome did fall through heresy, and that the second Rome, Constantinople, hath fallen into the keeping of the grandsons of the Hagarenes, the godless Turks. But thy great Tsardom of Rus doth surpass all in piety, and thou alone art known, throughout the universe, as the one Christian Tsar."

These various phenomena and impressions served to mould the Church community of Rus in a very original way. Towards the opening of the seventeenth century that community was thoroughly permeated with religious self-confidence, but a self-confidence which was fostered, not by the religious, but by the *political*, progress of Orthodox Rus, as well as by the political misfortunes of the Orthodox East. As the fundamental motive of this national self-complacency we see the notion that, in all the world, Orthodox Rus was now the sole cherisher and defender of genuine Christian truth, of purest Orthodoxy; and from this notion, through a certain transposition of ideas, the national conceit deduced the additional conviction that the Christianity whereof Rus was the possessor was, with all its local peculiarities and its native limitedness of understanding, the one true Christianity under heaven, and that no other pure Orthodoxy existed, nor ever could exist, than the Russian. Yet, according to our doctrine, the preserver of Christian truth is not a local Church, but the Church Universal, which unites in herself not only such believers as live at a given period or in a given locality, but *all* believers, of every period and every locality. Therefore, no sooner did the Russian Church community proclaim itself the sole preserver of true piety than it also proclaimed its local religious sense to be the standard of Christian truth. That is to say, it closelocked the idea of the Church Universal into the narrow geographical confines of a local Church, and the universal Christian sense into the narrow purview of the inhabitants of a single period and a single locality. I have said that Christian doctrine is abstracted into certain forms, that it is expressed in certain rites for the purpose of direct understanding, that it is formulated in certain texts for the purpose of education, and that it is preserved in certain practical Church rules. Both the comprehension of texts of doctrine and the practice of Church rules become deeper and more perfect with the growth of the religious sense and its motive force (such motive force being reason, reinforced by faith), since, with the help of rites, texts, and rules, religious thought is able to penetrate to the mysteries of doctrine, and so to explain them, and to direct the life religious. True, rites, texts, and rules do not constitute the *essence* of doctrine; yet, according to the growth of religious comprehension and knowledge, such rites, texts, and rules develop in close connection with doctrine, and so become, for every Church community, forms of religious outlook and attitude which are barely distinguishable from their religious inwardness. At the same time, if, in a given community, such rites, &c., become mutilated or deviate from the original norms of doctrine, there still remains a means for correcting them ; and that means of revision and correction, that corrective to a proper understanding of Christian truth in local Church communities, lies in the consciousness of the Church Universal—of the Church whose authority is potent to amend all local Church deviations. Unfortunately, as soon as Orthodox Rus proclaimed herself the sole possessor of Christian truth, that means of correction became lost to her, since, once it had declared itself to be the Church Universal, the Russian Church community could not very well permit any extraneous examination of its beliefs and rites. Hence no sooner did Russian Orthodox minds arrive at this standpoint than there became confirmed in them also an idea that the Russian local Church possessed, in all its plenitude, universal Christian recognition, and that the Russian Church community had acquired everything necessary for the salvation of believers, and had nothing more to learn, nothing more to borrow, from any source, in matters of faith, but could rest for ever the guardian of the treasure which it had received. Thus, not universal recognition, but the national Church antiquity of Rus became the standard of Christian truth ; the Russian Church community adopted for its rule the precept that a man ought to pray and to believe as his father and grandfather had prayed and believed before him, and that nothing more remained to the grandson but to hold unquestioningly to the tradition of his forebears. Yet that tradition only represented comprehension which had halted and become congealed where it stood ; wherefore to accept it as the standard of truth meant the rejection of all onward movement of the religious sense, all possibility of correcting its mistakes and shortcomings. Consequently, from the moment when that acceptance became a fact, every effort of religious thought in Rus perforce became directed, not to delving to the mysteries of Christian doctrine, nor to assimilating, as truly and as fully and as vividly as possible, the sense of universal religion, but to preserving intact the whole available local stock of religious conceptions and rites, and to safeguarding them from treason and unclean contact from without.

From this attitude, this bent, of religious ideas there issued two important results with which the origin of the schism was closely connected. The two results in question were that such Church rites as had been bequeathed by local antiquity acquired the significance of inviolate, immutable sanctities, and that there became established among the Russian community a supercilious, an overbearing relation towards any participation in questions of faith by reason or by scientific learning. Though such learning might flourish in other Christian communities—thus men reflected in ancient Rus—it had not succeeded in preserving those communities from heresy any more than the light of reason had served to hinder their faith from growing dim. Therefore, vaguely remembering that the original roots of lay erudition had sprouted on the heathen soil of Greece and Rome, the Russian of the day reflected with a shudder that that erudition had been nurtured on the impure juices of a soil that was evil; wherefore he became filled with a timid, squeamish feeling whenever he thought of the rhetorical and philosophical arts of Greece— of matters which were the outcome of a sinful mind which perforce had become abandoned to itself. For instance, we read in an old Russian "book of instruction": "Impious unto God is every man who loveth geometry, and a spiritual sin it is to study astronomy and the books of Greece; for, according unto his reason, will the true believer readily fall into diverse errors. Love thou simplicity rather than wisdom, and seek not that which is above thee, nor attempt that which is over-deep for thy understanding. Whatsoever is given thee of God shall be meet for learning, and cleave thou fast unto it." Also, in certain scholastic copybooks we find the injunction: "My brother, be not thou high-minded. If they shall ask of thee whether thou knowest aught of philosophy, make thou answer: 'With Greek swiftness have I not run, of rhetoric and astronomy have I not read, with wise philosophers have I not consorted, and from philosophy have I turned mine eyes away. Only the blessed Books of the Law do I study, to the end that I may cleanse my sinful soul of error.'" This view thrived the better on the conceit of ignorance. "Though I be not skilled in words," writes an old Russian bookman of himself, "nor in reasoning, nor in dialectic, rhetoric, and philosophy, *yet have I within me the wisdom of Christ.*" In this way the old Russian Church community lost not only all means of self-improvement, but also any desire for such means.

In their more artless form the views in which the Russian Church community of the seventeenth century became confirmed were the views of the populace, yet also views which embraced the bulk of the clergy, both white and black. Among the hierarchical directorate, however, they found less rude expression—they merely became a part of the Hierarchy's irresponsible ecclesiastical attitude. In joint liturgical service with visiting Greek prelates, even with the Greek Patriarch himself, Russian Church dignitaries would, while following the visitors' every movement, point out to them with vast condescension such departures in liturgical detail as they (the Russian dignitaries) had allowed to be made. "Such and such a *tchin*[1] do we not observe among us, and such and such a *tchin* hath never been received into our one true and Orthodox Christian Church." This practice supported in the Russian prelates a belief in their ritualistic superiority to the Greeks, and filled them with such complacency that they never thought of the temptation which their conduct afforded to the faithful—namely, the temptation to break in upon the serving of the Offices with ritualistic objections. In the attachment of the Russians to the Church rites which they had been brought up in there was nothing extraordinary : we ought to see in it a popular psychological inevitability, a natural historical condition of the Russian religious understanding, rather than an organic or chronic malady of the Russian religious sense. In fact, it was a sign of the historical growth of the nation. No ; the organic vice of the old Russian Church community lay in the fact that it considered itself the one true Orthodox community in the world, and its conception of the Deity the exclusively regular one ; that it put forward as the Creator of the Universe a peculiarly Russian god who belonged to and was known to no one else ; and that it elevated to the rank of the Church Universal a purely local Church. Resting presumptuously satisfied with this opinion, it also proclaimed its Church ritual to be an inviolate sanctity, and its religious understanding to be the norm of, and the only corrective to, all revelation. Naturally, the meeting of these views with what was happening in the State caused their provocative character to become enhanced the more.

We have seen that, with the accession of the new dynasty, Rus adopted certain political and economic innovations which had for their object the reorganisation of the national defence and the State's finances. Feeling the need of new, of borrowed, technical resources, the State summoned to its aid a multitude of foreigners who, in faith, were Lutheran or Calvinist. True, these foreigners were summoned only for the giving of military instruction, for the casting of guns, and for the building of factories, —all of which had little to do with moral ideas, still less with religious views ; yet the old-time Russian, with his concrete way of thinking, was not accustomed to draw fine distinctions between the relations of life,

[1] Order of service.

nor able or willing to separate one aspect of life from another. If the German commanded a Russian military force, and taught that force his military skill, then the Russian too must dress himself, and shave his beard, in German fashion, and adopt the German's faith, and smoke his pipe, and drink milk on Wednesdays and Fridays, and forsake his (the Russian's) old-time piety. In fact, his conscience stood halting between native antiquity and the German Quarter. All this rendered the Russian community, towards the middle of the seventeenth century, extremely uneasy and suspicious—an attitude which manifested itself on every possible occasion. For instance, in 1648, when the young Tsar Alexis was about to wed, a murmur arose in Moscow that the end of the old pious system was approaching, and that new foreign customs were about to be introduced. In the presence of such a frame of mind, any attempt to revise either the Church's ritual or the text of her service-books would seem to the distressed, nervous Church community an attempt against the faith itself; and it so happened that the prelate who applied himself to that revision was the man who, of all others, was constitutionally capable of bringing that frame of mind to the last pitch of tension. For this reason alone the Patriarch Nikon (who was consecrated to the Patriarchate in 1652) deserves a moment to himself in our sketch of the origin of the Great Schism.

Born, in 1605, a peasant, he was enabled by his skill in letters to become a village priest; but certain circumstances of his life soon led him to enter the profession of monasticism, where, after tempering himself by the stern ordeal of desert life [1] among the northern monasteries, he, through a capacity for influencing men, acquired the unbounded confidence of the Tsar, rapidly attained the office of Metropolitan of Novgorod, and finally, at the age of forty-seven, became Patriarch of All Rus. No leading man in Russia of the seventeenth century bulks more largely, and in a more distinctive way, than does Nikon. Yet he was not a man who could be understood at a glance, for he was a very complex character, and, beyond all things, an unequal one. Although in peaceful times, in the daily routine of life, he was difficult to deal with, capricious, fiery, arbitrary, and, above all things, selfish, these were not his permanent, his radical, characteristics, since, for one thing, he could produce a great moral impression upon men, and no really selfish person can ever do that. Again, because of his keenness in a fight he was sometimes accounted cruel; yet enmity of any kind distressed him, and he could easily forgive a foe if he

[1] See vol. ii. p. 153.

remarked in his antagonist a wish to meet him half-way. To a declared enemy Nikon was undoubtedly stern; yet even then he would forget everything at the sight of human tears and suffering. Beneficence, the helping of a weak or ailing neighbour, was, with him, not so much a duty of his pastoral service as the involuntary instinct of a kind nature. Also, his moral and intellectual strength caused him to be a great *doer* —to be a man who was both able and willing to accomplish great things, and nothing that was *not* great. What everyone could do he did worse than anyone else. Yet in him he had both the will and the power to do what no one else would even undertake, no matter whether that something were good or evil. For instance, his treatment, in 1650, of the Novgorodian rebels—rebels among whom he risked his life to bring them to reason—as well as, later, his conduct during the Muscovite plague of 1654 (when, in the Tsar's absence, he hurried the Imperial family out of the range of infection), shows him to have been a man who could boast of daring and self-possession. Yet, under the petty stress of life and the banalities of the daily round, he could easily lose his head and his temper; and in such cases the impression of the moment would, with him, develop into a complete attitude of mind. At difficult junctures which, though not created by him, demanded the whole exercise of his intellect, he would occupy himself with vanities, and at the same time, through those very vanities, prepare himself for some great and sounding deed. When, for instance, he was under a cloud, and had been banished to the Monastery of Therapont, he still continued to receive presents from the Tsar; yet on one occasion when the Tsar sent him a parcel of fish, Nikon actually took offence, and sent, by way of answer, a reproachful query whether he ought not, rather, to have been sent fruit, grapes preserved in honey, and apples! When in a good humour, he was both approachable and keen-witted; but when he was roused and offended, he would lose every vestige of tact, and mistake the whims of a heated imagination for realities. During his exile he set himself to tend the sick; yet, even then, to astonish the Tsar with his prodigies of healing, he could not refrain from sending him a list of the healed, and telling the Tsar's envoy that, even if he (Nikon) were deprived of the Patriarchate, he would not care so long as he was given a doctor's phial whereon there had been inscribed, "Heal thou the sick." In short, he belonged to the number of people who can bear the most terrible pangs without a murmur, yet will at once cry out and fly into hysterics on receiving a mere pin-prick. His was the weakness from which men who are strong, but ill-disciplined, so often suffer: he could neither endure inertia nor control his soul in patience during a time of waiting. On the contrary, he needed constant excitement, the constant distraction of a daring scheme or a comprehensive undertaking—even the diversion of a quarrel with some one who was distasteful to him. In fact, he was like a sail which is itself only in a storm, but which, during a season of calm, rattles, a useless roll of canvas, against the mast.

CHAPTER XV

ALMOST in the prime of life, and with a store of strength as yet untapped, Nikon became Patriarch of the Russian Church. Yet it was into a turbid, stormy mäelstrom of conflicting tendencies, political schemes, ecclesiastical misunderstandings, and Court intrigues that he fell when he did so. The State was preparing to make war upon Poland—to settle accounts which had been outstanding since the Period of Troubles, and to ward off from Western Rus the Catholic attack which was about to be delivered under the Polish flag : and to attain success in this struggle Moscow had need of the Protestants, of their military skill, and of their industrial guidance. On the other hand, there had arisen for the Russian Church Hierarchy two principal cares—namely, to encourage the Imperial Government in its struggle with the Catholics, and to prevent the Government from being seduced by the Protestants. Under the spur of these objects of solicitude certain signs of movement appear in the otherwise stagnant life of the Church, for, to prepare itself for the struggle, the Russian Church community had to hasten to take precautions, to put itself in order, to purify itself, to rally its forces, and to look to its shortcomings. Strict injunctions were issued against superstitious and heathen customs on the part of the people ; against unseemly conduct on holidays, against prize fights and lewd sports, against drunkenness, rudeness, and liturgical irregularities on the part of the clergy. Also, haste was made to do away with the dissensions which, for six and a half centuries, had been allowed to increase with the enrichment of the Church. Finally, the Church began to look for allies, for, if the State needed German artificers, the Church felt that she needed the Greek or the Kievan tutor ; wherefore her relations with the Greeks improved, and, despite the old distrustful, contemptuous view which Rus had long taken of their tarnished piety, the Greeks now began to be recognised by Moscow as strictly Orthodox. Intercourse with the Eastern Hierarchy grew more animated, and more and more frequently Eastern prelates visited Moscow with prayers and propositions—more and more frequently did men turn from Moscow to the Greek dignitaries of the East with questions concerning the Church's needs and doubts. That is to say, the Russian autocephalous Church now treated the Church of Constantinople with the respect due to her (the Russian Church's) late metropolis. Every attention was paid, in Moscow, to the opinions of Eastern Patriarchs, as to the opinions of the heads of the Church Universal, and no important ecclesiastical dilemma was ever resolved without their consent. In return, the Greeks hastened to answer any summonses which came from Moscow. While Moscow was thus seeking light of the Greek East there came thence a proposal that Moscow herself should become a source of light for the East—that she should become the foster-mother and diffuser of spiritual enlightenment for the whole Orthodox world, by founding a superior training college for the clergy, and organising a Greek printing-press. In addition, confidential use was to be made of the labours and services of Kievan *savants*. Yet it was easier to collect these various spiritual forces than to unite them, and adjust them for friendly co-operation. In Moscow Kievan academicians and Greek *savants* were haughty sojourners who looked askance at their hosts because of the latter's inferiority in learning ; while such Court supporters of Western culture as Morozov and Rtistchev, though valuing the Germans greatly as artisans, welcomed the Greeks and Kievans, rather, as ecclesiastical tutors, and assisted Nikon's predecessor, the Patriarch Josephus, in the reforming tendencies which he shared in common with the Tsar's confessor, Stephen Vonifatiev—tendencies which included an agitation for schools and the translation and publication of educational works. Also, to introduce better ideas and morals among the masses, Stephen summoned from different corners of Russia a number of popular preachers—Ivan Neronov of Nizhni Novgorod, Daniel of Kostroma, Loggin of Murom, Abbakoum of Yurievetz on the Volga, and Lazarus of Romanov-Borisogliebsk. Among this company there moved also Nikon—taking silent stock of his comrades and future opponents ; but Rtistchev, owing to his scientific leanings, became suspected of heresy, and the Tsar's father confessor, though at heart a magnanimous and peaceloving man, took occasion, on the first occurrence of collision, to denounce the Patriarch and the Holy Synod generally as thieves and iconoclasts, and to declare that in the Muscovite Empire

God's Church was not. Upon that the Patriarch petitioned the Tsar to make use of the article in the *Ulozhenïe* which decreed death for the utterance of slanders against the Synodal and Apostolic Church : the upshot of which was that the Imperial confessor's motley following ceased to obey their leader, "did speak with him harshly and contrariwise," cursed him to his face, and, with fanatical *abandon*, hurled themselves, in the name of the common Russian God, upon the Patriarch and all innovators, together with their new books, their new ideas, their new systems, and their new tutors ; sparing neither German, Greek, nor Kievan in the campaign. Truly the Tsar's confessor had been right when he said that in the Muscovite Empire God's Church was not, if by that Church we are to understand the discipline and liturgical order which were practised by the Hierarchy ! Here there reigned utter disorder and license. For instance, the pious Russian prelates, though supported by their clergy, grew weary of long standing in the Sanctuary ; wherefore, to meet their convenience, the clergy introduced an accelerated and unauthorised order of service whereby different portions of the Offices were read and sung by two or three voices at once ; or else, at one and the same time, a chanter intoned the canticles, a deacon spoke the *ektenia*, and a priest uttered the ejaculations, so that nothing at all could be distinguished amid the babel. The only proviso was that everything that was read or sung should be contained in the Liturgy. True, the Council of the *Stoglav* had forbidden such liturgical polyphony, but the clergy calmly disregarded the Council's injunction, and though, for such irregularities of ritual, the disorderly officiants could have been subjected to disciplinary correction, the Tsar, in 1649, commanded the Patriarch to convene a Church Council for the consideration of the matter. The result was that, through fear of murmurings both from the clergy and the laity, the Council sanctioned these irregularities ; and it was only in 1651 that the dissatisfaction of the upholders of ecclesiastical decorum forced the convening of a new Council, and the revision of the matter in favour of vocal monotony. The truth is that the higher pastors of the Church were afraid of their flock—even of their subordinate clergy, and, for their part, the flock thought nothing of pastors who, under the spur of treasonous influences, could deviate from side to side without differing in any way, as regards legislative looseness, from the Government of the State.

If, amid all this storm and stress of ecclesiastical unrest, Nikon had not imported so weighty a substance into his idea of the Church Universal and the relation thereto of the local Russian Church, one might still have marvelled at the spiritual force of a man who, under such circumstances, could work out an idea of that calibre, and hold to it until he had attained the Patriarchal throne. But in any case he entered upon his governance of the Russian Church with a fixed determination to re-establish complete concord between his own Church and the Greek Communion by annulling all those ritualistic peculiarities which distinguished the former from the latter. Of suggestions to support him in his sense of the necessity of such a union there was no lack, for the Eastern prelates who, during the seventeenth century, visited Moscow with increasing frequency more than once reproached the prelates of the Russian Church with those peculiarities, and declared them to be local innovations which must end by destroying all agreement between the local Orthodox Communions. Indeed, not long before Nikon's accession to the Patriarchate, there occurred an event which did in very truth point to such a danger. This was when, at a convention of the inmates of the Greek monasteries at Mount Athos, the bi-digital sign of the cross was declared heretical, the Muscovite service-books in which it had been promulgated were solemnly burnt, and a move was made to burn the friar in whose possession the books had been discovered. Consequently we can well conjecture the personal motive which led Nikon to devote his chief attention to the forming and consolidating of a close reunion between the Russian Communion and the Eastern Churches, as well as between the Russian Patriarch and the Patriarchs of the Church Universal, since he must have been aware that the fainthearted reforming blunders of the Patriarch Josephus and his fellow thinkers were never likely to deliver the Russian Church from its uncomfortable position. Knowing also, as he was bound to do, what a pitiable cipher a Patriarch of All Rus could come to be at Court, and how easily, on the other hand, a forceful personality could turn a young Tsar in any direction desired, his explosive self-conceit felt hurt at the thought that he, the Patriarch Nikon, should come to be a toy in the hands of a clever Imperial confessor, as his predecessor in the Patriarchate had been—a predecessor who, towards the close of his tenure of office, had stood in hourly expectation of dismissal. Therefore, on the height of the Apostolic throne in Moscow Nikon must have felt completely isolated, and, consequently, bound to seek extraneous support in the Church Universal of the East, and in a closer union with his fellow prelates of that Communion, since, despite the difficulty of bringing such a conception home to the Muscovite ecclesiastical mind, the authority of the Church Universal still acted as a

scarecrow to the piously nervous, but arrogant, Muscovite conscience.
Next, following his usual custom of working out his every idea, his every
sentiment, with the help of his imagination, he soon forgot the Morduine
country of the Nizhni Novgorodians whence he was sprung, and tried to
convert himself into a Greek.   Thus, at the Church Council in 1655 he
explained that, though he was a Russian and the son of a Russian, his
faith and his convictions were Greek; and in the same year he followed
up a solemn service in the Usspenski Cathedral by publicly divesting
himself of his Russian cassock, and donning a Greek,—a proceeding
which called forth, not smiles, but deep mutterings at this challenge to
those who believed that, in the Russian Church, everything had been
bequeathed by the Apostles at the suggestion of the Holy Spirit.   Even
in the matter of his table Nikon was for the Grecian fashion, and we read
that, in 1658, the Archimandrite of a certain Greek monastery in Nikolskaia Street, with his cellarer, "did order a banquet for my lord the
Patriarch even as the Greeks do," and that for their services the said
"orderers" received a *poltina*, or seven roubles in modern currency.
Thus strengthened with support that lay extraneous to his Muscovite
authority, Nikon attempted to become, not merely Patriarch of Moscow
and All Rus, but also one of the Universal Patriarchs, and to act independently.   That is to say, he attempted to give actual force to the title
"Great Lord" which he bore in common with the Tsar, no matter
whether his action had to take the form of a usurpation condescendingly
permitted or that of a favour which the Sovereign unguardedly conferred
upon his "beloved friend."   By this course Nikon placed the priesthood not only on a level with the Tsarship, but above the latter; and
once, on being accused of Popery, he answered nonchalantly : "Wherefore should the Pope not be honoured for that which is good?   The chief
Apostles of Rome were the Saints Peter and Paul; and now the Pope
doth serve where they have served."   Thus Nikon hurled a challenge not
only at the whole past of the Russian Church, but also at the Russian
actualities which surrounded him.   Yet of himself in connection with it
all he took no thought, for in the presence of the cherisher of the idea of
the Church Universal and Eternal there disappears everything which
is local and temporary.   In short, Nikon's whole efforts were directed
to re-establishing complete agreement and union between the Russian
Church and its fellow Orthodox Communions, and to occupying, as
Patriarch of All Rus, his rightful place among the Hierarchy of the
Church Universal.

Nikon entered upon the work of re-establishing inter-ecclesiastical agreement with his usual zeal and enthusiasm. As soon as ever he had ascended the Patriarchal throne he imposed upon the boyaral Government and the nation a solemn oath to accord him full license in the reorganisation of the Church's affairs. In other words, he exacted a kind of ecclesiastical dictatorship. Next, he spent whole days in seclusion in his library, to the end that he might examine and study the old books and disputed texts. In them he found, among other things, a charter of 1593 for the institution of a Patriarchate in Rus, signed by the Eastern Patriarchs, and saying that, as brother to his fellow Orthodox Patriarchs, the Patriarch of Moscow was in all things to consort with them, and to root out innovations from the pale of his Church, since innovations invariably proved a cause of ecclesiastical dissension. Upon this Nikon became seized with a dread lest the Russian Church should in times past have permitted departures to be made from the Orthodox Greek Law; and in his anxiety he set himself to examine and compare the Slavonic text of the Symbol of the Faith and the service-books with the Greek text, and everywhere found changes and discrepancies. Next, in the same belief that it was his duty to maintain complete agreement with the Greek Church, he decided to undertake a correction of the Russian service-books and Church rites; which task he, in 1653, began by sending to every parish church a rescript for regulating the manner wherein the obeisances were to be made when reading the well-known prayer of Saint Ephraim Sirin, together with an injunction that, during its course, the sign of the cross was to be made with *three* fingers. Next, he ran a tilt against the Russian church decorators of his day, who had departed from the Greek models, and adopted methods of Catholic ornamentation. Also, with the help of the monks of the South-West, he replaced the old Muscovite unison chant with Kievan part-singing, and also established the hitherto unprecedented custom of preaching sermons of his own composition. Such sermons were looked upon with suspicion in ancient Rus, for the reason that men saw in them a sign of arrogance on the part of the preacher; they considered it decent to read only the teachings of the Holy Fathers (though, as a matter of fact, that the Liturgy might not be delayed, those teachings were usually *not* read). But Nikon loved, and was a master in the art of delivering, his own teachings; and it was at his instigation, and by the force of his example, that Kievan priests in Moscow also were led to begin preaching sermons of their own composition, and sometimes sermons written around the themes of the day. The ferment into which Orthodox Russian minds—minds already sufficiently agitated by other matters—were thrown by these innovations is certainly intelligible, since, for the first time, Nikon's ordinances showed the Russian Orthodox community that it had never yet known how to pray or to paint an *ikon*, as also that the clergy had hitherto been ignorant of the proper way in which to perform the Offices. Upon one of the first leaders in the schism, the Archpriest Abbakoum, the ferment made a particularly great impression. After the order concerning the Lenten obeisances had been issued he writes that "we did gather together, and take counsel; and it was as though the winter season had come upon us, so greatly were men's hearts troubled, and so grievously were their members made to quake." Nor was the ferment likely to diminish when Nikon proceeded also to correct the service-books, — though it is true that he carried through this portion of his work with the help of a Church Council (1654) which was presided over by the Tsar himself, and attended by the *Boyar-skaia Duma*. In the result, the Council decreed that, in future, all Church books which should be printed should follow the ancient Greek and Slavonic texts. Now, bygone Rus drew little distinction between Church manuals and the Sacred Testament; wherefore Nikon's undertaking was bound to raise the question as to whether, after all, God's word was faulty, and, if so, whether *anything* in the Russian Church was altogether free from fault; and this fear was the more increased by the fact that the Patriarch introduced his new ordinances suddenly, and with an unusual amount of stir—he did so without in any way preparing the community for the same, but accompanied them, rather, with harsh measures against persons who should prove recalcitrant. To rend, to abuse, to curse, to destroy the opponent who displeased him—such were the customary methods of his forceful exercise of the pastorate. Even against Paul, Bishop of Kolomna, he employed those methods, in return for the Bishop's opposition to him at the Council of 1654; and without trial by the Council Paul was deprived of his See, handed over to "cruel beating," and sent into exile; all of which had the effect of unhingeing his mind, and leaving him to die an unknown death. Again, a contemporary tells us of the manner in which Nikon proceeded against the new fashion in church decoration. In 1654, when the Tsar was absent on a military expedition, the Patriarch gave orders that a domiciliary search should be made in Moscow, and all *ikoni* of the new painting seized, whether in the houses of the nobility or elsewhere; after which the eyes of the confiscated images were gouged out, and the disfigured images borne in procession through the city, to enforce an *ukaz* whereby stern punishment was threatened to all who should redecorate those *ikoni*. Soon afterwards a deadly pestilence broke out in Moscow, and an eclipse of the sun took place; whereupon the Muscovites became greatly alarmed, and held meetings whereat the Patriarch was blamed, on the score that the pestilence and the eclipse represented a visitation of God for the dishonour which Nikon had done to the images. Indeed, preparations were made to kill the iconoclast. However, in 1655 the Patriarch held a solemn service in the Usspenski Cathedral whereat two of the Eastern Patriarchs—those of Antioch and Servia—were present; and after the Liturgy was ended he read a homily on the paying of reverence to images, and then delivered a forcible speech against the new Russian church painting, and excommunicated, in advance, all persons who should paint or harbour any of its products. At the same time he had brought to him the *ikoni* which had been confiscated, and, after holding up each one of them to the people, he cast them down upon the iron floor with such force that they were shattered to pieces. Lastly he gave orders for the remains of the offending images to be burnt. But Tsar Alexis, who had been listening to the Patriarch the while, now approached him, and said in an undertone: "No, my father. Bid them not be burnt, but, rather, ordain that they be buried in the earth."

What was worse, this hostility of Nikon's to the ordinary rites and customs of his Church was governed by no conviction of the spiritual banefulness of those rites and customs, or of the exclusive spiritual salutariness of the new ritual and usage. Just as, until the question of the correction of the service-books arose, Nikon always crossed himself with two fingers, so, in later days, he permitted both the double and the triple Alleluia to be sung in the Usspenski Cathedral. In fact, as late as the closing days of his Patriarchate we find him saying to the then repentant Ivan Neronov, in a conversation concerning the old and the new service-books: "Both the one and the other of them are meet. Serve thou as thou mayest desire." Hence it was not ritual that the matter hinged upon, but opposition to ecclesiastical authority. Neronov was anathematised at the Council of 1656, not for the bi-digital sign or the older-printed service-manuals, but for the fact that he failed to show any deference to the Council of the Church. That is to say, the question had passed from ritual to the rule which enjoined the rendering of obedience to spiritual authority: and it was on the same basis that, at the Council of 1666–67, the Church's ban was laid upon the Old Believers.

The situation had reached the point that, if the spiritual power prescribed hitherto unaccustomed ritual, persons who proved recalcitrant were
excommunicated, not because they continued to observe the older ritual,
but because they showed a proper want of complaisance; but if they
repented and expressed their contrition, they could be reunited to the
Church, and at the same time permitted to observe the older ritual. In
fact, the whole thing was like a system of camp alarm which is designed
to teach soldiers the necessity of constant preparedness for attack. Yet
this never-ceasing trial of the community's obedience to the Church
seemed, to the religious conscience of the pastorate, a mere sport on the
part of its pastors. Only such men as the Archpriest Abbakoum found
their conscience insufficiently pliable to prevent them from becoming
schismatical preceptors. Yet if, at the outset of his campaign, Nikon had
said to the Church at large what he said to Neronov after the latter had
recanted, there would never have been a schism at all. Nikon contributed
to the schism chiefly through the fact that he misunderstood the men
with whom he had to deal—he undervalued his antagonists, Neronov,
Abbakoum, and others who had been his friends. These men were
not only popular preachers, but national agitators who could display their
educational gifts in lectures on the Holy Fathers, more especially on the
doctrines of St. John Chrysostom. Even Neronov, who ministered in
Nizhni Novgorod, did not dissent from those doctrines, but read and
expounded them both from the pulpit and in the streets and squares,
where the people gathered in crowds to hear him. Whether these exegetical
extempores contained much that was of theological import we do not
know, but certainly they contained a great deal of temperament. Against
the vices of the laity and the drunkenness of the clergy, against the
chicanery of mountebanks and the official abuses of *voievodi*, he declaimed
so vehemently that more than once his zeal won him a beating. Later,
when he had become Presbyter of the Kazan Cathedral in Moscow, the
entire capital came to hear him, and the body of the building and its
porch were filled to repletion, and the people besieged even the windows.
Nay, the Tsar himself attended in person, with his family, to listen to
the preacher. Others of the preaching brotherhood which was presided
over by the Imperial confessor there were who resembled their superior;
and popularity and Court favour combined to fill them with such boundless temerity that, from treating Nikon as their Patriarch, they took to
flouting him, to insulting him in his own Cathedral, and to telling
tales of him to the Tsar. To all this Nikon retaliated with the severest

penalties. For instance, when the Archpriest Loggin of Moscow was confirming the wife of the local *voievoda* in the house of the latter, he asked her why she had whitened her face; whereupon the offended husband and his guests cried out: " Dost thou, O Archpriest, blaspheme against the pigment wherewith the images be whitened?" To this Loggin retorted: "Take ye not so much delight in the painting of images, for it is in the Saviour Himself, and in the Mother of God, and in the Holy Fathers, rather than in their images, that honour doth chiefly lie." Thereupon the *voievoda* reported to Moscow that Loggin had given vent to railings against the images of the Saviour, the Holy Mother, and the Saints; and Nikon, without making any inquiry into the unseemly affair, subjected Loggin to close arrest in return for former reproaches on the score of pride and highmindedness which the Archpriest had uttered against his Patriarch. By thus introducing personal enmity into the affairs of the Church Nikon at once lowered his pastoral authority and crowned his antagonists with the halo of martyrdom; while, by persecuting those antagonists all over Russia, he furnished the dark corners of the country with a supply of daring propagators of Old Belief. This policy neither justified his dictatorship nor righted the ecclesiastical situation. On the contrary, it rendered the latter even worse. Power and Court company combined to extinguish in Nikon all the spiritual force with which he was so bounteously dowered by nature, and nothing new or of a reformative character did he introduce into his pastoral activity—least of all into his revision of the Church's ritual and manuals. Correction is not reform, and if it was only to bolster up new dogmas that Nikon's corrective amendments were adopted on the part of a section of the clergy and the community, the fact that those amendments called forth a rebellion in the Church renders Nikon and the Russian Hierarchy the more guilty. Why did he undertake such a work when he must have known what would come of it? What, too, had the Russian prelates been doing during the past century if they had not been teaching their pastorate to distinguish dogma from, say, the double Alleluia? Nikon did nothing to reconstruct the Church order in a new spirit and tendency: all that he did was to replace one Church form with another. The truth is that, he understood in too narrow and schismatical a spirit the idea of the Church Universal which he made the pretext for his work of correction; he looked upon it too exclusively from the standpoint of external ritual, and therefore failed to get the Russian Church community to take a broader view of it. Also, instead of strengthening his work through the medium of an ordinance passed by a Council of the Church Universal, he completed what he had begun by calling the Eastern Patriarchs who condemned him Oriental despots, rogues, and thieves, and, though jealous for the unity of the Church Universal, he placed his local branch of the Church in schism. In short, the fundamental string in the religious attunement of the Russian Church community—namely, inertia of the religious sense—he stretched to an excessive tension ; until, breaking and rebounding, it lashed the face both of him and of the Russian hierarchical-directorate which had been egging him on.

Over and above his particular form of policy, Nikon had at his disposal two auxiliary means of contending with the stubbornness of Old Belief— but two means which, in view of the setting which he gave to his work, greatly contributed to the spread of the schism. In the first place, Nikon's immediate assistants in the introduction of his ecclesiastical innovations were *savants* of Southern Rus of whom it was known in Moscow that they were closely in touch with the Polish Catholic world ; and to these there may be added Greek scholars like Arsenius, the wandering convert from Catholicism, who, after being recalled from correctional discipline in the Solovetski Monastery (he was known as "the banished black monk of dark Roman errors "), served as Nikon's confidential literary editor. Also, the introduction of ecclesiastical innovations was accompanied by serious mutual revilings between the visitors from Little Rus and the Eastern Empire and the people of Great Rus ; at every step the Kievan monk collided with the Great Russian public on the score of that public's boorishness and want of familiarity with literature, rhetoric, and the other scholastic sciences. Indeed, Simeon Polotski solemnly declared from the episcopal throne of the Usspenski Cathedral that wisdom had no place where it could lay its head in Russia, that the Russian people were hostile to education, and that the country despised the enlightenment which had been offered it of God. Also he spoke of "diverse clowns" who, though daring to call themselves teachers, were nothing, and never would be anything, of the sort. "Truly," said he, "they are not teachers, but tormentors." By these "clowns" he meant chiefly the Muscovite priests, and naturally enough, these reproaches raised among the guardians of Old Russian piety the two questions : Are we so gross as represented, and is all this imported learning really necessary for the preservation of the Treasure entrusted to the Russian Church? Already the community had been rendered sufficiently uneasy and suspicious by the influx of foreigners ; and to this there became added an angry feeling that the national dignity was being insulted by the community's Orthodox brethren. Finally, at a Council of 1666–67, the Russian and Eastern Hierarchies anathematised the bi-digital sign and other rites which, in 1551, had been recognised by the Council of the *Stoglav*, and solemnly declared that "the fathers of that Council did err in thought, through their rudeness." Thus the Russian Hierarchy of the seventeenth century handed over to revision the Russian Church antiquity which, for a notable portion of the Russian public, possessed the force almost of a universal institution. We can easily understand the dismay which these phenomena must have spread among Orthodox Russian minds which had been nourished on religious self-complacency, and were now so rudely disturbed : and that dismay led to a schism as soon as ever a key to the riddle of the mysterious ecclesiastical innovations was discovered. The participation in innovations by immigrant Greek and Western-Russian scholars who were suspected of being in league with Latinism ; their daring propagation of the scholastic learning which flourished in the Latin West ; the appearance of Church innovations upon the heels of the Western novelties ; the unreasoning attachment of the Government to apparently unnecessary borrowings from the very West whence numbers of heretics had been summoned to Rus, to live there on their sumptuous earnings,—all this diffused among the ordinary Russian public the idea that the Church innovations were the work of a secret Latin propaganda, and that Nikon, with his Greek and Kievan assistants, was an instrument of the Pope, who was once more intending to Latinise the Russian Orthodox nation.

It is sufficient to glance at the initial productions of the literature of Old Belief to see that it was the above impressions and apprehensions which chiefly ruled the early protagonists of Old Belief and their followers. Among such productions a notable place must be assigned to two petitions, whereof one was presented to Tsar Alexis, in 1662, by a monk named Sabbatius, and the other one to the same Tsar, in 1667, by the brethren of the Solovetski Monastery, who were opposed to Nikon's innovations. It seems that Nikon's publishers of the new service-books had reproached the adherents of the older, the non-corrected manuals with ignorance both of letters and of rhetoric ; wherefore, by way of answer, the monk Sabbatius writes to the Tsar, concerning the correctors of the new manuals : " Alas ! O Tsar, certain men are disquieted who do seek to despoil our books and have long been in error, in that their lack of learning, with the strange monks, hath rendered them foolish." Although Nikon could cite as justification for his innovations the encouragement of the Eastern Greek

Hierarchy, the Greeks had long been suspected by Rus of impure Orthodoxy, and in reply to a reference to Greek authority the petition from
Solovki remarks that the Greek teachers are unable to cross their fore-
heads "as it doth beseem," and that they walk in Church processions
without crucifixes ; wherefore it is *they* who ought to learn piety of the
Russian people—not the latter to learn piety of *them.* The introducers
of ecclesiastical innovations believed that the ritual of the Russian Church
was incorrect; yet the same petition confuses ritual with doctrine, and,
standing up for the ancient customs of the Russian Church, declares :
"To-day new teachers of doctrine are instructing us in a faith of which
we know not, nor have heard before. The same is like unto the Faith of
the Morduines or the Tcheremissians, who know not God. Forsooth,
such teachers are seeking to baptize us anew, and to cast out of the
Church both the means of grace and the doers of miracles. Thus
foreigners do laugh at us, and say that hitherto the Christian faith hath
been hidden from us." Evidently the Church innovations impinged upon
the most sensitive chord in the attunement of the Russian Church community—namely, upon its national self-complacency in ecclesiastical
matters. Of the fundamental point of view and fundamental motives of
the schism the Archpriest Abbakoum—one of the schism's first and most
ardent protagonists—appears to have been the best expositor, since in his
form of policy, as also in his writings, he expresses the whole essence of
the religious outlook of ancient Rus, according as that outlook had become
compounded during the period under study. The source of the ecclesiastical troubles which had overtaken the country Abbakoum discerns
in the new Western customs and new service-books. "Alas !" he
exclaims in one of his works, "what need hadst thou, O miserable
Rus, of Latin customs and German fashions?" Also, he is of opinion
that the Eastern Church instructors who had been summoned to instruct
Rus in the more knotty points of Church doctrine themselves stood in
need of instruction from Rus ; and in his autobiography he draws a
matchless, as well as a mocking, picture of the Church Council of 1667
which had condemned him, and of his own behaviour in the presence of
the Eastern Patriarchs. The latter he declares to have said to him on
that occasion : "O Archpriest, thou art stubborn. Both our Palestine
and the Serbs and the Albanians and the Roumanians and the Lithuanians
do cross themselves with three fingers. Only *thou* art for thyself, and dost
cross thyself with two. To do so is not befitting." Thereupon Abbakoum
retorted : "O preceptors of the Church Universal, Rome of old time did

fall, and the Lithuanians have come to naught, in that they did remain foes to the Christians unto the end. So too are *ye* wearing an Orthodoxy of many colours, and, through the onslaughts of the Turkish Mahomet, have been rendered impotent, yet are come hither to teach us. But, by the favour of God, we Russians do possess the Autocracy, and up to the time of the apostate Nikon did keep our Orthodoxy pure and without stain, and our Church without dissensions." After this the accused retired to the door, and fell upon his face, exclaiming: " Be ye now seated, and suffer me to creep in unto you." Some of those present smiled and said, " The Archpriest is mad, and doth show no respect unto the Patriarch "; but Abbakoum continued: " All of us are madmen for the sake of Christ. Ye are glorious, and we men without honour. Ye are strong, and we are weak." The fundamental idea which guided the first leaders in the schism is thus expressed by Abbakoum : " What though I be a man without sense, and without skill in letters, yet do I know that unto the fathers of the Church all things have been committed pure and without fault. Unto death, therefore, will I maintain, if it be my pleasure, that I may not set bounds unto the eternal. Thus it hath been charged unto us: ' Keep ye the truth for ever and ever.' " These main features of the religious outlook of ancient Rus— features to which the events of the seventeenth century communicated a peculiarly unfortunate motive and a peculiarly one-sided bent—passed into the schism wholesale, and came to form the basis of its religious purview.

I have now explained the origin of the schism. Once more let us recount what we have observed, that we may the more fully understand the factor and its importance.

The external disasters which overtook Rus and Byzantium consolidated the Russian Church by weakening its spiritual communion with the Churches of the Orthodox East ; and they gave rise, in the Russian Church community, to the idea of the Church Universal, with, as its underlying idea, the notion that the Russian Church was the one Orthodox Communion which had a right to figure as the Universal *Ecclesia*. In other words, the authority of the Christian consciousness was submitted to the authority of local and national antiquity. Also, the segregated order of Russian life led to an accumulation of local peculiarities in Russian Church practice ; while the exaggerated value set upon local Church antiquity communicated to those peculiarities the significance of inevitable sanctities. Likewise, the temptations of life, coupled with the religious perils which Western influence introduced, rendered the Russian Church community uneasy, and aroused in its directors a feeling that they must rally their forces for some impending struggle, and keep constant watch and guard, and strengthen themselves by means of closer communion with their fellow Orthodox communities. Thus at about the middle of the seventeenth century there came to life again, in the best Russian minds, the idea of the Church Universal—an idea which the Patriarch Nikon manifested in an intolerant and violent policy which had for its object the ritualistic approximation of the Russian Church to the Churches of the East. Like the idea itself, the circumstances of its rise—more especially the methods of its subsistence—evoked in the Russian Church community a grave amount of unrest. Indeed, the idea of the Church Universal carried that community out of its usual self-complacency in religious matters, its usual national and ecclesiastical conceit, while a violent, heated persecution of its familiar rites wounded the national self-esteem, yet afforded the troubled conscience no chance to consider matters, or to break with old customs and prejudices. Meanwhile, the thought that it was Latin influence which was giving the first impetus to those violent impulses towards reform filled men's minds with a panic born of an apprehension that in the breaking down of native antiquity there moved the hidden, insidious hand of Rome.

Thus, both as a religious attitude and as a protest against Western influence, the schism arose from the clashing of a reform movement in the State and the Church with the popular-psychological significance of ecclesiastical ritual and the national view of the position which was held in the Christian world by the Russian Church. In this respect, indeed, the schism constitutes a phenomenon of popular psychology, and no more. Yet in the popular-psychological composition of Old Belief it is necessary to distinguish three fundamental elements—namely, (1) ecclesiastical self-complacency, which led to a conversion of Russian Orthodoxy into a national monopoly (*Russian Nationalisation of the Universal Church*), (2) the obliquity and timidity of Russian theological thought, which found itself unable to adopt the spirit of the new knowledge which had come from abroad, and feared it as an unclean Latin suggestion (*Russian Latinophobia*), and (3) the inertia of Russian religious feeling, which found itself unable to renounce the customary methods and forms of its motives and manifestations (*Russian fear of bi-lingual ritualism*). Unfortunately, this schismatical attitude of protest against and antagonism to ecclesiastical authority became converted into a revolt within the Church at the moment when the Old Believers refused to submit to their spiritual pastors in the matter of the *rapproachement* with Latinism which those pastors had proposed; and upon this the Russian Hierarchy, with two of the Eastern Patriarchs, excommunicated (at a Muscovite Church Council held in 1667) the recalcitrant Old Believers from the Orthodox Church, for their schismatical opposition to the canonical authority of their ecclesiastical superiors : and from that time forth the schism acquired the import, not only of a religious attitude, but also of a Church association separate from the ruling Communion.

It was not long before the schism had its effect both upon the course of Russian enlightenment and upon the condition of Western influence. On the one hand, this influence gave a direct impetus to the reaction from which the schism had sprung, and, on the other hand, the schism gave an indirect impetus to the scholastic enlightenment against which the schism was chiefly directed. Both the Greek and the Western-European *savants* railed against the popular governors of Rus as the schism's root cause, until eventually they turned their attention to the question of the permanent, regular school. But of what bent and type was that school to be? At this point the schism helped two views to differentiate themselves which had formerly, through a misunderstanding, been one. So long as Rus had had only foreign heretics—Papists and Lutherans—before her eyes, she had summoned, for their confusion, Greek and Kievan scholars like Epiphany Slavinetski (who had brought with him the Greek tongue) and Simeon Polotski (who had brought with him the tongue of the Latins); but now there had arisen also *domestic* heretics, in the shape of Old Believers (who had seceded from the Church because of the Church's Latin novelties) and *Chliebopoklonniki* or "Bread Worshippers" (*i.e.* persons who preached the Latin doctrine of Transubstantiation of the Sacred Elements). In this latter heresy the leader was considered to be the Latinist Simeon Polotski. The result was that there arose a heated dispute as to which of the two languages—Latin or Greek—was to be the basis of Orthodox School education. In those days the two languages connoted not merely two distinct grammars and lexicons, but also two distinct systems of education, two mutually hostile methods of culture, two irreconcilable views of matters in general. Latin connoted "free teachings" and "freedom of seeking"—that freedom of inquiry to which we have seen a reference made in the benedictory charter which was conferred upon the parishioners of St. John the Divine; it connoted, in short, the learning which corresponds both to the higher intellectual needs and to the daily requirements of man. On the other hand, the Greek tongue connoted that aggregate of "sacred philosophy," literature, rhetoric, and dialectic which serves as so many auxiliary means to the understanding of God's word : and it need hardly be said that the Hellenists won the day. Thus, in the reign of Theodor II. there was written, in defence of the Greek tongue, a treatise which opens with a postulation of the question and an appended reply. "Is it more expedient for us," the author asks, "to study letters, rhetoric, philosophy, theology, and the art of verse, and thence to know the Writings of God, or in no way to study such cunning, but in all simpleness to act pleasingly unto God, and, through much reading, to know the inwardness of the Holy Scriptures? Of a truth it is better that the Russian people shall learn the Greek tongue rather than the Latin." According to the same treatise, study of the Latin language was an unconditionally harmful and pernicious pursuit, since it threatened two great dangers—(1) that, on hearing of the adoption of this study in Moscow, the crafty Jesuits would creep in with their "unseemly syllogisms and soul-corrupting arguments," and so cause a repetition in Great Rus of what had taken place in Little Rus, where "wellnigh all men had become Uniates, and few remained in Orthodoxy"; and (2) that if, among the people—more especially among the "simpletons"—word went abroad concerning the studying of the Latin tongue, "I know not"—so writes the author—"what good we may look for, save that may God deliver us from all calamities!" In 1681 there was opened at the Muscovite printing-press in Nikolskaia Street a school with two classes—the one for studying the Greek language, and the other one for studying the Slavonic; and over this school there presided for a long time a priest named Timothy (who had lived in Byzantium) and two assistant Greek tutors. At the time it was opened the school comprised only thirty pupils of different social standings; yet by the year 1686 those pupils had come to number 233. Later there became established also a higher school—a sort of Slavonic-Greco-Latin Academy, which was opened at the Zaikono-spassk Monastery in Nikolskaia Street, and over which two Greek brothers named Lichuda were invited to preside. To this institution there were transferred the older pupils from the other school, and thus the latter became a sort of lower section of the Academy proper. During the year previous to its opening a pupil of Polotski's named Sylvester Medviedev submitted to the Regent Sophia the Academy's charter of privileges—a document drawn up during Theodor's time; and from certain points in this document we can gather fairly well what the nature and the tasks of

the establishment were.   Opened for men of all classes, it conferred
service ranks upon its *alumni*, and admitted none but Russian and Greek
subjects to fill the posts of rector and tutors.   Western-Russian *savants*
in particular could fill those posts only when recommended thereto by
trustworthy persons of unimpeachable piety.   Also, the Academy was strictly
forbidden to maintain native teachers of foreign languages, or to harbour,
or to allow to be read, Latin, Polish, German, or other heretical books ; upon
which productions, however, as also upon the propaganda of other faiths
than the Orthodox, the Academy was to keep a watchful eye, and to try
persons accused of blasphemy against the Orthodox faith, and to subject
the guilty to the penalty of burning.   Thus the continued agitation for a
Muscovite nursery of " free teachings " for the whole of the Orthodox
East found its consummation in an ecclesiastical-police educational institution which became the original type of the Church school.   Yet,
though appointed to safeguard Orthodoxy from European heretics at large,
it lacked preparatory schools of any sort, and so was powerless either to
permeate with its enlightening influence the masses of the people or to
act as a menace to schism.

Still more strongly did the schism react to the advantage of the
Western influence by which the schism had been evoked.   The storm in
the Church to which Nikon gave rise did not embrace by any means the
whole of the Russian Church community ; for, beginning among the
Russian clergy, it raged, at first, only between the Russian Hierarchy
and that portion of the Church community which was led by Nikon's
ritualistic innovations to join a movement of opposition that was engineered
by agitators drawn from among the subordinate white and black clergy.
Nor, at the outset, was even the whole of the Hierarchy on Nikon's side,
for we see Bishop Paul of Kolomna, when in exile, incriminating three
other prelates who, like himself, had held to the old piety.   Indeed, in
this respect unanimity only became established in proportion as the
Church quarrel became shifted from the ground of ritual to the ground
of canonical authority, and converted into a question of the opposition
of the flock to its lawful pastors.   When that had come about the Hierarchy understood that the matter concerned, not an old nor a new cult
of piety, but the question of whether a prelate was to remain on his
episcopal throne without a pastorate, or to resign alike his pastorate
and his throne, as Paul of Kolomna did.   The Tsar and the bulk of the
community treated the matter in dual fashion.   That is to say, they
accepted the innovations in deference to their canonical obedience, but

disliked the chief innovator for his repellent character and the form of his policy; they sympathised with the victims of his intolerance, yet could not very well encourage his recalcitrant opponents in their unseemly sallies against the powers and institutions that were—the powers and institutions whom they were accustomed to look upon as the mainstays of the ecclesiastical-religious order. Yet serious folk could hardly fail to pause at the scene which took place in the Cathedral when Loggin was unfrocked—at the scene presented by the ex-Archpriest, when divested of his robes, spitting across the Sanctuary at Nikon, and then tearing off his shirt and hurling it in the Patriarch's face. Thinking men would endeavour to penetrate to the essence of the matter, and to find for their consciences the support which their pastors had failed to give them. Thus Rtistchev, the father of the literary enthusiast of whom I have spoken, said to Prince Urussov, one of the first sufferers for the Old Faith: "One thing doth trouble me, in that I know not whether it be for the *truth* that ye do thus endure." That is to say, he could ask himself whether such men were being *rightly* persecuted. Also we read that a deacon named Theodor—another of the schism's first protagonists—set himself, when in prison, to fast until he had found out what was wrong in the old piety, or right in the new. Doubtless, however, others of this kind passed openly into schism; although the greater number of them compounded with their consciences to remain devoted subjects of the Church, yet discern between her and the Hierarchy, and conceal complete indifference to the latter beneath an outwardly respectful bearing. On the other hand, ruling State circles adopted a more decided attitude. Here it was long remembered that the chief of the Hierarchy had tried to raise himself above the Tsar, and that, at the Universal Tribunal of 1666, he had shamed the wielder of the supreme power of Moscow. Such circles also recognised that from the Hierarchy there was nothing to be looked for but trouble; wherefore by common consent they decided tacitly to leave that body alone, and to accord it no real share in the administration of the State. This put an end to the old-time political *rôle* of the Russian clergy—a *rôle* which had always been ill-apportioned and still worse fulfilled; and thus there was removed at least one of the chief obstacles to the progress of Western influence. That is to say, inasmuch as, at this ecclesiastico-political crisis, the Tsar's quarrel with the Patriarch became inextricably entangled with the Church trouble which had been raised by Nikon, the effect of that quarrel upon the political standing of the clergy may be considered to have constituted an indirect service which the schism rendered to Western influence. A still more direct service was rendered to Western influence by the schism, through its weakening the action of a second obstacle to the reforms which, later, Peter accomplished under that influence. I refer to the attitude of suspicious hostility to the West which was so widely diffused throughout the Russian community. Even among the ruling circles who were peculiarly susceptible to Westernism native antiquity had not yet lost the whole of its magic force; and this factor had long given pause to the reform movement, and weakened the energy of the innovators. The schism, however, shattered the authority of that antiquity by raising, in antiquity's name, a revolt against the Church, and, consequently, against her ally the State. The greater portion of the Russian Church community now perceived the evil feelings and tendencies which antiquity could foster, and the dangers which lurked in a blind attachment to the same; wherefore the directors of the reform movement, though still wavering a little between native antiquity and the West, were enabled to go their way with an easier conscience, and with boldness and decision. Particularly strong, in this connection, was the action of the schism upon the Great Reformer himself; for, through the fact that, in 1682, when Peter had just been elected to the Tsarship, the Old Believers repeated their movement of revolt in the name of antiquity (*i.e.* of the Old Faith—I am referring to the quarrel in the Hall of Angles of the 5th of July), the movement, as an impression of Peter's childhood, remained bitten, all his life, into the Reformer's soul, and left in it some ineffaceably connected remembrances of native antiquity, of the schism, and of the revolt. Ancient custom, Peter would conclude, means schism, and schism means revolt: wherefore ancient custom means revolt. It is not difficult to conjecture the attitude towards antiquity which such a chain of impressions was bound to leave in the Great Reformer's mind.

CHAPTER XVI

Tsar Alexis—T. M. Rtistchev.

W<small>E</small> have now studied the movements which took place among the Russian community of the seventeenth century, and it remains for us but to glance at the men who acted as the social leaders of the day. This is indispensable if we are to review the period thoroughly. Of the two opposing tendencies which then agitated the Russian community, the one drew the community in the direction of antiquity, and the other attracted it towards the dim vista of unknown alienism. These two hostile influences aroused and diffused among the community at large only vague feelings and undefined attitudes of mind; but in the case of certain individuals who stood at the head of society those feelings and aspirations became clearer—they became converted into conscious ideas, and came to represent practical problems. These few representative, typical personalities help us to a better understanding of the sort of life from which they sprang, for in them we see collected, and prominently exemplified, all those interests and characteristics proper to their *milieu* which we only too easily lose sight of in the daily round, if they be sporadically diffused among the rank and file of men—*i.e.* among an aggregate of scattered and impotent accidents. So I will halt for a moment at the small band of individuals who marched at the head of the reform movement by which the way was prepared for Peter the Great. That will be sufficient for my purpose. In the ideas and problems which those reformers propounded we see manifested, as the essential results of the preparatory process which was effected by the movement, the identical ideas and problems which, later, Peter inherited, and embodied in his programme of reforms.

Undoubtedly the leading place among Peter's forerunners must be assigned to the Great Reformer's father, Tsar Alexis, for the reason that this Sovereign represents the first stage in the reform movement, before its leaders had yet bethought them of breaking with the past, and of shattering the existing order of things. In the movement Alexis adopted a pose which corresponded to this view of the matter; for, with one foot firmly planted upon native Orthodox antiquity, and the other one stretched out to cross the boundary-line of that foothold, he remained always in an attitude of transition and uncertainty. The reason for this was that he had grown up with the generation which, for the first time, was compelled to look carefully and attentively to the heretical West, in the hope of deriving thence such a means of escape from Russia's domestic difficulties as should not involve a renunciation of the conceptions, customs, and beliefs of pious antiquity. That generation was the only generation in Russian history to adopt this attitude. Men had never so done before its time, and they ceased to do so after it was passed away. The men of earlier generations had been afraid to borrow even *material* amenities from the West, lest they should do harm to the moral heritage which they had received from their fathers and grandfathers, as a sanctity which must never be parted with; but in later days they came to look upon that heritage more lightly, in proportion as they found the borrowed amenities of Western Europe to be more and more to their taste. Alexis and his contemporaries cherished Orthodox antiquity no less than their forefathers had done, except that they came to feel that it was possible to flaunt their persons in German tunics, and even to witness foreign "comedy acts," without doing an injury to the feelings and ideas without which a man could only with pious horror envisage the notion of, say, breaking his fast during Epiphanytide.

Tsar Alexis was born in 1629, and traversed the whole curriculum of ancient Russian education—of what was known as "the teaching of letters." That is to say, at the age of six he was put to study a hornbook which had been specially prepared for him (at the instance of his grandfather, the Patriarch Philaret) by one of that grandfather's *diaki*—a hornbook made up, as usual, of abbreviated moral maxims, the Shorter Catechism, and so forth; while as tutor (in so far as the term was then understood at the Muscovite Court) he was assigned a *diak* belonging to one of the Muscovite *prikazi*. A year later a move was made from the hornbook to the reading of the Breviary ; whence, when another five months were past, the pupil passed to the study of the Psalter, and thence, after a further three months, to the Acts of the Apostles. At this point—or, rather, when Alexis had devoted six months to the study of the Acts—the director of the Court choir introduced him (now aged nine) to the Chant-Book, and then to the study of the Church music which was used at Passiontide—music particularly difficult of assimilation. Lastly, arrived at the age of ten, the young Tsarevitch was "ready"

—he had passed through the whole course of the Russian school education of the day, he could read the Hours aloud in church, and with some success join the Cantor in singing the crooked notes of the Thanksgiving Hymn and Canon. At the same time he studied in detail the order of the Church Litany, until he could hold his own in the same with any monasterial or Synodal dignitary. Probably at this point a Tsarevitch of older days would have stopped, but Alexis was brought up at a period when men were yearning to proceed further, and to advance into the mysterious province of Latin and Greek learning which the pious Russian scholar of earlier ages had always scouted with a shudder, and with the sign of the cross. But the German, with his new-fangled inventions, had long ago been enrolled in the Russian army; and now he penetrated also into the nursery of the Imperial palace, until the hands of the little Alexis were stuffed with German toys—with horses of German workmanship, German pictures which had been bought for 3 *altini* 4 *dengi* apiece (about a rouble-and-a-half, in modern currency), and even German armour which had been specially made for the child by a Teuton artisan named Peter Schaldt. Also, by the time Alexis was eleven or twelve he possessed a small library which, composed chiefly of gifts from his grandfather, his uncles, and his tutor, numbered thirteen volumes. For the most part the tomes consisted of copies of Holy Writ and the Church's service-books, but among them there figured also a grammar which had been printed in Lithuania, a cosmography, and a lexicon of some sort which likewise hailed from the Lithuanian country. In the literary connection the Tsarevitch's head instructor was the boyar B. I. Morozov, who was a leading member of the aristocracy, and strongly attached to the learning of Western Europe. This man introduced into the curriculum of the young Alexis a system of ocular instruction,—*i.e.* he familiarised him with various subjects through means of German engravings; while a still more daring innovation which he introduced into the Muscovite palace of State was to clothe the Tsarevitch and his young brother in German costume.

Arrived at maturity, Alexis presented an exceedingly attractive combination of the good qualities of the old-time Russian who remained true to antiquity with the leanings of a man for whom useful and pleasant novelties had a powerful attraction. A model of piety—of that measured, ever-studied godliness to which the religious sense of ancient Rus devoted so much time and attention—he could argue with any monk on the subject of prayer and fasting; and during the seasons of Lent and the Assumption he observed Sundays, Tuesdays, Thursday, and Saturdays by partaking of one meal a day (at which his food consisted only of cab-bage-soup, mushrooms, and berries—never of meat), while on Mondays, Wednesdays, and Fridays he ate and drank nothing at all.   Also, he would spend periods of five or six hours in church—making, on some days, a thousand obeisances, and, on other days, fifteen hundred.   In short, he was a true "religious" who, in his efforts to save his soul, combined bodily toil with tense exercise of the religious sense.   This piety had a potent effect both upon his governmental ideas and his everyday relations. The son and successor of a Tsar who had enjoyed but a limited power, while he himself was a fully autocratic Sovereign, Tsar Alexis held stoutly to the exalted view of the Imperial authority which had become elaborated among the old Muscovite community.   Indeed, in his words we can hear an echo of the tradition of Ivan the Terrible.   "God hath blessed Us, the Tsar, and hath given unto Us to rule and to judge truly Our people, both in the East and in the West and in the South and in the North."   Yet his sense of autocratic power was mitigated, in some of its manifestations, by a pious kindliness of heart and a deep humility which strove always to remember the humanity within him.   In fact, he was tinged with none of that self-confidence, of that irritable, revengeful, sensitive love of ruling, from which Ivan the Terrible suffered so much. "Better is it to order the thoughts with tears, and with zeal and humility before God, than with strength and pride," writes he to one of his *voievodi;* and this union of forcefulness with complete absence of conceit helped the Tsar greatly in his relations with his boyars, to whom, under an autocratic supremacy, he yielded a large share of the administration. To share his authority with his nobles, and to act with them as a com-rade, was, for him, a rule and a custom, not a sacrifice, or a vexatious concession to circumstances.   "We, the Great Tsar," he wrote, in 1652, to Prince Nikita Odoievski, "do daily pray of the Creator, and of His Immaculate Mother, and of all the Saints, that the Lord God may grant unto Us, the Great Tsar, and unto you, the Boyars, that with one mind We do rule His people of the laity with equal justice unto all."   In par-ticular, there has come down to us a characteristic fragment, in the shape of an autograph sketch of what he proposed to say at a sitting of the *Boyarskaia Duma.*   From it we see how the Tsar prepared himself on such occasions—that he not only wrote down what questions were to be sub-mitted to the judgement of the boyars, but also that he made notes both of what he himself was going to say and of how this, that, or the other ques-tion was to be decided.   Also, wherever, in the document, he has made a

correction he has appended his initials. Thus about one matter he has
not quite made up his mind, nor does he know what the boyars are going
to say about it, while concerning another matter he has an undecided
opinion which he is prepared to renounce if it should be opposed. At
the same time there are questions on which his mind is *fully* made up,
and to which he means to hold fast in debate—*i.e.* questions of simple
equity or conscientious service. For instance, a report has had it that the
voievoda of Astrakhan has allowed the Kalmuks to keep some Orthodox
prisoners whom they have taken; wherefore the Tsar decides to write to
him " both with threatening and with kindness," and if the report be true,
to punish him with death, or at least to cut off his hands and exile him to
Siberia. In short, the document gives us the clearest possible picture of
the simplicity and openness with which the Tsar always treated his
councillors, while paying also the closest attention to his own administrative obligations.

On certain occasions, however, the manners and ideas of contemporary
society proved too much for the good qualities and addictions of Alexis,
for, in ancient Rus, the man in authority could all too easily forget that
he was not the only person in the world, and fail to mark the border-line
to which his own volition extended, but beyond which there began the
rights of others, and the decorum which was incumbent upon all. Old
Russian piety had a limited field of action, for, though it maintained the
religious sense, it did little to restrain the will. By nature spirited,
impressionable, and easily carried out of himself, Alexis suffered from an
ardent temperament which was apt to lose its self-control and afford too
free a rein to his tongue and hands. Once, during the time of his strained
relations with Nikon, the Tsar was so angered by the Patriarch's presumption that he seized a pretext of Church ritual to quarrel with him in
church on Good Friday, and hotly to reproach him in the terms of abuse
which were then customary among Muscovite grandees, the Patriarch himself (whom Alexis on this occasion called a peasant's son, and so forth)
included. On another occasion, when the Tsar was visiting his favourite
Monastery of Savvin Storozhevski (which he had recently built), for the
purpose of honouring the memory of the monastery's sacred founder and
celebrating the restoration of the establishment, the cantor at Solemn
Matins began, in the presence of Makarius, Patriarch of Antioch, the
customary reading from the life of the Saint with the ejaculation, " Bless
us, O Father ! " Thereupon the Tsar leapt from his seat, and cried out,
" *What* sayest thou, thou son of a peasant? '*Bless us, O Father !*'?

Nay! There sitteth the Patriarch. Say thou, rather, '*Bless us, O Great Lord!*'" Also, all through the service the Tsar walked up and down among the monks, and taught them how to read this, and how to sing that; and whenever they made a mistake he corrected them, performed the duties of choir-leader and church elder, lit and extinguished the candles, took from them the snuffers, and, throughout, never ceased to converse with the attendants of the visiting Patriarch, as though he were at home in the church and the eyes of all were not turned upon him. Neither his kindliness of nature nor the thought of the dignity of his office nor his efforts towards piety and refinement raised the Tsar a jot above the rudest of his subjects. Against his ill-restrained temperament his religious-moral sense broke in vain, and in the presence of that temperament even the best impulses of his intellect received but poor expression. But what chiefly aroused the Tsar's fiery nature was encounters with moral deformity—especially acts wherein there were disclosed arrogance or boastfulness. " He who exalteth himself, the same shall be abased," was what summed up Alexis' impressions of life. For instance, in 1660 Prince Chovanski was defeated in Lithuania, and lost almost the whole of his army of 20,000 men. Upon this the Tsar consulted the *Duma* as to what should be done next; and as he was doing so suddenly a boyar named I. D. Miloslavski, who had never in his life been in command on a campaign, exclaimed that, if his uncle the Tsar would permit him, he would take over the direction of the forces, and soon return with, as prisoner, the King of Poland himself. " How thou dost play the fool, thou slave, thou mean fellow ! " retorted Alexis. " To think that *thou* shouldest boast of thy skill in matters of war ! When thou di st go with the regiments, what victories didst *thou* gain over the foe ?" So saying, the Tsar leapt up, dealt the old man a blow on the cheek. pulled his beard, and, kicking him out of the chamber, slammed the door. In short, anyone who bragged or proved impudent enraged Alexis, who would descend even to fisticuffs if the culprit stood ready to hand, and abuse his adversary to his heart's delight, for he was a master of the art of that kind of raillery which the humour of the indignant, yet non-resentful, Russian loves to employ. Once the treasurer of the Savvin Storozhevski Monastery g t drunk, and, in that condition, picked a quarrel with some musketeers who were quartered in the Monastery, killed their officer, and commanded their weapons and clothing to be thrown out of doors. By this occurrence the Tsar was greatly moved—"he did come even unto tears, and did walk as in a mist" (so he himself confesses);

until at length, unable to contain himself longer, he wrote the mutinous monk a threatening letter whereof even the address is characteristic. "From the Tsar and Great Prince Alexis Michaelovitch of All Rus"—so runs the superscription—"unto the enemy and hater of God, and the betrayer of Christ, and the destroyer of the House of Miracles, and the upholder of Satan, and the accursed foe, and the evil spy, and the cruel and subtle doer of evil, the Treasurer Mikita." Yet against the flow of the Tsar's disdain there beat always the idea that in all the world there was no one without sin before God, and that before His judgement-seat all men were equals, and even Tsars were subject to His power. Yes, even in his moments of bitterest wrath Alexis never allowed himself to forget the man in his own person, or in that of the culprit whose Sovereign he was. "Look you, angel of Satan," he writes in his letter to the monasterial treasurer, "that to thee alone, and to thy father the Devil, is earthly honour dear and comely ; but to me, a sinner, such honour is but as dust so long as we be not dear unto God, and so long as, in our proud hearts, we fear not the Lord." Yet, further on, the same Autocratic Tsar who could blow Father Mikita off the face of the earth like dust is seen writing that "with tears" he will beseech the Abbot Savvin to turn away his wrath from the immoral treasurer, "in that one day God will judge both us and thee—otherwise had I never spared thee." This combination of goodness and kindliness of character with respect for the human dignity in the subject attracted both friend and foe, and earned for Alexis the name of "the gentle Tsar": nor could foreigners ever sufficiently admire the fact that, despite the Sovereign's unlimited power over a people which was fully inured to slavery, he made no attempt against the property, the life, or the honour of a single individual (I am quoting the words of the Austrian Ambassador, Meierberg). The evil acts of others affected him the more in that they imposed upon him the distasteful duty of meting out punishment. Yet his wrath was transient—it passed in a momentary flash, and never advanced beyond threats and kicks. Indeed, when it was over, he would meet the sufferer half-way, with pardon and reconciliation in his hands, and try to soothe away any resentful feeling which he had aroused. For instance, being prone to obesity, he, on one occasion, sent for a German doctor to tap one of his veins ; and, on experiencing relief from the treatment, he, as usual, wished to share his pleasures with others, and so proposed to all his boyars that they should be subjected to the same operation ! One such boyar, how-ever—a man named Strieshnev, and the Tsar's maternal relative—hung back, and pleaded, in excuse, old age ; whereupon Alexis fired up, and beat the old man, exclaiming : " Is thy blood, then, dearer than mine ? Or dost thou account thyself of more value than all the rest ? " Yet it was not long before the Tsar could scarcely do enough to recompense the offended boyar, nor send him sufficient presents to persuade him to forego his wrath, and forget the insult.

Alexis liked everyone around him to be cheerful and satisfied. To him the most unbearable thought was that anyone should be discontented, or murmuring against him, or oppressed through his agency. He it was who first began to mitigate the stilted Court etiquette which had long rendered Court relations in Moscow so irksome and strained. He would jest with his courtiers, visit their houses as a plain guest, and invite them to evening suppers of his own whereat he drank plentifully and entered intimately into their domestic affairs. Indeed, the ability to adopt the position of others, to understand and to lay to heart their sorrows and joys, was one of the best features in the Tsar's character, and it is necessary only to read his letters of condolence to Prince Nikita Odoievski (on the occasion of the death of the Prince's son) and to Ordin-Nastchokin (on the occasion of the flight abroad of a son of the latter) to see to what a height of delicacy and moral sensitiveness this man of whims could rise through his ability to divine the grief of a friend. In 1652 one of Prince Nikita Odoievski's sons (the Prince was then serving as *voievoda* of Kazan) died of a fever almost in the presence of the Tsar ; whereupon Alexis wrote to the old man to comfort him, and said, among other things : " Grieve not beyond measure, O boyar of mine, for it is not meet to grieve and to weep ; but if thou *must* weep, then do so in moderation, that the Lord God be not offended." At the same time, the author of the letter did not confine himself to a detailed disquisition on the untimely death, or to a flood of condolences to the father, for, in concluding the epistle, he cannot forbear adding : " Nay, do not grieve, O Prince Nikita Ivanovitch. Put thy trust in God, and thy hope in Ourselves." Again, in 1660 a young son of Ordin-Nastchokin —a boy upon whom his parent had built great hopes—had his head turned with tutors' tales of Western Europe, and ran away to foreign parts : which misfortune so grieved and abashed his father that he repaired to the Tsar in person, to tell him of his unhappiness, and to ask to be allowed to retire. But Alexis understood the situation better, and wrote the father a cordial letter in which he defended Ordin-Nastchokin from himself. " Thou askest," said the Tsar, among other things, " that

I should grant thee dismissal. But wherefore askest thou this? Methinks, it is through boundless sorrow. But wherefore shouldst thou marvel that thy son hath acted thus foolishly? He hath erred but through want of prudence, for as yet he is young, and would see the world, and the works of God. Even as a bird doth fly hither and thither, and, having flown, returns to its nest, so, before many days are past, will thy son bethink him of his home and his spiritual attachment, and return unto thee."

Yes, Tsar Alexis was a man of the purest loving-kindness; he was the best type of Russian. Indeed, I see in him the finest figure which ancient Rus ever produced, for I know no other character who could have produced so pleasing an impression, *had he not been the occupant of the throne.* For the latter position he was too passive a character. Nature or his upbringing led to the development in him of the very qualities which are most valued in the round of daily life, and impart so much light and warmth to domestic relations. Yet, for all his quickness of moral perception, Alexis lacked sufficient *moral energy.* True, he loved his fellow men, and wished them unbounded good, for the reason that he was averse to having his own quiet personal pleasures marred by their grief and discontent. He contained (if I may so express myself) too large an element of that moral sybaritism which loves what is good simply because what is good evokes pleasant sensations. Too feeble, or too little disposed, to persist in or to carry through a given matter, or to contend with anyone for long, he would appoint to important posts not only gifted and honourable agents, but also men upon whom he himself set the lowest value; with the result that observers who, though unprejudiced, were not devotedly attached to him derived from his conduct such mingled impressions as hardened into a general opinion that Alexis would have been a Sovereign of the best and wisest type had he not listened to bad and stupid counsellors. In him there was nothing of the warlike; least of all had he either the wish or the capacity to move forward, to spur, or to direct men in a given course of action—though for "abasing" a corrupt or a non-conscientious subordinate he had a pronounced weakness. On the whole, contemporary writers (including foreigners) recognised that he possessed rich natural gifts, as well as that his power of assimilation and love of knowledge assisted him to acquire a (for the period) remarkable erudition both in theological and secular literature. Of him they said that he was "accustomed unto many philosophical studies." In truth the spirit of the age and the needs of the moment were such as both to stimulate thought and to prove fertile of new questions; and these factors we see reflected in Alexis' literary bent. Fond of writing, he wrote more than any other Tsar who came after the period of Ivan the Terrible. He attempted to compose a history of his military campaigns—he even tried his hand at verses, and there have come down to us some lines in his handwriting which, to their author at least, may have appeared to be poetry. Most of what he has bequeathed to posterity, however, consists of letters to different people. In these documents there is simplicity, gaiety, and, at times, a sort of reflective melancholy; and the whole is illuminated both with a fine understanding of the daily relations of men and with a just appreciation of the trifles of life and the ordinary run of humanity. Yet these letters contain not a trace of those daring, combative turns of thought, or of that irony, wherein the epistles of Ivan the Terrible so much abound. Everything, with Alexis, is mildly expressed; everything, though prolific of words, and sometimes couched in lively and picturesque terms, is wholly restrained, gentle, vague, and a little sickly in its sweetness. Evidently the author was a man of system rather than of ideas and abstractions; yet also a man who was quite ready to set aside his system in favour of those ideas and abstractions. Everything attractive had for him a charm, and nothing exclusively, so long as by no manner of means was his peace of mind or his environment disturbed. Lastly, this spiritual and intellectual bent was strikingly reflected in his full, almost corpulent, figure, low brow, pale face, close-clipped red beard, puffy, high-coloured cheeks, sandy hair, kindly facial expression, and gentle eyes.

It befell this Tsar to have to withstand the impact of some very important internal and external movements. During his reign all relations —relations old, and of recent birth; relations with Sweden, Poland, the Crimea, Turkey, and Western Rus; relations social and ecclesiastical— became accentuated, thrown into opposition, and confused; they gave birth to insistent questions which called for an answer, without any regard to their historical order. Finally, over them all, as the key to their general resolution, towered the fundamental question: Are we to remain true to native antiquity, or are we to take lessons of the foreigner? That fundamental question was decided by Alexis in his usual fashion. In order not to be forced to choose between antiquity and the innovations he neither broke with the former nor turned away from the latter. By custom, as well as by family and other relations, he was attached to the older way of thinking; whereas, through the needs of the State, through his readiness to respond to anything that was desirable, and through his personal sympathy, he felt drawn, rather, towards the men of intellect and energy who, in the name of public welfare, wished things to be done after the new fashion. The Tsar did not hinder such innovators—he even supported them, but only until there came the first fluctuation of opinion, until the first energetic expression of views found voice on the part of the conservative element. Although it is true that the new influences so attracted him that in many things he departed from the time-hallowed order of Russian life; although it is true that for a time he rode in a German coach, and took his wife hunting with him, and conducted her and her children to witness foreign "comedy acts" (with music and dancing), and toasted his lords and father confessor to the point of intoxication at supper parties whereat German musicians played trumpets and organs; although it is true that he gave his sons, for their tutor, a Western-Russian monk of learning, who carried his instructions far beyond the limits of the Breviary, Psalter, and *Oktoich* (Chant Book), in that he taught the young Tsarevitches both Latin and Polish; although it is true that Alexis did all these things, it is also true that he was not the Sovereign to head the new movement, nor to impart to it a definite direction, nor to find the right men for its guidance, nor to indicate to them the best ways and means of action. That is to say, though powerless to lop the growing tree of alien culture, he had no mind to soil his hands with the dirty work of propagating it in Russian soil.

Yet, despite his passive character and his indifferent, undecided attitude towards the questions of the day, Alexis greatly contributed to the progress of the reform movement, since by his frequently ill-regulated and inconsequential impulses towards what was new, as much as by his ability to smooth away and assuage, he afforded timid Russian thinkers a helping hand in the direction of the influences which emanated from abroad. Though he himself could furnish no leading ideas in the matter of reform, he at least assisted the first reformers to come forward with *their* ideas, and made it possible for them to "find themselves," and to show their strength. In short, he opened up to them a broad road for their onward march, and, while imparting to the reformers neither plan nor direction, created for them an atmosphere in which they could flourish.

Next let us familiarise ourselves with a man who was not only one of the chief workers in the direction of reform, but also one of Alexis' most intimate coadjutors, and a statesman who greatly resembled his Sovereign as regards the main features of his character. Yet what a difference there was between the assortment and the general adjustment of their respective *traits*, as well as between the manifestations of their otherwise similar qualities!

During almost the whole of the reign of Alexis, son of Michael, there stood by his side—at first as chief gentleman-of-the-bedchamber, and, later, as major-domo and the tutor-uncle of the eldest Tsarevitch—Theodor Michaelovitch Rtistchev. Born nearly at the same time as the Tsar (their natal years were, respectively, 1625 and 1629), he ended his life in 1673, three years before the decease of his Sovereign. Upon outside observers he made little impression, for he never put himself forward—his rule of life was always to remain hidden in the shade; but, fortunately, a contemporary writer has bequeathed us a small "life" which, though it resembles a panegyric rather than a biography, contains some interesting particulars concerning the character and the career of him whom the work calls "a most gracious man." Rtistchev was one of those rare and peculiar persons who are absolutely lacking in self-conceit. Despite the natural instincts and the agelong habits of humanity, he fulfilled Christ's command that we should love our neighbour as we do ourselves only as regards the first part of the injunction. That is to say, for his neighbour's sake he put self-love altogether aside—he was one of those strict followers of the Gospel who, when their right cheek is smitten, offer also the left to the smiter with an air, not as though the act were an exercise in humility, but as though it were a sheer demand of the physical law. Of insults or revenge he knew nothing, just as other men are ignorant of the taste of wine, and unable to understand how their fellows can bring themselves to drink the disagreeable stuff. For instance, one Ivan Ozerov, who had once been befriended by Rtistchev, and, through his assistance, had received a good education at the Kievan Academy, later became his patron's foe. Yet, though Rtistchev was the official superior, he (Rtistchev) made no attempt to exert his power, but, on the contrary, did all he could, through humility and benevolence, to assuage his *protégé's* enmity. Often he would visit Ozerov's lodgings, knock quietly at the door, and, on being refused admission, depart, and return again. But at length, losing patience at such insistent and annoying kindness, the master of the house invited the guest to enter, and then turned upon and abused him; whereupon, without even noticing the insults, Rtistchev departed—only to return with an offer of goodwill, as though nothing had happened. Indeed, he continued so to do until the death of his stubborn *quondam* friend. Finally he buried him as men would bury their best of comrades. Of all the moral qualities derived by ancient Rus from Christianity, Rtistchev nourished in himself the quality which came hardest to, was the least inborn in, the Russian of those days—namely, the quality of humility. His influence as the Tsar's favourite was used simply to make peace at Court, to remove enmity, to avert collisions, and to hold in check such violent, overbearing, tenacious men as Morozov, Abbakoum, and Nikon. In this difficult *rôle* he succeeded the better in that he knew how to speak the truth without giving offence, never made a parade of his own superiority, took no account of family or official rank, hated calculations of *miestnichestvo,* and renounced the offer of a boyarship which the Tsar tendered him in return for teaching the young Tsarevitch. All these qualities combined to produce upon men an impression of rare good sense and unshakeable moral strength. In the former (so we are told by the Austrian Ambassador, Meierberg) Rtistchev, at forty, surpassed many a greybeard; while Ordin-Nastchokin looked upon him as the morally-strongest courtier whom Alexis possessed. Even the Cossacks so much respected him for his equity and incorruptibility that they desired to have him for their viceroy, as " Prince of Little Rus."

For the reform movement to succeed it was very important that Rtistchev should stand at the head of it. Combining within himself the best principles and traditions of old Russian life, he understood also its needs and shortcomings, and held a leading place among the agents of the new order of things. Indeed, nothing advocated by such a statesman could really be bad or unsuccessful. For instance, he was one of the first to hear the voices raised against the Liturgical irregularities of which I have spoken, and he also took a leading part in inducing Alexis to introduce education that was carried on with the help of Kievan *savants;* indeed, he may even have been the first to *suggest* that course. Continually before the Tsar's eyes, and able to inspire him with absolute confidence, he none the less never became a time-server, any more than he remained a passive witness of the movements which were springing up around him, but played a part in matters of the most varied kinds, either by Imperial command or on his own initiative. Thus he supervised the various *prikazi,* and once (in 1655) successfully carried through a diplomatic commission. In short, wherever an attempt was made to correct and ameliorate the position of affairs, there was Rtistchev with his help, his intercession, and his advice. Every demand for a reform he hastened to meet halfway; often he himself had raised the demand— though he would at once withdraw, and substitute for it a new plan, if, by so doing, he could facilitate matters for his fellow-workers, and avoid supplanting them. Peaceloving and benevolent, he had no stomach for anger and dissension, but lived on good terms with all the most prominent statesmen of the day—with Ordin-Nastchokin, Nikon, Abbakoum, Slavi-netski, and Polotski—despite dissimilarities of characters and tendencies. Lastly, he did his best to restrain the Old Believers and the Nikonians in the realm of theological thought and literary differences—to prevent, that is to say, matters from reaching the point of an actual ecclesiastical cleavage—by organising debates at his house at which Abbakoum "did contend with the apostates," more especially with Polotski, until he (Abbakoum) was worn out and almost beside himself.

Also, if we credit the statement that it was Rtistchev who inspired the idea of the copper currency, we must recognise that his administrative influence extended far beyond the limits of the Court department in which he served as an official. Yet it was not statesmanship, in the exact meaning of the word, which constituted his true life-work, for he likewise took upon himself a no less arduous, yet less prominent and more self-denying, order of labour—namely, the service of poor and suffering humanity. Of it his biography gives us several touching details. Thus, when accompanying the Tsar on the Polish campaign of 1654, Rtistchev took up so many beggars, sick men, and cripples into his carriage *en route* that he himself had to get out and ride on horseback, despite a long-standing affection of the legs from which he suffered. Also, in the towns and villages through which the army passed he arranged for these people temporary rest-houses, where they were fed and doctored, partly at his own expense, and partly out of money given him for the purpose by the Tsaritsa. In the same way, when in Moscow, he used to collect stray drunkards and sick persons into a special refuge, where he supported his charges either until they had become sober or until they had recovered of their ailments; while for incurable patients and very old and destitute persons he built a hospital which, in the same way, he maintained at his own expense. Again, he lost a great deal of money in ransoming Russian prisoners from the Tartars, and helped with loans both foreign prisoners who were residing in Russia and insolvent folk who had got into prison through debt. This philanthropy flowed not only from a sympathy for the helpless, but also from a sense of social justice. A particularly kind act of his was to present the town of Arzamas with a piece of land which he owned near the borough, and of which the citizens stood greatly in need, but could not afford to buy; and that although Rtistchev had been offered for it, by a private customer, what, in modern currency, would amount to about 14,000 roubles. Again, in 1671, on hearing of a famine in Vologda, he dispatched thither a train of bread-waggons, on the pretext that certain lovers of Christ had commissioned him to distribute the food to the poor and needy in remembrance of the donors' souls; after which he sent the impoverished town a further sum of 14,000 roubles, as the proceeds of the sale of some of his clothing and furniture. Also it is clear that he understood not only the needs of others, but the faults in the social structure of his time, for he was one of the first to give active expression to a condemnatory view of serf right. In his biography we read that he always took the greatest care of his domestic staff, especially of his peasantry. Always he tried to fit their tasks and tithes-payments to their means, and supported their industry with loans. Lastly, when selling a certain village, he lowered its selling value by forcing the purchaser to swear that never at any time would he increase the seigniorial tithes or tasks of *barstchina;* and before his death he not only freed the whole of his staff of household servants, but also besought his heirs—*i.e.* his daughter and son-in-law—to promise him that, in remembrance of himself, they would always behave well to the peasantry whom he was bequeathing to their charge. " For," said he, " they are our brethren."

What impression Rtistchev may have produced upon the public by his relation to his *krestiané* we do not know; but at all events his beneficent efforts had an influence upon legislation. During the reign of Alexis' successor there arose the question of State-ecclesiastical almsgiving, and by orders of the Tsar a census was taken of the poor and needy in Moscow who lived upon voluntary offerings. In the end the incapable and destitute were swept into two hospitals built for the purpose, and there maintained at the State's expense, while the able-bodied were assigned to one and another form of forced labour. Next, at a Church Council convened in 1681 the Tsar proposed to the Patriarch and the bishops that refuges and hospitals should be built in *every* town. To this the fathers of the Council agreed. Thus, through the private initiative of a good and influential man, there became founded the system of Church benevolent institutions which gradually arose at the close of the seventeenth century, while, through the activity of statesmen of the day who held progressive views, certain personal ideas and private efforts became converted into legislative questions which eventually developed into political tendencies or State institutions.

CHAPTER XVII

A. L. Ordin-Nastchokin

ANOTHER notable figure which stands out from among the coadjutors of Tsar Alexis and the statesmen of the seventeenth century is that of A. L. Ordin-Nastchokin.

A Muscovite statesman of the seventeenth century! The very expression would seem to be an abuse of the political terminology of the period, for a statesman connotes a highly developed political intellect which is capable of observing, understanding, and directing social movements, able to take an independent view of the questions of the day, ready with a detailed programme of policy, and possessed of a definite range of political action—a series of conditions which by no means we expect to find present in the old Muscovite Empire. In very truth those conditions never *are* observable in the Empire of the Muscovite Autocrats before the seventeenth century, and at their Court one might look long enough for a man worthy of the name of statesman, seeing that in those days the course of Imperial affairs was directed by the established order of things, and by the personal will of the Sovereign which lurked behind that order. The individual served merely as the instrument of the Sovereign's volition, and to the yet stronger influence of custom and of tradition that volition and the established order of things were alike subject. Yet during the seventeenth century Muscovite State life began to find other roads than this; ancient customs and the stereotyped system began to totter; and there gradually arose a quest for intellect and personal force of character which caused the will of Tsar Alexis to be inclined to submit, for the public good, to any strong and well-intentioned personality who might appear.

I have said that it was Alexis who founded, in the Russian community of the seventeenth century, a tendency towards reform; and the leading place among the statesmen whom that tendency embraced belongs, without a doubt, to the most brilliant of Alexis' assistants, the most energetic precursor of the reforming tendencies of the day—namely, to the boyar Athanasius Lavrentievitch Ordin-Nastchokin. For ourselves this statesman is doubly interesting, in that he doubly prepared the way for the reforms of Peter the Great. In the first place, none of the Muscovite statesmen of the seventeenth century expressed so many of the reformative ideas and schemes which Peter afterwards made good as did Nastchokin; while, in the second place, it fell to the lot of this Ordin-Nastchokin not only to act on new lines, but also to create the setting of his own policy. By origin he had neither part nor lot in the community among whom he was commissioned to act, since the privileged inheritors of the right of administration in the Muscovite Empire were the old boyar families of the *Rodoslovetz*, who looked down upon the bulk of the provincial *dvoriané*. Ordin-Nastchokin was practically the first member of these *dvoriané* to penetrate to the circle of the haughty aristocracy— but a pioneer in whose train a long bevy of his provincial brethren eventually beat down the serried ranks of the aristocratic caste.

Athanasius Lavrentievitch was the son of a very humble *pomiestchik* of Pskov; where, as in the neighbouring canton of Toropetz, there then flourished a *côterie* of Nastchokins which derived their descent from a fourteenth-century courtier of eminence: and it was of that same *côterie* —which had grown steadily poorer since the death of its founder—that our Ordin-Nastchokin came. As early as Michael's reign, he made a name for himself, for on more than one occasion he was appointed a member of certain Russo-Swedish boundary commissions; with the result that, by the time Alexis came to the throne, Nastchokin was already looked upon as a distinguished agent and zealous servant of the Muscovite Government. Indeed, that is why, during the Pskovian rebellion of 1650, the rebels took measures to kill him. During its suppression he showed both energy and good sense; and from that time forward he rose steadily. When, in 1654, war broke out with Poland, he was entrusted with a very difficult post, since, with but a small Russian force, he was sent to guard the Russo-Lithuanian-Livonian frontiers. Nevertheless he performed this duty with credit. Again, when, in 1656, Russia declared war upon Sweden, and, the Tsar having moved against Riga, the Muscovite troops took a Livonian town named Kockenhausen (the Kukeinos which had at one time belonged to the Princes of Polotsk), Ordin-Nastchokin was appointed *voievoda* both of this and of certain other conquered towns; in which capacity he performed important military and diplomatic exploits, held the frontiers intact, captured other small towns in Livonia, and carried on the necessary correspondence with the Polish authorities. In fact, in every important diplomatic affair he played at least a part, until, in 1658, his efforts came to an end with the Treaty of Valiesarsk, whereby Tsar Alexis gained from Sweden more than he had hoped to do.   Next, in 1665 Nastchokin was made *voievoda* of his native Pskov; after which we find him following up some eight months of wearisome negotiations with the Polish plenipotentiaries by concluding (in January, 1667) the Treaty of Andrusovo, which put an end to the devastating thirteen-years' struggle between Poland and Moscow.   In this difficult service on behalf of the Muscovite Government Nastchokin showed much diplomatic talent for conciliating the foreigners, for out of them he got not only the provinces of Smolensk and Novgorod Sieversski, with the eastern portion of Little Rus, but also part of the western portion of the latter, in the shape of Kiev.   Through this Treaty Nastchokin rose to a high position in the Muscovite Government, and won a great diplomatic reputation. By *otechestvo* (*i.e.* by origin) a mere provincial-urban *dvorianin*, he was soon promoted to the rank of boyar, and appointed chief director of the Office of Ambassadors, under the grandiose title of " Keeper of the Great Imperial Seal, and of the State Affairs of the Great Ambassadors." That is to say, he became Imperial Chancellor.

Such was Nastchokin's official career.   In these fortunes of his his birthplace played a considerable part, since the region of Pskov—which ran with the frontier of Livonia—had long been in close relations with its neighbours the Germans and the Swedes; and this early familiarity with the foreigner, these private dealings with the alien, enabled Nast- chokin to study and observe the two countries of Western Europe which lay nearest to Russia.   For him to do so was the easier through the fact that in his youth he had had the good fortune to be given an excellent educa- tion.   He knew (it was commonly said) not only mathematics, but also the Latin and German languages, and the circumstances of his later service forced him to familiarise himself also with the Polish tongue.   Thus both early and fundamentally he underwent a good preparation for the *rôle* which he was afterwards called upon to play in the relations of Moscow with the European West; so much so that his service colleagues used to say of him that he " doth know the German matter, and also hath know- ledge of the German customs."   In fact, close observation of foreign institutions, combined with a habit of comparing them with those of his own country, had rendered Nastchokin both a devotee of Western Europe and a keen critic of his own order of things : whence in time he came to renounce the national seclusion and exclusiveness, and to work out for

himself a special line of political thought. It was he who first promulgated the rule that "for a good man it is in no way shameful if he do
become accustomed unto what is abroad and of the foreigners, even
though they be his foes." Also, he has bequeathed to us a series of
documents—official reports, and notes or representations to the Tsar on
different political questions—which are of great interest, since they help
us to characterise both Nastchokin himself and the reform movement of
his time. From them it is clear that the author was loquacious, and that
he had an incisive pen, so that even his enemies had to acknowledge
that he was a "ready writer." A still rarer quality was his subtle,
tenacious, expansive intellect, which could envisage a given situation
swiftly, and summarise, unaided, the conditions of the moment. Also,
he was a master of the art of building original and unlooked-for political
structures. But he was not a man with whom it was easy to quarrel.
Introspective and imperturbable, there were occasions when he made
foreign *diplomats* with whom he happened to be treating lose all patience,
and set to and abuse him for making the transaction of their business so
difficult. Never did he make the least slip, or perpetrate the least incon-
sistency, in diplomatic conversations. In a moment he could trick or
nonplus a careless or shortsighted opponent, and poison the pure inten-
tions with which he himself had begun the discussion. With this bent
of mind there went also a restless conscience, and a habit of despising
people who did not agree with him. To grumble at the lack of truth
and of healthy judgement which was everywhere prevalent was, with him,
a duty, and he took pleasure in doing it. Indeed, the note most frequently
sounded in his letters and reports is the reiteration of bitter complaints
against the Muscovite people and Muscovite institutions. Always Ordin-
Nastchokin complains; never is he wholly satisfied, either with the
Government's enactments, the customs of the *prikazi*, the organisation of
the army, or the morals and ideas of the public. Naturally enough, these
sympathies and antipathies of his were so little shared by his fellows that
they created for him an awkward, ambiguous position among the Muscovite community. True, his attachment to Western-European systems,
and his renunciation of Russian institutions, pleased foreigners with whom
he became associated, and they condescendingly declared him to be
"not wholly a maladroit counterfeiter" of their customs; but the mere
fact of this earned him a host of enemies among his own countrymen,
and gave his Muscovite well-wishers an opportunity of laughing at
him and calling him "the foreigner." To this ambiguity of position

his origin and character contributed. Although his compatriots and foreigners alike recognised in him a man of keen intellect who would go far, this brought him into collision with many men's vanity, and the more so since he did not follow the accustomed road which his origin dictated. Needless to say, his stern and aggressive manner did nothing to mitigate these encounters. In short, he was an alien among the official world of Moscow, and, when a political novice, had to fight for his official position, since he knew that every step forward would increase the number of his enemies, more especially among the boyar aristocracy. In fact, it was his position which created his peculiar manner of treating the hostile community by which he was surrounded. He knew that his one support was the Tsar, a man who had no love for arrogance; wherefore, to secure himself that support, Nastchokin endeavoured to take refuge from his adversaries by assuming, in the Tsar's presence, an appearance of lowly discretion, and a humility which approached self-effacement. Upon his service position he set no great value, and appraised that of his aristocratic opponents even lower. Everywhere he complains bitterly against them. "Of all men who do labour for thy Empire," writes he to the Tsar, "none is so hated as I"; and in another passage he calls himself "a man slandered and hated who hath nowhere to lay his sinful head." Whenever a difficulty arose, or he came into collision with influential opponents, he begged of the Tsar to dismiss him from the service, as a failure and a blockhead through whom the State's interest was bound to suffer. "Now is the work of the State hated for my sake, who am thy slave," he again writes to the Tsar, and then prays his Sovereign "to remove from his labours thy vile slave." Yet Athanasius was perfectly well aware of his own value, and of his humbleness it may be said that it was a worse humility than pride, since it never hindered him from accounting himself a man not altogether of this world. "If I were of the world, the world would love its own," is what he writes to Alexis when complaining of the general ill-will shown him. Even the Councillors of the *Duma* would not listen to his representations and advice, "for the reason that they see not the ways of truth, and their hearts have grown fat with envy." Also an ironical note sounds in his words when writing to the Tsar concerning the administrative superiority of the boyar caste, as compared with his own lowborn person. "To none of the men of the *Duma* am I needful, for great matters of State are not meet unto me. . . . In matters of this sort it is more befitting to be of the trusty boyars; for they be of high birth, and have many friends, and in all things do know how to live, and to think spacious thoughts. Thus I do resign unto thee, Great Tsar, my oath upon the cross,[1] which I dare not hold longer by reason of the lackings of my sorry mind."

Long and steadfastly, however, did the Tsar support his wilful and irascible agent. Patiently he bore with his wearisome complaints and reproaches as he constantly assured him that he had nothing to fear, and that never would he be betrayed to anyone. Alexis even went so far as to threaten Nastchokin's adversaries with dire disgrace for their hostility, as well as left him complete freedom of action; which circumstance helped the statesman not only to display his administrative and diplomatic talents, but also to work out, and in part to consolidate, his political schemes. In all his letters to the Tsar the Chancellor either blames actuality or inveighs against his political opponents, but in no case sets forth his programme. Nevertheless there can be apprehended in these documents a notable stock of ideas and projects which, further elaborated, could become—and, indeed, did become—the principles which long ruled the foreign and domestic policy of Rus.

The first idea which Nastchokin strongly insisted upon was that in everything models should be taken from the West—that everything should be done "according unto the example of other and foreign lands." In fact, it was the starting-point of his schemes of reform. Yet there was no necessity to borrow of the foreigner *indiscriminately*. "What have we to do with the customs of alien peoples?" says he in one passage. "Their clothing is not of us, nor is ours meet unto them." In short, he was one of the few "Westerners" who gave a thought to what *could*, what *need not*, be borrowed—one of the few who ever sought to make general-European culture agree with the national conceit of Rus. Secondly, Nastchokin could not reconcile himself to the spirit and customs of Muscovite administration, the policy of which was hopelessly swayed by personal considerations and relations, rather than by the interests of the State which had been committed to the State's agents. "With us," he writes, "men do love a matter, or do hate it, not according unto the matter itself, but according unto him who doth work it. Me they do love not, and therefore also they do despise my work." Once, when the Tsar had expressed his dissatisfaction at his statesman's failure to get on with certain of his highborn detractors, Nastchokin replied that he cherished no personal hostility against them, but "my heart is sore for the work of the State, and doth permit me not to keep silence whensoever in

---

[1] *i.e.* my sworn commission.

that work I see remissness." Thus State management, and not the statesman, was what mattered : this was the second rule which guided Nastchokin in his policy. His chief field was diplomacy, and he was a
diplomatist of the first rank. Upon that point his contemporaries,
even those of them who were foreigners, were agreed. At all events he
was practically the first Russian statesman to inspire the alien with
respect. For instance, we find an Englishman named Collins, who was
physician to Tsar Alexis, calling Nastchokin a politician who was inferior
to no other great minister in Europe. Moreover, Nastchokin had a
respect for his own work. Diplomacy he conceived to constitute the
chief function in a State administration, and only men who were worthy
of the art to have a right to engage in it. "In matters of State," he
writes, "it is for honest and chosen men to look carefully to the en-
larging of the Empire: which is the work of the Office of Ambassadors
alone."

Meanwhile Nastchokin had his own diplomatic schemes, his own
peculiar views of the tasks which were incumbent upon Muscovite policy.
To his lot it befell to have to act at a time when a series of delicate
questions arose which helped the more to nourish the boundless hostility
already existent between Russia, Poland, and Sweden—namely, the questions of Little Rus and of the Baltic seaboard ; and circumstances set this
statesman in the very vortex of the negotiations and collisions which
those questions evoked. Yet that vortex never turned his head : even in
the most complicated affairs he could always distinguish the important
from the clamorous, the attractive from the expedient, the chimerical from
the attainable. He discerned that, as now situated, and possessed of her
present resources, the Muscovite Empire could never decide, in all its
bearings, the Little Russian question—the question of uniting South-
Western Rus to Great Rus ; wherefore he inclined, rather, to peace, and
even to a close alliance, with Poland ; he hoped, though he knew (so
he himself expressed it) "the exceeding unsteady, soulless, and incon-
stant Polish people," to gain considerable advantages from such a bond.
Among other things he hoped that, on learning of the alliance, the Turkish
Christians, the Moldavians, and the Wallachians would separate themselves
from Turkey, and that all the children of the Eastern Church who now
dwelt between the Danube and the confines of Great Rus, but were split
into two portions by hostile Poland, would then combine into a single
multitudinous Christian nation, under the protection of the Orthodox Tsar
of Moscow, and that of themselves they would put an end to those

Swedish wiles which only the Russo-Polish estrangement had made possible. Accordingly, in 1667, when the Polish Commissioners visited Moscow for the ratification of the Treaty of Andrusovo, Nastchokin unfolded to them his plans in a spirited speech, wherein he pointed out the glory which would cover the Slavonic peoples, and the great enterprises which might be crowned with success, if only the Slavonic stocks which now inhabited what in modern days has become the Russian Empire (almost all the stocks of which spoke the same Slavonic tongue) between the Adriatic Sea, the Baltic, and the Ocean of the North were to become united, and the glorious future which the two Empires might look to if, standing at the head of the Slavonic nations, they were to combine under a single Autocracy.

Thus agitating for a close alliance with Russia's most ancient enemy, and even dreaming of a dynastic union with the same under the authority of the Muscovite Tsar, or of his son, Nastchokin accomplished a sharp break in Moscow's external policy. Yet for this change in the course of affairs he had his own reasons. In his eyes the Little Russian question was a secondary matter altogether. "If," writes he, "the Cossacks be traitors, are they then worthy that we should stand for them?" As a matter of fact, the annexation of the eastern portion of Little Rus resolved the chief knot in the question, and Poland ceased to be dangerous for Moscow, who now held an assured position on the Upper and Middle Dnieper. Yet to make the temporary tenure of Kiev permanent, or to annex the western portion of Little Rus, would be impossible without the committing of an international wrong, and a breaking of the Treaty of Andrusovo ; whereas Nastchokin was one of those rare diplomatists who possess a diplomatic conscience—a quality which, even in those days, ill consorted with diplomacy. Nothing that was unfair would he do. "Better far," he writes, "if I were to put an end to my accursed life, and be for ever free, rather than to act contrary to truth." It was for this reason that, when the Cossack Deroshenko, with his followers of Western Little Rus, had separated from Poland, and, after swearing allegiance to the Sultan of Turkey, had expressed willingness to become subject to the great Tsar of Moscow, Nastchokin answered an inquiry from the latter as to whether it would be possible to receive Doroshenko and his people with a vigorous protest against any such infringement of treaties, as well as an expression of his personal displeasure that such an improper question should ever have been put to him. In his opinion the matter ought to be managed so that, after weighing their own and Moscow's interests, the

Poles should voluntarily seek a Russo-Polish alliance, and cede Kiev to Moscow, or even the *whole* of the western portion of Little Rus. "But of this," added Nastchokin, "it is not possible to write insolently unto Poland." Even before the Treaty of Andrusovo he persuaded the Tsar that "peace ought to be made according unto measure" (*i.e.* on certain carefully considered conditions) with the Polish King, for fear lest, later, the Poles should seek an early occasion of revenge. "Let us take Polotsk and Vitebsk," was Nastchokin's advice; "and then, if the Poles be stubborn, we shall have need not of those towns." At the same time he let fall an unguarded hint to the Tsar that, for the consolidation of a Polish alliance, it might be necessary to retire not only from the western portion of Little Rus, but also from the *whole* of the country; whereupon Alexis uttered a warm protest against any such want of spirit on the part of his favourite, and expressed his displeasure in a very energetic way. "This article," the Tsar said, "we do set aside, and command to be forsaken, in that it is unbecoming, and that we do find therein one mind and a half—a mind which is steadfast, and a mind which is shaken by the wind. It is not meet that a dog should eat even a morsel of Orthodox bread, and it is not meet that the Poles should possess even Little Rus of the West. That they now do so is not of our own will, but because it hath been so ordained for our sins. But if both morsels of the sacred bread shall fall to the dog, how will he who permitteth that justify himself? To him let there be apportioned, as recompense, only the lowermost Hell, the cruellest of fire, and the most merciless of pains! Good sir, depart thou with the peace of thy Tsar, and walk the middle road. As thou hast begun, so end. Swerve not unto the right, nor unto the left, and may God go with thee!" And the stubborn-minded statesman so far yielded to the pious aspirations of his master—of the master whom, at times, he declined even to listen to—that he made a bold bid for another morsel of "Orthodox bread," and extracted from the Poles, at Andrusovo, not only the eastern portion of Little Rus, but also the western portion and Kiev.

These schemes for a Panslavonic union under the joint directorship of Moscow and Poland were Nastchokin's political idyll; but, as a practical statesman, he occupied himself, rather, with interests of a real order as, with diplomatic eye, he scanned every quarter in the hope of finding and developing new gains for the Treasury and the nation. He tried to organise trading relations with Persia and Central Asia, with Khiva, and with Bokhara; he fitted out a mission to India; he looked to what could be done in the Far East and China; he conceived a plan for colonising the Amour region with Cossacks. Yet I need hardly say that, amid these quests, there was ever present to his eyes the nearest quarter of the West, the Baltic Sea. Guided by popular-industrial considerations, no less than by national and political, he comprehended the commercial and cultural importance of this ocean for Rus, and therefore turned his attention the more earnestly to Sweden, especially to Livonia, which, he opined, ought by hook or crook to be annexed, since its acquisition would prove of immense use both to the industry of the country and to the Tsar's Treasury. Attracted by the ideas of his agent, Tsar Alexis also looked to that quarter, and agitated both for the recovery of Russia's former possessions, and for the acquisition of the ports of Narva, Ivan, and Orieshk, as well as of the whole course of the Neva and the Swedish fortress which then stood where, later, St. Petersburg arose. But even here Nastchokin regarded the matter from a wider point of view, for he had lived to learn that trifles must not be allowed to obscure the main object, and that Narva, Orieshk, and the rest were but unimportant points. No; what he must do was that he must penetrate to the sea direct, and get possession of Riga—of the port which led by the straightest and nearest road to Western Europe. Consequently, to form a coalition against Sweden, and to deprive her of Livonia—*that* was Nastchokin's pet scheme, the scheme which constituted the soul of all his diplomatic devisings. To attain it he advocated peace with the Khan of the Crimea, an alliance with Poland, and the sacrifice of Western Little Rus; and though it was a scheme which never became crowned with success, Peter the Great succeeded wholesale to these ideas of his father's minister.

At the same time, Nastchokin's political purview was not confined solely to questions of foreign policy, for, in his own fashion, he had a care for the domestic admininistration of the Muscovite Empire. Yet he was dissatisfied with that administration, on account of its structure as much as on account of the way in which it was conducted. In the first place, he was against the excessive red-tapeism which prevailed. Everything administrative was based upon the most restrictive oversight of subordinates by the higher institutions of the centre, so that local executors were the blind instruments of instructions given them from above. Nastchokin, however, demanded a given range for executive officials. " Let them not in all things look unto the Tsar's *ukaz*," he wrote. " Everywhere let there be discretion of the *voievodi*"—*i.e.* action according to the plenipotentiary's individual ideas. For this he pointed to the example of the West, where at the head of armies there stood experienced generals who distributed their own orders to their subordinates, and did not ask, according as each trifle arose, for a dispensation from the centre. " Where the eye doth see and the ear doth hear," wrote Nastchokin, " the plan also should be held to, and delayed not." Yet, while demanding such independence for executors, he proposed to lay upon them responsibility in proportion. Not through *ukazi*, he considered, nor according to custom and routine, must administration act, but on consideration of the circumstances of the moment. Such a policy, founded upon the personal thinking power of the subordinate, Nastchokin called *promisl* or thought — in modern parlance, resourcefulness ; while rude force he deemed to be of little avail. " Better than strength is thought. 'Tis thought which availeth, and not a multitude of men : for where there be many men, and not one thinker, nothing doth come of the same. Here is this Swede who, of all rulers that do lie nigh unto us, possesseth the fewest people : yet in thought he doth surpass them all. No man dareth take from the man who thinketh his will. Therefore let us sell of our military one-half, and buy a man of thought, and 'twill be the better for us." Lastly, in Nastchokin's administrative activity there is to be noticed a feature which tells especially in his favour—namely, the feature that, in addition to being methodical and expeditious, Muscovite administration was extremely attentive to subordinates, sympathetic and humane towards those administered, and eager at once to spare their strength and to set them in the position wherein, with the least possible loss of efficiency, they should contribute the most to the advantage of the State. During the Swedish war the conquered territory on the Western Dvina became overrun with Russian soldiers of fortune and Cossacks of the Don, who took to robbing and harassing the inhabitants, despite the fact that the latter had sworn allegiance to the Muscovite Tsar. This brigand's method of carrying on war Nastchokin (who was then serving as *voievoda* of Kukeinos) loathed to the depths of his soul, and his very heart bled as he listened to the complaints of the wronged population. At length he wrote to the Tsar that the Crown must send help both against its enemies and against the robbers who were of its own people. " Rather I had seen wounds upon myself than these guiltless folk enduring such bloodshed. Rather would I be cast into a dungeon whence there is no return than that I should live here and see such evil calamities come upon the people." This *trait* in his assistant was greatly valued by Alexis, and in a patent of 1658 which raised Nastchokin to the rank of Councillor the Tsar praises him "in that he doth feed the hungry, and give drink unto the thirsty, and clothe the naked, and favour the troops, and let no malefactor escape."

Such were Nastchokin's administrative views and methods. Yet he attempted also to make practical application of his ideas, for his observations into the life of Western Europe had led him to recognise the chief fault which lurked in the State administration of Moscow. The fault in question lay in the fact that the administration was directed solely to exploitation of the popular labour, and not to development of the productive forces of the country. Popular industrial interests were sacrificed to fiscal aims, and valued by the Government merely as so many auxiliary resources for the Treasury. His recognition of this fault led to Nastchokin's eternal agitation on the subject of the growth of industry and trade within the Muscovite Empire, for he was one of the first to adopt the notion that the popular industry ought, of its essence, to constitute an object of the State's care. In fact, he was one of the first political economists to appear in Russia. Yet, in order that the industrial class should act more productively, it was necessary that that class should be freed from the pressure of administration through *prikazi*. Consequently, while Governor of Pskov, Nastchokin attempted to put into local execution a project of urban self-government which he had borrowed "from the example of other and alien lands"—*i.e.* from Western Europe: which represents the only known instance of local government of any kind obtaining in the Muscovite Empire of the seventeenth century. Not without a certain dramatic element, the scheme characterises both its originator, Nastchokin, and the system under which he had to act. On reaching Pskov (in March, 1665), the new *voievoda* caused a great commotion in his native town on perceiving that fierce dissension existed among the townsmen—that the "best men," the substantial merchants, were availing themselves of their strength in the local public administration to wrong "the middle and small men" in apportioning taxes and allotting fiscal posts. He perceived that the "best men" were doing as they liked with the town's affairs, and that their inferiors were unaware of this; the result being that both parties were incurring ruin, through lawsuits as much as through departmental malfeasance. Goods were passing to and fro between Pskov and the German frontier without paying customs, and traders whose means did not permit of their possessing any working capital were secretly borrowing money of the Germans at contract rates, and then buying up Russian goods cheaply, and selling them as their own (or, rather, handing them over to their creditors) at a profit which represented no more than an infinitesimal commission; which proceeding was resulting in a beating down of the value of Russian merchandise to the lowest possible limits, a sapping of the resources of genuine capitalists, an incurring of unpayable debts to the foreigner, and a ruining of the local community. Accordingly, soon after his arrival, Nastchokin proposed to the people of Pskov that they should adopt a series of measures which, first of all, the local *starosti*, assembled " for a general council of the people at large " in the town's public offices, were carefully to consider ; the upshot being that, with the *voievoda's* help, there became worked out certain " articles relating to the ordering of the town " which, together, formed a sort of charter, in seventeen sections, for the self-government of Pskov and its suburbs. This charter was subsequently approved at Moscow, and won for the *voievoda* the Tsar's commendation of his zeal and care, while the local *starosti* and townsmen at large were rewarded with the Imperial thanks " for their excellent counsel, and their readiness in all good works."

The more important articles in this charter related to reforms in the public administration and legal dispensation of the town, and to the regularisation of external trade—*i.e.* to one of the most active nerves in the economic life of the Pskovian region. The urban community of Pskov was to select from among itself, for three years, fifteen burghers, of whom five were, in turn, and for the space of a year, to carry on the town's affairs in the *zemskaia izba* or local townhall. To these " territorial chosen men " there were to be committed the town's industrial management, the supervision of the sale of liquor, the collection of customs, and the direction of Pskov's trading relations with foreigners. Also, these commissioners were to judge their fellow townsmen in all commercial and other cases, save only cases which related to treason, robbery, and sacrilege, which were to remain within the jurisdiction of the *voievoda*. Thus the latter voluntarily surrendered a large portion of his authority in favour of local urban self-government. In specially important cases the five local administrators who were on duty were to confer with the other two, and even to invoke the advice of the " best men " of the urban community at large.

Nastchokin saw the chief faults in Russian commerce in the fact that " Russian men who do trade are weak before one another "—*i.e.* are not to be depended upon, are unaccustomed to treat their fellows in friendly fashion, and are not proof against falling into debt to the foreigner. Of that unreliability Nastchokin considered the chief causes to be lack of capital, mutual distrust, and the absence of satisfactory credit; and it was to remove such shortcomings that the articles relating to trade with foreigners were inserted into the Pskovian charter. The weaker traders were to be distributed, "according unto substance and unto acquaintanceship," among the larger capitalists, who were to superintend their (the weaker traders') businesses, while the *zemskaia izba* was to allow the latter occasional loans out of the town's funds, for the purchasing of Russian export merchandise. Also, for trading with foreigners there were to be established, near Pskov, two annual markets of non-dutiable goods which were to begin on, and to last for two weeks from, the 6th of January and the 9th of May respectively : and to those markets the small merchants were, with the aid of their loans from the urban authorities and the support of the large capitalists to whom they happened to be assigned, to bring their export merchandise, to register it at the *zemskaia izba*, and then to hand it over to their principals—the latter subsequently paying their clients the purchase value of the goods received, in order to enable those clients to purchase a fresh stock at the ensuing market, and handing them a certain "added sum" over and above the said purchase value, "for maintenance." Lastly, the large capitalists were to sell the goods which had been entrusted to them at high prices fixed by regulation, and to hand over to their clients what they reckoned to be "full profit" thereon, after the manner of a modern company's dividend. This organisation of the commercial class would have the merit of concentrating foreign trade in the hands of a few strong individuals, who would be able to maintain at a proper height the values of native goods.

The device of these peculiar trading partnerships was based upon the possibility of friendly association of the upper commercial *stratum* with the bulk of the townspeople—*i.e.* upon the possibility of an assuagement of the social hostility which Nastchokin found to be existent in Pskov. Also, the device may have been based upon the mutual advantage of the two parties, patrons and clients, since the strong capitalist would offer excellent profits to the weaker members of his group, of his "company," and the latter would still not spoil values for their patrons. Another important point was that these associations were to be formed under the auspices of the urban administration, which was thus to become a lending bank for the smaller commercial folk, and a control upon the larger. Also, the dependence of the town's suburbs and attached boroughs upon the town itself would enable the community of the latter to direct, through its judicial-administrative organs, the foreign trade of the *whole* of the Pskovian region. Unfortunately, the success of these reforms was marred by social dissension. The lesser townsmen accepted the new position readily, as a favour granted by the Tsar, but the "men of sub-stance," the arbiters of the town, opposed the innovations, and obtained support in the metropolis, where it is to be imagined with what dis-like Nastchokin's enterprise was received by the world of boyars and *prikaznïe liudi*, who saw therein a daring attempt against the ancient rights and customs of *voievodi* and *diaki* in favour of the taxpaying urban peasantry. Yet it is a matter for admiring wonder that, within eight months of his appointment to Pskov, Nastchokin should have succeeded not only in conceiving the idea and the plan of a complicated system of reforms, but also should have made himself master of the troublesome details of its execution. His successor at Pskov—Prince Chovanski, the braggart champion of boyar pretensions, whom "every man did name as a fool" (to quote Alexis' own expression)—represented Nastchokin's affair to the Tsar in such a light that the Sovereign then and there annulled it, despite what he had said about the Prince. In fact, Alexis yielded to his customary weakness for deciding a matter according to the latest impression received.

But Nastchokin had no mind to give in, either to adversaries or to adverse circumstances. So strong was his faith in his Pskovian reforms that, though his critical intellect had been well schooled by study of foreign mistakes, he himself made the mistake of self-deception. Con-sequently in the Pskovian charter he expresses a hope that, when, upon the Pskovians, "there shall be imposed civic rights of the people, and they be duly ordered," the inhabitants also of other towns may look to receive similar organisation. Nevertheless the reverse was decided upon in Moscow: it was there resolved that it was not right for Pskov to have a special system to itself. In return, when become director of the Office of Ambassadors, and engaged in introducing a charter which, in 1667, he drew up for the town of Novotorg, Nastchokin could not deny himself the pleasure—albeit a fruitless one—of repeating his Pskovian ideas as to the making of loans to poor traders by the Muscovite customs authorities and local town bodies, the associating of those traders with larger capitalists in order to maintain the high prices of Russian merchandise, and so forth. Also, in this charter Nastchokin took yet another step forward in his plans for reorganising Russian trade and industry. In 1665 the townsmen of Pskov had petitioned at Moscow for management by a single *prikaz*, instead of being tossed to and fro among different institutions of the metropolis, and thus enduring useless affronts and loss ; and now, in this charter of Novotorg, Nastchokin reintroduced the idea of a single *prikaz* to superintend all the local trading communities, to serve them in the frontier towns as a protection, and in the other towns as a bulwark and police authority against the oppressiveness of *voievodi*. This Central Office of Commercial Affairs was the forerunner of the Muscovite "Burghermeister's Hall" or "Chamber" which Peter the Great instituted to superintend the whole of the urban trading and industrial population of the Empire.

Such were Nastchokin's schemes for and attempts at reform. Truly one may marvel at the breadth and originality of his projects, and at the diversity of his activity ! His was a fruitful mind which always took the simple, the direct view of things. Upon whatever sphere of State administration he had chanced, he would still have subjected the established order to stern criticism, and given that order a more or less clear-cut plan of reform. Even in military matters he made attempts in this direction, for he noted the faults in the organisation of the army, and proposed a scheme for their correction. For one thing, he recognised that the mounted militia, composed of provincial-urban *dvoriané*, was entirely useless, and that it ought to be replaced with a foreign-trained force of "given men" or recruits—*i.e.* a regular army which was to be formed by the enlistment of members of all classes in the community. In short, no matter what novelty was conceived in Moscow—whether the establishment of a fleet on the Baltic and the Caspian, the organisation of a foreign postal service, or the laying out of public gardens with trees and flowers imported from abroad—it was Ordin-Nastchokin who headed or suggested the innovation. Once, even, a rumour ran through Moscow that he was busy upon a revision of the Russian laws, with the supposed intention of reorganising the whole State in the direction of decentralisation, and of weakening that tutelage of local administrations by the metropolitan *prikazi* against which he had all his life contended. It is to be regretted that he did not succeed in doing all that he might have done, but his unyielding, perverse bent of character entailed a premature end to his governmental activity. This was because he and the Tsar could not agree in their views on foreign policy. The author of the Treaty of Andrusovo was too correct in his diplomacy not to advocate the exact execution of that document. That is to say, he contemplated a possible restoration of Kiev to Poland; upon which course Alexis, on the other hand, looked with distaste, and even with horror, as a sin. This difference of opinion caused the Tsar gradually to cool towards his favourite; until finally, when commanded, in 1671, to enter into new negotiations with Poland which were to shatter his own work and infringe the Polish compact which, a year earlier, he had ratified with his oath, Nastchokin refused to fulfil the commission, and in February, 1672, became enrolled an inmate of the Kripetski Monastery of Pskov, under the name of Brother Antonius. The day of his retirement—December 2nd, 1671— was marked by a ceremony whereat the Tsar, in the presence of the boyars, "did graciously dismiss" his statesmen, "and publicly free him of all worldly vanities." The last secular care to which Brother Antonius gave his attention was the task of building a hospital in Pskov. He died in 1680.

In many things Ordin-Nastchokin forstalled Peter the Great, for he was the first to express ideas which Peter, later, made good. Though Nastchokin was a bold, self-confident bureaucrat who knew his own worth, he was none the less solicitous for and benevolent to those whom he administered, and of an active, practical turn of mind. In everything, and before everything, he had in view the State's interest, the public good. Never content with mere routine work, he peered keenly into the faults in the existing order of things, devised means for their removal, and looked ahead to see what other problems confronted him. Possessed of strong common sense, he never applied himself to aims that were too remote, or to tasks that were too comprehensive. Able to make himself active in many different spheres, he strove to effect those aims through existent resources. Yet, though ceaselessly insisting upon the faults in the established order, he left its bases untouched, and devised schemes for correcting it, rather, piecemeal. It was in his brain that the dim impulses towards reform which characterised Alexis' period first began to crystallise into concrete projects, and to shape themselves into a connected scheme of amelioration. Yet Nastchokin's was no radical scheme which called for a general breakage—he was anything but an indiscriminate innovator. Rather, his programme of reforms combined only three fundamental demands—namely, a demand for the improvement of administrative institutions and service discipline, a demand for the selection of bolder and more conscientious administrators, and a demand for an increase of the Treasury's profits and the State's income by means of augmentation of the people's substance through a quicker growth of trade and industry.

I began this chapter by remarking upon the rare appearances of statesmen in Russia of the seventeenth century : but if we consider the fluctuations, the thoughts, and the feelings of the period, the wanderings through statesmanship of the exceptional intellect and character which I have described, the struggle of Ordin-Nastchokin with the conditions which encompassed him,—if we consider all this, I say, we shall understand why these fortunate accidents were so rare in Russia of that period.

In spite of the dissimilarity of natures and activities, one common feature brings Rtistchev and Ordin-Nastchokin into close approximation with one another. That common feature is that both of them were modern for their day, and that both of them did modern work—the one in politics, and the other in the moral sphere. Thus they differed from Tsar Alexis, who, by heart and intellect, was a son of old Russian antiquity, and was attracted by innovations only in so far as he could use them to adorn his outward circumstances, or smooth his political relations. Yet in that same Russian antiquity Rtistchev and Nastchokin were able to discover something new, to open up resources as yet unused and untouched, and to turn those resources to the common good. Western models and scientific learning they directed, not against their native antiquity, but to the saving of its bases of existence from an over-hard, over-narrow interpretation of the same—an interpretation which arose from the bad governmental and ecclesiastical guidance of the masses, and from the routine which was so destructive to those bases. Nastchokin, the diplomatist, insistently and truculently promulgated the idea that external success, both military and diplomatic, would never prove but fleeting if it were not prepared for and supported by thorough-going internal organisation, and that foreign policy ought to conduce to the growth of the productive forces of the nation without also exhausting their energy ; while Rtistchev, the wealthy courtier, supplemented his aggressive friend's ideas with a kindly form of policy which instilled the notion that economic progress is little worth in the absence of the principal conditions necessary to well-ordered life in common—the conditions which are built upon equitable relations between the social classes, upon an enlightened sense of morals and a religion which is not darkened by invented rites and superstitions, and upon a beneficence which manifests itself, not in chance personal impulses, but in the creation of social institutions. Lonely soldiers in the field, Rtistchev and Nastchokin yet were not voices crying in the desert; and though both of them continued to hold fast to the old forms and sympathies—the one founding a monastery, and the other one ending his days in a monastic establishment—their ideas, for all that they were half-comprehended and half-accepted by the men of the day, stretched forward to another period, and helped to bring about a revolution in the political and religious life of ancient Rus.

CHAPTER XVIII

Prince V. V. Golitzin—The preparation and programme of his reforms.

THE youngest of the forerunners of Peter the Great was Prince V. V. Golitzin. Yet he made greater departures from the existing order of things than his seniors had done. While still a young man, he was a notable personage in governmental circles under Tsar Theodor II.; while during the time of the Tsarevna Sophia (who, on the death of her elder brother, became Regent of the State) he figured as one of the most influential men in Rus. The ambitious and cultured young Regent was incapable of overlooking any boyar of wits and education; and thus by personal friendship Golitzin contrived to link his political career with that of the Tsarevna. A warm admirer of the West (for which he renounced many of the time-hallowed traditions of Russian antiquity), he, like Nastchokin, could speak Latin and Polish with fluency; while in his house—which foreign writers reckoned to be one of the finest in Europe—everything was arranged on the European scale. In the great *salons* the walls between the window-apertures were furnished with huge mirrors; on the side walls there hung pictures—portraits of Russian and foreign sovereigns, and German maps in gilded frames; on the ceilings there were painted systems of the planets; and a multitude of clocks and thermometers of artistic workmanship completed the adornment of the apartments. Also, he possessed a large and varied library of manuscript and printed books, in the Russian, Polish, and German languages, and among its Polish and Latin grammars there stood a Kievan chronicle, a German geometry, an Alkoran translated from the Polish, four manuscripts concerning the staging of plays, and a manuscript work by Yuri the Serb (Krizhanitch). The mansion also served as a *rendezvous* for educated foreigners who chanced to be in Moscow, and in their entertainment their host went further than other lovers of the foreigner, for he received even Jesuits, with whom the former had never been able to agree. It follows that such a man was bound to be on the side of the reform movement. One of Nastchokin's successors in the direction of the Office of Ambas-

sadors, Golitzin developed the ideas of his predecessor. With his
assistance there was drawn up (in 1686) a treaty for a lasting peace with
Poland; by which document the Muscovite Government was to embark
upon a coalition struggle with Turkey, in company with Poland, the
German Empire, and Venice. This caused Moscow formally to enter
into the concert of the European Powers. In return, Poland permanently
ceded to Moscow both Kiev and the other Russian acquisitions which had
been temporarily surrendered after the Treaty of Andrusovo. In questions also of *domestic* policy Golitzin went further than had been the case
with former statesmen of the reforming tendency. As early as Theodor's
reign he was made president of a Commission upon which there was
imposed the drawing up of a scheme for reorganising the Muscovite
military system; and, to accomplish this end, the Commission recommended that the German system should be introduced and the *miestnichestvo* abolished (the Law of January 12th, 1682). Also, Golitzin never
ceased to urge upon the boyars that they ought to have their sons
educated either by sending them to Polish schools or by obtaining Polish
tutors for their home instruction. Indeed, there can be no doubt that
many broad schemes of reform sprang to birth in Golitzin's brain; and
the pity is that we know nothing of them except fragments or vague
jottings which were noted down by the Polish Ambassador Neuville, who
arrived in Moscow in 1689, not long before the fall of Sophia and
Golitzin. Neuville used often to visit the Prince, and to chat with him (in
Latin) concerning the political events of the day, but more especially concerning the English Revolution; and this enabled the Ambassador to
gather something of the position of affairs in Moscow, and also to collect
Muscovite evidence and reports on the subject. Golitzin was greatly
concerned about the question of the Muscovite army, the shortcomings of
which he knew well, since on more than one occasion he had commanded
troops. According to Neuville, his chief desire in the matter was that the
dvoriané should travel abroad, and there learn the military art, since he
intended to replace the now useless peasant conscripts (whose lands, while
their holders were on service, had to be left unworked) with trained soldiers,
and then to impose upon the peasantry, in lieu of their useless military
obligations, a graded poll-tax. This means that the peasant and slave
conscripts who had hitherto constituted the bulk of the *dvorianstvo* regiments were to be removed from the latter, while the army (in contravention
of Ordin-Nastchokin's idea) was to retain its strictly class constitution as
a body drawn principally from the *dvoriané*, and, though possessed of a

regular character, to be commanded by *dvorianin* officers who had been specially trained to war. With this military-technical reform Golitzin's ideas connected also a social-economic revolution. His principal notion of reorganising the Empire was to emancipate the peasantry, by presenting them with the lands which they now worked, subject to an interest payable to the Tsar (*i.e.* to the Treasury) in the form of an annual tax. This, he calculated, would increase the Treasury's income by over one-half. Unfortunately, Neuville did not succeed in hearing all the conditions of this agrarian operation, and has not recorded them ; but since the *dvoriané* were still to have imposed upon them the compulsory and hereditary obligation of military service, it is probable that, in proportion to the agrarian State tax which was to be levied upon the peasantry, the monetary salaries of the *dvoriané* were to be increased, as compensation both for the incomes from peasantry which *pomiestchiki* would be deprived of and for the lands which would be made over to *krestiané*. Thus Golitzin's plan was to effect the operation of ransoming serf labour and the allotted plots of the peasantry through replacement of the capital redemption sum with constant incomes of the service-official class, received from the Treasury in the shape of increased remuneration for military service. Similar ideas for the decision of the serf question only began to circulate among Russian statesmen as long as a century and a half later. Much else as to Golitzin's plans did Neuville hear, but has failed to hand down to us. In fact, in this respect he confines himself to the following rather idyllic passage : " If I were to attempt to write all that I have heard concerning this Prince, I should never reach the end thereof. Sufficeth it to say that he did strive to people the waste lands, to enrich the poor, to change barbarians into men, cowards into heroes, and shepherds' huts into stone mansions." Yet in truth, as one reads Neuville's tales in his " Account of Moscow," one cannot fail to be struck with the boldness of the schemes of " the great Golitzin," as Neuville grandiosely calls him. Though communicated to the author but in fragments, and without any internal connection between them, those schemes show that at their basis there lay a broad and, apparently, well thought-out plan of reforms which touched not only the administrative and economic order, but also the class organisation of the State, and even popular education. Yet these were no more than fancies —no more than the result of fireside talks with friends, and not legislative projects, since Golitzin's personal relations prevented his even beginning the practical working out of his ideas of reform. The truth is that, his fortunes being bound up with those of the Tsarevna Sophia, he fell with her, and took no part in the work of Peter the Great, although he had been the latter's immediate forerunner, and might have acted as a good helpmeet to him, if not the best. Nevertheless the *spirit* of his schemes found a reflection in legislation, for the conditions of slavery for debt became mitigated, and the burying alive of murderers and the death penalty for utterance of sedition were alike abolished. As for the hardening of punitive measures against Old Believers, this cannot be altogether attributed to the Government of the Regent Sophia, but, rather, to the professional zeal of the ecclesiastical authorities; which zeal usually utilised the State Administration as its punitive instrument. At about the same period the pressure exercised by the Church bore fruit among fanatics of the Old Believing persuasion, and thousands of perverts burnt themselves to save their souls, while the Church's pastors burnt, for the same reason, thousands who advocated self-burning. Nor did the Regent Sophia's Government succeed in doing anything for the serfs, since she was too busy intimidating the turbulent *Strieltsi* with the *dvoriané*, and then, with the aid of the *Strieltsi* and the Cossacks, attempting to do the same with the *dvoriané*. Yet it would be unfair not to admit that Golitzin's ideas played a certain part in the State's life; only, we must seek evidence of the fact, not in new laws, but in the general character of the Regent's seven years of rule. Peter's brother-in-law (consequently, Sophia's opponent), Prince B. I. Kurakin, has left us, in his memoirs, a notable judgement on that rule. " The administration of the Tsarevna Sophia Alexievna did begin with every sort of diligence and right judgement unto all, and to the satisfaction of the people, so that never did such wise government abide in the Russian State; and during the seven years of her rule the whole State did come to a flower of great wealth, and commerce and all handicrafts did multiply, and the learning of the Latin and Greek tongues did begin to be established, and the people did rejoice in their sufficiency." This testimony as to "a flower of great wealth " receives clear support from a statement by Neuville that, in old Moscow of the wooden houses, which were then reckoned to contain upwards of half a million inhabitants, there were built, during Golitzin's ministry, more than three thousand edifices of *stone :* and it would hardly be rash to suppose that what called forth the above encomium upon Sophia's term of rule was the form of her policy. That stout, uncomely woman— a woman who had a large, clumsy head, a coarse face, a short, squat figure, and, at twenty-five, looked forty—sacrificed ambition to conscience, and temperament to sense of shame. Yet, having acquired power through shameful intrigues and bloody crimes, she, as a Princess " of great mind and great policy " (to quote Kurakin once more), needed an excuse for her usurpation, and therefore turned an attentive ear to the advice of her first minister and gallant, who also was a man " of great mind," and beloved by all. Surrounding himself with lowborn, but devoted, coadjutors like Nepluev, Kasogov, and others, he, with their help, attained the administrative success to which Kurakin refers.

Golitzin was the direct continuer of the work of Ordin-Nastchokin; but, as a member of another generation and another type of education, he went further than did his predecessor in schemes of reform. Though devoid of Nastchokin's intellectual power, administrative genius, and business adroitness, he was the more booklearned of the two, and, though less active, thought more. His mind, though not so much supported by experience, was bolder, and penetrated further into the existing order of things, and touched its foundations. That is to say, his type of thought identified itself with general questions of State—with State problems, and with the organisation and adjustment of the community; nor was it for nothing that his library contained a manuscript work "on civic life and the direction of all matters which pertain in general unto the people." He was not, like Nastchokin, the man to be satisfied with mere administrative and economic reforms, but took thought for the spread of enlightenment and toleration, freedom of conscience, the free entry of foreigners to Russia, and the improvement of the social structure and moral conditions of life. In short, his plans were more comprehensive and daring than Nastchokin's, yet, at the same time, more idyllic. Representatives of two contiguous generations, they were founders of the two types of statesmen which arose in Russia during the eighteenth century—all of whom were either of the Nastchokin or of the Golitzin stamp. Nastchokin was the founder of the practical statesmen of Peter's era; in Golitzin we see the outlines of the liberal and slightly imaginative ministers of Katherine's day.

I have now completed my survey of the period preparatory to the reforms of Peter the Great. Permit me to summarise what I have said.

We have seen with what fluctuations the preparatory period proceeded. The Russians of the seventeenth century kept taking a step forward, and then stopping to think what they had done, and whether the step had not been too long a one. A spasmodic movement onwards, a halt for thought, and a timid look backwards—that is the manner in which we might define the cultural march of the Russian community of the seventeenth century. Yet, though that community considered each step, it did not progress so far as it imagined itself to be doing. The idea of reform was evoked in it by the need for national defence and State income; which demands called for extensive improvements in the State's organisation and industrial conditions—*i.e.* in the people's labour. In both the one and the other the men of the seventeenth century confined themselves to timid experiments and irresolute borrowings from the West; yet amid those experiments and borrowings they wrangled and fought, and considered first one thing, and then another. Their military and industrial needs clashed with their agelong beliefs, deeply-rooted customs, and time-honoured prejudices, and it seems as though they needed more than they could, or would, or were prepared to, accomplish—as though, to secure their political and economic existence, they needed to revise their ideas and feelings—in short, their whole outlook. Thus they were in the awkward position of men who shrink from their own demands. They needed technical knowledge, military and industrial, yet not only lacked it, but were convinced that it was unnecessary, and even sinful, since it did not lead to the salvation of the soul. What success, then, did they attain in this dual struggle with their needs, and with themselves, and with their own prejudices?

To satisfy their material necessities these men introduced into the State order a few successful changes. Summoning to their help some thousands of foreign officers, soldiers, and artisans, they placed a large portion of their troops on a regular footing (though in a poor way, and without the necessary equipment), and built a few factories and ordnance works. Then, after much fuss and effort, they, with the help of the reorganised troops and the factories which I have mentioned, recovered, with some difficulty, the two provinces—Smolensk and Sieversski—which they had lost. Also, they managed to obtain a certain hold upon half Little Rus—the half which made voluntary surrender to them. That sums up the essential fruits of seventy years of sacrifices and efforts! The State order these men in no way improved: on the contrary, they made it more oppressive than before, by abolishing local self-government, by, through segregation of the classes, increasing social dissension, and by sacrificing the freedom of peasant labour. At the same time, in the struggle with themselves they gained one or two victories which lightened that struggle for later generations: and this fact may, without dispute, be accounted a service to the cause of reform. These men prepared the way, not so much for the reforms themselves, as for the assimilation of those reforms by the minds and consciences of the day—a less prominent, but none the less a both difficult and necessary, task. Let me shortly enumerate those moral and intellectual victories.

In the first place, the men of the seventeenth century recognised that they were ignorant of much of what ought to be known to them. This was their most difficult victory over themselves—over their own conceit and their own past as they concerned themselves with questions of a moral and religious order, discipline of the conscience and will, subjection of the mind to dogmatical obedience, and all that related to the salvation of their souls. Yet conditions of mundane existence they left quite out of account, since they saw in those conditions the lawful province of fate and of sin, and therefore, with impotent humility, resigned them to the mercy of rude instinct. The men of those days could not understand how it was possible to import, nor how it could ever be worth while to import, any good thing into a world which Holy Writ has described as plunged in evil, and, consequently, bound always to remain in that condition. They felt certain that the existing system of human life depended as little upon human efforts, and was as unchangeable, as was the system of the world itself. But this belief in the destined immutability of human existence on earth gradually began to waver under the influence of two factors—of factors which operated both within and without. The inward influence in question proceeded from the shocks administered to the Empire during the seventeenth century. The Period of Troubles dealt a first, and a very rude, blow to the drowsy Russian mind; it forced men of capacity to think, to open their eyes to their environment, to look life in the face with clear, direct gaze. In the works of every writer of the day—of Palitsin, Timotheiev, and Prince Chvorostinin—there shines forth what might be called historical reflection—an inclination to investigate the conditions of Russian life, the bases of the tangle of social relations, in order to discover the causes of the calamities which had come about. And even when the Period of Troubles was over, the ever-growing burdens of State maintained this inclination, by feeding the dissatisfaction which broke forth into a series of rebellions. Both at *Zemskïe Sobori* and at class conferences with the Government we see deputies of the community pointing out various disorders, and disclosing a despondent sense of the state of things, and proposing means for its correction. Evidently contemporary thought was being moved to attempt a stirring of all this stagnant life, although it saw in the latter only what was divinely appointed and unchangeable. On the other hand, Western influence brought ideas which led men to think of the conditions and amenities of life in common, and to set before them the perfecting of that life as the principal task of the State and the community. But for this there was needed such learning as ancient Rus neither possessed nor respected—more especially the study of nature, and of what nature could furnish for man's needs. Hence the increased interest of the Russian community of the seventeenth century in cosmographies and similar works. The Government itself supported that interest, and began to consider how it might exploit the untouched wealth of the country by discovering minerals. For this, however, technical knowledge was needed. The new impulse embraced even weak individuals like Tsar Theodor, who is reputed to have been a great lover of learning, more especially of mathematics, and of whom Sylvester Medviedev relates that he concerned himself not only with theology, but also with technical education. During his reign he enlisted, for his Imperial workshops, " artists of every craft and handiwork," gave them good wages, and himself superintended their labours with assiduity. From the close of the seventeenth century the idea of the necessity of such knowledge became the ruling conception of the leading men of the Russian community, and their complaints of the absence of that knowledge came to be common ground in their pictures of the condition of Russia. Yet it must not be supposed that that consciousness or those complaints led at once to the adoption of the required knowledge, or that that knowledge, on becoming a standing question, speedily became converted into an insistent demand. Far from it. In Russia men long and cautiously considered the matter of deciding the problem : throughout the eighteenth century, as well as during the bulk of the nineteenth, men continued to meditate and to dispute as to what knowledge was good for us, and what full of peril. But the intellectual demand, when once raised, soon changed the relation of the community to the existing order of life. As soon as men had assimilated the idea that learning could help to make life flow more smoothly than at present, faith in the immutability of things underwent a decline, and there arose a desire to arrange matters so that life should be bettered. In fact that desire came into being sooner than the right method of reorganisation had been properly apprehended; learning came to be believed in at an earlier period than it was properly laid hold of. Then men set themselves thoroughly to examine the existing system, and found in it, as in a house long neglected, decay, litter, and rubbish of all kinds. Those aspects of life which had formerly stood the strongest now ceased to excite any faith in their durability. Hitherto men had thought themselves assured in the belief that, without literature or rhetoric, they could assimilate the mind of Christ; but now we see the Eastern prelate Ligarid pointing out the necessity of scholastic education in the war with schism, while the Russian Patriarch Joachim repeats his words when, in a treatise aimed against schism, he writes that many pious men through "sorriness of mind"—*i.e.* lack of education—are inclined towards schism. Thus intellect and learning came to be recognised as the mainstays of godliness. In 1683 a translator who was employed in the Office of Ambassadors translated the Psalter, and, in so doing, made this avowal of the necessity of reorganising the ecclesiastical system with the help of education: "Our Russian people are gross and unlearned. Not only plain men, but also men of the clergy, do seek not the verities, or understanding of Holy Writ, but do slander those who be learned, and call them heretics."

In the rise of this ingenuous belief in science, and of this trustful hope that it might one day right everything, there lay, in my opinion, the chief moral success which was attained in the matter of paving the way for Peter's reforms. That belief and that hope guided also the Great Reformer in his work; and the same inspiration supported Russia when he was gone, on every occasion when, failing in her pursuit of the progress of Western Europe, Russia felt ready to fall in with the idea that she was not born for civilisation, and must, in her vexation, plunge into self-abasement.

But in the men of the seventeenth century these moral acquisitions had the effect of causing them to shape the community anew. Hitherto the Russian public had lived upon influences of native origin, upon the conditions of its own life, upon what the nature of its country revealed; and when to that public there came wafted also alien culture, which was rich in experience and knowledge, it clashed with the native systems, and entered into a conflict therewith which agitated the population, confused Russian ideas and customs, and complicated the life of the people by communicating thereto a movement at once violent and unequal. Disturbing men's minds with a flood of new conceptions and interests, foreign influence evoked, during the seventeenth century, a phenomenon which threw Russian life into even greater confusion. Hitherto the Russian community had been remarkable for the homogeneity, the wholeness, of its moral and religious composition. Despite differences of social position, the Russian people of olden days all resembled one another in their spiritual complexion, and satisfied their spiritual needs at one and the same source. True, the boyar and the slave, the literate man and the illiterate, had not an identical mental store of sacred texts, prayers, hymns, exorcisms of the devil, tales, and old traditions—they did not all understand things in the same way, or study their catechism of life with equal strictness; but at least they all affirmed the *same* catechism, sinned with equal indifference, and, with an identical fear of the Almighty in their hearts, went to confession and Communion. This varied tortuosity of an automatic conscience helped the old Russians to understand one another, and to form a homogeneous moral body. It established among them a certain spiritual harmony, despite social cleavage—it brought about a constant repetition of a fixed type. Just as, in the palace of the Tsar and the mansions of the boyars, cunning devices of gilding and of carving concealed the fact that there was present the same architectural plan as belonged to the peasant's rude hut of wood, so in the florid diction of the Russian bookman of the sixteenth and seventeenth centuries there glimmers the unpretentious, hereditary spiritual substance " of the rural blockhead who is simple of mind, yet more simple of understanding." This moral wholeness of the old Russian community was shattered by Western influence. Although that influence did not penetrate deeply into the nation, among the higher classes of the community—which, through their position, were the more open to external influences—it gradually acquired a commanding eminence. As a window cracks which is unequally heated in various portions, so the Russian community fell apart under the unequal action of Western influence. The schism which took place in the Russian Church of the seventeenth century was an ecclesiastical expression of this moral cleavage of the Russian public which arose from Western culture. As soon as it broke forth there arose in opposition to one another two points of view, two hostile orders of ideas and feelings. The Russian community became split into two camps —that of the respecters of native tradition in Church matters, and that of the adherents of foreign, or Western, innovations. The ruling classes of the community, though remaining within the pale of the Orthodox Church, began to trust in the antiquity in whose name the schismatics declared war with indifference, and so fell the more easily a prey to foreign influence; while the Old Believers, expelled beyond the pale of the Church, hated the imported innovations the more, and attributed to them the ruin of their Orthodox Russian Church. This indifference of some and hatred of others became part of the spiritual composition of the

Russian community, as new causes which complicated the social movement whereby men were attracted in different directions.

A specially fortunate condition for the success of the reforming influence was the active part taken in its diffusion by individuals. They were the last men, yet the best men, in ancient Rus to place their stamp upon the tendencies which they had first furthered or supported. Tsar Alexis felt the attraction of the new movement without breaking with the older system, and he was followed by Ordin-Nastchokin, Golitzin, and others. The most important points in the political programme which they consecutively followed were (1) peace and an alliance with Poland, (2) a struggle with Sweden for the eastern seaboard of the Baltic, as well as with Turkey and the Crimea for Southern Russia, (3) a reforming of the troops into a regular army, (4) a replacing of the old complicated system of direct taxes with a poll- and an agrarian-tax, (5) the development of foreign trade and domestic manufactures, (6) the introduction of urban self-government, with the aim of increasing the productiveness and prosperity of the commercial-industrial classes, (7) the emancipation of the serfs from their lands, and (8) the establishment of schools, not only of a general-educative and ecclesiastical character, but also of a technical nature that should be adapted to the needs of the State. All this was to be done on foreign models, and with the help of foreign guides. It is manifest that it was a programme which was practically the programme also of Peter, but one which became completed before he entered upon his activity. In that lies the true importance of the statesmen of the seventeenth century. They not only created the atmosphere wherein the Great Reformer was brought up, and which he afterwards breathed, but they also outlined for him the scheme of his work, though in some respects they went further than he did.

INDEX

END OF VOL. III.

Printed by BALLANTYNE, HANSON & Co.
at Paul's Work, Edinburgh

THE
ECONOMIC HISTORY
OF RUSSIA

IN TWO VOLUMES

Vol. I. THE RISE AND FALL OF BONDAGE
RIGHTS
„ II. INDUSTRY AND REVOLUTION

BY

J A M E S   M A V O R , Ph.D.

PROFESSOR OF POLITICAL ECONOMY IN THE
UNIVERSITY OF TORONTO

THE aim of this work is to present to English
readers the main results of recent historical re-
searches which have been conducted by various
Russian scholars.

No such great attempt to bring into one
work so great a mass of material upon Russia has
hitherto been made. The fullest reference is
provided to original as well as to secondary
authorities, to make both volumes as useful to the
accomplished special historian as to the student of
general history.

[P.T.O.

THE
REPUBLICS OF CENTRAL
AND SOUTH AMERICA

THEIR RESOURCES, INDUSTRIES, SOCIOLOGY
AND FUTURE

BY

REGINALD C. ENOCH, C.E., F.R.G.S.

With Maps and Illustrations.   Square Demy 8vo.

BOOKS upon the Latin-American Republics have largely been confined to accounts of travel.   The present work affords a comprehensive survey and source of exact information for all interested in any way in the eighteen independent states of Central and South America — Argentina, Brazil, Mexico, Peru, Chile, Bolivia, Colombia, Venezuela, Uruguay, Paraguay, Guatemala, &c.   The natural resources, topography, people, races, government, industries, railways, mines, openings for investment, trading and manufacture, are set forth interestingly and succinctly.   The traveller, merchant, engineer, capitalist, land-seeker, emigrant, archæologist, concessionaire, prospector, and all others will find matter of absorbing interest in its pages as well as the general reader.   Finally, the present and future of this great region of growing activity and importance is fully surveyed from the point of view of the sociologist and political economist—a field which hitherto has been neglected.

J. M. DENT & SONS, LTD., BEDFORD ST., W.C.

RICHMOND COLLEGE LIBRARY

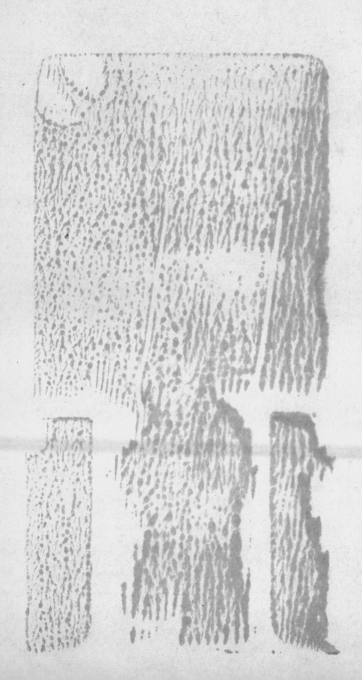